D0141371

THE TWO NATIONS AND THE EDUCATIONAL STRUCTURE 1780–1870

STUDIES IN THE HISTORY OF EDUCATION

THE TWO NATIONS AND THE EDUCATIONAL STRUCTURE 1780–1870

by

BRIAN SIMON

LAWRENCE & WISHART
LONDON

First published under the title
'Studies in the History of Education, 1780–1870'
1960

Reprinted 1964

Reprinted under new title
'The Two Nations and the Educational Structure, 1780–1870'
1974

First Paperback Edition 1976
Reprinted 1981

Printed in Great Britain by
The Camelot Press Ltd, Southampton

PREFACE

This volume was originally published in 1960 under the title 'Studies in the History of Education, 1780–1870'. But two others have since appeared to make a three-volume series of *Studies in the History of Education* which together cover the period 1780 to 1940. Accordingly the first volume acquires another title and the pattern of the series, chronologically arranged but centring on key themes, is as follows:

Volume 1, *The Two Nations and the Educational Structure, 1780–1870*, discusses the attitudes of changing social classes during this period, as expressed in educational outlook and policies, and the extent to which an organised system of schools for different classes developed up to the point when a compulsory system of elementary education was established.

Volume 2, *Education and the Labour Movement, 1870–1920*, looks at developments during this period from the standpoint of the Labour movement which, as its influence grew, formulated demands for access to education in all its aspects, as against allocation of merely elementary instruction.

Volume 3, *The Politics of Educational Reform, 1920–1940*, is concerned with the crucial years between the wars. The Conservatives sought to contain developments within strict limits in face of the rising demand for secondary education for all from a now fully enfranchised working class with considerable representation in Parliament. Attention turns accordingly to decision-making at the administrative and top political levels—a process subjected to close analysis.

There is a volume of readings covering the same period as Volume 1, *The Radical Tradition in Education in Britain* (1972), which has full excerpts relating to education from the writings of William Godwin and Thomas Paine referred to in the first chapter; from Robert Owen, Robert Dale Owen, Richard Carlile, William Thompson, referred to in chapter 4; and from William Lovett's *Chartism*, discussed in detail in chapter 5.

March 1974   B. S.

CONTENTS

INTRODUCTION

HISTORIES of education are often mainly concerned with the organisation of schools and colleges and the ideas of reformers, and as such, addressed to educationists rather than the ordinary reader. But, looked at more generally, the history of education is full of incident and interest, touching on all sides of life, on the outlook and interests of all classes of society. It is to draw attention to those aspects which are often neglected, and in an attempt to relate the ideas of reformers and the changes introduced to contemporary social and political conflicts, that this book has been written.

The framework of the present educational system was constructed in the nineteenth century and it is with this period that the book is chiefly concerned. But, though a roughly chronological treatment is preserved, there has been no attempt to write a complete history of educational legislation, theory or institutions. Instead, attention is focussed on some of the more important ideas and trends which profoundly affected education at the time and have often influenced all subsequent developments.

The educational ideas which achieved a wide currency in the early nineteenth century derived to a considerable extent from an earlier age. The first chapter is, therefore, concerned with the educational outlook of late eighteenth-century reformers and the ways in which this found expression as England moved into the age of the Industrial Revolution. Attention is concentrated on two main centres where industry and science were developing rapidly; and at these centres on groups of men who, in a society still dominated by the landed aristocracy, represented the developing professions and the rising industrial middle class.

There follow four chapters covering the first half of the nineteenth century, but each approaching the educational concerns of the time from a different angle. Two deal with the preoccupations of the middle class, both as concerns their own education and the education of the workers; the theories they developed, the criticisms of old institutions, the attempts to provide for new needs—all these as an accompaniment of the movement for Parliamentary reform, the struggle for political power. Similar questions are then approached from the workers' point of view. They also sought education, criticised what there was and attempted to build afresh. During the period up to 1832 these activities were, to a considerable extent, behind the scenes; later, with the emergence of an organised working-class movement, they took an increasingly prominent place and the demand was advanced for a universal system of education.

The final chapters cover the separate reforms carried out during the period 1850 to 1870 which marked a crucial moment of change in English education. It is often suggested that there was no effective state intervention until the passage of the Education Act of 1870. On the contrary, this was the culmination of a series of measures. It was only after the education of the upper and middle classes had been brought into some kind of order that attention was turned to evolving a system of elementary schools for the working class.

With the 1870 Act there was completed the structure of a national system of education which, to all intents and purposes, has persisted unchanged. Additions have been made, developments have taken place in many directions, but the essentials remain. Oxford and Cambridge still stand at the apex of the system, the "public" schools continue to provide only for the upper class, maintained secondary schools are still divided according to the age the children leave and the professions they are likely to enter—just as was planned in the 1850s, '60s and '70s.

If the particular themes and periods selected appear arbitrary, it must be noted that they are, to a great extent, forced on the student. The leading reformers of the late eighteenth century in fact disappear from the scene in the 1790s as a result of acute political reaction. Those who, at a later period, take up once more the demand for educational advance do so for different reasons, in the light of conflicting class interests which dictate opposing policies.

If the middle class begins by advancing radical ideas, it is the workers who take these to their logical conclusion after 1832. Working-class leaders now take over and develop the heritage of eighteenth-century materialism and nineteenth-century political economy to develop a new view of society. It is primarily in the working-class movement that there is expressed the fervent belief in the power of human reason, in science, in education as an essential means to individual and social development, which is earlier to be discerned among the reformers of the 1780s.

The story of the working-class struggle for education is itself chequered because it is, once more, interrupted or forced underground by persecution and intimidation. But if newspapers are suppressed, books censored and those who attempt to disseminate them gaoled, there is nothing like a period behind bars for writing a book. So from Dorchester gaol in the 1820s, from Warwick prison in the 1840s, come books which express the ultimate optimism and belief in education of men who have espoused the cause of the working class and are looking towards socialism.

If this book directs attention to neglected aspects of educational history, it will have achieved its aim. It is, however, no more than a foray into fields rich in material. Much still remains to be discovered; the picture can only be filled out when there has been a great deal more research. On this basis, each chapter could easily be lengthened into a book, or even a series of books, for the material is available. Meanwhile my debt to those who have worked in this field, in particular to the works of Elie Halévy, are obvious; as also to specialist studies to which acknowledgement is made in the text. I am also much indebted to James Klugmann, who has constantly encouraged the writing of this book, as to others who have also read the manuscript in whole or in part and made valuable suggestions, notably A. L. Morton, George Rudé, S. Lilley and Aubrey Black; to the latter I am particularly grateful for generously putting at my disposal unpublished essays on the educational activities of the early co-operative movement, as well as other material, on which I have drawn freely. My thanks are due also to the Librarians at the University of Leicester and to Dr. Higson of the Leicester Institute of Education; and to Miss Langton who has undertaken the main burden of typing the M.S. To Joan Simon, who has assisted greatly with the final draft of this book, my debt cannot be adequately acknowledged.

June 1959   BRIAN SIMON

CHAPTER I

FORERUNNERS OF EDUCATIONAL REFORM
1760–1800

IN the closing decades of the eighteenth century a new interest in education arose among forward-looking industrialists and professional men in the chief manufacturing centres of the Midlands and northern England, most notably in Birmingham and Manchester. The projects advanced were primarily those of a class which was experiencing at first-hand the potentialities and effects of a now rapidly developing capitalist industry; both as concerned the integration of science with production, which brought revolutionary developments in industrial techniques, and in relation to the rapid expansion of urban communities, resulting in a variety of new civic problems and responsibilities. As a preliminary to discussing their educational ideas and activities, therefore, it is worth examining briefly who these men were and some of the influences at work which sharply differentiated the leading citizens of Birmingham and Manchester from the England of Whig and Tory, parson and squire, Established Church and traditional universities.

1. INDUSTRY, SCIENCE AND EDUCATION

(i) *The Lunar Society and the Manchester Literary and Philosophical Society*

The far-reaching changes initiated in industry at this time rested primarily on the introduction of power engineering. While the use of the steam engine as a source of power in the textile industry "joined together the two originally separate strands of heavy and light industry and created the modern industrial complex", its development represented "pre-eminently a conscious application of scientific thought".[1] It was at Matthew Boulton's works in Birmingham that the major problems involved in perfecting the steam engine were overcome by a brilliant group of men who were often at the same time both scientist and technician and who made the mane of

---

[1] J. D. Bernal, *Science in History* (1954), 370.

Soho famous throughout the western world. This was the group which formed the nucleus of the Lunar Society, first established as an informal grouping in 1766 or before, when meetings were held to conduct experiments and discuss scientific topics, and which continued in existence for a quarter of a century. From a profound interest in the advancement of science and technology, members of the Lunar Society moved on to an interest in wider social and political questions, not least in education.

It was not only technological and scientific interests and developments that opened new horizons. Industrial expansion and the opening up of new markets brought a development of banking and commercial undertakings; public buildings and housing, as well as factories of a new kind and improved transport, helped rapidly to change the face of what had been small towns. Between 1760 and 1801 the population of Birmingham doubled, rising to 70,000; in Manchester, where the output of cotton goods increased fivefold in twenty years, the population had increased from 20,000 to 58,000 by the close of the century. With this rapid expansion many problems of local government arose and professional men found themselves faced with radically new tasks. In particular, the doctors began to come together as a group with a new civic concern with the founding of the provincial hospitals—at Manchester in 1752, at Birmingham in 1773; many of these were also keenly interested in scientific investigation and became involved in industrial developments, particularly in chemical technology.[1]

There was, then, much in common between the circumstances and outlook of rising manufacturers and professional men, and shared interests and aspirations were to find expression in other bodies similar to the Lunar Society, the various Literary and Philosophical Societies which sprang up after 1780. The most famous of these was founded in Manchester in 1781. It first met in the schoolroom of the Unitarian chapel in Cross Street. Here was another of the bonds uniting the middle class of the industrial cities—the tradition of dissent, in which many had themselves been brought up. The Unitarians, the most rational and advanced of dissenting sects, numbered among their adherents members of leading middle-class families; their ministers took a prominent part in intellectual and social life and their chapels became the centres of philosophical, scientific and literary discussion and enquiry.

[1] A. and N. Clow, *The Chemical Revolution* (1952), *passim*.

The central figure of the Lunar Society, so named because it met on the night of the full moon, was the genial and expansive Matthew Boulton, F.R.S., scientist, inventor, engineer; others concerned with the Soho works were James Watt and James Keir, both Fellows of the Royal Society, and Dr. William Small. Members living in Birmingham included the two doctors, William Withering and Jonathan Stokes, both Fellows of the Royal Society and both particularly interested in botany, Samuel Galton, F.R.S., manufacturer and chemist, and later Joseph Priestley, F.R.S., scientist, Unitarian minister, philosopher and educationist. From Lichfield and its neighbourhood came three members with whom we shall be particularly concerned: the famous doctor, Erasmus Darwin, F.R.S., Richard Lovell Edgeworth and Thomas Day. Josiah Wedgwood, F.R.S., whose pottery works at Barlaston were too distant to allow him to make the monthly journey to a meeting, was a close personal friend of all the leading members of the society.

Of these men, Edgeworth was to record in his memoirs:

"Mr. Keir, with his knowledge of the world, and good sense: Dr. Small, with his benevolence and profound sagacity: Wedgwood, with his unceasing industry, experimental variety, and calm investigation; Bolton, with his mobility, quick perception, and bold adventure; Watt, with his strong inventive faculty, undeviating steadiness, and unbounded resource; Darwin, with his imagination, science and poetical excellence: and Day, with his unwearied research after truth, his integrity and excellence:—formed altogether such a society, as few men have had the good fortune to live with; such an assemblage of friends, as fewer still have had the happiness to possess, and keep through life."[1]

If we take this remarkable group as a focal point, it is possible to illustrate the width of interests developed by this section of the middle class and to trace strands linking their groupings in different centres.

The forward-looking industrialist of this age was often a scientist-innovator as well, abreast of and developing science in its practical

[1] R. L. and Maria Edgeworth, *The Memoirs of Richard Lovell Edgeworth* (2nd edn, 1821), Vol. I, 180-1. In listing membership of the Lunar Society I have followed the conclusions of Robert E. Schofield, M.S., Ph.D., in a valuable article "Membership of the Lunar Society in Birmingham", *Annals of Science*, Vol. XII, No. 2, June 1956. Schofield includes Wedgwood in the Lunar Society and concludes that it had 14 members (including William Small, the "founding father", who died in 1775). The two not mentioned in the text are John Whitehurst of Derby, geologist and clock maker, an early friend of Boulton's who shared his practical scientific interests, and the Rev. R. A. Johnson, F.R.S., from Kenilworth.

applications. If Matthew Boulton and James Watt are outstanding examples, Wedgwood also, an extremely competent chemist, completely revolutionised the pottery industry on the basis of modern technique and the introduction of classical art. Watt's first partner, John Roebuck, a medical man turned scientist, was founder of the famous Carron Iron Works, which changed the face of Clydeside, and subsequently solved the problem of large-scale manufacture of sulphuric acid, thus cheapening a raw material that was vital to the progress of the textile, metal-finishing and many other industries. James Keir, another man with a medical training who turned to scientific research and industry, discovered a method of soda manufacture which was also to play a major part in the enormous increase of output of textiles. Murdock, an employee of Boulton and Watt, played a major part in the practical development of Watt's engines; Galton, who was made a Fellow of the Royal Society as a result of his experiments in optics, was also vitally interested in both chemistry and botany, and, through his firm, made a major contribution to the development of the armaments industry.

Among many links with advanced sectors of industry in other centres was that with the great ironmaster John Wilkinson, a major figure in the expansion of the iron industry, who married Priestley's sister. In Manchester, among prominent members of the "Lit. & Phil." engaged in industrial innovation, were Thomas Walker, Thomas Cooper, who developed the new chlorine method of bleaching pioneered by Watt, and Thomas Henry, doctor and scientist, closely concerned also with the development of the bleaching industry in Lancashire.

Lunar Society members were also engaged in scientific research in other fields. Joseph Priestley, described by Thomas Henry as "this excellent philosopher, to whom . . . Nature takes delight in revealing her secrets", was in many ways the doyen of the whole movement; largely responsible for the pneumatic revolution, his experimental work covered a wide range of science. Erasmus Darwin is chiefly notable for his scientific speculations concerning the evolution of life, his *Zoonomia* anticipating his grandson's theories by fifty years. Galton wrote a three-volume *Treatise on Birds*. Dr. Withering, who combined the interest in medicine and botanical science typical of the time, was a friend of Linnaeus; his book on the medicinal value of digitalis in the treatment of heart disease, based on a careful analysis of a large number of case histories, has been described as "the first scientific treatise on the treatment of disease written in English".[1] He is also well known for his general treatise on British flora.

William Small, whose wide knowledge of physics and mechanics was put to good use at Boulton's Soho works, had formerly been tutor to Thomas Jefferson and Professor of Moral Philosophy at Williamsburg, Virginia, and came to Soho with an introduction from Benjamin Franklin. Here was one of a number of direct links with scientists in America. There was also close contact—through the chemist, Joseph Black, the philosopher, David Hume, the geologist, James Hutton, the economist, Adam Smith—with men who had made Glasgow and Edinburgh centres of intellectual life, in close touch with continental learning and of international reputation.

Dr. Thomas Beddoes, a leading chemist of the day, who married one of Edgeworth's daughters, was another close associate; he drew crowds of students to his lectures at Oxford and later was to become the centre of a local society in Bristol. Direct efforts were made to promote societies in other towns and keep contact with them. Erasmus Darwin, who founded the Botanic Society in Lichfield, which published translations of the work of Linnaeus, later moved to Derby and established the Philosophical Society there in 1784; Priestley is said to have been associated with the activities of the Leeds Literary and Philosophical Society founded in 1783, Matthew Boulton corresponded with the Newcastle Philosophical Society, founded by William Turner, a Unitarian minister, while the sons of both Priestley and Watt were members of the Manchester "Lit. & Phil", the latter acting for a time as secretary.

Manchester itself could boast of a galaxy of experimental scientists, beginning with Dr. Thomas Percival, friend of Diderot and Voltaire and founder of the "Lit. & Phil." With many others—including Cooper, Henry, Dr. Ferriar, John Aiken and Charles White—he published his work in the famous *Memoirs* of the society, the first volume of which appeared in 1785. It is not without significance that the Praelector of Chemistry in the University of Cambridge, who was more of a classicist than a chemist, is found in 1782 "paying the greatest respect to the rising scientific authorities in Manchester, and writing with great deference".[2]

The advancement, dissemination and application of science was, then, the chief bond linking these groups, and they found a field of

[1] T. Whitmore Peel and K. Douglas Wilkinson, *William Withering of Birmingham* (1950), 68.
[2] R. Angus Smith, *A Centenary of Science in Manchester* (1883), 99-100.

application not only in industry but also in civic affairs, in particular in public health. Matthew Boulton took a keen interest in the Birmingham dispensary. Thomas Percival was described as "a leader in every medical, hygienic, literary and educational movement in Manchester"; he was among those who persuaded Peel to bring in his first Factory Act. With the aid of other leading doctors he developed the Manchester Infirmary, with out-patients' department and dispensary, founded the Manchester Board of Health in an attempt to ameliorate conditions, concerned himself with other projects for sanitary improvement, and advanced propositions for smoke abatement.

Many had a vision of the development of new industrial cities which should be not only clean but well planned and beautiful. Indeed, the planning and building of the Soho works and Wedgwood's Etruria were practical examples of a linking of eighteenth-century ideals of order and proportion with modern industrial requirements.[1]

The fusion of art with science and industry was evident at Soho and at Etruria. Both Boulton and Wedgwood employed artists on a considerable scale; the famous dinner service produced for Catherine of Russia, for instance, required more than a thousand separate paintings. Wedgwood also personally encouraged and employed one of the best of contemporary painters, Joseph Wright of Derby, whose work brilliantly expressed the scientific, humanist and moral outlook of the Lunar grouping,[2] as well as the leading sculptors, Flaxman and Roubillac.

In so far as they lived before the full social impact of industrial development was felt, such men were able to imagine and work for —and to this extent to create—a marriage of industry, science and

---

[1] Cf. J. Bisset's description of Soho in his *Poetic Survey round Birmingham* (1812):

"On yonder gentle slope, which shrubs adorn,
Where grew, of late, 'rank weeds', gorse, ling & thorn,
Now pendant woods and shady groves are seen,
And nature there assumes a nobler mien.
There verdant lawns, cool grots and peaceful bow'ers,
Luxuriant, now, are strew'd with sweetest flow'rs,
Reflected by the lake, which spreads below,
All Nature smiles around—there stands Soho!

Soho!—where Genius and the Arts preside,
Europa's wonder and Britannia's pride. . . ."

[2] "Joseph Wright's 'Orrery', 'Air-Pump' and 'Alchymist' are the first paintings to express the enthusiasm of the eighteenth century for science," writes F. D. Klingender, *Art and the Industrial Revolution* (1947), 47-8; referring to the painting entitled "A Philosopher giving that Lecture on the Orrery in which a Lamp is put in the place of the Sun" he adds, "rarely before had the thrill of scientific exploration been expressed as dramatically as this".

art. They themselves often personified this, as has already been suggested. Erasmus Darwin, for instance, was accepted by many as a
leading poet of the age; how *The Botanic Garden* (1789-91) brought
science into poetry is exemplified in its sub-titles—"The Economy of
Vegetation" and "The Loves of Plants"—and it was specifically designed by its author to "inlist Imagination under the banner of Science;
and to lead her votaries from the looser analogies, which dress out the
imagery of poetry, to the stricter ones, which form the ratiocination
of philosophy".[1]

But perhaps the most outstanding example in this sense, and in
his civic endeavours, is William Roscoe of Liverpool—banker, poli-
tician, poet, historian, art collector—who sought to make his native
city the "Venice of the North". It was Roscoe whose works on the
Italian Renaissance so astonished the aristocracy,[2] who founded the
Liverpool Society for the Encouragement of the Arts of Painting and
Design (1773) which organised the first exhibition of pictures in any
English provincial town, and who characteristically tried to reclaim
Chat Moss for agriculture. Like the Lunar Society members, with
whom he was associated, Roscoe had connections with the London
publisher Johnson and so with the brilliant group surrounding him,
which included William Godwin, the philosopher, Mary Wollstonecraft and many other leading thinkers and artists. Among the latter
was Fuseli, befriended by Roscoe when he first came to England and
later commissioned (with William Blake) to illustrate Erasmus Darwin's poems collected in *The Botanic Garden* (William Blake was also
called upon to provide illustrations of Mary Wollstonecraft's *Tales
for Children*). Elsewhere, artists and writers formed part of provincial
groups; the young Southey and Coleridge found congenial spirits
among the Bristol society sponsored by Dr. Beddoes in the early 1790s,
while the painters Crome and Cotman were drawn into a group at
Norwich.

Absorbed in the creation of new industrial processes and in developing civic life, deeply involved in scientific enquiry and often
directly engaged in art and literature, this section of the middle class
was profoundly at variance with many aspects of the prevailing social
order. Regarded as an inferior class by the great landowners who still
had an influence in many towns, and by the old-established merchant

---

[1] Quoted by Klingender, *ibid.*, 31.
[2] Cf. H. Maxwell (ed), *The Creevey Papers* (1904), Vol. II, 256. Roscoe's works included
his *Life of Lorenzo de Medici* (1795) and the *Life and Pontificate of Leo the Tenth* (1805).

families, they were often, as nonconformists, excluded under the Test Acts from holding any public office. By the same token, they had been debarred from taking degrees at the English universities, and so had sought a higher education either in dissenting academies or in the Scottish universities which retained a civic connection and, unlike Oxford and Cambridge, moved with the times.

Many were dissenters of a Unitarian trend, rationalist in outlook, supporters of what Priestley called "the great and glorious doctrine of necessity", advocates not so much of "toleration" but of the widest liberty of thought. With this background, and largely cut off from traditional and official culture, they were open to the influence of, stimulated to seek and develop, new ideas and values. It was to the writings of the great French *philosophes* of the Enlightenment that they most eagerly turned and they also enthusiastically acclaimed the works of Rousseau with their social and educational implications. In addition, they took up and developed the psychology of associationism, advanced by David Hartley (1705-57), which provided a firm basis for asserting the formative power of education. Armed with these ideas, and with a firm belief in the potentialities of the scientific and technical advances they were promoting, they confidently looked forward to the "heavenly city" where men would be free and equal and able to develop their talents for the public good.

Inevitably, these men were drawn increasingly into the political conflicts of the time; indeed, they often took a leading part in political agitation. They were in the forefront of the long-drawn struggle for the abolition of the Test Acts; one in which Priestley was particularly prominent and which aroused violent political passions after 1789. They were to be found supporting every other struggle for liberty—the movement against slavery, in which Thomas Day and Roscoe were particularly active, and the American war of independence. Many were fully engaged in the great movement of the late eighteenth century for the reform of Parliament through more equal representation of the counties and shorter Parliaments, and by pamphlet, petition and other means, courageously and consistently exposed the corruption of aristocratic government. They were, therefore, eventually to acclaim the fall of the Bastille and to welcome the French Revolution as the beginning of a new era in the history of mankind.

It is against this background that their contribution to educational ideas and practice was made. Rejecting the values of eighteenth-century aristocratic society, and breaking out of the narrow circle of provincial dissent, they picked up the strands of materialist philosophy and psychology and attempted to advance new and relevant designs for social living. Not only were they concerned to extend teaching to cover science and modern subjects, but also to define a new purpose and new scope for education. "He that undertakes the education of a child", wrote Thomas Day, "undertakes the most important duty of society."

Of the fourteen members of the Lunar Society, three wrote educational works of wide significance. Joseph Priestley is best known as a scientist; he was, however, a practising educator throughout most of his life, first in his own school at Nantwich, later as tutor at the famous Academy at Warrington, later still as tutor to the Earl of Shelbourne's sons, and finally as lecturer in the shortlived Academy at Hackney. In many of his writings he made important contributions to the theory and practice of education and to psychology—developing the ideas of Hartley, who had been the first to advance a scientific system of psychology. Edgeworth, in *Practical Education* (1798), written with his daughter Maria, produced what was certainly the most significant contemporary work on pedagogy. Thomas Day advanced radical educational and social ideas in *The History of Sandford and Merton* (1783-9), first begun in collaboration with his friend Edgeworth, one of the most popular children's books of all time. In addition, Erasmus Darwin, among his many other pursuits, wrote his *Plan for the Conduct of Female Education in Boarding Schools* (1797) to popularise a school kept by his two illegitimate daughters; though his claims as an educationist also rest on his *Zoonomia*. Thomas Percival's *A Father's Instruction to his Children* (1775), of the same *genre* as Day's famous book, and indeed the first of its kind in the country, also exercised a wide influence in the whole development of children's literature having an educative and moral purpose.

Coupled with writings which achieved an extensive circulation—*Sandford and Merton* passed through at least fifty editions in the hundred years following its publication—were practical efforts to extend educational facilities. It was in Manchester, Birmingham and Liverpool that subscriptions were collected from leading manufacturers to found Warrington Academy (1757-86) which provided a modern education for laymen as well as dissenting ministers. When this closed, a new academy was opened in Manchester itself, the first two tutors being Thomas Barnes and Ralph Harrison of Cross Street Unitarian

Chapel, respectively secretary and vice-president of the "Lit. & Phil."
In addition, in 1783, largely through the initiative of Thomas Barnes
and Thomas Henry, a Manchester College of Arts and Sciences was
established to teach science, technology, medicine, law and literature
to young men and to artisans already employed in industry.

These educational activities stemmed, to a considerable extent, from
the dissenting tradition in education, in which many of the men
concerned had been educated, and which now took a new direction.
It is worth, therefore, considering briefly how this tradition had developed during the previous century and what other educational
practices and theories contributed to shaping the outlook of this
section of the middle class.

(ii) *The Educational Tradition of Dissent and Its Development*

The growing interest in the study, advancement and application
of science, coupled with advocacy of wider educational reforms, represented in a sense the revival of an educational outlook which had
been obscured for over a century; one originally associated with the
name of Francis Bacon and widely propagated during the revolutionary era 1640-60.

Bacon, the first great English materialist philosopher, was a popu-
lariser of science and the scientific attitude with all that this implied;
advocate of "the advancement of learning" at a time when universities were tied to old beliefs and outlooks, and of application of the
fruits of learning "for the relief of man's estate" as the means both
to social progress and to deeper understanding of the world. But
Bacon specifically separated science from religion, holding that human
knowledge must not "presume by the contemplation of nature to
attain to the mysteries of God", and this enabled puritans to support
his scientific approach wholeheartedly, while at the same time furthering religious ends. In the outcome the "advancement of piety and
learning" became a watchword of educational reformers who advocated the provision of a useful and relevant education and the
extension of schooling to all.

One of the most active groups came together at Oxford where
men engaged in scientific enquiry became heads of colleges during
the Commonwealth and met regularly to undertake experiments and
discuss the study and teaching of science. In London a closely associated
group published a series of works on education, calling not only for
complete reorganisation of the school system but also for a more

humane attitude to children, new teaching methods, the replacement of an exclusively classical curriculum by one which gave attention to history, geography, modern languages, science and technology.

With attacks on the scholastic learning of Oxford and Cambridge were coupled demands for new universities in London and Manchester, York and Durham, and reformers looked towards a national system of education. When bishops, deans and chapters were swept away, Parliament did in practice direct the affairs of schools and colleges and diverted some of the money from confiscated Church lands to increase the income of schoolmasters, the smaller colleges of Oxford and Cambridge and the Scottish universities and to found a new university at Durham.[1]

But after 1660, with the restoration of king, court and Established Church this educational movement was eclipsed. The foundations of recent educational advance were in turn swept away with the return of confiscated lands to the Church which now reasserted the closest control over all education, limiting the right to graduate at the university and to teach in school to those who subscribed to the Thirty-nine Articles. While scientists found new support and scope for their work in the Royal Society, established in 1662, the plans of educational reformers had been too closely associated with puritan and republican policies to survive. Penal legislation now prevented nonconformists from becoming teachers in established schools or colleges and created a new and permanent division in education. Henceforth Oxford and Cambridge ceased to be national educational institutions; they tended to become seminaries for the clergy of a Church which was now only the most powerful of a variety of religious sects, a Church which had reached a low moral and intellectual condition by mid-eighteenth century. If, for various reasons, Cambridge never sank so low as Oxford and supplemented the traditional curriculum with some teaching of mathematics and science, in general neither university contributed materially to the advancement of science or education.

Meanwhile those who were excluded by law and conscience from taking degrees at the ancient universities founded and supported academies for the education of ministers to serve dissenting congregations. But what had been a live and all-embracing educational theory, informing plans for the development of a national system of schools

---

[1] Joan Simon, "Educational Policies and Programmes (1640-60)", *Modern Quarterly*, Vol. IV, No. 2 (1949), 154ff.

of a new kind, had lost both its philosophical background and its field of application. Now that the puritan middle class, which had provided the chief impetus towards reform, had lost its predominant position, nonconformism inevitably tended to become provincial in outlook and educational ideas narrowed. New subjects and methods of teaching found a place in the dissenting academies, and to this extent the ideas of the Commonwealth reformers were put into practice; but the advancement of piety was necessarily the main consideration, the provision of a suitable training for future preachers and pastors.

Elsewhere mathematics and navigation were sometimes taught, for instance at Christ's Hospital and at local schools in some of the great ports, while modern subjects of a kind necessary for a commercial career could be studied in private institutions of various kinds. But most established grammar schools, under the control of small governing bodies or corporations which at this time became increasingly corrupt, tended to stagnate, retaining virtually unchanged the classical curriculum and methods of teaching grammar which had been assailed as obscurantist and outdated by John Milton, William Petty and many others in the 1640s.

With some exceptions—notably the developing "public" schools in or near London, the old collegiate schools of Winchester and Eton, and some well placed local schools under masters of some reputation —the grammar schools no longer attracted the gentry as they had done in the late sixteenth and early seventeenth centuries. A recognised form of education for the upper classes became tutoring at home, often followed by the Grand Tour of the continent. Lesser gentlemen sent their sons to board with some local vicar, rather than keeping a tutor themselves, and though they might still apprentice younger sons to a respectable calling, did not think in terms of a useful education in school or college. It was, in fact, pre-eminently the mark of a gentlemanly education not to acquire any specialist knowledge; the aim was, rather, acquaintance with polite literature through study of the classics.

The early dissenting academies were often forced to move from one place to another and some were shortlived. But a tradition was established and a body of teachers created who carried on some institutions for two or three generations, if sometimes in different towns. After 1750, however, the position in the north of England deteriorated rapidly; with the death of the famous Dr. Doddridge, the Northampton Academy moved to Daventry, and within the next four years, also as a result of the death of men who had spent a lifetime teaching, both the Kendal Academy and that at Findern, near Derby, closed down altogether. It was in this situation that the young dissenting minister at Warrington, John Seddon, proposed the establishment of a new academy and gained support from leading nonconformist industrialists and merchants in Manchester, Warrington, Liverpool and Birmingham.

It was a sign of the times that Warrington Academy was much more than a replica of former institutions of this kind, being overtly designed to educate not only intending ministers but also laymen. Embodying the outlook of the section known as the "wide" dissenters, favourable to scientific enquiry and open to the influence of new needs, the academy's stated aim was to provide for the education of ministers who should be "free to follow the dictates of their own judgments, in their enquiries after truth, without any undue bias imposed on their understandings", and at the same time to give to those intended for commercial life and the learned professions

"some knowledge . . . in the more useful branches of literature, and to lead them to an early acquaintance with, and just concern for the true principles of religion and liberty, of which principles they must, in future life, be the supporters."[1]

Here, in the 1760s, Joseph Priestley became tutor in languages and literature, lecturing on the theory of language, oratory and criticism. But he also initiated a course on the history, laws and constitution of England, encouraging the fullest discussion among his students. His widely read *Essay on a Course of Liberal Education for Civil and Active Life* was to be based on these lectures and later editions included the syllabus he had followed. This was the first regular introduction of history as an academic discipline in a higher educational institution; while the lectures of Priestley's colleague, John Aiken, were the first systematic treatment of English literature. Mathematics, science in the form of natural history, German, were also part of the Warrington curriculum.

This was the educational tradition in which some of the key men composing the groups we have described were themselves brought up. One of the first students at Warrington was Dr. Percival of

---

[1] William Turner, "Historical Account of the Warrington Academy," published in *The Monthly Repository*, 1813-15, and re-published in *Warrington Academy* (ed G. A. Carter, 1957), 4.

Manchester, who eventually completed at Edinburgh and Leyden an education which owed nothing to accepted English institutions; here also were educated Thomas Barnes and Ralph Harrison, later to become the original tutors at the Manchester Academy, Warrington's successor. In fact, of the twenty-five original members of the Manchester "Lit. & Phil." only one was educated at an English university, and this was the "father" of the society, Peter Mainwaring, who became its first president at the age of eighty-five. Of the leading lights of the Lunar Society, Edgeworth and Day had been at Oxford and Darwin at Cambridge, but Priestley had received his education at the Daventry Academy (1752-89) which was second only to Warrington in influence, while it was at Warrington itself that Samuel Galton, as his daughter wrote later, "received his first introduction to the intellectual world, and to that habit of scientific scrutiny, that ardent spirit of free unshackled enquiry, which subjects everything to the alembic of discussion and criticism".[1] William Turner, the Unitarian Minister who founded the Newcastle Philosophical Society, was also educated at Warrington, while such men as the ironmaster, John Wilkinson, and the philosopher, William Godwin, were also products of dissenting academies.

The other educational institutions which exercised a key influence were the two chief Scottish universities, themselves closely connected with new industrial and social developments. Glasgow in particular had become one of the main centres of trade with America by 1750, when university professors were already involved in solving some of the technical problems of the linen industry. With the opening of the Carron Iron Works in 1760 heavy industry and mining sprang into prominence and enterprises producing all kinds of consumption goods for export grew up around the expanding port. This was a centre which, with Birmingham, was the chief herald of the Industrial Revolution and centre of scientific enquiry.

But Calvinistic Scotland had also the benefit of a network of schools, developed since the days when John Knox had first advocated universal education. Its colleges—or universities—were in the streets of busy towns, closely linked with civic life, and charging low fees. Rich endowments enabled the English universities to ignore changing opinions, wrote Adam Smith, and so they often became "the sanctuaries in which exploded systems and obsolete prejudices found shelter and protection, after they had been hunted out of every other

[1] C. C. Hankin (ed), *Life of Mary Anne Schimmelpenninck* (1858), Vol. I, 254.

corner of the world"; but the teachers of the poorer Scottish universities "depending upon their reputation for the greater part of their subsistence" were forced to pay attention to current needs.[1]

What gave Scottish intellectual life its particular vigour was this interest in contemporary changes, which extended over the widest field of social activity and learning, and was inspired by the belief (which Bacon had first propagated) that the advancement of knowledge depends on its application, that learning must be put to social use. Scotland's chief new contribution to knowledge was made by those who, stimulated by radical industrial and social changes, turned to historical investigations which laid the basis for a new science of society. It was Adam Smith's lectures on Natural Theology, Ethics, Jurisprudence and Political Economy at Glasgow, where he became Professor of Moral Philosophy in 1752, which provided the kernel of *The Wealth of Nations* (1776); a close analysis of the origin and functioning of industrial civilisation and the role of labour, in the process of which the case was put for state provision of education. At the same time John Millar was also engaged in the studies which gave rise to his *Historical View of the English Government* (1787) and other works, while at Edinburgh were William Robertson and Adam Ferguson, author of *An Essay on Civil Society* (1766).

Not only did the Scottish universities occupy a leading place in philosophy but also in science and in medicine; possessing, in the Edinburgh medical school, a centre towards which all progressive young doctors looked. Of those who attended dissenting academies several, like Percival and Barnes, ended by qualifying at Edinburgh; others, predominantly medical men, sooner or later found their way either to Glasgow or Edinburgh, if not to graduate at least to attend lectures for a time—among Lunar Society members, for instance, James Keir, William Small (both of whom were Scotsmen), William Withering and Erasmus Darwin. Many of the other prominent members of this and the Manchester group also came directly under the influence of the great Scottish teachers, whether during their most formative years or in later life.

If, then, this generation of industrialists and professional men fully grasped the implications of science, if the men who directed a decisive stage of the Industrial Revolution were "thoroughly imbued with the scientific spirit",[2] it was in no small part due to the influence of Glasgow and Edinburgh; not least to a medical training which

---

[1] Quoted by Klingender, *op. cit.*, 27.   [2] Bernal, *op. cit.*, 372.

provided a scientific discipline and was an excellent preparation for scientific research, in particular in chemistry and chemical technology.

To these more formal educational influences must be added the formative effect of training in the course of active work, in industries where the separation between scientist and technologist was yet to come, where there was the closest alliance between theory and practice. Many of the Lunar Society members were almost entirely self-educated against this background. Josiah Wedgwood, the youngest of a family of thirteen, left school at eight to work as a potter, Roscoe finished his schooling at twelve, Matthew Boulton at sixteen when he went into his father's business. William Murdock, when first appointed at Soho in his early twenties, had no scientific qualification; he learned both science and technology literally on the job. So also, James Watt, son of a Greenock carpenter, left school to become a professional instrument maker at fifteen, was appointed to Glasgow University in this capacity and so was able to use the knowledge gained from discussions with the chemist Black and other University professors in solving the initial problems of the steam engine. It is, indeed, characteristic of this period that engineers and scientists whose inventions changed the course of industry and so the nature of society itself, owed little or nothing to formal education. John Metcalfe, James Brindley, Thomas Telford, John Rennie, George Stephenson, all began their careers as ordinary mechanics and learned as they went along; picking up experience and ideas in the workshops and on the the new construction sites of developing capitalist industry.

It was from the vantage point provided by their own education and their industrial experience that the men of the Manchester and Birmingham groupings criticised traditional educational institutions and practices, in much the same spirit as the Commonwealth reformers of a century before. So remote from the business of life was the general course of study at recognised centres of education, wrote Priestley in 1765:

> "that many gentlemen, who have had the most liberal education the country could afford, have looked upon the real advantage of such a liberal education as very problematical. . . . Indeed, the severe and proper discipline of a Grammar-school is become a common topic of ridicule, and few young gentlemen, except those who are designed for some of the learned professions, are made to submit to the rigours of it."[1]

[1] *An Essay on a Course of Liberal Education for Civil and Active Life* (1768 edn), 6.

Arguing that the curriculum must be fundamentally changed—that education must cover modern history, policy, arts, manufactures, science, mathematics, commerce—Priestley adds:

> "the necessity of the thing has already, in many instances, forced a change, and the same increasing necessity will either force a greater and more general change or we must not be surprised to find our schools, academies, and universities deserted, as wholly unfit to qualify men to appear with advantage in the present age."[1]

The whole course of education advocated by the Edgeworths is an indirect criticism of rote methods of learning and the narrow classical curriculum of the contemporary grammar and public school; while, of the universities, citing Adam Smith's criticisms, they write:

> "without depreciating or destroying the magnificence or establishments of universities, may not their institutions be improved? May not their splendid halls echo with other sounds than the exploded metaphysics of the schools; and may not learning be as much rewarded and esteemed as pure *latinity*."[2]

Objections to the schools are also grounded on the fact that "too little attention is paid to the general improvement of understanding and formation of the moral character" and to the individual propensities of pupils.[3] Why, they ask, do so many children, on whom much care is spent, learn so little and prove so incapable of applying their knowledge? Their answer is, in part, restrictive and harsh discipline.

> "In a certain number of years, after having spent eight hours in 'durance vile' by the influence of bodily fear, or by the infliction of bodily punishment, a regiment of boys may be drilled by an indefatigable usher into what are called scholars; but, perhaps, in the whole regiment, not one shall ever distinguish himself, or ever emerge from the ranks."[4]

It is, however, Thomas Day who launches the sharpest attack on the moral outlook inculcated by the public school. The mother of his young hero, Tommy Merton, is urged by friends to place him "in some polite seminary; where he might acquire a knowledge of

---

[1] *An Essay on a Course of Liberal Education for Civil and Active Life* (1768 edn), 23.
[2] R. L. and M. Edgeworth, *Practical Education* (2nd edn, 1801), Vol. II, 383-4.
[3] *Ibid.*, Vol. II, 360.   [4] *Ibid.*, Vol. II, 186.

the world and make genteel connections". But Day exemplifies the
kind of education provided by polite seminaries in Master C—

> "reckoned a very genteel boy, though all his gentility consisted in
> a pair of buckles so big that they almost crippled him, in a slender,
> emaciated figure, and a look of consummate impudence. He had
> almost finished his education at a public school, where he had
> learned every vice and folly which is commonly taught in such
> places, without the least improvement either of his character or
> understanding."[1]

The resultant morality is vividly illustrated in the arrogant and ill-
mannered behaviour of Mash and his friends with whom Tommy
comes into contact.

It was, then, not only the obscurantism and uselessness of public
school education that was criticised, but also its moral worthlessness,
indeed decadence. Hence the necessity of evolving a completely new
approach to the theory and practice of education, one which would
take account both of the man as a human being and of the functions
he must fulfil in a changing and advancing society. So Priestley, outlining the aim to be worked for, found it "beautifully expressed in
the following lines of Mr. Thompson, describing the future happy
state of Great Britain:

> "Instead of barren Heads,
>   Barbarian Pedants, wrangling Sons of Pride,
>   And Truth-perplexing metaphysic Wits,
>   MEN, PATRIOTS, CHIEFS, and CITIZENS are formed."[2]

In common with Godwin, however, and indeed all other dissenters,
Priestley was adamantly opposed to education becoming a function
of the state. Should it do so, it would not achieve the object he desired, on the contrary, it would be used to promote uniformity of
thought and belief; in command of a state system of education,
Godwin argued, government would not fail "to strengthen its hands,
and perpetuate its institutions".[3] Already, in the grammar schools,
the spirit of free enquiry is stifled and the pupils' minds "cramped
by systems, habituated to servitude, and disinclined to think for them-

---

[1] T. Day, *The History of Sandford and Merton* (9th edn, 1812), Vol. II, 237.

[2] J. Priestley, *op. cit.*, preface (the quotation is from the poem "Liberty", Part V).

[3] William Godwin, *Enquiry Concerning Political Justice and its Influence on Morals and Happiness* (3rd edn, 1798), Bk. 6, Ch. 8; Vol. II, 302.

selves in their early years".[1] Godwin echoed the view that such an education "actively restrains the flights of mind" and produces an individual who "is no longer a man, (but) the ghost of a departed man".[2] "Let all the friends of liberty and human nature", wrote Priestley, "join to free the minds of men from the shackles of narrow and impolitic laws. Let us be free ourselves and leave the blessings of freedom to our posterity."[3]

If the major task was seen as the freeing of English life from the shackles of the established order in church and state, then Priestley and his friends looked only to the middle and upper classes to achieve this purpose. Locke had advanced the conception towards the close of the seventeenth century: "that most to be taken care of is the gentleman's calling. For if those of that rank are by their education once set right, they will quickly bring all the rest into order".[4]

It is in much the same spirit that Priestley—a great admirer of the "judicious philosopher"—specifically addresses himself not "to low mechanics, who have no time to attend to speculations of this nature, and who had, perhaps, better remain ignorant of them", but to persons of future rank and influence, to "young gentlemen, who now have leisure for studying the history and interests of their country, and who will not want opportunities to recommend schemes of public utility, or influence to assist in carrying them into execution".[5] It is true that Priestley urged "effectual provision" for teaching every child to read, write and cast accounts, reiterating Adam Smith's plea for parish schools and referring to their success in Scotland and America.[6] But his attitude to education for the people is as conservative as his general educational ideas are progressive. If, he writes, "those who have the poorest prospects in life can be taught contentment in their station, and a firm belief in the wisdom and goodness of providence . . . and consequently, apply themselves with assiduity and cheerfulness to the discharge of their proper duties, they may be almost as happy, even in this world, as the most virtuous of their superiors and unspeakably happier than the generality of them".[7]

This was essentially the outlook of a man who, while he found much to criticise in the prevailing order, was concerned to do away

---

[1] J. Priestley, *The Proper Object of Education in the Present State of the World* (1791), 7.
[2] Godwin, *op. cit.*, Bk. 6, Ch. 8; Vol. II, 298, 300.
[3] J. Priestley, *Remarks on a Proposed Code of Education* (1765), 203.
[4] J. Locke, *Some Thoughts concerning Education* (ed R. H. Quick, 1899), lxiii.
[5] J. Priestley, *Essay on a Course of Liberal Education*, 72.
[6] J. Priestley, *Lectures on History and General Policy* (1793), Vol. II, 51.
[7] J. Priestley, *Miscellaneous Observations relating to Education* (1778), 129.

with aristocratic prejudices and limitations rather than with aristo-cratic precedence; to make way for the new without destroying the old. It was an outlook shared by most of his colleagues. The Man-chester Academy and College were expressly set up to meet the needs of "gentlemen who are designed to fill the principal stations of active life". Edgeworth and Darwin both had in mind the upper stratum of the industrial middle class and those above it. Even Thomas Day reluctantly admits that "distinctions of rank may indeed be necessary to the government of a populous country"; though he adds that it is "for the good of the whole, not of individuals, that they have any just claims to be admitted" to high rank and those who do so should show "by the courtesy and benevolence of their manners, that they lament the necessity of their elevation, and would willingly descend nearer to an equality with their fellow-creatures".[1] It is, indeed, this approach which colours most of Tommy Merton's education.

Such men as Percival, Priestley, Boulton, Watt, Galton, Wedgwood and Edgeworth rejected the traditional educational institutions for their own children, and it was not least the need to provide education for their own families which first prompted and kept alive an interest in educational ideas and methods, and enhanced the enthusiasm with which Rousseau's books were received. Edgeworth's family eventually numbered nineteen. First a father at the age of twenty-three, for five years he applied the whole system advocated by Rousseau in *Emile* to the upbringing of his eldest son. Day's attempts to create a Rous-seauesque wife for himself by taking over the education and upbring-ing of the two orphan girls, Sabrina and Lucretia, are too well known to bear repetition. The same influence is clearly brought out in Mary Anne Galton's fascinating autobiography, which describes the educa-tional methods employed in one of the Lunar families.[2]

Others of these circles determined that their children should receive an education in line with the needs of the time. Percival's eldest son Thomas, for instance, was educated at Warrington Academy, while the first name on the roll of regular students at Manchester Academy was that of James Percival. Thomas Henry's more famous son, William, was also educated at Warrington; he then spent five years in Percival's house, attending at Manchester Academy, proceeding to Manchester Infirmary and finally to Edinburgh University. Thomas Butterworth Bayley, a member of the Manchester "Lit. & Phil.", himself Vice-President of the Warrington Academy, also sent his son there, as did

[1] *Sandford and Merton*, Vol. II, 214.   [2] Schimmelpenninck, *op. cit., passim.*

Wedgwood, whose eldest son John proceeded from Warrington to Edinburgh University and then to the continent to continue his studies. Both Wedgwood and Priestley took great care with the education of their children: a resident tutor at the Wedgwoods', for instance, later becoming Professor of Natural Philosophy at Edinburgh and a distinguished Scottish scientist.

The close attention given by Boulton and Watt, especially the former, to the education of their sons, is of particular interest. Each stage of the boys' education was specifically designed to prepare them for their future role in the development of science and industry. Thus James Watt junior, after finishing his early schooling, spent a year gaining industrial experience at Wilkinson's ironworks, followed by three years' schooling at Geneva and in Germany, where he attended science courses as well as learning foreign languages; there followed two years at Manchester to improve his knowledge of business. The young Matthew Boulton also continued his education on the continent—in France and Germany—where he studied science, mathematics and literature. The many very human letters from Boulton to his son are of extreme interest, and, as has been remarked, "reflect a great deal of light on the (educational) ideas held by the midland philosophers as a group". Modern languages, mathematics and science together with its practical applications formed the core of their education, as well as history and literature (including classical literature). Their experience abroad gave them a European outlook, while their contact with philosophers and scientists at home must have also had a powerful effect on their development.[1] When Boulton and Watt junior took over the Soho works, they pioneered entirely new industrial methods; their educational experience differed profoundly from that available in the contemporary grammar school and university.

[1] S. Smiles, *Lives of Boulton and Watt* (1865), 403-6; the education of Boulton's and Watt's sons is fully described in Eric Robinson, "Training Captains of Industry; The Education of Matthew Robinson Boulton (1770-1842) and the younger James Watt (1769-1848)", *Annals of Science*, Vol. X (1954), 301-13. Erasmus Darwin's son, Charles, was also early educated in science and mechanics. According to a memoir by his father, he later "acquired a complete knowledge of the latin and greek languages, chiefly by reading books of useful knowledge, or which contained the elements of science." At the same time he studied botany, fossil history, chemistry and anatomy, and applied himself "to natural philosophy experimentally." After a year at Oxford he "sigh'd to be removed to the robuster exercises of the medical schools of Edinburgh", where, after spending the greater part of the day "in accurately dissecting the brain of a child, who had died of hydrocephalus internus", he was suddenly taken ill and died. Charles Darwin, *Experiments establishing a criterion between mucilaginous and purulent matter* (ed Erasmus Darwin, 1780), 127-34. I am indebted to Dr. S. Lilley for drawing my attention to the memoir by Erasmus Darwin, published in this book.

In the same way, educational writings and practical efforts to found new institutions were predominantly concerned with advancing an enlightened education for the middle class; one whose influence might spread to the established educational system. Within this framework, the ideas advanced were often radical and progressive, inspired by the scientific spirit typical of the men concerned and expressing also their moral outlook and social aspirations.

2. EDUCATIONAL ATTITUDES AND ACTIVITIES

The educational ideas of Priestley and Darwin, Edgeworth and Day, were based first on a definite conception of the kind of people education should produce, of the moral qualities it should endeavour to inculcate. Second, the possibility of shaping young people by education was affirmed in the light of the psychological theory of associationism which provided a rational explanation of the learning process, and the idea arose that education itself could become a science. Third, depending on both these standpoints, a curriculum was outlined, and methods of teaching were advocated of a kind adapted both to the subject matter proposed and to the needs of the child. Some of these ideas were put into practice at the Warrington and Manchester Academies, and, later, at Hackney College, the last of these institutions to come into being, and also in the education given at home and in certain private schools such as that run by the Unitarian minister, David Williams, and by Priestley's friend, Thomas Wright Hill of Birmingham.

(i) A New Morality

Priestley defined his educational aim as the provision of a "proper course of studies" for young gentlemen "designed to fill the principal stations of active life", one which would fit youth "for the business of manhood". This stress on "active life", the "business of manhood", is typical of the Lunar Society outlook. To men fully involved in the scientific and industrial, the social, religious and philosophical issues of the time, life had many facets. What drew all these together was, above all, science. In all the writings with which we are concerned, the emphasis on science—on the understanding of nature and its laws —is all-pervading. This emphasis extended to an attempt to understand the nature of children, and then to seeking means to develop that nature in a human and moral direction.

Here, the influence of Rousseau's works, which expressed a point of view diametrically opposite to that of prevailing educational practice, was at first decisive. *La Nouvelle Héloïse* became known in England in 1761, the first translation of *Emile* appeared in the following year; both aroused tremendous interest and enthusiasm. "Were all the books in the world to be destroyed," wrote Day to Edgeworth in 1769,

> "the second book I should wish to save, after the Bible would be Rousseau's Emilius. It is, indeed, a most extraordinary work—the more I read, the more I admire—Rousseau alone, with a perspicuity more than mortal, has been able at once to look through the human heart, and discover the secret sources and combinations of the passions. Every page is big with important truth."[1]

So impressed was Edgeworth with Rousseau's system by contrast with "the obvious deficiencies and absurdities . . . in the treatment of children in almost every family" with which he was acquainted, that he determined to leave "the body and mind of my son . . . as much as possible to the education of nature and of accident".[2] In this course he continued for five years until the child was eight years old, when, on a visit to Paris, he introduced him to Rousseau, who took the boy for a walk and pronounced himself in general satisfied with his development. From Paris Edgeworth proceeded to Lyons where, characteristically, he applied all his energy to a scheme for turning the course of the Rhone, leaving the supervision of his son's education to Thomas Day, who took on the task with enthusiasm.

Not long afterwards, however, Edgeworth abandoned the experiment. The boy had developed considerable abilities, he recalled later in his *Memoirs*:

> "uncommon strength and hardiness of body, great vivacity, and was not a little disposed to think and act for himself. . . . Whatever regarded the health, strength, and agility of my son, had amply justified the system of my master; but I found myself entangled in difficulties with regard to my child's mind and temper. He was generous, brave, good-natured, and what is commonly called good-tempered; but he was scarcely to be controlled. It was difficult to urge him to anything that did not suit his fancy, and more difficult to restrain him from what he wished to follow. In short, he was self-willed, from a spirit of independence which had been inculcated

[1] Edgeworth, *Memoirs*, Vol. 1, 221.   [2] *Ibid.*, Vol. I, 172-3.

by his early education, and which he cherished the more from the inexperience of his own powers."[1]

Edgeworth, therefore, rejected Rousseau's conception of natural virtue and, though continuing to consider the child's needs, stressed in his writings the importance of forming human and moral qualities. The child should be brought up to be pure, honest, truthful, inventive and self-reliant, interested in the world around him, usefully engaged and concerned with his own improvement. He was to be capable of hard work, perseverance and concentration, able to use his hands and to unite theory and practice; he must develop an affection for humanity and be concerned to better the human condition. This implied a close concern with the content of education and methods of teaching, and it is in the chapters on this theme in *Practical Education* that Edgeworth develops his ideas; the many chapters on what may more strictly be called moral education, contributed chiefly by his daughter Maria, have less interest.

It is to Thomas Day, described by his friend Edgeworth as "the most virtuous human being whom I have ever known",[2] that we may turn for a detailed analysis of moral purposes in education. Indeed, *Sandford and Merton* is essentially an essay in moral education, specifically intended and framed "to form and interest the minds of children".[3]

Written to popularise Rousseau's educational method, the theme was presented for children in such a way as to engage their interest and arouse their amusement; and, though the book is essentially didactic, it succeeded in its aim in so far as it became one of the most widely read children's books, constantly reprinted to meet a steady demand.

The story concerns the reclamation and education of Tommy Merton, a boy with a naturally good disposition but corrupted by the wealth, extravagance and values of upper-class society. Tommy is taken from his home and brought under the constant educative care and control of a tutor, Mr. Barlow, and so also under the influence of Harry Sandford, a farmer's son who is a paragon of all natural virtue. The account of his re-education, which is not without setbacks, is interspersed with a variety of stories—which Day finds in sources ranging from Plutarch to the latest *Memoirs* of the Manchester Literary and Philosophical Society—each of which is not only

---

[1] Edgeworth, *Memoirs*, Vol. I, 268-9.   [2] *Ibid.*, Vol. I, 177.
[3] *Sandford and Merton*, Vol. I, ix.

instructive (and indeed still interesting), but specifically chosen to illustrate Day's notions of truly moral, or immoral, behaviour. From the start of the book to its close, therefore, the reader never ceases to be concerned with the fundamental question as to what is and what is not a moral act—how one *ought* to behave.

Fundamentally, following Rousseau, Day is concerned to challenge the values of "civilised" society which he holds up to obloquy. When Mr. Barlow rode about the country he

> "used to consider with admiration, the splendid stables which the great construct for the reception of their horses, their ice-houses, temples, hermitages, grottoes, and all the apparatus of modern vanity. All this, he would say, is an unequivocal proof that the gentleman loves himself, and grudges no expense that can gratify his vanity."

But he would then wish to see what this gentleman

> "has done for his fellow-creatures, what are the proofs that he has given of public spirit or humanity; the wrongs which he has redressed, the miseries he has alleviated, the abuses which he has endeavoured to remove."[1]

The tutor would draw other lessons from contemplation of the countryside; the lesson, which owed much to the teaching of Adam Smith, that labour is the source of all wealth, all production:

> "Without labour, these fertile fields which are now adorned with all the luxuriance of plenty would be converted into barbarian heaths or impenetrable thickets; these meadows, the support of a thousand herds of cattle, be covered with stagnated waters. . . . Even these innumerable flocks of sheep, that feed along the hills, would disappear along with that cultivation, which can alone support them, and secure their existence."

There was an essential moral to be drawn from this analysis:

> "For this reason, would Mr. Barlow say, labour is the first and most indispensable duty of the human species, from which no one can have the right entirely to withdraw himself."[2]

The wealthy and idle were, therefore, to be both despised and pitied. Day prefaced the second volume of his book with a quotation from Lord Mondobbo:

---

[1] *Sandford and Merton*, Vol. II, 210.   [2] *Ibid.*, Vol. II, 268-9.

"I do not know that there is upon the face of the earth a more useless, more contemptible, and more miserable animal than a wealthy, luxurious man, without business or profession, arts, sciences or exercises."

He himself represents the rich as concerned only to increase their wealth at the expense of the poor: "a thousand cottages are thrown down to afford space for a single palace".[1] But this state of luxurious living fails to bring happiness:

"What, said he, shall a wretch, a peasant, a low-born fellow that weaves bulrushes for a scanty subsistence, be always happy and pleased, while I, that am a gentleman possest of riches and power, and of more consequence than a million reptiles like him, am always melancholy and discontented?"[2]

It is in the poorer classes alone that desirable human qualities are to be found; among independent farmers and in all societies that have not been corrupted by excess of wealth, luxury and easy living—the Arabs, Spartans, American Indians, Greenlanders, Scotsmen, Negroes. Their virtues comprise the classical qualities of simplicity in life and behaviour; independence, initiative, fortitude in adversity. They have human compassion and active benevolence, integrity, moderation, self-command, clemency, generosity; above all, public spirit, which is the product of a true humanity.

It follows that the most important task in the education of the gentleman is to extirpate any idea of his natural superiority, his natural right to command others, replacing it with the desire for self-improvement. Thomas Day illustrates that this can be achieved: "I now plainly perceive", says Tommy towards the close of his education, "that a man may be of much more consequence by improving his mind in various kinds of knowledge, than by all the finery and magnificence he can acquire."[3]

And it is the most important outcome of his training that he comes "to consider all men as his brethren and equals".[4] His education completed, many of his early illusions have been shattered, his system of values overturned; he has become mild, obliging, engaging, developing the qualities of composure and fortitude; he has learned:

"how much better it is to be useful than rich or fine; how much more amiable to be good than to be great."[5]

[1] *Sandford and Merton*, Vol. I, 37.   [2] *Ibid.*, Vol. I, 63.   [3] *Ibid.*, Vol. III, 255.
[4] *Ibid.*, Vol. III, 298.   [5] *Ibid.*, Vol. III, 311.

Defining the human qualities that required development in this way, and finding them in every section of society except the aristocracy, Day gave clear expression to the outlook of a new and rising class as it began to challenge the ruling morality and those subservient to it. "The pool of mercenary and time serving ethics was first blown over by the fresh country breeze of Mr. T. Day," wrote Leigh Hunt in his autobiography, "a production that I well remember and shall ever be grateful to."[1] Instead of bowing to established values, accepting the prevailing social morality, men must find new ethical values to inform enlightened behaviour; this was Thomas Day's message and, for him, ethical behaviour rested on the doctrine of enlightened self-interest—if you do good to others, others will do good to you. This simple precept, central to the bourgeois morality of the late eighteenth century, is often explicitly stated and also drawn as a moral from many of the tales recounted and many of the events in the book.[2] It is on the foundation of this precept that Day builds his whole system of morality; though mention is made of the precepts of religion and the tutor, Mr. Barlow, is a clergyman, this morality owes little to religious inspiration; it is essentially rational and secular.

Day's only predecessor in this *genre* of literature in England was Dr. Percival of Manchester, one of whose moral tales, told personally by Percival to De Quincey when still a child, had so profound an effect on the latter that he published it many years later in his autobiography.[3] Day acknowledged the influence of Percival's book, but his own had much wider repercussions. Highly recommended by the Edgeworths and Erasmus Darwin, it was to have an immediate success which was by no means confined to this country; its very sharp social criticism exactly fitted the mood of the democratic movement of the 1780s, and it is with some reason that a French writer has commented: "*Il y a, le mot n'est pas trop fort, la Révolution qui gronde en Thomas Day.*"[4]

If, however, this was the objective significance of Day's work, he

---

[1] J. E. Molpurgo (ed), *The Autobiography of Leigh Hunt* (1949), 51; he goes on: "It came in aid of my mother's perplexities between delicacy and hardihood, between courage and conscientiousness. It assisted the cheerfulness I inherited from my father; showed me that circumstances were not to crush a healthy gaiety, or the most masculine self-respect; and helped to supply me with the resolution of standing by a principle, not merely as a point of lowly or lofty sacrifice, but as a matter of common sense and duty, and a simple co-operation with the elements of natural welfare."

[2] For instance, the story of Hamet, and of the good and cruel boy.

[3] D. Masson (ed), *Collected Works of Thomas De Quincey* (1889), Vol. I, 131-3.

[4] J. Pons, *L'Education en Angleterre entre 1750 et 1800* (1919), 189.

and his colleagues were rather intent on preaching for the conversion
of the aristocracy; and at the same time, promoting a system of ethics
which would bring up the younger generation of their own class to
live an active and influential life. "I was very fond of *Sandford and
Merton*," wrote Mary Anne, Galton's daughter, "and this book, together with my mother's instructions grounded upon it, formed a
decided phase in my tastes and habits of mind. I thus early learnt to
abhor finery, and to consider it as contemptible. . . . I held also in
the greatest contempt all aristocratic distinctions. I loved Harry Sandford for contemning the rich and the fashionable at Mr. Merton's,
and for helping the poor. I had the utmost enthusiasm for his refusing
to denounce the poor hare to Squire Close; and for Hamet, the
generous Turk."[1] It was not in ostentation and self-indulgence but
in useful work, in acquiring useful knowledge, that men added to
their human qualities and so became whole and happy human beings.
"Let us be satisfied", Priestley had written earlier, "if we can make
our children good men, and truly valuable members of society,
whether the reception they meet with in the world be favourable
or unfavourable."[2] "There is nothing on earth I so much wish for",
wrote Matthew Boulton to his son, "as to make you a *man*, a good
man, a useful man, and consequently a happy man."[3]

Not only in the works of Edgeworth and Day, Priestley and
Darwin of the Lunar Society, in those of Percival, Barnes and Harrison
of Manchester, but also in William Godwin, Mary Wollstonecraft
and others of their circle, the same aim is apparent; the same striving
towards a rational, secular, human morality, which would inspire
men and women to usher in a more truly human era in the history
of man.

(ii) *Education as a Science*

All that has been said about moral training, the formation of
character, implies a belief that education can change men's nature.
This was a conviction that eighteenth-century educationists owed to
materialist philosophers; the belief that man was a rational being and

---

[1] *Life of Mary Anne Schimmelpenninck*, Vol. I, 10-11.

[2] J. Priestley, *Miscellaneous Observations* (1780 edn), xv.

[3] S. Smiles, *op. cit.*, 405; in another characteristic letter Boulton adjures his son not "to
be polite at the expense of honour, truth, sincerity, and honesty; for these are the props
of a manly character, and without them politeness is mean and deceitful. Therefore, be
always tenacious of your honour. Be honest, just, and benevolent, even when it appears
difficult to be so. I say, cherish those principles, and guard then as sacred treasure."
Ibid., 340-1.

therefore capable of advancing to perfection, the firm conviction that it was not only possible but also essential to "form children's minds", a faith in the all-powerful influence of education—these were fundamental to their thought.

The roots of these ideas are to be traced to the works of Hobbes, Descartes and Locke, who first elaborated a materialist theory of knowledge. But Priestley and his associates drew more directly on a psychological theory which, though stemming directly from materialist philosophy, also owed much to advances in anatomy and dicimene; that advanced by David Hartley in his *Observations on Man* (1749). In this work, psychology began to emerge as a distinct discipline, separate from philosophical enquiry. Elaborating the theory of associationism as the basic process of learning, and basing this theory firmly on the physiology of the nervous system so far as it was then understood, Hartley produced what was the first scientific treatise on psychology. His influence on educational thought, on philosophy itself, in the late eighteenth and early nineteenth centuries cannot be exaggerated. It is the key to a grasp of the educational optimism so characteristic of this time.

Writing of psychology, Priestley could say: "Something was done in this field of knowledge by Descartes, very much by Locke, but most of all by Dr. Hartley, who has thrown more useful light upon the theory of the mind than Newton did upon the theory of the natural world."[1] Priestley, who embraced and developed Hartley's theories, reprinted his book in 1775 with an introduction of his own. "I think myself", he wrote, "more indebted to this one treatise, than to all the books I ever read beside, the scriptures excepted."[2] What was of particular moment to Priestley was the application of psychological theory to use, and, he wrote, "the most important application of Dr. Hartley's doctrine of the association of ideas is to the *conduct of human life*, and especially the business of education".[3]

Associationism provided a rational, materialist theory of human learning; one which led logically to the conclusion that man's mind is formed by his circumstances, that is, by education conceived of in its widest sense. Locke had advanced the view that the mind is a blank

[1] J. Priestley, *An Examination of Dr. Reid's Inquiry into the Human Mind on the Principles of Common Sense* (1774), xv.

[2] *Ibid.*, xix.

[3] *Ibid.*, xiii. Priestley's contribution to educational theory and practice has been assessed by J. Wootton, "The non-conformist contribution to educational thought and ideas in the eighteenth century with special reference to the writings and work of Joseph Priestley", unpublished M.Ed. thesis (1955), Leeds University.

sheet at birth, Hobbes had argued that the foundation of all knowledge is to be found in sensations caused by the action of external objects on the senses. Hartley went on to show that ideas, originally arising in this way and developing on the foundation of physiological processes in the brain, inevitably become "associated" together in a certain order in the mind. From this it followed that, by organising a child's experiences according to a definite pattern, it was possible to exercise a formative influence on his mental development.

Taking up these ideas, Priestley developed them a stage further in relation to education. Hobbes had argued convincingly that nature is governed by laws and that these laws can be discovered; this was the foundation for all scientific hypothesis and experiment. There must also, Priestley argued, be laws governing the working of the human mind which was part of nature, as man himself was; taking Hartley's theory as a basis, further laws could be discovered by observation and experiment—education itself could become a science.

It was chiefly Priestley who, in his philosophic controversies, took associationism to its logical conclusion in the "great and glorious doctrine of necessity". But his colleagues were also, in effect, thoroughgoing determinists. In an interesting passage on the educational significance of the opposing theories of freewill and necessity, Priestley shows that only to the extent that the educator's actions have a necessary effect on his pupils can his labours have any purpose.[1] *Sandford and Merton*, indeed Rousseau's *Emile*, may be regarded as expositions of educational determinism in this sense. The story of the two dogs who develop opposite characteristics in different environments, and whose characters change diametrically when they are exchanged,[2] is paralleled by the change in Tommy Merton as he moves first to Mr. Barlow's house, then back to his own and finally to Harry Sandford's. Each exchange has its necessary effect; Tommy is the product of his circumstances—nor could it be otherwise.

But these circumstances include a planned course of education, the educator's purpose brought to bear through specific methods of teaching. Here the way must be lighted by science. The Edgeworths roundly claim that progress in education depends on patiently reducing it to an experimental science, which must be the labour of many generations. For themselves, they write, as "we rely entirely upon practice

---

[1] J. Priestley, *The Doctrine of Philosophic Necessity Illustrated* (2nd edn, 1782), Vol. II, 84-8.

[2] *Sandford and Merton*, Vol. I, 75ff.

and experience, we have chosen the title of *Practical Education*". In fact, this title was chosen by Edgeworth's second wife, Honora, who first kept a register of her children's remarks and reactions which was carried on after her death by her husband and daughter and freely drawn upon in their book.[1]

It is in the same spirit that David Williams—Unitarian, friend of Priestley, who ran his own school—acclaims Hartley's attempt to understand the human mind and affirms that until this is achieved there can be "no rule to go by in education"; men "must proceed, as they do now at random". He adds: "It is necessary that a man should have a clear and distinct idea of the manner in which habits are formed before he can pretend to regulate that formation; and before he should pretend to interfere in education."[2]

Meanwhile, as a result of observation and practical experience, ideas about habits of learning were formulated; in particular the view that failures resulted from deficiencies in teaching rather than from lack of ability in children. Thus the Edgeworths write:

> "It is not from want of capacity that so many children are deficient in arithmetical skill and it is absurd to say 'such a child has no genius for arithmetic, such a child cannot be made to comprehend anything about numbers'. These assertions prove nothing, but that the persons who make them are ignorant of the art of teaching."[3]

Edgeworth does not deny that differences between children, whether natural or acquired, appear early; the fact that they increase with age "seems to prove that during the interval the power of education has operated strongly to increase the original propensities".

The important task of the educator is to avoid allowing the child to lose confidence in his ability. If a child is experiencing difficulties, Edgeworth advised, point out that "attentive patience can do as much as quickness of intellect, if they perceive that time makes all the difference between the quick and the slow, they will be induced to persevere".

This precept arose from practical experiments in educating his own children:

> "the same problems have been frequently given to children of

---

[1] "She was of opinion that the art of education should be considered as an experimental science, and that many authors of great abilities had mistaken their road by following theory instead of practice." *Practical Education*, Vol. III, 324.

[2] David Williams, *Lectures on Education* (1789), Vol. I, 23.

[3] *Practical Education*, Vol. II, 246.

different degrees of quickness, and though some have succeeded much more quickly than others, all the individuals in the family have persevered until they have solved the questions; and the timid seem to have been more encouraged by this practical demonstration of the infallibility of persevering attention, than by any other methods which we have tried."[1]

The Edgeworths, therefore, were led to place attention at the centre of the educational scheme, as did Helvétius, and to regard its presence or absence as the primary cause of intellectual success or failure. It was part of their practice to make the children themselves conscious of this, and to this end they advise reading the works of Benjamin Franklin and others who stress that achievement is due to perseverance. This positive approach is coupled with the general view that all children—all human beings, even to the most ignorant savages— have the power of abstracting and generalising; all, then, are capable of intellectual development through education.

These ideas were a challenge to prevailing views that men are born with certain innate ideas and instincts, with mental and moral faculties which unfold during life but are insusceptible to educational influence. A hundred years earlier, Locke had opened his *Essay Concerning Human Understanding* with a devastating assault on the contemporary theory of innate ideas, and propounded instead that of the *tabula rasa*—the mind as a blank sheet at birth. His *Essay* is an attempt to interpret how the mind, "void of all characters, without any ideas . . . comes to be furnished . . . by that vast store, which the busy and boundless fancy of man has painted on it with an almost endless variety".[2]

In Priestley's time, the theory of innate instincts was being propagated anew specifically in opposition to materialist ideas. It was in actively challenging this doctrine that Priestley chiefly developed his psychological ideas, as for instance in his *Examination of Dr. Reid's Inquiry*, whose title page bears the challenging quotation:

"As some men have imagined *innate ideas*, because they have forgot how they came by them, so others have set up almost as many *distinct instincts* as there are *acquired principles* of acting."

The theory of instincts, Priestley maintained, implies that ultimate principles have been reached, checks all further enquiry into behaviour, and so is a disservice to science. Behaviour ascribed to instincts,

[1] *Practical Education*, Vol. I, 137-9.
[2] *An Essay Concerning Human Understanding*, Bk. 2, Ch. 1, Sect. 2.

and therefore supposed to be innate, is in fact, Priestley reaffirms, acquired behaviour. Of the allied theory that the child's innate reasoning and moral faculties "unfold themselves by degrees", he comments drily "this hypothesis of the gradual *unfolding* of the powers of the mind very much resembles the gradual *acquisition* of them, from the impressions to which we are exposed". He buttresses this standpoint with examples of the association of ideas leading to new forms of behaviour, and with a wealth of psychological evidence.

The rationalist viewpoint was given its most complete expression—and its widest circulation—by the philosopher, William Godwin, in *Political Justice* (1793). Men will only begin to know themselves, to realise their full potentialities, Godwin proclaimed, when they come to recognise that there are no obstacles to improvement which they cannot overcome by their own efforts. They will only exert the energy necessary to success when they have got rid of fettering prejudices of "the chilling system of occult and inexplicable causes, and consider the human mind as an intelligent agent" guided by explicable causes and not by some unknown force. The argument applied with particular force to education:

> "How long has the genius of education been disheartened and unnerved by the pretence that man is born all that it is possible for him to become? How long has the jargon imposed upon the world, which would persuade us that in instructing a man you do not add to but unfold his stores?"

Failures in education, Godwin reaffirmed, are in no way due to the limitations of its powers but stem "from the mistakes with which it is accompanied":

> "Education will proceed with a firm step and with genuine lustre, when those who conduct it shall know what a vast field it embraces; when they shall be made aware that . . . the question whether the pupil shall be a man of perseverance and enterprise or a stupid and inanimate dolt, depends upon the powers of those under whose direction he is placed, and the skill with which those powers shall be applied."[1]

This was the argument, above all others, which the educationists were concerned to drive home. They had embraced the theory advanced by English materialist philosophers and developed by their

[1] *Enquiry concerning Political Justice and its influence on morals and happiness* (3rd edn, 1798), Bk. I, Ch. 4, 43–4.

French successors, that man is the product of his circumstances; a theory propounded in social terms by Adam Smith when he asserted that the wide differences between the philosopher and the street porter arise not so much from differences in natural talents as from "habit, custom and education". They accepted Hartley's psychological theory of associationism, which, within this framework, set out to explain how mental life is formed. All this implied rejection of the traditional view that human powers are inborn, the unchangeable attributes of an indivisible soul; and led to the affirmation that an enlightened education could be the most vital of circumstances making man. If it were to be genuinely enlightened, education must become a science. It remained to discover, in so far as possible by observation and experiment, how education could best be planned to develop moral and intellectual powers in desired directions. In the process, Priestley, the Edgeworths, Godwin, voiced their profound belief, not only in men's rights and duties, but also in human powers; the belief that, once freed from the bonds of outmoded ideas and educational practices, there was no limit to human abilities, to what men could do and achieve.

(iii) *The Content of Education and Methods of Teaching*

As might be expected, in detailing the subjects to be studied and how they should be taught to children, the Edgeworths, Darwin and Day lay great emphasis on science and its practical application.

In *Sandford and Merton* the truly human individual is personified in the old philosopher Chares, who comments on the worthlessness of riches and pleasure and spends his life, so far as possible, in observation of nature, cultivating the land, investigating the nature of vegetables and the qualities of soils; in addition, applying science for the benefit of his fellow men by cleansing a noxious marsh and reclaiming the land for the village. During the course of his education Tommy Merton learns to work on the land, goes botanising, visits a windmill to see how it works and builds a house with Harry, so learning the principles of effective construction against wind and rain. Besides learning to read, and to apply arithmetic to practical use, he also studies astronomy, making a star-globe and learning the use of stars for navigation. He finds out, from practical experience, the qualities of lever, wedge and pulley; and the properties and practical applications of magnetism, which leads on to study of the compass and thence, through navigation, to commerce and the exchange of products. He also uses lenses and studies the phenomenon of the bending of light.

In addition to scientific knowledge of this kind, Tommy also learns about natural history—the characters, habits and uses of the elephant, camel, crocodile, monkey, reindeer, seal and whale; while, otherwise, Day is constantly referring to human geography—the conditions of life and economic activities of Egyptians, Laplanders, Kamchatkans, American Indians and Negroes. Tommy himself declares that he will never rest until he has become acquainted with everything of interest in every branch of knowledge. "A man," he decides, "should know how to do everything in the world." "The more knowledge he acquires", replies Mr. Barlow, "the better."

Day evidently followed this method with his orphaned wards, for Sabrina writes to Edgeworth: "I know how to make a circle and an equilateral triangle—I know the cause of night and day, winter and summer."[1] In other households there was the same preoccupation. Matthew Boulton, writing to Watt, describes how their two boys had spent the holidays erecting a Savery's engine to work a forge below his duck pond. "They are both exceedingly keen on it," he writes, adding: "We have killed many poor robins by pouring fixable air upon them, and had some amusement in our electrical and chemical hobby-horsery which the young men like much better than dry Latin."[2] So also, it is characteristic that Josiah Wedgwood, considering a portrait of his three sons to be painted by Joseph Wright, planned that the eldest should be shown "standing at a table making fixable air with the glass apparatus, and, etc., and his two brothers accompanying him, Tom jumping up and clapping his hands in joy and surprise at seeing the stream of bubbles rise up just as Jack has put a little chalk to the acid. Jos with the chemical dictionary before him in a thoughtful mood, which actions will be exactly descriptive of their respective characters".[3] Galton's daughter, Mary Anne, describes her early education in detail in her autobiography and refers particularly to her father's delight in teaching her science and natural history, both in his laboratory at home, during walks in the country and at the seaside where "everything around furnished new materials for knowledge and for scientific exploration".[4] "I have lately", wrote John Dalton of Manchester, "had the pleasure of undertaking to

[1] Edgeworth, *Memoirs*, Vol. I, 220.　　[2] Smiles, *op. cit.*, 404.

[3] E. Meteyard, *The Life of Josiah Wedgwood*, Vol. II (1866), 441. Unfortunately this painting was never finally commissioned, the Wedgwood family portrait being painted by Stubbs.

[4] Schimmelpenninck, *op. cit.*, Vol. I, 62.

instruct some very amiable and accomplished young ladies in chemistry, namely Dr. Percival's daughters."[1]

Erasmus Darwin also held that such interests were not only for boys but should be extended to girls as part of their regular education in school. In *Female Education*, he advocates a curriculum covering grammar, languages, arithmetic, geography, civil and natural history, arts and sciences; for instance botany, an outline of chemistry, "a sketch of mineralogy" which should refer not only to precious stones but also to mining and the composition of soils, a necessary foundation for the theory and practice of agriculture. The girls should also be introduced to astronomy, mechanics, hydrostatics and optics; while "electricity and magnetism" should be acquired by attending lectures in experimental philosophy given by "itinerant philosophers"—the travelling lecturer being a feature of the age. The arts and manufactures "which adorn and enrich this country" and contribute to the "convenience of life" should be "exhibited to young ladies by their parents in the summer vacations"—the cotton mills on the Derwent, potteries in Staffordshire run by his friend Wedgwood, the iron foundries at Coalbrookdale, and the factories at Birmingham, Manchester and Nottingham.

Answering the charge that he is putting too great an emphasis on these subjects, Darwin counters that

"as in male education the tedious acquirement of ancient languages for the purpose of studying poetry and oratory is gradually giving way to the more useful cultivation of the modern sciences",

it may be an advantage to ladies to acquire this understanding, since it will assist them to attain a reciprocal understanding with their future life companion.[2] While the female should be pliant, mild and retiring, single women may later cultivate the arts and sciences "for their amusement or instruction"; the married woman "may need energy in the care, education and provision for a family" if her husband should die or be otherwise useless. Therefore women need to be able to transact the business of life. Education, then, should prepare a girl for her future life, uniting "health and agility of body with cheerfulness and agility of mind" and providing for the acquirement "of the rudiments of such arts and sciences, as may amuse ourselves,

---

[1] W. C. Henry, *Memoirs of the Life and Scientific Researches of John Dalton* (1854), 47.

[2] Erasmus Darwin, *A Plan for the Conduct of Female Education in Boarding Schools* (1797), 40-5.

or gain us the esteem of others; with a strict attention to the culture of morality and religion".[1]

But it is above all the Edgeworths who base their educational practice on a full grasp of the achievements of contemporary science and who are concerned to prepare children for a predominantly scientific culture. It is impossible here to do justice to the extraordinary richness of ideas concerning pedagogical methodology outlined in certain chapters of their book, perhaps particularly the chapter entitled "Toys" ("the first hint" of which, they acknowledge, "was received from Dr. Beddoes")[2] and that on mechanics, the latter written by R. L. Edgeworth.

Above all, the child is encouraged to find things out for himself, to make models illustrating mechanical principles, to try every kind of chemical and physical experiment. "In the papers of the Manchester Society," they write, "in Franklin's letters, in Priestley's and Percival's works, there may be found a variety of simple experiments which require no great apparatus, and which will at once amuse and instruct."[3] For Percival's experiments, for instance, "oil and water, a cork, a needle, a plate and glass tumbler are all the things necessary. . . ."[4] Children should be given small stills, tea-kettles and lamps, for boiling, evaporating, distilling and subliming; they should be shown simple experiments which they can later undertake themselves: evaporation, crystallisation, calcination, detonation, effervescence and saturation. The experiments should be rational; all trick effects—popular at the time—should be avoided.

The children should fill their shelves with specimens of ores logically arranged. Cheap microscopes should be produced, so opening up a world of new delights. They can be interested in optics. "In Dr. Priestley's *History of Vision* many experiments may be found which are not above the comprehension of children of 10 and 11 years old",[5] so developing a taste for science by making it exciting. "In Dr. Franklin's *Letters* there are numerous experiments which are particularly suited to young people; especially as in every instance he speaks with that candour and openness to conviction, and with that patient desire to discover the truth, which we should wish our pupils to admire and imitate." In mechanics, chemistry, geometry and the arts, "instead of showing young people the steps of a discovery, we should

[1] Erasmus Darwin, *A Plan for the Conduct of Female Education in Boarding Schools* (1797), 9-11.
[2] *Practical Education*, Vol. I, xi.   [3] *Ibid.*, Vol. I, 45.   [4] *Ibid.*, Vol. I, 46.
[5] *Ibid.*, Vol. I, 49.

frequently pause to try if they can invent. In this our pupils will often succeed beyond our expectations".[1]

But in particular, following Edgeworth's own dominating interest, it is in mechanics and technology that many of the most original ideas are to be found. At an early age the child should be provided with "card, pasteboard, substantial but not sharp-pointed scissors, wire, gum and wax". He should make models of furniture which can be taken to bits. Later he should be given "all manner of carpenter's tools, with wood properly prepared for the young workman, and with screws, nails, glue, emery paper", etc., making architectural models, and then simple machines, beginning with "wheelbarrows, carts, cranes, scales, steelyards, jacks and pumps, which children ever view with eager eyes".[2] So to models of more complicated machinery, such as spinning wheels, looms, paper mills, windmills, watermills. While working on such models they should be taken on factory visits, under the care of someone properly qualified to explain the various processes. The workmen might assist the teachers on these visits, which should concentrate on a limited number of processes, involving as many as four or five visits for a complete understanding of the processes studied. Later, their ingenuity may be excited by setting particular mechanical problems, and asking the children to invent a model illustrating the practical solution to the problems posed. So the children will learn to compare various contrivances and to discern which parts of a machine "are superfluous and what inadequate, and they will class particular observations gradually under general principles".[3] The child should work in wood, brass and iron, he should learn the use of the turning lathe and the work bench, so gaining constant active employment and pleasure in carrying projects through to a successful conclusion, in "executing their own plans". The child will gain by constant manual and physical exercise.

Edgeworth develops these points on the methodology of teaching mechanics in the chapter on this subject, describing in detail some of the apparatus he evolved and some of the very complex questions, for instance, on velocity, he set to his children, together with the models they constructed to prove the thesis. Apart from practical mechanical work and perspective drawing (necessary for understanding prints of machines, of architecture and of tools), he is concerned with teaching the theory and practice of the wedge, the lever, the pulley, the inclined plane, friction, and resistance of air and water,

---

[1] *Practical Education*, Vol. I, 50-1.   [2] *Ibid.*, Vol. I, 36-8.   [3] *Ibid.*, Vol. I, 40.

and later with the ideas of space, time, velocity, momentum, force and gravity. His aim is primarily to lay a sure foundation for future improvement, hence his emphasis on the construction of machines and models by the children themselves. "Children who are thus induced to invent machines or apparatus for explaining and demonstrating the laws of mechanism, not only fix indelibly those laws on their own minds, but enlarge their powers of invention, and preserve a certain originality of thought, which leads to new discoveries. We therefore strongly recommend it to teachers, to use as few precepts as possible in the rudiments of science, and to encourage their pupils to use their own understandings as they advance. In acquiring a knowledge of mechanism a general view of the powers and uses of engines is all that need to be taught; where more is necessary, such a foundation with the assistance of good books, and the examination of good machinery, will perfect the knowledge of theory and facilitate practice."[1]

One of the features of Edgeworth, Darwin and Day is that, although they certainly placed considerable emphasis on the acquisition of knowledge, or, more accurately, of the means to knowledge, they were also deeply concerned with the child's all-round moral, cultural, aesthetic and physical development, and indeed were pioneers in these fields as well as in that of science and technology. In fact, in their writings, the sections on the acquisition of knowledge are relatively short compared to the space devoted to other aspects of education. If their interest in science is brought out here, it is because this is perhaps the most significant aspect of their general outlook.

Erasmus Darwin was, however, one of the first to study the effect of physical circumstances on mental development, and was given full credit for his pioneering work by James Mill in his famous article on education, published in 1818 in the *Supplement* to the *Encyclopaedia Britannica*. Mill refers particularly to Darwin's *Zoonomia* as the main source of these observations, and indeed there is much in this work which has an application to education, some of which was drawn on by the Edgeworths. In Darwin's work on *Female Education* a good deal of attention is given to the need for exercise, fresh air, effective ventilation of bedrooms, the most healthy kind of clothing for girls, and diet, together with advice as to how to cure lisping, stammering, squinting, involuntary motions (what we call "tics"), swelled fingers and kibed heels. Edgeworth constantly emphasised the need for bodily

[1] *Practical Education*, Vol. II, 315-16.

exercise,[1] while Tommy Merton and Harry Sandford are never still. It is this all-round approach to education which is one of the chief features of their educational theory and practice.

(iv) *The Academies*

If ideas about the education of children could only be put fully into practice in the home, and to some extent in such small schools as those run by David Williams and Darwin's daughters, there was more scope for developing a new curriculum in higher education. The innovations introduced at Warrington Academy (1757-86) have already been referred to. This tradition was continued at the Manchester Academy, its direct successor. It was carried further, particularly as regards the teaching of philosophy, at Hackney College (1786-96), another creation of the "wide" dissenters; while a new effort to further the advanced teaching of science was embodied in the Manchester College of Arts and Sciences initiated by the Literary and Philosophical Society.

It was on his experience at Warrington that Priestley primarily drew in outlining detailed proposals for widening the curriculum of higher educational institutions. When he joined the staff in 1761, the Academy was already giving a broad general education designed not only for students intended for the Ministry, but also those preparing for business and commerce, medicine and law, who represented to a considerable extent a new element in the dissenting academy.

The full course for the latter in 1760 covered, in addition to the classical languages, grammar and rhetoric, mathematics (including trigonometry), natural philosophy (including astronomy and chemistry), English composition, French, commercial and economic geography. "A short system of morality . . . concluding with the evidences for the Christian religion", was given in the final year. Exercises included dissertations on moral, political and commercial subjects. Special attention was given to English pronunciation, and instruction was available in writing, drawing, book-keeping and shorthand.

As we have seen, Priestley was originally appointed to lecture on the theory of language, oratory and criticism. But to this he soon added his remarkable series of lectures on "History and General Policy", "Laws and Constitution of England" and "History of England". The syllabus of these courses, which represented an entirely new departure in educational practice, was first published in 1765, and later included with

---

[1] Cf. his plan of a school; *Memoirs*, Vol. II, 430.

his *Essay on a Course of Liberal Education for Civil and Active Life*, itself "written to recommend and explain" the courses but in fact ranging more widely. This book, reprinted many times, had a far-reaching influence on the transformation of educational practice.

In putting the case for the teaching of history, Priestley advises that more attention should be given also to geography, particularly economic and commercial geography, where the various products of the different countries should be studied, and commercial links and opportunities brought out. Law also deserves attention for similar reasons, while the practical utility of the study of chemistry is made clear. Without a knowledge of chemistry, Priestley writes, "a man might for instance be digging for . . . a baser metal, and overlook another of much more value, which might lie in his way. So great an advantage might he miss for want of knowing such ores. And it is more than probable, that the countries to which we trade for articles of small account are capable of furnishing us with commodities of much greater value, and will be found to do it, as soon as our attention is sufficiently awake to discover them".[1]

Like all educational innovators, Priestley devoted special attention to methods of teaching, aiming, in particular, at securing the active participation of students in the educational process. At his own school at Nantwich he conducted experiments with the air pump and electrical machines. "These I taught my scholars in the highest class to keep in order to make use of, and by entertaining their parents and friends with experiments, in which the scholars were, generally, the operators, and sometimes the lecturers too."[2] When lecturing at Warrington, he encouraged and welcomed interruptions, questions and discussion, encouraging his students to express their own point of view "and to urge any objections to what he had delivered, without reserve", his object being "to engage the students to examine and decide for themselves, uninfluenced by the sentiments of any other persons",[3] Themes for orations and essays were set on questions raised in the lectures. Priestley also pioneered the use of biographical and historical charts, and was interested in the use of models and other aids in the teaching of history, geography and other subjects. Many of these ideas found their practical expression at Warrington, more particularly in the 1760s, when Priestley himself was tutor there; they

[1] J. Priestley, *Essay on a Course of Liberal Education*, 68.
[2] *Memoirs of the Rev. Dr. Joseph Priestley written by himself* (1809), 36.
[3] W. Turner, *Warrington Adademy*, 25-6.

reached a much wider audience through his *Essay* and other works.[1] In later years, the official historians of the Dissenting Academies were to applaud the dissolution of this Academy on the grounds that the education was altogether too liberal in outlook.[2] In the closing years of the eighteenth century, however, the experience gained there had a formative influence on educational theory and practice.

When Warrington was forced to close down, owing to practical and financial difficulties, the Academies at Manchester and Hackney took its place. But in the Manchester College of Arts and Science (1783) we have a new specialised institution which, though shortlived, is full of significance for the future; a forerunner of the Owens College of seventy years later, which eventually evolved into Manchester University.

The close connection between Manchester College and the Literary and Philosophical Society was marked by the appointment of the nine officers of the latter as Governors, with Dr. Percival himself as President, "a mark of respect to the (Society) . . . which has so fully discussed the merits, and so zealously encouraged the plan of this Institution".[3] In fact, the Society published a number of articles on education, and on the plan itself, in the first two numbers of the *Memoirs*.

The intention of the founders was to encourage the furtherance of science and its application to industry. Thomas Barnes first proposed the formation of an institution which would develop the relations between theory and practice, science and technique.[4] In his view the sciences most relevant to local industry were chemistry and mechanics. Barnes envisaged a kind of instructional and experimental educational museum, where models of all such machines "as seem to bear the most

[1] These included *A Course of Lectures on the Theory of Language and Universal Grammar* (1762), *Lectures in Oratory and Criticism* (1777), *A Description of a Chart of Biography* (1785), *A Description of a New Chart of History* (1786), *Lectures on History and General Policy* (1793), *A Course of Experimental Philosophy* (1794).

[2] "The dissolution of the Academy at Warrington, was a fatal blow to the wide dissenters, of whom it was the pride and the boast. The tutors were, indeed, worthy to be entrusted with the education of youth, if talents and learning and respectable character were all the qualification required in a tutor; but those who wish to hear Ministers declare with the apostle, 'I am determined to know nothing among you but Jesus Christ and him crucified' will not regret to see such tutors quit the academic chair." D. Bogue and J. Bennett, *History of the Dissenters, from the Revolution in 1688 to the year 1808* (1808-12), Vol. IV, 284.

[3] *College of Arts and Sciences* (1783), a pamphlet on its constitution. Percival later became Chairman of the Governors of Manchester Academy.

[4] "On the affinity subsisting between the arts, with a plan for graduating and extending manufactures, by encouraging those arts on which manufactures principally depend." Read on January 9th, 1782, *Memoirs*, Vol. I (1785), 84ff.

distant relation to our own manufactures" and those which show "the astonishing effects of mechanic genius in other branches" would be collected together, with the materials required for experimental work in dyeing, printing, etc. The museum would have a full-time super-intendent "well versed in chemical and mechanic knowledge", who would be prepared to advise local industries, to communicate the results of research by lectures, and to undertake the education of young men preparing for industry.

Barnes' plea for a deeper understanding of chemistry and its prac-tical applications was based to some extent on ideas already put for-ward by Thomas Henry, F.R.S., at this time one of the secretaries of the Society, in a paper "On the advantages of Literature and Philo-sophy generally (and their consistency with industrial pursuits)".[1] Henry had taken a broader view, being concerned to argue the case for extending interest in technology to cover related subjects which were also closely relevant to the interests of the industrial middle class. But his primary object was still to emphasise the utility of the various sciences. Referring to chemistry as "the corner-stone of the arts", Henry shows a profound grasp of the relations between scien-tific education, chemical research and industry. In particular, he analyses in detail the connection "between chemistry and those manu-factures which are the pride and the glory of this respectable commercial town"—primarily the textile industry, in which he him-self was engaged—with the object of impressing on those engaged in industry the need to acquire scientific knowledge. He first stresses the importance of chemical processes as a result of recent developments in the cotton industry:

"Bleaching is a chemical operation. . . . The materials for this process are also the creatures of chemistry, and some degree of chemical knowledge is requisite to enable the operator to judge of their goodness. Quick-lime is prepared by a chemical process. Potash is the product of the same art, to which also vitriolic and all acids owe their existence. The manufacture of soap is also a branch of this science. All the operations of the whitster, the steeping, washing and boiling in alkaline lixiviums, exposing to the sun's light, scouring, rubbing and blueing, are chemical operations, or founded upon chemical principles. . . . (Also) dyeing and printing, by which those beautiful colours are impressed on cloths, which

[1] Read on October 3rd, 1781, *Memoirs*, Vol. I, 28ff.; R. Angus Smith, *A Centenary of Science in Manchester* (1883), 79-85.

have contributed so largely to the extension of the manufactures of this place."

But all these developments, Henry continues, have taken place in a haphazard way as a result of purely empirical procedures; a sound theoretical knowledge of science has too often been absent in those conducting industrial processes.

Henry goes on to discuss the difficulties in developing and utilising new theoretical knowledge; nevertheless, with the aid of qualified chemists these have been overcome. Much more needed doing, particularly to discover ways of ensuring the permanency of colours, and it was up to industrialists to acquire the necessary knowledge: "Sensible as our manufacturers are of this defect, is it not strange that so few of them should attempt to acquire a knowledge of those principles which would probably supply them with the means of improving and fixing their dyes?"

Besides this attempt to bring home the practical importance of science, Henry also stressed the importance of "the Polite Arts", especially drawing and design, in the manufacture of finer and more elegant wares. "It is . . . supereminent taste," he writes, "that has distinguished the products of a Wedgwood and a Bentley . . . such a taste would doubtless be equally beneficial to the manufacturer of the fine cotton and silk goods of Manchester."

These ideas inspired the "Proposals for establishing in Manchester, a plan of Liberal Education, for young men designed for Civil and Active Life, whether in trade, or in any of the Professions", drafted by Barnes for the Literary and Philosophical Society and published in 1783.[1] On July 6th of that year, the institution opened its doors as an evening college with lectures from 6 p.m. to 9 p.m. on four evenings a week.

A note in the second volume of the *Memoirs* of the Manchester Society, published in 1785, states that the scheme had been carried through "with considerable success": "during the last two winters the lectures have been delivered in different branches of science to numbers of gentlemen, who have thus given the most respectable sanction to the undertaking".[2] The Society drew on its own members as lecturers, the prospectus announcing courses on "Chemistry, with a reference to Arts and Manufactures" by Thomas Henry, F.R.S.; "On the Theory and History of Fine Arts" by George Bew, a medical

---

[1] This paper was republished in the Society's *Memoirs*, Vol. II (1785), 30ff.
[2] *Ibid.*, Vol. II, 42.

man; "On Practical Mathematics, the Principal Branches of Natural and Experimental Philosophy" and on geography, by Henry Clarke, a well-known mathematician and schoolmaster, and "On the Origin, History and Progress of Arts, Manufactures, and Commerce" and commercial law, by Thomas Barnes.[1] Lectures on anatomy were also given by Charles White, F.R.S., assisted by his son Thomas White, M.D.[2] The most successful courses appear to have been those undertaken by Thomas Henry on chemistry and on bleaching, dyeing and calico printing, since there is evidence that these continued independently for some years after the closure of the College, being attended also by "the better educated among the operative artisans."[3] Under Thomas Henry's direction, the College also took up the scientific development of chlorine bleaching and, as a direct result, several firms near Manchester began to operate the process.[4] Though, therefore, the College itself only remained in existence for a few years, it established a precedent and helped to prepare the way for later institutes of the same kind in the industrial towns.

The Manchester Academy, established in 1786, was originally intended to complement the College, providing full-time education for students, while the latter provided part-time education for those in employment. This, at least, was Thomas Barnes' idea: "The friendly correspondence which subsists between the patrons of our College of Arts and Sciences and the supporters of our Academy, is a circumstance naturally favourable to both establishments, and to the common cause which gave them birth. By this friendly co-operation the circle of studies which young men may attain among us is agreeably enlarged, and opportunities offered which could not have been equally enjoyed in a single institution, or in a more confined sphere."[5] The Manchester Academy was promoted by some of the most active members of the Literary and Philosophical Society—chiefly Barnes, Harrison, Henry and Percival, but other members belonged to the Church of England, and deprecated the idea that the Society as such was conducting a Dissenting Academy. Accordingly the Society—affirming that as a body it had no religious bias—disclaimed any connection

---

College of Art and Sciences (1783).

[2] J. Thompson, *Owens College: its Foundation and Growth* (1886), 8.

[3] James Wheeler, *Manchester, its Political, Social and Commercial History, Ancient and Modern* (1836), 491.

[4] A. and N. Clow, *The Chemical Revolution*, 189.

[5] T. Barnes, "Free Teaching and Free Learning" (1786); quoted in Thompson, *op. cit.*, 10.

with the Academy by a resolution passed in March, 1786, which was ordered to appear in both the Manchester newspapers.

In fact, the Academy, following the example of Warrington, provided a five-year course for intending ministers, and a three-year course for those proposing to enter one of the professions, commerce or industry. The original syllabus was sufficiently comprehensive, including, besides the classical languages, Hebrew, and the usual religious instruction, logic, psychology, moral philosophy, English, modern languages, commerce, history, and the laws and constitution of England. Special attention was given to mathematics and science, a mathematical tutor being appointed from 1787; in 1793, John Dalton was persuaded to accept the post of Professor of Mathematics and Experimental Philosophy, holding it for six years with evident success.[1]

While, therefore, the Academy students were initially expected to attend Charles and Thomas White's lectures on physiology, and Thomas Henry's on chemistry, delivered at the College of Arts and Sciences, some of this work was later carried on at the Academy itself. Dalton himself taught mathematics, mechanics, geometry, algebra, natural philosophy and chemistry, among other subjects. The Manchester Academy inherited the Warrington Library, but had to provide its own scientific equipment; a "reflecting telescope" was presented in 1787 and in the same year electrical equipment was purchased. Five years later the Committee voted a sum "not exceeding £100 for an apparatus proper for a course of lectures in experimental philosophy".[2]

3. THE ECLIPSE OF THE REFORMERS

The educational outlook of the most advanced section of the middle class has been described, together with its relation to their social, and to some extent to their political aims. What, then, became of these groups, of their educational perspectives and of the institutions they set up?

According to Thomas Walker, friend of Boulton, Watt and Priestley, cotton manufacturer, Boroughreeve of Manchester in 1791,

[1] "In the province of Mathematics, natural philosophy and chemistry, Mr. Dalton has uniformly acquitted himself to the entire satisfaction of the trustees; and has been happy in possessing the respect and attachment of his pupils. It is hoped and presumed that he will continue, with zeal and ardour, his scientific exertions, and that with the growing prosperity of the New College he will enlarge his sphere of reputation and usefulness." *Monthly Magazine*, August, 1797, 105-7; Thompson, *op. cit.*, 11.

[2] H. McLachlan, *English Education under the Test Acts* (1931), 262.

whose trial for treason took place in 1794, it was during the agitation for the repeal of the Test and Corporation Acts in 1789 that virulent party feeling against the friends of reform began to manifest itself in Manchester. July 14th of that year saw the outbreak of the French Revolution and the fall of the Bastille, an event greeted with acclamation by democratic circles in this country. Galton's daughter, Mrs. Schimmelpenninck, records with what hope and anxiety the latest news from France was received by members of the Lunar Society before 1789.[1] Later, she wrote: "One evening in this summer towards the end of July, we saw at a distance a vehicle . . . returning at more than its usual speed. After some minutes the door of the drawing-room opened, and in burst Harry, William Priestley's brother, a youth of sixteen or seventeen, waving his hat and crying out, 'Hurrah! Liberty, Reason, brotherly love for ever! Down with kingcraft and priestcraft. The Majesty of the People for ever! France is free, the Bastille is taken'. " Her father, Samuel Galton, "hailed the French Revolution as the auspicious day-star of social regeneration". "I have seen", she adds, "the reception of the news of the victory of Waterloo and of the carrying of the Reform Bill, but I never saw joy comparable in its vivid intensity and universality to that occasioned by the early promise of the French Revolution."[2] Support for the French Revolution, and increased activity at home for Parliamentary reform and religious liberty, went hand in hand. A period of crisis had been reached, one where the struggle for a reformed education fused with the political and religious struggle, and where members of the groupings with which we are concerned were fully involved, sometimes playing a leading part on a national scale.

[1] In 1788, Matthew Boulton's son, who had just returned from France, was present at a meeting of the Lunar Society. "I well remember," writes Mrs. Schimmelpenninck (Mary Anne Galton, who was only eleven at the time), "my astonishment at his full dress in the highest adornment of Parisian fashion; but I noticed as a remarkable thing, that the company (which consisted of some of the first men in Europe) all with one accord gathered round him and asked innumerable questions, the drift of which I did not fully understand. It was wonderful to me to see Dr. Priestley, Dr. Withering, Mr. Watt, Mr. Boulton himself, Mr. Keir, manifest the most intense interest, each according to his prevailing characteristics, as they almost hung upon his words; and it was impossible to mistake the indications of deep anxiety, hope, fear, curiosity, ardent zeal, or thoughtful gravity, which alternately marked their countenances, as well as those of my parents. My ears caught the words, 'Marie Antoinette', 'the Cardinal de Rohan', 'diamond necklace', 'famine', 'discontent among the people', 'sullen silence, instead of shouts of "Vive le Roi".' All present seemed to give a fearful attention. Why, I did not then well know, and in a day or two, these things were almost forgotten by me: but the rest of the party heard, no doubt, in this young man's narrative, the distant, though as yet faint, rising of the storm which, a year later, was to burst upon France, and, in its course, to desolate Europe." Schimmelpenninck, *op. cit.*, Vol. I, 149-50.
[2] *Ibid.*, Vol. I, 216-18, 252.

"Now is the time to speak out without any fear, both on Civil and religious subjects, while the advocates for tyranny are overawed", wrote Priestley in a letter to his friend Dr. Lindsey.[1] Dr. Price, leading dissenter and friend of Priestley's, whose *Essay on Civil Liberty* had had a tremendous effect in rallying support for the American revolutionaries some thirteen years before, chose November 4th, 1789, anniversary of the "Glorious Revolution" of 1688, to preach his famous sermon "On the Love of our Country" to the Revolution Society. At the banquet in the afternoon, a Congratulatory Address was sent to the French National Assembly. It was as an answer to this sermon, later published, that Burke composed his *Reflections on the French Revolution*, a document that played a decisive part in stirring up hatred against the "Jacobins", as all the supporters of the French Revolution came to be called. Priestley immediately answered Burke in the sharpest terms,[2] and at the same time continued, in a series of pamphlets, the struggle for Unitarianism and for the repeal of the Test Acts. These writings contained some of Priestley's most open attacks on the state and the Established Church. Tom Paine's *Rights of Man*, which became the rallying centre of the democratic movement, also appeared in 1791. "Have you seen Mr. Paine's answer to Mr. Burke?" wrote Priestley to Wedgwood, "it is most excellent, and the boldest publication that I have ever seen."[3] In 1792 the French Convention not only gave Joseph Priestley the rights of French citizenship, but also offered him a seat in the Convention itself (with Tom Paine, who took his seat for Calais); a year later he was offered, as a residence, a monastery in the South of France "which reason has recovered from superstition".[4]

But if the Radicals took the offensive, this brought an immediate reaction from the Church and Tory party, assisted by Burke and other Whigs who made common cause with their former enemies in order to hold back the expression of popular feeling. The political temperature rose with the formation of such societies as the Constitution Society, of which, in Manchester, Thomas Walker and Samuel Jackson, both of the "Lit. & Phil.", were President and Secretary and later, in Manchester, of the Patriotic and Revolution Society,

[1] J. T. Rutt (ed), *Life and Correspondence of Joseph Priestley* (1832), Vol. II, 49-50.
[2] J. Priestley, *Letter to the Rt. Hon. Edmund Burke* (1791), Burke was also answered by Paine's *Rights of Man*, Mackintosh's *Vindicae Gallicae*, Mary Wollstonecraft's *Vindication of the Rights of Men*, and many other works, including, in a lighter vein, Roscoe's poem: "The Life, Death and Wonderful Achievements of Edmund Burke".
[3] Carrington Bolton (ed), *The Scientific Letters of Joseph Priestley* (1891), 106-7.
[4] *Ibid.*, 117.

which worked for a liberal and reform policy in opposition to the Church and King Club. On July 14th, 1791, on the occasion of the Revolution Society's dinner, presided over by James Keir, there took place the famous riots at Birmingham, beginning with the destruction of Priestley's Unitarian meeting house, and culminating in the looting and burning of Priestley's and other leading Unitarians' houses —the crowd also attacked the houses of members of the Lunar Society who were not Unitarians (for instance, William Withering's). It was here that Priestley suffered the loss, not only of his entire—and very extensive—scientific apparatus, but also of notes collected over a period of twenty years. James Watt was said to have attended the first meeting of the Lunar Society held after the riots with pistols in his pockets.[1]

In spite of this setback, in Manchester the reform movement gathered strength. In the spring of 1792 the *Manchester Herald* was launched, a weekly paper propagating the views of Tom Paine and the reform movement generally, edited by Matthew Faulkner and Thomas Kershaw, a manufacturer and member of the "Lit. & Phil.", financially supported by Thomas Walker and his brother, and contributed to largely by Thomas Cooper, all of whom had been members of the "Lit. & Phil.",[2] the latter a particularly close friend of Priestley's.[3] In May and June, the Patriotic and Revolution Societies were formed. And, also in the spring of that year, two members of the Constitution Society visited France as delegates of that society— Thomas Cooper and James Watt, junior.

It was the visit of Cooper and Watt to Paris, when they presented an Address to the Society of the Friends of the Constitution sitting at the Jacobins, that was to be made an issue precipitating the political crisis of 1792-3, leading to the suppression and defeat of the reform movement. On April 30th there took place a debate in the House of

---

[1] Carrington Bolton (ed), *The Scientific Letters of Joseph Priestley* (1891), 213.

[2] Priestley had been elected an honorary member of the "Lit. & Phil." in 1782, and the Society had supported his scientific work financially. After the burning of his house, Samuel Jackson moved a vote of sympathy with him: "That the Society do write to Dr. Priestley, expressing their concern at the losses he has sustained by the late disgraceful riots at Birmingham." Nicholson writes: "The Society was evidently afraid of doing anything that would connect it with the politics of the day, and postponed the resolution, whereupon, as a protest, Thomas Cooper, a Vice President, James Watt junior, Thomas Walker and Samuel Jackson, resigned their membership, as also did Joseph Priestley, junior, Dr. Priestley's son, who had only just been elected." F. Nicholson, "The Literary and Philosophical Society, 1781-1851", *Memoirs*, Vol. LXVIII, (1923-4), Part 1, 105.

[3] Priestley had recommended Cooper for F.R.S., and was convinced the refusal was due to political prejudice. As a protest against political discrimination, he ceased giving his scientific papers to the Royal Society. Cf. Carrington Bolton, *op. cit.*, 100-2, where Priestley's letters of protest to Sir Joseph Banks are published.

Commons, arising from Lord Grey's announcement of a motion for Parliamentary reform, during which Pitt, ably seconded by Burke, made it appear that the demand for Parliamentary Reform was the preliminary to revolution. Referring to the Manchester delegates, Burke opened his attack, and is reported to have said, in substance:

> "That there were in this country men who scrupled not to enter into alliance with a set in France of the worst traitors and regicides that had ever been heard of, the Club of the Jacobins. Agents had been sent from this country to enter into a federation with that iniquitous club, and those were men of some consideration here; the names he alluded to were Thomas Cooper and James Watt (here Burke read an address presented to the club of the Jacobins by those men on April 16th). . . . He likewise could name others who avowed similar principles; for instance, Mr. Walker, of Manchester."[1]

From this moment, events began to move fast. Cooper published his *Reply to Burke's Invective*, a very effective pamphlet.[2] On June 4th, 1792, the Birmingham riots were repeated at Manchester, if on a lesser scale. Large crowds assembled in Saint Anne's Square, uprooted trees, and, using these as battering rams, attacked both the Cross Street Chapel—the original seat of the "Lit. & Phil."—and the new Unitarian chapel in Moseley Street. On December 11th, crowds again assembled and attacked the premises where the *Manchester Herald* was printed, and, among others, attacked Thomas Walker's house several times.[3]

The situation of the liberal democrats was becoming untenable. The rapid growth of the Corresponding Societies, in which the working class for the first time organised themselves for a political purpose, determined the government on an active policy of political repression. There followed the period of the treason trials and on April 2nd, 1794, Thomas Walker, along with Samuel Jackson and other Manchester men, stood their trial at the spring assizes at Lancaster, on a charge of conspiring to overthrow the constitution and government, and to aid and assist the French (being the King's enemies) in case they should invade this kingdom.[4] The trial took place six

---

[1] Angus Smith, *op. cit.*, 172.

[2] Dumas Malone, *The Public Life of Thomas Cooper* (1926), 44-5.

[3] Cf. Frida Knight, *The Strange Case of Thomas Walker* (1957), for a full description of contemporary struggles in Manchester.

[4] Archibald Prentice, *Historical Sketches and Personal Recollections of Manchester* (2nd edn, 1851), 13.

months after the savage sentences on Muir and Palmer of the Edinburgh Society of Friends of the People, but in this case the prosecution fell to the ground, since it was proved that the principal witness had been bribed to make false charges. Walker and the others, who were ably assisted by Thomas Cooper in their defence, were honourably acquitted and returned triumphantly to Manchester.[1]

Six months after the trial of Walker, Hardy was acquitted on a charge of high treason by a London jury; eleven days later, John Horne Tooke was similarly acquitted, and then John Thelwall, the government abandoning the remaining prosecutions by which they hoped to prove the existence of treasonable activity.[2] Nevertheless, the trials had had their effect. The political situation had sharpened with the advent of Robespierre's régime in France (1793), and the subsequent declaration of war. The cause of reform was pushed further and further into the background, and, as political repression intensified, more and more of its erstwhile friends deserted; others, such as Faulkner and Birch of the *Manchester Herald*, threatened with prosecution, and Thomas Cooper himself, emigrated to America. In Liverpool, Roscoe's circle had to go underground, and others elsewhere were forced to tread warily as political feeling against dissenters, reformers, liberals and freethinkers generally was roused almost to fever pitch. The long period of severe political repression was at hand.

With these events, the efforts of the more radical dissenters to develop their educational institutions inevitably ran into difficulties. Nowhere is this more evident than in the short and turbulent history of the New College at Hackney, set up near London on the demise of Warrington Academy, and, in many ways the most ambitious educational undertaking of the wide dissenters.

Hackney College numbered among its tutors during its short life a galaxy of talent, men as well known for their democratic political views as for their literary, mathematical or scientific culture. Among these were Richard Price (in 1786-7), whose later outspoken support for the French Revolution provoked Burke's reply. Shortly after Priestley was forced to flee from Birmingham in 1791, he lectured gratis at the College in science. Both of these came under the whiplash of Burke's oratory in the House of Commons. Gilbert Wakefield,

[1] Angus Smith, *op. cit.*, 173; Knight, *op. cit.*, 153-65.
[2] Watt, junior, to Matthew R. Boulton, junior, May 23rd, 1794: "The citizens here are all in very high spirits since the late trials; and I had the honour of dining with two of the *acquitted felons*, on Sunday last." Smiles, *op. cit.*, 417n.

previously a tutor at Warrington, was at Hackney in 1790-1. In the latter year he published his *Inquiry into the Expediency and Propriety of Public or Social Worship*, which gave rise to a storm of public controversy and resulted in a remonstrance by the students against the rule of compulsory services.[1] In 1789 the College staff was joined by Thomas Belsham, earlier a tutor at Daventry, a strong believer in the doctrine of philosophic necessity, who acted as divinity tutor. "We are now engaged", he wrote in January 1790, "in the great and glorious doctrine of Necessity. My class consists of upwards of thirty students. Many of them enter thoroughly into the subject, and will, I doubt not, be confirmed philosophic Necessarians."[2] Hazlitt, a student under Belsham, reported in a letter to his father that he read David Hartley for four and a half hours a week.[3]

Many of the tutors, then, were public figures, fully involved and committed in the political struggles.[4] But the students were not far behind and they made their standpoint clear in no uncertain manner: "Rules to the contrary notwithstanding," writes McLachlan, the historian of the College, "students were present in Westminster Hall during the memorable trial of Warren Hastings in 1788-9 for misconduct in the government of India, and they flocked to the gallery of the House of Commons on the night of 2 March 1790, when Charles James Fox, arriving booted and spurred from Newmarket, delivered his two great speeches in favour of the Repeal of the Test and Corporation Acts. There was hardly any length to which the students would not go except in the matter of attending divine service under compulsion on Sundays. About that they exhibited serious scruples. Protests against the ordinances of the Committee and resolutions to resist their tyranny were passed, and kings, priests and aristocrats, without much distinction of foreign or domestic, were the objects of their hearty execration."[5]

In the summer of 1792, shortly before he was forced to flee the country, Tom Paine was a guest at a Republican supper at the college. But, with the growing persecution of the radical movement, the

1 "The fever reached its climax when a bold young spirit delivered a warm defence of the remonstrance in an oration at the public examination before the assembled tutors, committee and supporters of the institution. Several students were sent down, others withdrew, alleging their abandonment of religious belief." H. McLachlan, *op. cit.*, 249.

2 *Ibid.*, 251.

3 J. W. Ashley Smith, *The Birth of Modern Education* (1954), 177.

4 Other tutors included Abraham Rees, F.R.S., John Corrie, F.R.S. and Andrew Kippis, F.R.S.

5 McLachlan, *op. cit.*, 253.

situation began to grow acute. "I cannot give you an idea of the violence with which every friend of liberty is persecuted in this country", wrote Priestley to a friend in America in April, 1793, announcing his determination to emigrate.[1] After the suspension of the Habeas Corpus Act in May, 1794, an ex-student of the College, with other members of the Corresponding Society, was arrested, and only acquitted at his trial which took place several months later. A member of the College Council was later tried on a charge of treason, and although he also was acquitted, the position was becoming increasingly untenable. Financial support was withdrawn, and, in the summer of 1796, the College was closed: "The spirit of the times was against it", wrote Belsham. "It fell—and the birds of night, ignorance and envy, bigotry and rancour screamed their ungenerous triumph over the ruins of this stately edifice; whilst virtue, truth and learning mourned in secret over the disappointment of their fond hopes and of their too highly elevated expectation."[2]

The closure of New College, Hackney, and the emigration of Priestley to America mark a significant stage in the educational history of this country. Although other Dissenting Academies weathered the storm, these were affected by the changed attitude to religion which marks the transition from the rationalism of the eighteenth century to the evangelicism of the early nineteenth, and began once more to concentrate on the narrow training of ministers for the various sects which maintained them. Even the Manchester Academy, where John Dalton, F.R.S., George Walker, F.R.S. and William Johns[3] taught in the 1790s, was removed to York in 1803, where it could not fulfil the functions its original promoters had in mind. And, although the Edgeworths, from the fastnesses of Edgeworthstown in Ireland, produced *Practical Education* in 1798, many of the most significant parts of this work—those written by R. L. Edgeworth himself—were based on twenty years' notes and experience, and had their origin in the general outlook of the Lunar grouping of an earlier period.

In fact, the political reaction which accompanied the French Revolution marked the end of the particular phase of social development which gave rise to the educational theory and practice outlined here. "For all their patronage," writes Bernal, "both the old régime in France and the Church and King party in Britain, with their base in

---

[1] Carrington Bolton, *op. cit.*, 136.   [2] McLachlan, *op. cit.*, 254.

[3] Dalton and Walker acted as President, and Johns as Secretary, of the Literary and Philosophical Society.

landed property, had necessarily to stand against science. The advancement of science accordingly became associated in the latter eighteenth century with rising industry, political reform, and liberal theology, serving largely to justify an optimistic and progressive outlook."[1] The educational standpoint of those who had direct links with science and industry could at this stage comprehend a broad humanity together with a positive and scientific outlook. In particular, the application of science had not yet brought about "the blight and ugliness of industrial areas, and with it an awareness, hostile or conscience stricken, of the mob, of the new proletariat",[2] neither had there developed those features of internecine struggle first pointed out in *Labour Rewarded* by the economist William Thompson, which were to mark the progress of industry in the nineteenth century. At this particular stage, therefore, the men most concerned with advancing science and with social and political reform were able to evolve a rational, moral, human and cohesive educational theory.

The class which had created Warrington Academy, Manchester Academy and New College, Hackney, though temporarily on the defensive at the close of the eighteenth century, was to emerge later, and to carry all before it. But it was to emerge as a class whose characteristics had changed, whose purposes were narrower, and who were engaged in a sharp struggle on two main fronts—against the landed aristocracy on the one hand, and against the emerging proletariat on the other. In these conditions the educational tradition of the late eighteenth century took on a new form, tending towards a narrower utilitarianism and having, to some extent, an abstract, doctrinaire quality. Nowhere is this more apparent than in what a critic has described as the "grotesque deformation" which overcame the type of children's literature initiated by Percival and Day—that of the moral tale, which poured from the press from the hands of numerous authors in the early nineteenth century, with an increasing emphasis on religion and punishment. So, inevitably, with the increasing class divisions consequent on the growth of factory production, the dominant educational theories of the middle class lost the humanism and all-sidedness that had been their chief characteristic earlier. In the Corresponding Societies, for the first time, the working class was beginning to develop its own independent educational forms serving its own independent class interests. From now on, education became divided against itself.

[1] J. D. Bernal, *Science in History*, 481.   [2] *Ibid.*, 482.

But though it is possible, in the most general terms, to mark the stages of this evolution, the old attitudes persisted into the new period. In Manchester, the "Lit. & Phil." continued to bring together the foremost scientists, industrialists and professional men and, as the eighteenth century turned into the nineteenth, John Dalton, George Walker, William Johns and many others carried on and developed the work which had begun in Percival's house before 1781. When Dalton died in 1845, 40,000 of Manchester's citizens turned out to line the route followed by his funeral cortège, so to mark the passing of the Quaker scientist who had brought such honour to the town, and who was so greatly loved by the people. In Birmingham, where Thomas Wright Hill, Priestley's friend, was already developing his famous school at Hill Top (later at Hazelwood) which at first put into practice many of the ideas of the Lunar educators, the influence of the Lunar Society persisted more than forty years after its first foundation. Its epitaph was written by Francis Horner, after a visit to Soho in 1809:

"The remnant of the Lunar Society, and the fresh remembrance in others, of the remarkable men who composed it, are very interesting; the impression which they made is not yet worn out, but shows itself, to the second and third generations, in a spirit of scientific curiosity and free inquiry, which even yet makes some stand against the combined forces of Methodism, Toryism, and the love of gain."[1]

[1] Leonard Horner (ed), *Memoirs and Correspondence of Francis Horner, M.P.* (1843), Vol. II, 2.

CHAPTER II

EDUCATION AND THE STRUGGLE FOR REFORM, 1800-1832

THE forerunners of educational reform in the closing decades of the eighteenth century were individuals, usually banded together in local societies or institutions in the pursuit of a common interest in science, education and progressive causes. Those who took up the cause of educational change in the early nineteenth century represented a new political grouping on a national scale. Adherents of the Radical movement, representing middle-class interests, they played a leading part in the struggle for Parliamentary reform which culminated in the passing of the Reform Act of 1832. The demand for educational reform developed as an essential aspect of this movement.

What were the forces engaged in this struggle? Two parties dominated political life—the Whigs and the Tories. Both, in the eyes of the politically conscious middle class, were aristocratic "factions" which retained power solely as a result of an outmoded and corrupt political system by which the franchise was denied to the large majority of the people, and whose one concern it was to uphold the interests of the large landowners as against those of all other sections of the community.

This standpoint was adopted by increasing numbers after 1815. Up to this time a measure of harmony existed between capitalist and landlord; the former, for instance, accepting the continuance of prohibitive duties on corn so long as, in return, the government swept away the old legislation which fettered masters in their relation with workmen. But the war with France had much strengthened the position of the manufacturers and brought some concrete advances. In 1811, a campaign led by the Liverpool merchants successfully reversed a government move to restrict imports; two years later pressure from northern industrialists brought the East India monopoly to an end.

There was, however, a setback in the same year when agricultural interests demanded higher import duties. These were immediately granted by Parliament in the teeth of violent opposition from the manufacturers who even invited the populace to riot in their support. Whatever temporary harmony there might have been between landlord and capitalist, underlying it was a fundamental economic opposition. This Ricardo made clear in his *Principles of Political Economy* (1817) when he pointed out that goods and services were distributed to landlords on the one hand, to capitalists and workers on the other, in inverse ratio; the higher the rent of land, the lower the rewards accruing to capital and labour in the form of profits and wages. In 1815, when economic dislocation brought high rents, low profits and lower wages accompanied by widespread distress, this potential conflict became actual.[1]

It is from this time that there begins an open, conscious struggle of capitalist (sometimes supported by worker) against landlord; one that was to be fought up to the achievement of political reform in 1832 and later through to conclusive victory with the repeal of the Corn Laws in 1846. In the course of this struggle the middle class emerged as a class-conscious force. Its political expression was Radicalism. With spokesmen in Parliament such as Sir Francis Burdett, Henry Brougham, and more particularly David Ricardo, Joseph Hume and Arthur Roebuck, and theorists such as James Mill and Jeremy Bentham, the Radicals rapidly gained influence and public support. Their fight for reform—regarded essentially as the means to political power—took the form of demands for a radical overhaul of the machinery of the state; of Parliament, the Church, the judiciary, and of old-established corporations—including the semi-ecclesiastical colleges at Oxford and Cambridge and the endowed grammar schools.

Middle-class reformers of this epoch were, then, no longer concerned to civilise the upper classes, to advocate the education of the aristocracy so that it might perform a more useful role and set a higher moral tone; rather they denounced all aristocratic pretensions and advanced the superior claims of the middle class, outlining a specific middle-class approach to the content and organisation of education. They were, in addition, much more acutely aware of the necessity of educating the growing working class than were their eighteenth-century predecessors.

In order to assess the nature of the movement for educational reform it is necessary briefly to consider the general ideas advanced by the Radicals and how they were applied to the educational field. The existing situation in the schools and universities may then be considered in conjunction with Radical criticisms of current organisation and

[1] E. Halévy, *The Growth of Philosophic Radicalism* (1928), 336-7.

practice. The middle class also attempted to further practical reforms, particularly in the grammar schools. With such attempts were coupled much more far-reaching activities, namely, the founding of new types of school and, in 1828, of University College, London, which presented a living challenge to the prevailing educational order.

These steps were concerned specifically with the education of the middle class. The plans advanced for working-class education, and carried through equally energetically, belong to another chapter of the story.

1. RADICAL POLITICS AND THE THEORY AND PRACTICE OF EDUCATION

(i) *James Mill, Spokesman of the Middle Class*

Every class has its spokesmen, its ideologists; those who generalise the experience of the class as a whole, chart the way forward, and so, especially during a period of sharp political struggle, contribute to the development of class consciousness. In the early nineteenth century it was *par excellence* James Mill who filled this role for the middle class. As his nineteenth-century biographer makes clear, he

"got hold of the more intelligent minds of the growing middle class in our great centres of industry. To them his views and reasonings were adapted in many ways. He seconded their natural demands for better government and better legislation to suit the extension of manufactures and commerce . . . and insisted on their having a share of political power for their own defence."[1]

A Scotsman, educated at Edinburgh University, Mill first came to London in 1802 to earn a living as a journalist. It was six years later that he met Jeremy Bentham and there began the close partnership which, for a quarter of a century, was to act as a nucleus of the Radical movement. At a time when there was no hard and fast division between philosophy and political theory, between politics, economics and sociology, Mill developed an outlook which covered all the main fields of social life. Basic to his thought was Hartley's concept of associationism, which had so profoundly influenced Priestley at an earlier stage, and this underlies both his political and educational theory. But, if he was the leading educational theoretician of the Radical movement, Mill was also closely concerned with educational practice and, throughout this whole period, envisaged educational change as

[1] Alexander Bain, *James Mill, a Biography* (1882), 446.

an essential aspect of a wider social transformation. In all the educational plans and programmes advanced Bentham was closely associated, making his particular contribution both in the realm of theory and in the field of internal school organisation. It was the activities of these two men which were primarily responsible for bringing education into the mainstream of political life.

Mill's ideas began to make a particular impact on politics in the 1820s. It was he who developed the theory of "democracy"—of universal suffrage—specifically as a means of uniting the mass of the people behind the middle class for the destruction of aristocratic oligarchy; and with it the idea of universal education which will be considered later. It was the guiding aim of the utilitarians—as the theorists of the middle class became known—to transform what was a closed society controlled by hereditary landlords in their own interests into a "free" society directed by those most qualified to govern in the interests of all. The latter were, without doubt, the middle class who furthered useful knowledge, amassed capital, developed industry and trade, lived frugally; who, all in all, were capable of bringing about the unification of the interests of all sections of society and so of promoting the greatest happiness of the greatest number.

Mill established this point by a consistent and detailed attack on aristocratic pretensions and morality coupled with what was no less than eulogy of middle-class qualities and achievements. His open contempt for the two aristocratic factions which dominated Parliament reflects the Radical determination to create a new political force capable of bringing about fundamental changes in the political and social structure. This standpoint is nowhere more clearly stated than in an article written for the newly founded Radical journal, the *Westminster Review*, in 1826. Intended as an enquiry into the state of the nation, this is, in essence, a sustained attack on the aristocracy and its politics.

"The composition of our legislature, the main spring of government, is pretty nearly the same as it has been for ages. A great majority of it is composed of the landed aristocracy; and a still greater majority is nominated and sent there by the will of that aristocracy. The consequences hardly need to be pointed out. . . . It is substantially as much an aristocratical, hereditary assembly as the House of Lords. Why continue the farce of election? Let the principal land holders, by hereditary right compose the House of Commons."[1]

[1] *Westminster Review*, Vol. VI, No. XII, October 1826, 265.

After exposing the monopoly of power, Mill deals with its consequences. The war with France he characterises as a war fought purely in the interests of the aristocracy, and he condemns outright the national debt incurred in its prosecution. In militant, polemical language he denounces the class morality of an aristocracy which by imposing the national debt and increasing taxation to pay for its war, is prepared to live on the labour of others. In addition, aristocratic policy has led to the suspension of cash payments—so depreciating the currency; to the Corn Laws—which operate solely in the interests of landowners; to the usury laws—which are disastrous for commerce and industry. Turning to a measure proposed by the government to scale down payments on the debt, brought forward because of the alleged "impossibility" of maintaining the former plan of repayment, Mill characterises this as the sheerest fraud —"an almost unparalleled disregard for the rights of property". His threats and language here reflect the rising militancy of the sober middle class.

"Impossibility! Is that plea to be listened to on the part of the debtor who is all the time rioting in boundless extravagance? Oh no! Before the people of England will think of the impossibility of paying their debts, they will cut off every atom of wasteful expenditure, and apply to their discharge the last penny of public property. All sinecure places must be abolished. All overpaid places must be retrenched. All extravagant establishments must be reduced. Army, navy, ordnance, all must come down to a fraction of what they are. What a breaking up of the resources of the aristocracy! . . . Even then, we should not be at the end of our resources. There is, first of all, the crown lands, which should be sold to the last acre, and the last brick. Next we shall be able to do, and much better than we do now, with a far less costly ecclesiastical establishment; and the whole of the tythes and church-lands may be rendered available to the discharge of the national debt. Even 'the decent splendour of royalty' must part with some feathers to avert the calamity of a national bankruptcy. We therefore believe we have said enough on the subject of impossibility."[1]

Since Mill's chief object was a Parliamentary reform which would oust the aristocracy from power, it was above all necessary to clarify the class issues, to expose the pretensions of the aristocracy in general, and especially to show that the "liberal" Whig party (then in

[1] *Westminster Review*, Vol. VI, No. 12, October 1826, 274-5.

opposition) was no less determined to maintain aristocratic rule than the Tories; though, in the course of the internal political struggle, the Whigs often spoke in terms calculated to win the support of the popular movement. This necessary task was carried out in a series of brilliant articles analysing in detail the content of the Whig *Edinburgh Review* and the Tory *Quarterly*. Particularly significant is Mill's insistence that, even though individual aristocrats may take up a position which appears opposed to the interests of the aristocracy in general, this does not mean that the aristocracy as a class ceases to put its own interests foremost. It is necessary, he writes,

"to caution unwary reasoners against allowing those motives which may predominate in the breast of individuals, from occupying that place in their reasonings which belongs to those motives which act upon the class as a class, and by which, as a class, they must be governed. It would be absurd to say that a comparatively small number of men formed into a class by possessing all the powers of government over the great number, and the means of using those powers for their own advantage, will not, as a class, be actuated by the desire to render that advantage as great as possible. This being admitted, and it being clear that a man would render himself contemptible by denying it, the only care of the rational man is to ascertain the course of action to which that desire must conduct the class; and having done so, to make it known to others."

Do not then, Mill urges his readers, be directed by those who attempt to distract your attention "from the consideration of the motives which must govern the class, by holding up to attention the other motives, which always may, and very often do, actuate individuals. There is not a more fertile source of false reasoning, in matters of government, than this".[1]

In Mill's view, then, the aristocracy was engaged in the defence of vital class interests. Opposed to them stood the middle class, also engaged on a struggle for *their* vital interests. But here the case was different. Unlike the aristocracy, the middle class, "this vast and unspeakably important portion of our population", contributed everything of value to the nation. It was by constantly elaborating on this theme that Mill—and, too, such men as Francis Place, artisan turned master—contributed to forming the class consciousness of that section of the population for whom they spoke:

[1] *Westminster Review*, Vol. I, No. 1, January 1824, 216-17.

"The value of the middle classes of this country, their growing numbers and importance, are acknowledged by all. These classes have long been spoken of, and not grudgingly by their superiors themselves, as the glory of England; as that which alone has given to us our eminence among nations; as that portion of our people to whom every thing that is good among us may with certainty be traced."[1]

So wrote James Mill, referring to the first steps being taken on an ambitious scale to provide a suitable education for the middle class —the University of London; and so the *Westminster Review* had written two years earlier:

"Of the political and moral importance of this class, there can be but one opinion. It is the strength of the community. It contains, beyond all comparison, the greatest proportion of the intelligence, industry, and wealth of the state. In it are the heads that invent, and the hands that execute; the enterprise that projects, and the capital by which these projects are carried into operation. The merchant, the manufacturer, the mechanist, the chemist, the artist, those who discover new arts, those who perfect old arts, those who extend science; the men in fact who think for the rest of the world, and who really do the business of the world, are the men of this class. The people of the class below are the instruments with which they work; and those of the class above, though they may be called their governors, and may really sometimes seem to rule them, are much more often, more truly, and more completely under their control. In this country at least, it is this class which gives to the nation its character."

"The proper education of this portion of the people", the article concluded, "is therefore of the greatest possible importance to the wellbeing of the state."[2]

So educational change is once more placed in the centre of the picture, as a specific demand of the middle class—as an essential aspect of the overall transformation of the government and institutions of society. But the traditional, and powerful, educational institutions of the country, the endowed grammar and "public" schools and universities, were closely linked to church and state; they acted as bulwarks of the *status quo*. Further, the whole educational position was in a state of confusion; in particular, as we have already seen, the

[1] *Westminster Review*, Vol. VI, No. 12, October 1826, 269.
[2] *Ibid.*, Vol. I, No. 1, January 1824, 68-9.

character of the schools and universities was such that the education there given was irrelevant to the life of the middle class. To enter these institutions—to transform them to meet their needs—this was the fundamental educational strategy of the bourgeoisie, one having a political as well as an educational significance.

This long-drawn struggle had, at this stage, a twofold aspect. It involved first, a sharp ideological attack against existing institutions, and, with this, the formulation of a positive alternative educational policy both as regards form and content; second, the establishment, by the middle class, of its own institutions under its own control, serving its own purposes, and untrammelled by ancient statutes and clerical control. On both these matters, the ideas and plans most closely in line with the requirements of the middle class were worked out in detail by Jeremy Bentham. *Chrestomathia*,[1] published in 1816-17, was to have a seminal influence on the educational thought and practice of the Radical bourgeoisie. It embodies the essence of the utilitarian outlook in educational terms.

(ii) *Jeremy Bentham and the Chrestomathic School*

The immediate impetus for Bentham's book arose from the practical necessity of creating new forms of education for the growing middle class. The Radical grouping in London, including James Mill, Francis Place and Edward Wakefield, were, in 1815, working actively to develop elementary education. But Francis Place could find no school suitable for the education of his nine children. Bentham had immediately offered room in his garden and set about "tracing the architectural, administrative and pedagogic plan"[2] of a radically new kind of school; a day school designed to extend "the new system of instruction to the higher branches of learning, for the use of the middling and higher ranks of life".[3]

Deliberately setting aside all existing educational practice, Bentham embarked on a survey of the whole field of human knowledge, including the most recent advances in science and technology; this he systematised and set down in tabular form—an "encyclopaedic table".

---

[1] Meaning "Conducive to Useful Knowledge".   [2] Halévy, *op. cit.*, 287.

[3] J. Bowring (ed), *The Works of Jeremy Bentham* (1838-43), Vol. VIII, 1ff. The "new system of instruction" was the monitorial system; Bentham, Place and others felt that this could be extended to secondary education. The basis of their belief lay in the great success which attended the application of these methods to the teaching of Latin and Greek at the Edinburgh High School and at Charterhouse (*Ibid.*, Vol. VIII, 59-63); Bentham constantly refers to the "matchless excellence" and certain success of these methods.

He then proceeded to reduce the various fields of knowledge to a logical order, or *priorities*—"the order in which they are most advantageously taught". This was determined by the two principles of utility and facility. Those subjects which had the clearest application "to the several purposes of common life"[1] should be included, while the principle of facility required that development should be from the simple to the complex, from the particular to the general.

In Bentham's scheme, therefore, science and technology are an integral part of the content of education—indeed the central core of the educational process. He completely accepted the vocational principle in education, not in the sense of a narrow specialised training, but by advocating a general survey and understanding of science and technology as the basis for a future choice of occupation—a point he specifically makes. After a preparatory stage learning the three Rs, science forms the major part of each of the five stages of instruction advocated; study begins with the descriptive and classificatory sciences (mineralogy, botany, zoology), proceeds through the various branches of mechanics, chemistry and physics (concentrating especially on electricity) and ends with the application of these sciences in the "school of technology" (mining, surveying, architecture, husbandry, etc.). History, geography, and languages are taught from the second stage onwards; at the fourth stage "the art of preserving as well as restoring health, including the arts and sciences thereto belonging" forms the body of teaching. Mathematics, on account of its difficulty, is postponed to the end of the course.

Bentham justifies all these subjects by reference to their utility in normal life. Knowledge, in his view, must serve a social function; it must prepare children to earn their future livelihood, be capable of application. All other knowledge is useless. Thereby Bentham specifically excludes all teaching of the classical languages; these may, he admits, be "a matter . . . of necessity" for the learned professions, but are useless for those for whom his Chrestomathic school is designed. In place of the dead languages, from which "at this time of day" nothing is to be learnt, he substitutes science and technology as essential aspects of a general education; and lays special stress on chemistry and electricity where the first important advances had only recently been made.

The Benthamite approach, based on Hartley's associationist psychology, led also to certain other important conclusions regarding content

---

[1] J. Bowring (ed), *The Works of Jeremy Bentham* (1838-43,) Vol. VIII, 24.

and method. The educational process must, above all, be systematic. The body of knowledge which the child is expected to master, set out in the encyclopaedic table, is systematised and, of course, imposed by the educator. According to the principle of facility, it is arranged in a certain order which is determined by the preparedness of the child to master the ideas involved, starting from simple, concrete teaching and advancing later to complex, abstract ideas. There remain problems of method, of how to present this ordered body of knowledge to the child so that he will find it most easily comprehensible. Here Bentham emphasises the need to accompany teaching with the exhibition of animals, plants, stones, charts, diagrams, the use of working models of machinery, and actual experimentation by the pupils. He also insists on consistently testing the pupils' knowledge, in such a way as to ensure that concepts have been fully grasped and understood, and not merely verbally memorised.

Bentham's interest extended, in addition, to all the details of school management, and he defined forty-three principles which, in his view, would provide the conditions necessary to ensure that learning took place with maximum efficiency. Many of these were derived from the ideas of Andrew Bell, one of the founders of the monitorial school; others are of interest since they presage what was to become normal practice. Symptomatic of the capitalist epoch is the great emphasis put on individual competition as the main incentive for work. The "comparative proficiency principle" and the "place capturing principle" are basic to Bentham's idea of school organisation—he refers specifically to their "exciting and invigorating effect". A full record is to be kept of the place of each boy in each class he attends. He advocates the modern system of "setting", whereby a pupil may belong to a different class for each subject according to his proficiency—while he goes up in one he may go down in another.

Stress is laid throughout on maximising the efficiency of learning. Thus the "distraction prevention principle" provides that all the windows should be of such a height that no child could look out, while the "tabula exhibition principle" lays down that the walls of the classroom be covered with instructive charts and diagrams—if a child finishes his work and has, for a few moments, nothing to do, he still cannot fail to imbibe knowledge wherever he looks. Discipline is to be maintained by various means; assistance to the backward pupils by the more advanced, short lessons containing a variety of matter and method, rewards and punishments (which should, however, be minimised). Above all, there should be self-government by the pupils themselves; this will counteract the tendency of pupils subject to coercion "to unite in a sort of standing conspiracy" against their teachers. These measures, Bentham affirms, should lead to good order; corporal punishment is to be entirely abolished.

If the Chrestomathic school had been set up in Leicester Square (which, but for the opposition of the shopkeepers it might have been)[1] a visit to it would have been a remarkable experience. In fact, the idea of founding such a school, which at one point gained considerable support, foundered on Bentham's insistence on the exclusion of religion. It was a fundamental point that the school should be open to everyone whatever their religious beliefs or disbeliefs, and clerical influence ensured that "the more opulent persons" who first encouraged the project later abandoned it.[2] It is possible, however, to form an idea of utilitarian theory in practice by reference to a description of Hazelwood school, first initiated at Hill Top, Birmingham, by a friend of Joseph Priestley, Thomas Wright Hill, but at this time run with the help of his more famous son, Rowland Hill. The description indicates both the positive and the negative features of this entire outlook.

At Hazelwood the bell was rung 250 times a week, on each occasion signalling a definite action. The first bell, at 6 a.m., marked the start of the day—except for defaulters who were kept fully occupied from 5 a.m. "The Monitor goes into each dormitory and blows a horn to awake such as may be sleeping. All the boys leave their beds at the word of command; and, when dressed, arrange themselves in each room in a certain order for marching downstairs."[3] At 6.10 the bell rings again, the word of command is given, and the boys march down. At 6.17 the bell rings for prayers, the classes then form for mental arithmetic, practised early in the morning "because it does not require much light". At 7.00, the bell rings two minutes for school, when the day-boys join the boarders.

Further bells at 7.20, 7.50, 8.00 and 8.20 signify class changes until, at 8.45, "a bell for washing". The boarders form up in four sections in the schoolroom, the first section marches to the wash-house, the others "at the same time, begin to repeat the multiplication table, all speaking

[1] P. Sraffa, *The Works of David Ricardo* (1952), Vol. VII, 198n. Ricardo was to have bought the ground, but abandoned the project due to this opposition.

[2] Bowring (ed), *op. cit.*, Vol. VIII, ii.

[3] M. D. Hill, *Public Education of Boys; Plans for the Instruction and Liberal Education of Boys in Large Numbers* (1822); this book was published anonymously. M. D. Hill was a son of Thomas Wright Hill.

in unison". When the first section is washed, the second follows, the other two sections "still repeating the tables" until all are washed. At 9.5 the bell rings for breakfast, the cook being aware "that she must be ready to a moment".[1]

Each minute of the day is similarly organised; though there was scope for individual and group activities outside the class organisation of the school, no time was lost. In short, just as Boulton and Watt junior were at this time developing a highly efficient system of factory organisation at Soho—evolving the first approach to the scientific routeing of materials[2]—so their contemporaries, the Hill brothers, were efficiently routing human materials at the Hazelwood school.

This parallel should not, perhaps, be taken too far; Hazelwood was certainly a pioneer school in evoking the children's activity in their trigonometrical surveys, the running of a school magazine, self-government, and in certain definite innovations in teaching method. But the main incentive to activity—the accumulation of penal marks (given for good work and voluntary labour) which could be used to pay fines imposed for bad behaviour or work—reflects the acquisitive nature of the society for which the boys were being prepared: "prudent boys are careful never to be without some hundreds of these marks; and there are those who have thousands. Indeed it is an object of ambition to possess the greatest number".[3] If fines could not be paid, penalties were doubled, up to solitary confinement in the dark for a time proportionate to the debt (a mode of punishment used also by the Quakers at Ackworth and the Presbyterians at Mill Hill). The "public treasure" (i.e. the counters representing penal marks not in circulation) was kept by a boy called the banker, who kept accounts in the normal way—the revenue column showing marks paid each day on penalties, the expenditure column, marks paid in cheques drawn on the bank by teachers—while the banker himself was "paid for his trouble by a commission of one per cent on his receipts and issues".[4] Thirty or forty years earlier Thomas Day had sought in enlightened self-interest the basis for a fully conscious approach to moral behaviour. For this, Hazelwood substituted the accumulation of capital, and the formation of mechanical habits "fixed" by association.

To the *Westminster Review*, however, the whole system advocated by Bentham and practised at Hazelwood had a "great moral advantage." It "places and keeps boys in a condition in which there is little

[1] Hill, *op. cit.*, 52–7.   [2] C. Gill, *History of Birmingham* (1952), Vol. I, 108–9.

[3] Hill, *op. cit.*, 25.   [4] *Ibid.*, 26.

opportunity of doing wrong. Their time is completely occupied: their attention is constantly fixed; they are never idle: they never deviate from a steady and regular course: whence the habit is founded of doing everything in its proper hour and place." If the whole of the middle class were educated in this manner "the improvement which would immediately take place would be universal, and without any bound which it is possible to fix".[1]

In fact, both *Chrestomathia* and Hazelwood—and later the Hills' second school at Bruce Castle—represented an outright challenge to the whole spirit and structure of the old-established schools and universities; a challenge flung down specifically in the interests of a class. Whatever the criticisms that may be levelled at it, *Chrestomathia* breathes a positive optimism, and advocates a coherent educational policy based on the all-embracing philosophy of utilitarianism. From the standpoint of this conception of education—with its clear purpose, its efficiency, its close links with the widest spheres of social activity—most current educational practice appeared sterile, pedantic and obsolete. The old endowed schools and universities were condemned as both useless and pernicious.

The Chrestomathic school never came into being. But when the middle class were in a position to start educational institutions under their own control, they had ready to hand a clear theory of education. Again, when they turned their attention to existing universities and schools, the middle class had clear political and educational aims. The utilitarians, or "philosophic radicals" as they came to be called, were, then, the spearhead of a general middle-class attack which included dissenters and other excluded religious groupings, and extended to the more radical wing of the Whig party. Each and all of these were profoundly dissatisfied with the state of the universities and schools.

2. THE RADICAL ATTACK ON ESTABLISHED EDUCATIONAL INSTITUTIONS

(i) *The Universities*

There had been stirrings in the university world before the publication of a series of articles in the *Edinburgh Review* from 1808-10 made university reform a national issue. At Cambridge, which had been more affected by eighteenth-century rationalism than Oxford, there

---

[1] *Westminster Review*, Vol. I, No. 1, January 1824, 74, 79. It is significant that Bentham's *Chrestomathia* and Hill's *Public Education of Boys* were reviewed together in the first number of this Radical journal. The reviewer was Southwood Smith.

was a radical intellectual movement of considerable significance in the 1780s.[1] Certain colleges, particularly Jesus where William Frend, an intimate friend of Joseph Priestley, was a fellow, became the centre of intellectual ferment and there developed an important movement for political and university reform. But, just as Priestley was driven from Birmingham, so Frend (who became a Unitarian) was deprived of his fellowship, ostensibly for publishing a radical pamphlet in 1793. So also Thomas Beddoes, another of Priestley's associates at Oxford whose lectures on chemistry had attracted many students, found it necessary to resign his fellowship in the wave of reaction that followed the war with France. All attempts at university reform were defeated.

Both universities were, of course, closely identified with the Established Church. At Oxford, all students were required to subscribe to the Thirty-nine Articles before taking up residence; they must subscribe again before taking the B.A. degree and once more before taking an M.A. At Cambridge, no subscription was required on entrance but before taking a degree the student had to declare himself a *bona fide* member of the Church of England.[2] Nonconformists could, in theory, study at Cambridge without taking a degree; but in practice they were "all but excluded from the colleges. The masters and tutors would in most cases have either directly refused admission to a nonconformist, or if he had been admitted would probably have forced him to attend the College chapel";[3] where, of course, services were Church of England.

As with all institutions—and particularly such complex ones as Oxford and Cambridge—generalisation is difficult. But there is ample evidence that, in the period 1750-80 in particular, the universities had fallen on evil days. Adam Smith's complaint that "professors had altogether given up even the pretence of teaching", while exaggerated, is in general confirmed by contemporary evidence. "The story for the most part", writes the historian of Cambridge University, referring to the professors, "is one of broken oaths, violated statutes and cynical disregard of testamentary wishes; and unfortunately the sinners were sufficiently numerous to keep one another in countenance."[4]

It was the colleges which effectively controlled not only entrance

---

[1] See B. R. Schneider, *Wordsworth's Cambridge Education* (1957) for an interesting and valuable study of this movement.

[2] This declaration was substituted for subscription to the Thirty-nine Articles in 1772. A similar proposition at that time at Oxford was rejected.

[3] A. V. Dicey, *Law and Public Opinion in England* (2nd edn, 1914), 349.

[4] D. A. Winstanley, *Unreformed Cambridge* (1935), 179.

to the university but also nearly all teaching. Founded for the most part in the fifteenth and sixteenth centuries as self-governing corporations for a certain number of fellows and students, they still maintained their semi-ecclesiastical character and reflected all the worst features of a Church long overdue for reform. The fellows, whose task it was to act as tutors, were rarely chosen for intellectual qualities or scholastic achievement; many fellowships were restricted to a particular school, county or even family and awarded by patronage. Moreover, it was not to success as university teachers but rather to the award of one of the Church livings in the hands of the college that fellows looked for advancement. Such men, together with past members of the university, the majority of whom were clergymen, dominated Convocation at Oxford and the Senate at Cambridge—the bodies which ultimately governed the universities.

Under such conditions, educational reform was at a discount. Teaching in the colleges was at a very low ebb and students seeking academic distinction were forced to have recourse to private tutors in the town. Further, the whole examination system, which was still based on the mediaeval practice of disputation, had lost all relevance and often degenerated into a farce. Such was the position that critics were to be found even among those who did not wish to see the ecclesiastical control of the universities broken and who had no fundamental objection to a curriculum based primarily on the classics in the early stages and which, at more advanced levels, bore no relation to the advancement of knowledge. As a result of such criticisms, advanced towards the close of the eighteenth century by Vicesimus Knox[1] and others, some minor adjustments were made. Thus at Oxford, a new examination statute came into force in 1802 making possible a voluntary public examination for a "class". Three years later there was only one candidate for examination but the system gradually became more popular;[2] further examinations were introduced and the number of students, which had long been at a low level, began to increase.

The effect of this development, however, was that the student's education became more narrow than before, since he was likely to concentrate only on examined subjects. As a result, such lectures as were given by university professors, who alone covered more general subjects, in particular science, ceased to attract students. Neither

[1] Vicesimus Knox, *On some parts of the Discipline in our English Universities* (1778); *Letter to the Rt. Hon. Lord North*; C. E. Mallet, *A History of the University of Oxford* (1927) Vol. III, 163-5.
[2] Mallet, *op. cit.*, Vol. III, 168.

university was abreast of modern knowledge in the fields of learning it mainly cultivated. At Oxford, the home of theological and classical studies, there was almost complete ignorance of the great advances in historical criticism and philology in Germany, where scholars had developed a new and more scientific approach to classical scholarship since the 1780s. At Cambridge, where mathematical studies had held an important place since the days of Newton and formed the main subject in honours degrees, the recent advances of French mathematical physicists were comparatively unknown. Critics were quick to seize on these points.

The first full-scale assault came, not from the Radicals associated with Mill and Bentham in London, but at an earlier stage and from the centre of intellectual activity in the north. It was conducted over a period of three years, from 1808 onwards, in the pages of the *Edinburgh Review*, recently founded organ of the more radical Whigs, which was widely read not only in influential political circles but also among the manufacturing class. The series of articles, written by Sidney Smith and two associates, advanced arguments supported by an intimate knowledge of the universities and developed them with a thoroughness and civilised wit seldom equalled in the history of journalism.[1]

Here was an attack which could not be ignored and a reply duly appeared from Oxford University, which had been particularly singled out for criticism, in a series of pamphlets.[2] But this only spurred Smith and his associates to greater efforts. The standpoint from which their merciless criticism was levelled was that of the Baconian tradition. The purpose of knowledge was "the relief of man's estate"; to ignore this was to ignore that "one of the greatest objects of human wisdom" has always "been to turn the properties of matter to the use of man".[3] The fundamental criterion to be applied in estimating the value of education must, therefore, be its "usefulness". Judged by this criterion the universities failed on nearly every count.

The authors, in common with Priestley in an earlier age, proclaim themselves to be concerned only with the education of a governing class—the future "Judges, Senators, Noblemen". Accordingly emphasis is laid on the value of a true classical education as opposed to the crabbed

[1] *Edinburgh Review*, Vol. XI, No. 22, January 1808; Vol. XIV, No. 28, July 1809; Vol. XV, No. 29, October 1809; Vol. XVI, No. 31, April 1810.

[2] E. Copleston, *A Reply to the Calumnies of the Edinburgh Review against Oxford* (1810); *A Second Reply to the Edinburgh Review* (1810); *A Third Reply to the Edinburgh Review* (1811).

[3] *Edinburgh Review*, Vol. XVI, No. 31, April 1810, 185.

sterility of contemporary practice and a broad, comprehensive plan for a liberal education is outlined. But, while there was little in common with the Benthamite utilitarian outlook, nothing with which an enlightened Whig aristocrat need disagree, the insistence on "modern studies" and originality of thought was as congenial to the middle class as it was anathema to the Church and Tory party which controlled the universities. In this sense the articles represent a restatement, in a new context, of the rationalism of the eighteenth century, so clearing the way for utilitarianism.

The main point of criticism was the "extravagant and overacted attachment" of the universities to classical knowledge and its effect in producing "narrow and limited beings". While the authors accepted that classical scholars were necessary, they could not, in the light of the criterion of usefulness, find any case for the monopoly of the classics in education.

From the age of six to the age of twenty-four, the pupil's "sole and exclusive occupation is learning Latin and Greek", except at Cambridge where mathematics is included. Scholars have come "to love the instrument better than the end" and aim at a "needless perfection", particularly in the production of Latin verses. In the authors' view, Latin and Greek should be placed "upon a footing with many other subjects of study". To the "very curious" argument sometimes put in justification of classical education: "What are you going to do with a young man up to the age of seventeen?" they answer: "As if a young man within that period might not acquire the modern languages, modern history, experimental philosophy, geography, chronology, and a considerable share of mathematics;—as if the memory of things was not more agreeable, and more profitable, than the memory of words". While the classics may have some value for those going into the church, those entering public life would be better occupied in learning about the making of laws, and about such matters as wealth, foreign trade, manufactures, agriculture, paper money, population, poverty, monopoly, taxation and the public debt.[1]

What of the stifling of the student's initiative? One article quotes an ironical comment; the universities "are of this service to the country at large, that they are the great schools by which established opinions are inculcated and perpetuated."[2] A later article places the blame for this

---

[1] *Edinburgh Review*, Vol. XV, No. 29, Art. 3, October 1809, *passim*.

[2] *Ibid.*, Vol. XI, No. 22, January 1808, 378-9. The book quoted, *Letters from England*, was written (anonymously) by the poet Southey.

squarely on "the English clergy, in whose hands education entirely rests . . .":

"There is a timid and absurd apprehension, on the part of ecclesiastical tutors, of letting out the minds of youth upon difficult and important subjects. They fancy that mental exertion must end in religious scepticism; and, to preserve the principles of their pupils, they confine them to the safe and elegant imbecility of classical learning. A genuine Oxford tutor would shudder to hear his young men disputing upon moral and political truth, forming and pulling down theories, and indulging in all the boldness of youthful discussion. He would augur nothing from it, but impiety to God and treason to Kings. And yet, who vilifies both more than the holy poltroon, who carefully averts from them the searching eye of reason, and who knows no better method of teaching the highest duties, than by extirpating the finest qualities and habits of the mind? . . . An infinite quantity of talent is annually destroyed in the Universities of England, by the miserable jealousy and littleness of ecclesiastical instructors."[1]

The *Edinburgh Review* is concerned to make clear that the universities, with their "spacious and comfortable abodes," their "ample revenues," their many advantages for the pursuit of learning, are "public institutions of England . . . from which knowledge is supposed to radiate over all the rest of the island". But, and this is the burden of the complaint, they are failing to serve this purpose, and resist any attempt to turn them to more useful ends. "When an University has been doing useless things for a long time, it appears at first degrading to them to be useful." Thus, the teaching of political economy or chemistry would be considered undignified at Oxford.

"and yet, what other measure is there of dignity in intellectual labour, but usefulness? And what ought the term university to mean, but a place where every science is taught which is liberal, and at the same time useful to mankind? Nothing would so much tend to bring classical literature within proper bounds, as a steady and invariable appeal to utility in our appreciation of all human knowledge."[2]

The *Edinburgh Review*, then, was primarily concerned with clerical control of the universities in so far as it restricted the development of a liberal education. It stood for the free play of the intellect in matters relating to morals and politics; for the reform of classical studies according to the criterion of usefulness and for the introduction of

[1] *Edinburgh Review*, Vol. XV, No. 29, October 1809, 50.   [2] *Ibid.*, 51.

those modern studies necessary to produce a cultivated man-of-the-world concerned with current events and changes.

When James Mill entered the field ten years later it was to deliver a much more outright attack on what he regarded as survivals of mediaevalism. His primary concern at this period was to lead the non-conformist middle class in an assault on the clerical domination of education. In his eyes the inculcation of religious opinions from an early age, opinions for which no evidence of any kind was offered, was the worst of intellectual crimes; as a result of such teaching, people were led habitually to disregard evidence and became, in effect, intellectual slaves. When teaching of this kind was pursued while no attention whatsoever was paid to the development of modern knowledge, then there was nothing to be said in favour of the educational institutions concerned.

"That he is a *progressive* being", wrote Mill, "is the grand distinction of man." Universities so constituted that they can make no provision for change are "a curse rather than a blessing"; they develop "a strong spirit of resistance to all improvement, a passion of adherence to whatever was established in a dark age" and a hatred of those who advocate any change. Education by its very essence contributes to the progress of man. "An institution for *education* which is hostile to progression, is, therefore, the most preposterous, and vicious thing, which the mind of man can conceive." Nothing could be worse than a university "united with an ecclesiastical establishment"; for "whatever the vices of the ecclesiastical system", and Mill's readers were in no doubt about these, the universities will "bend the whole of their force to the support of those vices". Under such conditions, the universities were inevitably led "to vitiate the human mind, which can only be rendered the friend of abuses in proportion as it is vitiated intellectually, or morally, or both".[1]

Bentham added his voice, in criticism not only of classical learning but also of Cambridge mathematics. "Even miraculous", he observed sardonically in 1819, "is the command, which, by the sacrifice of health and comfort for five or six years to the prospect of a rich fellowship, a young man acquires over Greek particles, and x's and y's, and lines right and curved applied to useless purposes."[2] Even Samuel Butler, now headmaster of Shrewsbury school, was led to ask how many

[1] James Mill, article on "Education", *Supplement to Encyclopaedia Britannica* (1818); reprinted in F. A. Cavenagh, *James and John Stuart Mill on Education* (1931), 67-8.
[2] "Jeremy Bentham to Lord Somebody: the Particular Lord not remembered," *Black Dwarf*, Vol. III, No. 51, 22nd December 1819.

Cambridge mathematicians were able to apply their mathematics to any useful purpose. If a bridge is to be built across the Thames, he enquired, who will do it best, a committee of Senior Wranglers, or Mr. Rennie? As for classical learning, "we weary ourselves with adjusting iambics and trochaics and anapaests, and twisting mono-strophics into choruses and dochmiacs, and almost seem to neglect the sense for the sake of the sound".[1]

By the early 1830s, all publications in any way expressive of the middle-class standpoint are in full cry against the state of university learning at Oxford in particular. The *Quarterly Journal of Education*, established in 1831 by the Society for the Diffusion of Useful Know-ledge (a Liberal-Whig organisation in which James Mill and Henry Brougham played a leading part) was particularly sharp in its criticism. "Nobody hangs up bars in semicircles, or flings perfectly elastic glass balls against perfectly hard walls", it wrote, ridiculing the teaching of mathematics. The student "knows himself to be living in a country abounding in applications, direct and indirect, both of mathematics and physics, to everything he wears and eats, to everything he reads of or sees. And yet he finds, to his discouragement, that though he is spending much time on these two great branches of human knowledge, his tutors never furnish him with any but make-believe problems, the circumstances of which are for the most part impossible, and the results nearly always useless".[2] Even the classical examinations at Oxford are full of "meagre, ill-sorted, unmeaning questions". The College tutors are quite inadequate and fail to exert themselves. One will lecture for ten years on Aristotle's *Ethics* without having ever read his *Politics*, wrote an Oxford graduate; "while Germany, with far less means, is daily making rapid advances in literature, and sending forth productions of great ability, the university of Oxford is obliged to the labours of German writers for the mere class-books which she prints for the use of her alumni." Logic and rhetoric are no better; the student gains nothing from his instruction. "No one who reflects upon the value of youthful years can fail to lament the time thus mis-spent, or cease to regret that so unsystematic and careless a mode of education exists in this university."[3]

Criticism of the state of the universities was, by the 1830s, being

---

[1] *Thoughts on the present System of Academic Education in the University of Cambridge* (1822), by Eubulus (Samuel Butler), 7-8, 19; the pamphlet is partly republished in S. Butler, *Life and Letters of Dr. Samuel Butler* (1896), Vol. I, 211-15.

[2] *Quarterly Journal of Education*, Vol. IV, No. 8, October 1832, 204.

[3] *Ibid.*, Vol. V, No. 10, April 1833, 334.

voiced not only from outside. In 1832 Baden Powell, Savilian Professor of Geometry at Oxford, criticising contemporary defects, and maintaining that not more than two or three Oxford degree candidates could add vulgar fractions, tell the cause of day or night, or the principle of the pump, made a strong plea for the inclusion of science and mathematics in the basic core of education. Full support was forthcoming from the *Quarterly Journal* which quoted an argument frequently to be repeated at a later stage. University College, London, founded by Bentham, Mill and their circle, had now been open for four years. The middle class were not only knowledgeable about industry and science in general but had also founded an institution of higher education designed to further that knowledge. Sections of the working class were also mastering science and technology in various institutions. Baden Powell sounded the warning:

> "Scientific knowledge is rapidly spreading *among all classes* EXCEPT THE HIGHER, and the consequence must be, that that class *will not long remain* THE HIGHER. If its members would continue to retain their superiority, they must preserve a real *pre-eminence in knowledge*, and must make advances at least in proportion to the classes who have *hitherto* been below them. And is it not a question, whether the same consideration does not in some measure apply to the ascendancy and stability of the *University* itself?"[1]

From now on this note was increasingly struck by the less radical critics of the University; failure to reform at this stage would irrevocably mean the loss of pre-eminence, perhaps worse. But more than this was needed to move Oxford to action. In 1833 a group of Oxford M.As. put up a scheme for including some study of mathematics and science in the degree course. The measure was rejected. For the *Quarterly Journal* this was the last straw. Even those students who passed through the university with credit left in "a fearful state of ignorance". Now Oxford University had solemnly declared "that physical knowledge neither is nor ought to be an essential part of a liberal education". "Bigotry and prejudice have doubtless had their share in leading to the formation of such a decision," declared the *Quarterly Journal*, "but indolence and incapacity exercise even a wider and more pernicious influence; and an ascendancy of privileged inertness represses all attempts towards amelioration on the part of the more enlightened few."[2]

[1] *Quarterly Journal of Education*, Vol. IV, No. 8, October 1832, 197-8.
[2] *Ibid.*, Vol. VII, No. 14, April 1834, 368; Vol. VIII, No. 15, 61-2. See also Vol. VII No. 13, 47-55.

The *Westminster Review* was less restrained, finding evidence of "a hideous laziness, an enormous and insatiable greediness, and a crapulous self-indulgence".[1] Meanwhile men who could further learning and application were refused admittance because they were dissenters. Nothing will ever be done, warned the *Quarterly Journal*, "without the vigorous interference of the legislature".[2] Although the University "may sleep in real or pretended indifference to the strictures of a strictly-judging public, a day must come when an account of her conduct will be demanded"; then "the ignorant will be obliged to give way to the well-educated . . . an enemy will one day appear at the door of convocation-house, who will be found stronger than the proctor, and to whose proceedings *non placet* will be no bar".[3] The *Westminster Review* roundly demanded that the King's Commissioners descend on Oxford and transfer the entire control of the university to laymen so that "these fair domains" might be rescued "from the withering sway of ecclesiastics".[4]

In 1831, twenty-three years after its first assault, the *Edinburgh Review* published the first of two major series of articles by Sir William Hamilton, Professor of Civil History at Edinburgh, who had studied at Balliol College, Oxford, after taking a degree at Glasgow, and who was also familiar with the character and work of the most advanced German universities. The first of these famous articles opened with a direct challenge and threat of state intervention:

"This is the age of reform. Next in importance to our religious and political establishments, are the foundations for public education; and having now seriously engaged in a reform of 'the constitution, the envy of surrounding nations,' the time cannot be distant for a reform in the schools and universities which have hardly avoided their contempt."[5]

The professed aim of this, and of the second series of articles published in 1834, was to break the power of the Church over the universities; to re-establish these as national institutions. Oxford was, as always, the particular target and the two main lines of criticism of the university—

---

[1] *Westminster Review*, Vol. XV, No. 29, July 1831, 59.

[2] *Quarterly Journal of Education*, Vol. X, No. 19, April 1835, 8.

[3] *Ibid.*, Vol. V, No. 10, April 1833, 336; Vol. IV, No. 8, October 1832, 198-9.

[4] *Westminster Review*, Vol. XV, No. 29, July 1831, 59.

[5] "On the State of the English Universities," *Edinburgh Review*, Vol. LIII, No. 106, June 1831, 384. Hamilton's articles were republished in *Discussions in Philosophy and Literature, Education and University Reform* (1852).

the inefficiency of collegiate teaching and the injustice of religious exclusion—were followed up in a mature and powerful exposure which paved the way to the demand for an overall reform. The thesis was quite simple. The colleges were "private institutions" that had sprung up later than the university itself; they had illegally usurped the teaching function of the university and transformed it into an institution closed to all but members of the Church of England. The remedy was to re-establish the primacy of the university. This might be done initially by re-establishing the ancient Halls and so admitting to the university all who qualified for entry whatever their religious beliefs. But since university affairs were, in fact, governed by the colleges, even this measure required interference by the state. With the political victory of 1832 in sight, there seemed every reason that this would be forthcoming:

"With a patriot king, a reforming ministry, and a reformed Parliament, we are confident that our expectations will not be in vain. A general scholastic reform will be, in fact, one of the greatest blessings of the political renovation, and perhaps, the surest test of its value."[1]

(ii) *The Grammar Schools*

If the Radicals were the spearhead of an attack on the universities which looked for nothing less than a complete change of government and educational outlook, they also played an important part in exposing the state of the grammar schools and demanding a like remedy here.

In 1819 the *Edinburgh Review* quoted an opinion of the Lord Chancellor, Lord Eldon, on the conduct of various charities, including endowed schools: "It is absolutely necessary that it should be perfectly understood that Charity Estates all over the Kingdom are dealt with in a manner grossly improvident; amounting to the most direct breach of trust."[2] It was the initiative of Henry Brougham, associate of Mill and the Radicals[3] which had led to the disclosure of this state of affairs. He had, in 1816, secured the appointment of a Select Committee on the Education of the Lower Orders in the Metropolis, whose terms of reference were shortly widened to include the whole country. In the

---

[1] *Edinburgh Review*, Vol. LIV, No. 108, December 1831, 499; Hamilton, *op. cit.*, (3rd edn, 1886), 467.

[2] Quoted in *Edinburgh Review*, Vol. XXXI, No. 62, March 1819, 502.

[3] Brougham, a Whig politician, worked closely with the Radicals at certain periods, particularly on educational issues. Leslie Stephen described him as "a kind of half-disciple" of Bentham's (*The English Utilitarians* (1900), Vol. I, 226).

outcome the committee investigated not only schools for the working class but also the affairs of various grammar schools, including what were known as the "great" schools—Eton, Winchester and Westminster. Flagrant abuses were found in the administration of many schools; endowments were often misapplied, some masters took salaries without performing any teaching at all, such teaching as there was, was often of the lowest standard. As a result of this enquiry and its findings Charity Commissioners were appointed to investigate charitable trusts throughout the country; the bill enabling appointment of a Charity Commission being sponsored by Brougham in 1818.

Like the universities, many grammar schools were largely under the control of the Church; their masters were usually clerics, prominent among their governors were vicars and members of the landed gentry, and not infrequently their visitors were bishops or the fellows of some Oxford or Cambridge college. The disclosures of Brougham's committee naturally provoked a strong reaction. A host of pamphlets and public letters denouncing the Committee's activities and opposing the proposal to appoint Charity Commissioners was published. The Tory *Quarterly* took up the cudgels against the Committee's work while the *Edinburgh Review* strongly supported it in a series of articles published in 1819. This matter, it declared, was above party, yet an attempt is being made to blacken Brougham's character. Opposition to the appointment of Charity Commissioners was inspired by a mixture of "political hostility" and "misplaced theological hatred". But whatever the "interested animosity" aroused, "the enquiry must, and will go on".[1]

In fact, Charity Commissioners were to be appointed and to tour the country for the next two decades or more, amassing an immense amount of information which, all in all, strongly substantiated the original findings. Extreme examples of the general laxity and corruption are afforded by the once famous and flourishing school at Pocklington in Yorkshire and Berkhamstead school founded in emulation of Colet's St. Paul's. At Berkhamstead, two clergymen in orders —a father and son—exploited between them a revenue of £3,000 a year belonging to the school; neither had done any teaching for years, indeed the son lived in Hampshire, but there was no governing body to remedy the matter. An independent enquirer found, in 1818,

---

[1] *Edinburgh Review*, Vol. XXXI, No. 62, March 1819, 497-550. See also Vol. XXXII, No. 63, July 1819, 89-111.

that Pocklington commanded an income of over £1,000 a year, two-thirds of which accrued to the master; but the latter had not attended the school for a year and, since his assistant was deaf, "the children have necessarily been sent to other schools". Here was a sixteenth-century school with statutes vesting considerable powers in the master; he held all the documents and failed to answer any enquiry.[1] But those ultimately responsible were the fellows of St. John's College, Cambridge, who had been appointed visitors of the school. When this body finally summoned up the energy to conduct a visitation (according to the *Edinburgh Review* the first for three centuries)[2] it was only to confirm this deplorable state of affairs.

These were outstandingly bad examples which may be balanced by examples of adaptation to the times to be recorded later. Nevertheless, the picture given by reports of the Charity Commissioners of the position throughout whole counties is melancholy enough. Leicestershire may be taken as an example.[3] At Leicester the ancient grammar school, originally the largest in the county and controlled by the municipal corporation, was attended by one boarder and three or four day boys; whereas, within the memory of older citizens, it had had 300 pupils. Here the master was afflicted with partial loss of memory, but the corporation claimed that he could not be removed as he had a freehold of his place. At Market Harborough the commissioners found four boys but no free scholars at all—the school had long since ceased to be a classical school. The affairs of Ashby-de-la-Zouch school had been under examination by the Court of Chancery over a period of nearly forty years during which successive headmasters were in constant conflict with the governors. Market Bosworth school was virtually in abeyance from 1808 to 1826; for over fifty years the endowments were subject to litigation in the Court of Chancery due to allegations of corruption.[4] The school at Melton Mowbray, which once sent a stream of local boys to the university, now taught only the three Rs, although the master had ten private pupils who boarded in his house. Kibworth school had forty scholars, most of them also in the elementary school; its affairs had been reorganised through the Court of Chancery in 1819. At Loughborough

[1] Nicholas Carlisle, *A Concise Description of the Endowed Grammar Schools in England and Wales* (1818), Vol. I, 532-42; Vol. II, 863-5.

[2] *Edinburgh Review*, Vol. XXXI, No. 62, March 1819, 526-7.

[3] *32nd Report of the Charity Commissioners, Part 5, Leicester and Leicestershire* (1839) *passim*.

[4] S. Hopewell, *Bosworth School, 1320-1950* (1950), 61-2.

there were only eight or nine boys in the grammar school, the head-master having a freehold and refusing (in common with his colleagues at Ashby and Leicester) to meet the request of the trustees that he teach modern subjects. Appleby Parva school, provided with a sub-stantial building with room for dormitories, had twenty boarders but only seven day boys in the grammar school. Hinckley school had disappeared, as also, to all intents and purposes, had those at Shawell, Stoke Golding, Wymondham, Kegworth and Osgathorpe.

Most of these had been flourishing grammar schools in the six-teenth and early seventeenth centuries, administered by governing bodies of local men and sending scholars on to the universities. But after 1660, as has already been suggested, the grammar schools be-came subject to a narrow ecclesiastical control and ceased to consti-tute a national system of education; while in the eighteenth century many reflected the laxity and abuses of the Church. At this period, in so far as the teaching of modern subjects developed, it was mainly in dissenting academies and private commercial schools and academies; and, with the growing middle-class demand for education, many more private schools came into being in the early nineteenth century. This brought into sharper relief the stagnation of the average grammar school, which, even if not corrupt and inefficient, was educationally in a rut. "Whoever will examine the state of the Grammar Schools in different parts of the kingdom", said Lord Kenyon, who, as Master of the Rolls, had to give judgment on many cases brought before him in the Court of Chancery, "will see to what a lamentable condi-tion most of them are reduced. If all persons had equally done their duty, we should not find, as is now the case, empty walls without scholars, and everything neglected but the receipt of salaries and emoluments."[1]

To turn from Bentham's educational ideas to the practice of a relatively flourishing grammar school is to realise the immensity of the gulf between middle-class aspirations and established institutions. A sixteenth-century scholar would have been altogether at home in Louth School (Lincolnshire) in the second decade of the nineteenth century. The Latin grammar used was that of Lily (first drafted for St. Paul's School in 1515) and, after memorising the first rules, the pupil, according to the description of an evidently quite complacent master, "begins to construe Valpy's *Delectus,* and to render into Latin the Eton *Exempla Minora,*—he is almost incessantly employed in

[1] Quoted in the *Edinburgh Review,* Vol. XXXI, No. 62, March 1819, 502.

parsing,—the *Exempla Minora* he first parses into English, then rends it (*sic*) into Latin, and in the evening writes it as a Latin exercise. . . . The pupil being now completely master of every other part of the Eton grammar, commences prosody—and to Valpy and Phaedrus, succeed Caesar, and the Eton *Selections* from the Epistles and Metamorphoses of Ovid, Cornelius Nepos, Sallust,—these are followed by Virgil, Horace, Juvenal,—by Cicero's *Orations, Offices*, the Eton *Scriptores Romani*, and by some books of Livy and Tacitus". The pupil is taught versification "by first giving the scholar the words of some Latin poet thrown into disorder, to reduce into verse,—and then by his forming Nonsense verses from the words of his Latin prose exercise"; at the age of eleven or earlier "he is introduced into the Greek". Each day has its appointed tasks, beginning with a "Sacred Reading": "the first and second [top—B.S.] classes read a portion of the Latin Testament into the original Greek,—the third construes some part of the gospels in Greek, the fourth and fifth construe the Latin Testament,—and those who are not equal to this, read the lessons of the day in English". After prayers "the Senior classes then repeat lines from Greek and Latin authors, which have been committed to memory on the preceding evening. . . . The other classes repeat a portion of Greek or Latin grammar, history or geography". Compositions in English, Latin or Greek done the previous evening are then looked over. "Every lesson, except in the first class, is construed twice over, and is parsed very carefully. . . . In the last month of the half-year, the whole work of the half-year is again gone over,—all the lines also are again repeated."[1]

There was, then, no genuine teaching, no conception of the processes of education, of learning; nothing but continuous memorising of a series of classical texts whose content was rarely expounded or understood. The same was true of the largest and most famous schools where the aristocracy were educated, such as the collegiate school of Eton founded in the fifteenth century; and also of those local grammar schools which had, through exploitation of the master's right to take in private boarders, developed into "public" schools with a considerable number of pupils. But among these, Harrow—which by contrast with the Church and Tory flavour of Eton had developed as the favoured school of the Whig aristocracy—made some provision for accomplishments regarded as necessary to a noble education. It had, besides the head, his deputy and five classical masters, teachers of

[1] Carlisle, *op. cit.*, Vol. I, 828-30.

French and Italian, writing and arithmetic, drawing, fencing and broadsword, dancing and music; a lecturer in natural and experimental philosophy, also attended "once in every two or three years".[1] Smaller schools catering mainly for the sons of professional men emulated this where they could; Louth grammar school, for instance, employed "a native of France" to teach French at a guinea a quarter and provided for teaching of writing, arithmetic, algebra, trigonometry and Euclid for an extra two guineas a year.[2]

The "great" schools, however, by reason of their large bodies of boarders, also presented other problems which had been forcibly brought to the public eye. These were something in the nature of schoolboy republics, with their own morality and law. Schoolboy rebellions reached major proportions during the period 1790-1810. At Rugby, the military were called out on one occasion to quell an uprising. At Winchester—according to the account of Dean Hook, a respectable High Churchman in later life—the boys took control of part of the school for a day and a night; armed with pickaxes, clubs and stones, they smashed windows, sang revolutionary songs, made forays into the town for meals and generally held the school to ransom.[3]

It was not long before changes began to be made, in particular at Rugby by Dr. Thomas Arnold. Meanwhile, chaos and indiscipline, exclusively classical teaching, religious observances based on the tenets of the Church of England, were hardly features likely to recommend these schools to the middle class.

The *Westminster Review* moved into the attack in 1825 with a condemnation of the educational system as pernicious, useless, purposeless and antiquated. Though "the church had fled before Luther, and the monks before Henry", there were still battles to be fought and won; "Westminster and Harrow, Winchester and Eton, are seminaries for monks".[4] This was an attack consciously directed against the aristocracy, in particular the Church and Tory party, but it was pursued also, in detail, on educational grounds. Following in the steps of Priestley and his colleagues, the Radicals assaulted the whole conception of an exclusively classical education at the secondary stage; though it might have some relevance to some learned professions, the *Westminster Review* objected to it "forming part of the education

---

[1] Carlisle, *op. cit.*, Vol. II, 153.   [2] *Ibid.*, Vol. I, 833.
[3] W. R. W. Stephens, *Dean Hook, his Life and Letters* (1880), 18-20, 608
[4] *Westminster Review*, Vol. IV, No. 7, July 1825, 147-9, 150-1.

of a very important part of the community, to whom, at least as it is at present communicated, experience proves it to be utterly useless".[1]

The criticism levelled at the curriculum and methods of teaching was of the same nature as that directed at the universities.

"From six to eight, till sixteen or seventeen, nine or ten months in every precious year of youth are occupied for six or eight hours of every day, in learning, or trying to learn, a little Latin and less Greek; in attempting, in fact, not to read and understand the matter of a classical author, to know the history, the poetry, the philosophy, the policy, the manners, and the opinions of Greece and Rome, but the grammar, the syntax, the parsing, the quantities, and the accents; not in learning to write and speak the languages, but in getting by rote a few scraps of poetry, to be again forgotten, and in fabricating nonsense, or sense verses, it is indifferent which. In ten years of this labour, privation, punishment, slavery, and expense, what is gained even of this useless trash? Nothing."[2]

Coupled with the denunciation of classical teaching at English schools as irrelevant to the middle class are descriptions of educational institutions on the continent and in America much better adapted to their needs. In article after article in the *Quarterly Journal* these points are driven home, and, when no action supervenes even after 1832, the attack is pressed more aggressively; the claims of the middle class affirmed more decidedly. In 1832 the *Quarterly Journal* is asking:

"Is it reasonable or creditable, or decent, that boys of fifteen years of age and more should know absolutely nothing of the simplest laws of mechanical philosophy? That they should know nothing of the growth, production and manufacture of the various objects which are daily subservient to their necessities and pleasures? That they should be absolutely or almost altogether ignorant of the climate, productions, and geographical distribution of the animal, vegetable, and mineral kingdoms, and even of the moral and social condition of their fellow-creatures scattered over the globe? Is it reasonable that they should not even know arithmetic, or be able to write their own language with tolerable accuracy? Such are very common results of the education misnamed 'liberal'. And finally, is it reasonable that all this should be sacrificed to the supposed attainment of two dead languages?"[3]

[1] *Westminster Review*, Vol. I, No. 1, January 1824, 46.
[2] *Ibid.*, Vol. IV, No. 7, July 1825, 156.
[3] *Quarterly Journal of Education*, Vol. III, No. 6, April 1832, 268-9.

"A new race of men" has sprung up, writes Professor Long of University College, the editor of the *Quarterly Journal*, "a race of men whose ingenuity and perseverance have, by one victory after another, subjected to our control the stubborn resistance of matter, and increased in a thousand ways the material sources of enjoyment—and another race of men, whose business it is to perform with their hands what the heads of the others have contrived." But there are no schools adapted to the needs of this new class.[1] Where, asks Frederic Hill, can the middle-class parent find for his child "the inducement, or even the opportunity, for the pursuit of mechanics, architecture, navigation, sculpture, chemistry, mineralogy, or that one among a dozen other branches of knowledge for which he may have a special aptitude?"[2] "If we find in the country and town schools little preparation for the occupations, still less for the duties of the future agriculturist or mechanic, we find in the grammar schools much greater defects", wrote the educational reformer, Thomas Wyse, M.P.:

> "The middle class, in all its sections, except the mere learned professions, finds no instruction which can suit their special middle-class wants. They are fed with the dry husks of ancient learning, when they should be taking sound and substantial food from the great treasury of modern discovery."[3]

Meanwhile the *Quarterly Journal* and the *Westminster Review* turned afresh to the vices of the public schools, particularly at Eton. Fagging, flogging, the lack of moral superintendence and actual sexual immorality in public schools are all deplored in articles based on personal experience. At Eton the boy "oscillates between tyrant and slave", and all the vices acquired by the aristocracy from early childhood are developed. "Before an Eton boy is ready for the University, he may have acquired, at a place of education where there is much less effective restraint than at the University, a confirmed taste for gluttony and drunkenness, an aptitude for brutal sports, and a passion for female society of the most degrading kind. . . ." The horrors of the Long Chamber, where some forty scholars of all ages were locked in together for ten hours at a stretch each night, were vividly described. Eton, claimed the *Quarterly Journal* in 1835, "does not belong to the

[1] G. Long, "On Endowments in England for the Purposes of Education," *Central Society of Education, Second Publication* (1838), 88.

[2] Frederick Hill, *National Education* (1836), Vol. I, 209.

[3] "Education in the United Kingdom," *Central Society of Education, First Publication,* (1837), 59-60.

present age. It is the effect of a system of jobbing and corruption in all departments of church and state, when patronage was the all-in-all of our aristocratic institutions, and when the system of representation which was destroyed only three years ago was the main instrument for working this patronage. Eton belongs to that old political system; it was part and parcel of it. The system is gone, but Eton remains unchanged".[1]

Hitherto little or no progress had been made, but here was a threat which portended what was to come now that the political power of the aristocracy had been undermined.

3. MIDDLE-CLASS EDUCATION

(i) *The Attempt to Transform the Grammar Schools*

Even after the passage of the Reform Act a long campaign had to be conducted—public opinion aroused and forces gathered—before Eton and Oxford fell to the reforming onslaught. Meanwhile there were other ways open to the middle class to promote educational advance in their own interest.

Unlike the universities and public schools, the grammar schools were local institutions at least partially open to the pressure of local opinion. Changes could, therefore, be demanded at this level. So also, the middle class could, and did, support other schools which set out to provide a relevant education; while the leaders of radical thought were themselves among the chief promoters of a new university.

There was little, or no, possibility of any considerable change in those grammar schools which were governed by the local clergy and squirearchy. A few were controlled by municipal corporations, but these, too, were ripe for reform; Leicester school is but one example of how borough schools were neglected and left to decay by unrepresentative and corrupt municipal bodies. But elsewhere the middle class gained some foothold on governing bodies, and it was here that demands for changes in the curriculum were chiefly pressed.[2]

As has already been suggested in the case of Leicestershire schools,

---

[1] *Westminster Review*, Vol. XXIII, No. 46, October 1835, 314; *Quarterly Journal of Education*, Vol. VIII, No. 16, October 1834, 286, 292-3. See also Vol. IX, No. 17, on "Flogging and Fagging at Winchester," and Vol. X, No. 19, "On the Discipline of Large Boarding Schools."

[2] It was not more than a foothold. James Bryce's report on Lancashire to the Schools Inquiry Commission revealed that the middle classes were often still excluded from the government of the grammar schools even in Lancashire as late as the 1860s. *Report of the Schools Inquiry Commission* (1868), Vol. IX, 441.

such demands were likely to be met with refusal to comply on the part of the master. Owing to the practice of freehold tenure, school-masters could not easily be dismissed and therefore gained considerable control over the affairs of the school. Making a reasonable living out of the fees of private pupils and the fixed salary due from the endowment, most had no wish to teach arithmetic, accounting, geography, history, modern languages to all comers; even if, as was doubtful, they were qualified to do so. They tended, therefore, to ignore the children of local inhabitants and the demands for a broader education. In taking this stand they could often quote sixteenth or seventeenth century statutes which laid it down that the business of the school was to teach the classical languages and literature.

A few examples, however, show that statutes could be changed or modified. Macclesfield Grammar School obtained an Act of Parliament regulating certain of its affairs in 1774 and the opportunity had then been taken to widen the basis of teaching; this by inserting a clause empowering the governors to appoint masters paid out of the revenues of the school to teach "not only in Grammar and Classical Learning, but also writing, arithmetic, geography, navigation, mathematics, the modern languages, and other branches of literature and education" as shall from time to time, in the judgment of the governors, be proper and necessary "to render the said Foundation of the most general use and benefit" according to the available revenues.[1] Here was a conception of education which had much in common with that advanced by Joseph Priestley. In the early nineteenth century Macclesfield School was patronised by the neighbouring aristocracy and gentry as well as by merchants and industrialists from nearby towns; though classical literature was still "the first object" of the school, mathematics, geography and French were also taught.[2]

Several other schools followed this example to the letter, incorporating exactly the same clause in Acts regulating their affairs; such were Bolton (1784), Haydon Bridge (1785), Wigan (1812), though the original statutes for the latter clearly stated that the school was founded for study of the classics. Elsewhere the changes made were less far-reaching, but still of some significance; the Act covering Rugby school (1777), for instance, permitting payment out of the school revenues of a master of writing and arithmetic.

Some schools, however, had no statutes. Many of these were now

[1] Carlisle, *Endowed Grammar Schools*, Vol. I, 120.
[2] *Ibid.*, Vol. I, 121.

providing a form of elementary education. Others modified the teaching of classics while developing commercial or "modern" subjects in response to local demands. Examples are four grammar schools in or near Lancashire. Lancaster and Congleton were borough schools, under the control of the corporation. While in both cases classics formed the main part of the education given, at Congleton this was supplemented by the teaching of writing, arithmetic, merchants' accounts, elementary mathematics, French and geography. At Lancaster, where a contemporary investigator notes in 1818 that "the scholars are of a mixed sort; the sons of Merchants and Tradesmen forming a considerable majority", English, history, geography, writing and arithmetic were included. Chorley frankly provided a commercial education; "as this is a manufacturing district, all the youth educated here at the present are intended for business". The same was true at Middleton.[1]

Where the statutes definitely laid down a classical education, they were sometimes evaded by the simple expedient of charging a fee (quarterage) for teaching modern or commercial subjects (so that the teaching was not "on the foundation" and therefore free), or sometimes simply by ignoring the statutes altogether. At St. Bees, Cumberland, while the established master and usher taught classics, writing, arithmetic, geography, English grammar and mathematics were taught by a third master "who has a quarterly charge on those who receive such instructions, the school being only free for the classics". At Wisbech instruction in writing, arithmetic and English grammar might be had for a guinea a quarter each. At Rochdale, where the statutes laid down the teaching of Latin "and true piety", all scholars paid a guinea and a half a quarter, "as they are instructed in other branches of literature besides what is required on the foundation". Even at Bury St. Edmunds, where the statutes laying down the teaching of classics and nothing else had recently been confirmed by the Visitor (the Bishop of Norwich), "mathematics and other branches of useful knowledge" had recently been introduced in 1818.[2]

Such teaching was, however, normally an extra, and sometimes quite a costly one at that. Nor did the majority of schools introduce additional subjects; in most cases the power of conservative interests successfully held up reform. Indeed, their position was strengthened after 1805 by a judgment in the Court of Chancery which operated

[1] Carlisle, *Endowed Grammar Schools*, Vol. I, 668, 106, 649, 707.
[2] *Ibid.*, Vol. I, 167, 102, 719; Vol. II, 513.

to maintain the grammar schools as classical schools. It is worth examining what is known as the Leeds Grammar School case[1] in some detail, tince it shows clearly the conflict of class interests which arose over she question of school reform.

At Leeds the governing body of the school, representative of local mercantile interests, had been trying since 1777 to broaden the curriculum, only to be met with the flat opposition of the master. In 1795 the governors finally decided on a suit in the Court of Chancery.

Their case was that Leeds "had a very extensive foreign trade" and that the teaching of subjects "usually considered to form the basis of a mercantile and commercial education" would be useful to the inhabitants and increase the number of scholars. They proposed that a master be financed out of the endowment to teach "low algebra and mathematics" and that French and German should also be taught.

The case went before the Lord Chancellor, Lord Eldon, in 1805. In his judgment he stressed that he must consider the founder's intent; that the Court could not change the nature of the charity simply because to do so might be beneficial to the inhabitants. He then pointed out that the endowment was originally made for a "free grammar school", and gave Samuel Johnson's definition of such a school as one "in which the learned languages are grammatically taught". There was no precedent, he claimed, whereby the Court could sanction "the conversion of that Institution by filling a school intended for that mode of Education with scholars learning the German and French language, Mathematics, and anything except Latin and Greek". The governors desired to convert this old school into a commercial academy. But this change was not proposed in order to benefit the poor (for whom the school was originally endowed). "This is a scheme to promote the benefit of the merchants of Leeds. It is not that the poor inhabitants are to be taught reading and writing English, but the clerks and riders of the merchants are to be taught French and German to carry on trade. I fear that the effect would be to turn out the poor Latin and Greek scholars altogether."

A triple conflict of interest stands out particularly clearly in the case. Eldon himself, the highest of Tories, would naturally be concerned to maintain the established order and the primacy of classical education, although it is doubtful whether there were any "poor" scholars learning

---

[1] A. C. Price, *A History of the Leeds Grammar School*, (1919), 133-50 (from which the quotations in this section are taken).

Latin and Greek at that time. The Committee, representing the manufacturing and commercial class, were concerned not so much, perhaps,
with the education of their own children as with ensuring a supply
of efficient clerks and accountants. They desired to re-interpret the
statutes in two important respects: first, by introducing commercial
subjects, and second, by excluding "poor" children (they stated
explicitly that the teaching of writing "should be wholly excluded".)
The third group, the parents of the potential "poor" scholars, the vast
majority of the Leeds population, required schools which gave an
elementary education; but it was impossible for them at this stage to
act as an articulate pressure group at all, and, in the event, their needs
were not consulted.

As Lord Chancellor, Eldon was able to invest his interpretation of
the statutes with all the force of the law. But such judgments must be
evaluated in the light of contemporary conflicts of interest. Certain
statutes, reflecting the founder's intent, but no longer expedient, had
already been abrogated by the Court of Chancery, among them those
laying down celibacy as a condition of appointment as a master; in
other instances also the Court had modified the application of endowments in such a way as to violate the will of the founder. One Master
of the Rolls had given a judgment at odds with that of Eldon, when
he ruled that a grammar school could finance the teaching of writing
and arithmetic out of its endowment.[1] At Eton, Winchester and the
Oxford and Cambridge Colleges, many mediaeval statutes were, of
course, no longer observed, since changing customs had rendered them
obsolete. There is no doubt that the founder's intent at Leeds and
elsewhere was to found a school that would be useful to the inhabitants;
in the sixteenth century, in pursuance of this end, he endowed a school
to teach the classics. But while the Governors stressed the former point
as overriding, Eldon took his stand on the letter of the statutes and,
insisted on the latter.

The end result was a form of compromise, for, in a rider to his
judgment, Eldon suggested that the conflict of interest might be
partially overcome. "If," he said "according to the Plan, every boy to
be brought to the school was to be taught the learned languages, and
the circumstance that these other sciences were to be taught would
induce persons to send boys to the school to learn Greek and Latin
also, that purpose might have a tendency to promote the object of the
foundation." With this legal quibble the governors had to be content.

[1] Long, *op. cit.*, 46-51.

Though bound to maintain classical teaching as the central business of the school, they had permission to introduce new subjects. But such subjects were, in fact, being taught even before the judgment and though they were now developed, there could be no transformation of the school's character, as had been desired. In 1815 the school was reorganised under a new head; apart from the introduction of mathematics (for which the boys *petitioned* in 1817—presumably because teaching of this subject had lapsed) it appears to have developed as a normal classical school.

The immediate practical significance of the Leeds Grammar School case is that it greatly strengthened the resistance of masters of schools to any attempt by the middle class to introduce curricula changes and discouraged further efforts to transform the grammar schools. No small governing body could risk the enormous charges involved in a suit in Chancery, especially when judgment was likely to go against them; nor was the more likely course of obtaining an Act of Parliament within their scope. Accordingly they were in a weaker position to overcome the objections, or control the actions, of masters in command of schools.

Such was the position in the Leicestershire schools already mentioned. At both Loughborough and Ashby, trustees who wished to introduce modern subjects and turn the schools to local needs met with an obstinate refusal from masters who now felt strong enough to pursue their own course. Mr. Lloyd, headmaster of Ashby (1811-14) "filled his House with boarders, kept them in the room in which he sat himself, apart from the free scholars, and interdicted them from having the least communication with each other;—and refused to instruct the free scholars, either in mathematics or geography, except as a matter of *favour*, not of *right*".[1] On his dismissal by the trustees he applied to the Court of Chancery, claiming that the Trustees had no power either to remove him, or to interfere with the internal management of the school. Though he was unsuccessful, the master appointed in his place felt able to take much the same attitude.

At Loughborough the majority of the trustees passed a resolution in 1828 pointing out that the foundation deed contained no directions for the establishment of "a mere grammar school", and requiring the master to teach ". . . in addition to the Latin and Greek languages, arithmetic, English composition, geography, history, natural philosophy, political economy, and the lower branches of mathematics".

[1] Carlisle, *op. cit.*, Vol. I, 350.

When the master refused to comply with this somewhat ambitious order, he was called upon to resign. This, however, he also declined, with the result that no further steps could be taken in the matter. "There can be no doubt", wrote Brougham's Charity Commissioners in 1837, "that if the scheme of the trustees had been acceded to, the school would have been fully attended, whereas it is now comparatively useless, the number of boys varying between five and fourteen, although the salary of the master much exceeds what is received by the masters of the other schools."[1]

The same story could be told of many other towns. At Wolverhampton, for instance, nonconformist bodies requested a town's meeting in 1820 to protest against alienation of the endowment and the fact that most pupils were boarders from outside the town. Their declaration required that no boarders be admitted in future and that the endowment be administered by Wolverhampton men only; it added that since "the population of this town consists of manufacturers and traders; a classical education . . . is only a partial and limited benefit; but the advantages would be general and incalculable, if the teaching of mathematics, the English language, history, and, etc., were combined with the learned languages as at present taught".[2] This relatively modest claim brought no result.

From this time there was little or no check on those masters of local grammar schools who were prepared to exploit the advantages of private boarders to the detriment of local residents. Nor could the grammar schools be turned into useful centres of education for the locality by way of replacing concentration on the classics by study of modern subjects. It was the same story at this level as in the higher realms of politics where the *Westminster Review* was continuing its exposures and complaints without effect.

But in 1831 the Birmingham Grammar School Act passed through Parliament, empowering the governors of what had become a vastly increased endowment to build a new school (next to the grammar school) to teach modern languages, the arts and sciences. Here, as the *Quarterly Journal* was quick to point out, was concrete recognition of the principle that endowments originally settled to provide a grammar school could be turned to new ends.

By the mid-1830s, the frustration of the middle class was becoming nation-wide. "The numerous cases reported and unreported in which

1 *32nd Report of the Charity Commission*, Part V, 389-90.
2 G. P. Mander, *History of the Wolverhampton Grammar School* (1913), 218.

attempts have been made to adapt charitable endowments for education to the wants and uses of the actual generation, are sufficient to show that the necessity for some change in such institutions is generally felt", wrote Professor Long in a detailed article examining the whole position, published by the Central Society for Education, an influential organisation set up in 1837 to promote educational reform.[1] In the cases brought before the Courts, the latter, he claimed, had no option but to uphold the intention of the original founders. Control when exercised by visitors (and therefore outside the jurisdiction of the Court) had proved to be extremely ineffective. Basic changes in the content of education and in its control could not, therefore, legally be made. "The legislature alone can remedy most of the evils complained of and a remedy ought to be provided which shall reach the full extent of the evil." Only a general measure covering all schools could ensure a modification of ancient statutes; and do it in such a way as to sweep the ground from under the feet of those who stoutly resisted any encroachment on their vested interests, and who had found support for their obduracy in the Courts.

Meanwhile, the increasing number of middle-class parents who sought a useful education for their sons were looking elsewhere than to the local grammar school for the upbringing of their children.

(ii) *The Private Schools*

When the Irish economist, William Thompson, at this time profoundly interested in education, first arrived in England in 1822, he was sent off post haste by Jeremy Bentham to Birmingham.[2] Here was Hazelwood school, a private school, which as we have seen, embodied much that Bentham held dear. Individual emulation was the main incentive; pupils were placed in sets according to their proficiency in different subjects, might study optional subjects, were actively involved in learning; there was a concrete approach to teaching, a wide curriculum, precise organisation and controlled movements about the school; an earnest approach to moral development. Above all, in contrast to the typical endowed school, here was a vitality and purposefulness which paralleled—and so prepared for—the active, bustling life of the middle-class manufacturer. The school, in the eyes of the director, was a blueprint for future educational development. "It was

---

[1] G. Long, "On Endowments in England for the Purposes of Education," *Central Society of Education, Second Publication* (1838), *passim*.

[2] R. K. P. Pankhurst, *William Thompson* (1954), 14-17.

the height of my ambition", writes Rowland Hill, looking back on his headmastership, "to establish a school for the upper and middle classes wherein the science and practice of education might be improved to such a degree as to show that it is now in its infancy."[1] Here, then, was the utilitarian conception of education in operation in one of the main centres of industry.

If Hazelwood school was unique at this time in its approach to teaching and school organisation, it was by no means unique in being set up by a private individual as a private school. Such schools had abounded since the sixteenth century; indeed in the early seventeenth century some of the most famous educational reformers had been private schoolmasters. With the exclusion of the dissenters from the endowed schools after the Test Act of 1665, this movement naturally developed, if in a new form. In spite of the obstacles put in their way, dissenting ministers and others not only set up Academies for higher education, but turned also to school teaching both to meet the demand for education among their congregations and as a means of livelihood. When, in 1779, Protestant nonconformists were allowed by law to follow the teaching profession "a great number of new private schools, partly modelled on the older Academies, were established, especially in the towns, to meet the needs of merchants and manufacturers who demanded a more practical education for their sons than that provided in the endowed schools".[2] So we find men of the calibre of Ralph Harrison, Henry Clarke and William Johns of Manchester, Joseph Priestley, John Corrie, John Aiken, the Barbaulds, Williams, Lant Carpenter and many other dissenters running private schools, some of considerable standing, towards the close of the eighteenth century and later.

Most of these men, educated at nonconformist Academies, brought into their schools a broad curriculum and enlightened approach to learning. John Corrie, for instance, successively pupil and tutor at Hackney College, elected F.R.S. in 1820, kept a successful school at Birmingham, including geography, English, history, and political economy as well as classics in the curriculum.[3] His assistant, Lant Carpenter, educated at Northampton Academy, was able to charge 100 guineas a year at his own school at Bristol; among his pupils were many sons of middle-class families who became leading public men,

[1] D.N.B., art. on Rowland Hill.

[2] H. McLachlan, English Education under the Test Acts (1931), 5.

[3] Ibid., 249-50; H. McLachlan, The Unitarian Movement (1934), 128.

including James Heywood, M.P. for North Lancashire, who was to introduce a decisive motion on the universities in the Commons in 1850. Another ex-pupil, Robert Nathan Phillips, M.P. for Bury, once claimed that at a Speaker's dinner he "found more Members of Parliament who had been at Dr. Carpenter's small school than had been at Rugby". The philosopher, James Martineau, intending at that time to take up civil engineering, studied physics, chemistry, mathematics, geology, and physiology under Carpenter, who gave this teaching a practical turn through the use of specimens, diagrams and charts, and actual scientific experiments.[1] Carpenter, an educationist of considerable standing, published in 1815 an extremely comprehensive book entitled *Systematic Education* dealing in particular with the teaching of science. His collaborators were two former tutors of Hackney Academy one of whom, Dr. William Shepherd, became a Unitarian minister and a well-known schoolmaster; to his private school, Sir H. E. Roscoe was later to recall, "my Roscoe uncles, the Booths, the Thorneleys, and a number of the sons of the best Liverpool nonconformist families were sent".[2]

Such schools, providing for the more affluent among the middle classes, played an important part in the early education of men who were to take the leadership in science and industry as well as in public life. Their very success contributed to the stagnation of the endowed grammar schools. But, if they stood in a class apart, there were innumerable other privately controlled schools serving different religious and social groups. Many day schools, usually called Academies, prepared for commercial and industrial occupations at relatively modest fees. Others were set up specifically to provide an education comparable with that available to the upper classes; or, beginning in a relatively modest way, gained status as the community they served grew in wealth and standing.

One such was the Quaker boarding school at Ackworth. Founded in 1777 "for the education of children of parents not in affluence" (the money was given by Dr. Fothergill, close friend of Priestley and Franklin), it had become, by 1805, "a 'middle-class school' with a high reputation among Friends". Among others, John Bright was educated

[1] J. Estlin Carpenter, *James Martineau* (1905), 16-22. James Martineau became Principal of Manchester New College, London, in 1869. This College was the direct descendant of the Manchester Academy, founded in 1786. It now exists as Manchester College, Oxford.

[2] McLachlan, *The Unitarian Movement*, 131-2; H. E. Roscoe, *Life and Experiences of Sir H. E. Roscoe* (1906), 12.

there in the 1820s. The aim of "getting on in life" was put before the pupils as an ideal, records the school's historian; "sterling men and women emanated from the Ackworth scholars of the twenties and thirties. They were successful in business, several founding firms of world-wide repute".[1] Three other Quaker boarding schools were established between 1808 and 1815 and other sects were also active. The Presbyterians established Mill Hill in 1807 in order to substitute one substantial school for several separate academies.[2] The Methodists had their own schools at Kingswood and Woodhouse Grove, the Primitive Methodists at Elmfield.[3] It may be added that, apart from schools founded by the nonconformist middle class, the Moravian community set up a school at Fulneck, the Jewish community two schools at Finsbury and Palestine Place, while the Roman Catholics founded Stonyhurst and Oscott. These were boarding schools to meet the requirements of specific religious communities. Other private boarding schools catering for the gentry and even the aristocracy were of course, Church of England in outlook; for instance, John Gilpin's famous school at Cheam originally founded in 1647. Indeed the sons of gentry and aristocracy were more frequently educated in schools of this kind, or by tutors at home, than at the public or grammar schools.

The lower strata of the middle class sent their children either to lesser boarding schools established near the larger towns, or to one of the many day schools in the town itself. Some of these maintained an existence over a considerable period. They varied greatly in quality; but were by no means all as bad as the schools rightly held up to obloquy by Charles Dickens. The provincial newspapers of the period are full of advertisements for such local schools. In three issues of the *Leicester Journal* for January 1819, for instance, schools located in and around Leicester are advertised, an appeal being consciously made to different classes of the community. The Reverend Nicholson advertises his "old-established seminary" where "young gentlemen are expeditiously instructed in every branch of classical, polite and useful literature, as may best suit their future destination, whether the Church, Army, Navy, Commerce, or the more retired scenes of private life" at a cost of 30 to 35 guineas per annum, or as parlour boarders, 50 guineas.[4] The Classical and Commercial Academy at Billesdon, conducted by a dissenting Minister, announces its advantages in terms

---

[1] I. H. Wallis, *Frederick Andrews of Ackworth* (1924), 1-8.
[2] N. G. Brett James, *The History of Mill Hill School* (n.d.), 6.
[3] F. C. Pritchard, *Methodist Secondary Education* (1950), 35-57, 74-91, 132.
[4] *Leicester Journal*, December 31, 1819.

more carefully calculated to attract the middle class. The establishment

> "is patronised by gentlemen of high respectability. . . . Instruction is communicated on an improved system, which has been tried for years with success, which expedites the student's progress, and which embraces every kind of education usually in request. While suitable exertions are made to promote the improvement of the pupils in French, and in classical literature, those parts of learning more necessary to trade and in commercial pursuits, receive a large share of attention. Many young gentlemen have left the seminary highly accomplished in English grammar, a qualification of peculiar importance in every respectable station in life. . . . The situation is retired, pleasant and healthy. Terms, 21 guineas per annum."[1]

Other schools detail such practically useful subjects as book-keeping and land-surveying as part of the curriculum, while the "Classical, Commercial and Mathematical Academy" in Leicester announces a "regular course of lectures on the leading branches of Natural Philosophy and Chemistry, illustrated by extensive apparatus, delivered to the pupils gratis".[2] Faced with this sort of competition, it is not surprising that the endowed grammar school at Leicester finally expired in the 1830s.

An assessment of the number and nature of "superior private and boarding schools" in a northern industrial city is given in a Report produced by the Manchester Statistical Society in 1834, based on a thorough survey of local facilities.[3] There were thirty-six boys' and seventy-eight girls' schools with a total of 2,934 pupils; just under 7 per cent of the total number of children attending school in Manchester. The majority of these schools, eighty-nine, had been established since 1820 and a high proportion of teachers were dissenters. An analysis of the curricula showed that the average boys' school provided teaching in reading, writing, grammar, arithmetic, geography, history, mathematics and languages, up to the age of about fifteen. A few schools also taught natural history and drawing and in some there was a little moral and religious teaching. Contemporary Manchester directories indicate the nature of individual schools. Some called themselves "Classical and Commercial Academies", as, for instance, that run by Dalton's friend, the Rev. William Johns of the Manchester Literary and Philosophical Society; others, also run by ministers, were normally

---

[1] *Leicester Chronicle*, January 7th, 1832.   [2] *Ibid.*

[3] *Report of a Committee of the Manchester Statistical Society on the State of Education in the Borough of Manchester in 1834.*

called academies or, as the case of the Rev. John Clunie's establishment in Salford, a "grammar school".

Such schools were the more numerous successors of institutions which had developed in the previous century[1] and which, breaking free from the traditional curriculum, evolved a new approach to the content of education to meet the needs of the class they served. "During the nineteenth century", writes J. W. Adamson, "the conception of what constituted secondary instruction underwent a profound change; so far as professional theory and practice influenced the change, it was due, not to any Public School or Public School master, but to the enterprise of the private schools."[2]

Yet all was not well. The private school was, of necessity, an ephemeral institution, depending for its very existence on individual initiative: for its owner-schoolmaster it was essentially a means of livelihood and not all schoolmasters were scrupulous as to the means employed in securing a profit. Further, lack of capital meant that schools were often small and ill-equipped. The *Quarterly Journal* sharply criticised the quality of assistant teachers in private boarding schools, many of whom were utterly incompetent and whose moral character was open to question.[3] Undoubtedly many such schools gave a very limited education, while some were unbelievably bad. Such, at least, was the view of one observer, who wrote to Thomas Wyse: "The schools for the trading and mercantile classes are very frequently mere egastula, to which boys are sent out of the way to be boarded and birched at £20 a year. . . . The actual business of tuition is made over by the ignorant master to the more ignorant and ill-paid ushers: and the acquirement of the scholars, even in the rudiments of learning, would disgrace any Lancastrian school." He added that the neighbourhood of London "swarms with establishments of the kind, in which every abuse of omission and commission is allowed to flourish".[4]

These comments referred primarily to schools for the lower ranks of the middle class. By the time they were written, ambitious attempts had already been made to establish schools on a more stable basis for a higher stratum. Out of the chaos of competing private schools there had begun to emerge, in the late 1820s and early 30s, the new, specifically middle-class proprietary schools.

[1] N. Hans, *New Trends in Education in the Eighteenth Century* (1951), *passim*.

[2] J. W. Adamson, *English Education, 1789-1902* (1930), 47-8.

[3] Cf. "English Boarding Schools", Vol. VII, Nol 13, January 1834; "On the Discipline of Large Boarding Schools," Vol. X, No. 19, July 1835.

[4] Wyse, *op. cit.*, 59-60.

(iii) *New Proprietary Schools*

The proprietary school movement marks a transition from mere seeking out of schools offering a relevant education to the actual founding and control of schools of the type desired. It reflects not only a demand for systematic education but also for more stable educational forms. The method used was that of establishing a joint stock company; one such school, for instance, was financed by £25 shares bearing interest at 5 per cent. This implied the banding together of like-minded people, and circles connected with the Church of England as well as the nonconformist middle class were now active in the matter. Why, asked the *Quarterly Journal* in 1831, were so many such schools erected? Because parents thought it better "to found a school, and make it good, than run the doubtful chance of placing their sons where they may learn nothing to any purpose".[1]

The Liverpool Institute was probably the first of the proprietary schools to become established, in 1825. Thereafter they multiplied rapidly both in and near London—at Pimlico, Hackney, Islington, Kensington, Blackheath—and in the provinces—at Bristol, Rochester, Wakefield, Hull, Leicester and elsewhere. Leicester provides an interesting example of competition between dissenters and secularists on the one hand and a Church of England foundation on the other.

"The Proprietary School for the Town and County of Leicester", founded in 1837, was promoted chiefly by a group of businessmen, tradesmen and manufacturers who controlled the city after the Municipal Corporations Act of 1835; indeed the first six mayors after the passing of the Act, all nonconformists, were closely connected with the school.

What was intended was no less than an educational revolution. The school was provided with an imposing building in the style of a Graeco-Roman temple; the headmaster received a salary of £500 a year (by comparison with the stipend of £75 18s. 6d. received by the master of the old grammar school) and had two well paid assistants. The school, proclaimed the first report of the directors, had "broken in upon the monastic system of education and substituted natural philosophy, English composition and literature for the monopoly so long held by the dead languages"; the course they had entered, they added, "was novel and untried—it was a complete innovation upon old and time-hallowed systems . . . a complete departure from the dull

[1] *Quarterly Journal of Education*, Vol. I, No. 2, April 1831, 264-5.

insipid and lifeless forms in which instruction is too generally communicated".

In the preceding year Church of England circles had founded the Collegiate School, also a proprietary school constituted on a joint stock basis. This was appropriately housed in a large Gothic type building, the Bishop of Lincoln was appointed visitor, while many of the gentry and aristocracy of the county figured as vice-presidents and in other official positions. It was not, however, for the aristocracy and gentry that the school was primarily intended; among the original subscribers were tradesmen and many professional men (solicitors and doctors as well as the local clergy). It was to these that a local clergyman addressed himself at the opening ceremony when he pointed out that the benefits of a sound education were now available at a moderate expense. Here there was no desire to overturn the established order, for he added: "The public schools of our country, with Eton at their head, I regard with unfeigned admiration. But it is not in the power of every one to go there. These schools are more particularly the resort of the young members of the noblest and wealthiest families. . . . But we of the middle classes, must strive to *hold our own*, we will labour to maintain our proportionate rank—to support our middle station, and if possible, to elevate that station. This school will doubtless have that powerful tendency".[1]

From an educational and from a political point of view, the most challenging school was that founded in connection with University College, London, in 1828, which served as a model elsewhere, particularly for those schools inspired by the Radical middle class.[2] Here there was no religious teaching whatsoever, nor any flogging. Benthamite principles were also applied in the organisation of teaching, there being no rigid "form" system but "setting" for different subjects. Further, no subjects were compulsory, a free choice was open to the children most of whom, however, studied Latin, many German, and practically all French. English was especially emphasised and applied mathematics, chemistry, physics, botany, physical geography and social science were also taught.[3]

Elsewhere, most schools under Radical control set out to teach science systematically. At Leicester Proprietary School the second master

[1] *Leicester Journal*, August 12th, 1836.

[2] Before the Hull Proprietary School opened in 1837 the head and assistant teacher visited University College School to study its methods; these were closely followed by the new school. J. Lawson, "Two Forgotten Hull Schools", *Studies in Education*, May 1952.

[3] H. H. Bellot, *University College, London* (1929), 169-71.

gave what were, by all accounts, brilliant scientific lectures, using scientific apparatus to demonstrate experiments. There is the testimony of Sir Henry Roscoe (professor of chemistry at Owens College, Manchester and a grandson of William Roscoe) as to the effectiveness of teaching at the Liverpool Institute in the early 1840s: "Even in those days we had a chemical laboratory in which the boys worked, and besides chemistry we learned drawing, natural history and French, as well as the stock subjects of English, mathematics or classics". After describing the highly effective method by which he was taught chemistry, Roscoe pays tribute also to his physics teacher from whom he learned "the history of the steam-engine and the properties of gases as well as the rudiments of mechanics and dynamics"; as a result, at the age of ten, he could write "a fairly good account of the rise and history of the steam-engine, including the atmospheric engine of Newcomen". Another of his teachers went on to become professor of political economy at Edinburgh University.[1]

Although the *Quarterly Journal*, referring to the Church of England proprietary schools, deplored that many "will be content with nothing less than a man in holy orders"[2] as master, yet these, and the schools under Radical control marked not only a sharp break with the traditional educational institutions of the country, but also represented, in the minds of many, a threat to their continued existence. "The traffic in joint stock company schools" confided Samuel Butler of Shrewsbury to the Bishop of Chichester "is ruining, and will ultimately ruin, the old foundations."[3] "University College school, the Proprietary school at Bristol, the High School of the Corporation of London, that about to be opened at Liverpool, with numerous other foundations emanating from the same desire . . . all intimate that the tide is far more advanced than we could calculate, from the old endowments of the country",[4] wrote Thomas Wyse in 1837. The fact that many of the day proprietary schools only maintained themselves for one or two decades does not detract from their educational significance. With the development of the railways and the changing political and social scene, the middle class turned to the boarding school in the mid-1840s. During the period 1830-40, however, the day proprietary schools fully embodied their educational aspirations.

[1] Roscoe, *op. cit.*, 15-16.
[2] *Quarterly Journal of Education*, Vol. X, No. 19, July 1835.
[3] Butler, *op. cit.*, Vol. II, 96.
[4] Wyse, *op. cit.*, 62.

(iv) *The Founding of University College, London*

By the late 1820s and early 30s, then, an educational revolution was under way—around the endowed grammar schools and ancient universities was growing a new system of education with new aims and perspectives, closely connected with the vigorous upthrust of the middle class. But the private and proprietary schools and academies were not the only example of these new trends in education. In other spheres also a new content and new methods of education were being enforced as necessity. Nowhere can this be more clearly seen than at the college of the East India Company at Haileybury, and in the various military and naval colleges and schools set up or reorganised in the early years of the nineteenth century.

The East India Company was now responsible for the government of an Empire, its servants "from being clerks, factors or writers, . . . are now advanced to the situation of judges, Ministers of State, and governors of provinces".[1] For such tasks untrained men were manifestly unsuitable. It was "the absolute necessity of applying an immediate remedy to the evil"[2] that led the Company to found a college at Hertford.

This college was designed for students aged sixteen to nineteen and among the first professors were such men as Hamilton and Malthus. The course included a modicum of classical literature but also Oriental languages, mathematics and science, the laws of England, general history and political economy, a course of study far wider than that at Oxford and Cambridge, as the *Edinburgh Review* did not fail to point out. It was, of course, a curriculum directly related to the practical needs of the parent company.

In the same way, institutions for technological education were brought into being to meet the immediate practical needs of the armed services. With such men as Bonaparte, products of the military academies of France, leading the French to victory in the 1790s, the significance of scientific training for warfare was forced on this country. Woolwich Academy had already been founded in 1741 for the training of engineers; here the distinguished mathematicians Charles Hutton and Olinthus Gregory were successively professors. But in 1799 and 1802 the Duke of York sponsored two new military schools, at High Wycombe and Great Marlow, modelled on those of France,

---

[1] *Edinburgh Review*, Vol. XXVII, No. 54, December 1816, 512.
[2] *Ibid.*, 519.

Austria and Prussia.[1] In 1809 the Naval College at Portsmouth was established, with the aim of forming an expert body of naval engineers; there was a stiff entrance examination to fill the twenty-five places and students learned the theory and practice of shipbuilding.[2] At the Gosport Naval Academy, founded in 1791, there were in 1818 eighty young gentlemen training to be officers in the Navy; these were "boarded, lodged, and instructed in the classics, mathematics, algebra, navigation, nautical astronomy, marine surveying, French, drawing, fencing and dancing".[3] It was, then, accepted that more than a knowledge of Latin versification was needed to produce "brave and scientific officers"[4] likely to succeed in their profession.

If we recall the continued existence of dissenting academies giving an education at a university level which included science and mathematics, and add to the military academies the medical schools which began to be established in the large provincial cities in the 1820s, it is clear that the claims of a higher education adapted to the needs of the professions was becoming increasingly recognised. The stage was now set for a more decisive advance—into the university field itself. When, in October 1828, the "University of London" first opened its doors, it translated into practice a conception of university education which, while it owed nothing to the example of the ancient universities of England, constituted a direct challenge to their monopoly of learning and higher education.

University College, as it was later to be called, was born on the crest of a wave. Supporting it, as members of the original Council, were not only the leading philosophic radicals, but also dissenters, catholics and Jews—excluded from Oxford and Cambridge; at the nominal head of the movement stood the Whig leaders who looked to Radicals and nonconformists to help them to return to power. The College was from the first designed to meet the needs of the growing middle class of the capital. In London, said James Mill, "is an aggregate of persons of middle rank collected in one spot . . . the like to which exists in no other spot on the surface of the earth".

---

[1] Halévy, *A History of the English People* (Penguin Edn 1937), Vol. I, 117. Henry Clarke, who had lectured in science and geography at the Manchester College of Arts and Sciences, was appointed as the first Professor of these subjects at the Royal Military College, Marlow, in 1802 (Hans, *op. cit.*, 97).

[2] *Ibid.*, Vol. I, 75.

[3] Carlisle, *op. cit.*, Vol II, 442-3. See also Hans, *op. cit.*, 101-5, for further examples of naval and military schools.

[4] The phrase is taken from Carlisle's description of the Academy.

This "vast and unspeakably important portion of our population", he added, had until now had a deplorably defective education. "Those who projected the University of London" were taking the first essential steps towards remedying this state of affairs.[1]

It was, of course, the utilitarians who played the leading part in drawing up the design and forming the character of the new institution. Though Bentham himself was then too old to take an active part, it is not for nothing that his skeleton is still a prized possession of the College. "It is difficult now to imagine the labour and anxiety undergone at that time by the pioneers of a movement that has had the effect of transforming the whole higher instruction of the country", writes the biographer of Grote, one of the inner circle of philosophic radicals. "The records of the self-styled 'University' prove the astonishing ardour displayed by the three men, Mill, Grote and Brougham . . . who took the lead in all that was done."[2]

This intellectual leadership, together with the political and religious affiliations of the groups in support, ensured that the new foundation was dubbed the "Godless College" and regarded in some quarters as part of "a great system that is to overthrow the altar and the throne".[3] Extremists apart, a University College which drew its inspiration "in part from the University of Edinburgh and the tradition of (Presbyterian) Scotland, in part from that liberal movement of which Priestley is a representative, and in part from the teaching of Jeremy Bentham"[4] was unlikely to promote anything but hostility from the established authorities in church and state. "The new institution is the legitimate produce of the disgust universally entertained for the absurdities of the old ones", wrote a contributor to the *Westminster Review* in 1829. "It has risen triumphantly through all the opposition and scurrility of its enemies." It was not, however, to be granted its charter of incorporation for another seven years.

The founders altogether ignored Oxford and Cambridge as models of university education and organisation. Instead, they turned to those new or reformed institutions outside England which most nearly embodied their aims and purposes. Chief among these was Edinburgh

[1] *Westminster Review*, Vol. VI, No. 12, October 1826, 270.
[2] *D.N.B.*, art. on George Grote.
[3] C. Knight, *Passages of a Working Life* (1864), Vol. II, 81.
[4] Bellot, *op. cit.*, 12.

University, with its flourishing schools of medicine, philosophy, political economy. Both Brougham and Mill were Edinburgh graduates; so also was Leonard Horner, the first warden, and eight of the original professors; not one Oxford graduate found a place.

There is evidence also that Jefferson's university at Virginia, established in 1819, was influential, especially through the "Rockfish Gap Report", where the ideas behind this new university were clearly discussed. Virginia embodied a liberal conception of education in a wide curriculum which covered science, medicine, modern languages, law, politics, economics and history. Finally the new or reformed German Universities, visited by the first progenitors of University College, the poet Thomas Campbell and others in the 1820s, profoundly influenced the founders.[1] In particular, Berlin University, established in 1809, reflected the aspirations of a bourgeoisie striving to remove the relics of a feudal order and build a modern nation; as also did the universities at Bonn, Breslau and Munich. It was at this stage that the great discussions on the purpose and character of university education in Germany first began to influence British opinion.

University College was designed to serve what Campbell called the "middling rich"—those with "small comfortable trading fortunes" varying from £400 and £500 to £4,000 and £5,000; it must, therefore, be relatively cheap. As it was situated in a great population centre it need not be residential. Since it was non-residential it could the more easily be entirely secular—without religious test or religious instruction. Moreover, in place of tutoring it could revert to the lecture system and a professoriat as the basic means of education, as practised in Scotland and Germany. Finally, since, like the proprietary schools, it was financed by a joint stock company, control could be vested in a lay council, so ensuring close contact between the university and the life of the city it was to serve. In all these respects University College differed fundamentally from Oxford and Cambridge. But, perhaps most important was the attempt to create a University of "Chrestomathic" type, spanning the whole field of modern knowledge, and concerned both with its diffusion and its practical applications. Medicine, engineering, mathematics, the various branches of science, political economy, law, philosophy, modern and classical languages— all these were represented in a "professoriat of unexampled width of range" for which Mill, as leader of the education committee, tried to secure men of the highest distinction and ability. The following table

[1] Bellot, *op. cit.*, 7ff.

lists the original professoriat, appointed before the opening of the College in October 1828:

Greek language, literature and Antiquities.

Roman Language, literature and Antiquities.

British Language and Literature.

Mathematics.

Natural Philosophy and Astronomy.

Zoology.

Chemistry.

Botany.

Political Economy.

Italian.

Hindustan.

Sanskrit.

Hebrew.

Spanish.

German.

French.

Jurisprudence and the Law of Nations.

English Law.

Engineering and the Application of Mechanical Philosophy to the Arts.[1]

Nature and Treatment of Disease.

Anatomy.

Anatomy, Surgery and Physiology.

Materia Medica and Pharmacy.

Midwifery and Diseases of Women and Children.

Clinical Medicine.

Pathological Anatomy.

Medical Jurisprudence.

Of the original professors, twelve came from Scotland, six from Cambridge, six from abroad. They included men of remarkably wide interests and considerable energy, many of whom were deeply interested in fundamental problems of education. Long, for instance, Professor of Greek, became editor of the *Quarterly Journal of Education* in 1831 and, as has been seen, took a leading part in the struggle for educational reform. De Morgan, fourth wrangler at Cambridge, and

[1] The professor appointed to this post resigned before the College opened; courses in engineering were first given in 1833, and the Chair finally established in 1841. (Bellot, *op. cit.*, 38-9). In addition the following Chairs were projected: Mineralogy and Geology; Surgery (filled in 1830); two Chairs in Philosophy (one filled in 1829, after considerable controversy); Education; Arts and Design.

appointed Professor of Mathematics at the age of twenty-one, contributed all the important articles on the teaching of arithmetic, geometry and mathematics to this journal, as well as writing some 850 articles for the *Penny Cyclopaedia*; he was particularly concerned with the teaching of mathematics with a view to the practical needs of accountants, civil engineers, surveyors, draughtsmen, navigators and military men. Key, Professor of Latin, was joint founder of University College School and, as its first headmaster, holds a distinguished place among practising educational reformers. Both McCulloch, Professor of Political Economy, and John Austin, Professor of Jurisprudence, were well-known followers of Bentham and Mill. To turn to the scientists, Lindley, Professor of Botany, was Secretary to the Royal Horticultural Society, editor of the leading gardening journal and author of many textbooks on horticulture. The Rev. Dionysus Lardner, Professor of Natural Philosophy and Astronomy, widely known as a writer of educational works on mathematics and science, was also an innovator in teaching method, collecting a large quantity of scientific instruments and working models of machines which he used for instruction. His inaugural lecture was a remarkable statement of the scope and methods of physics, of its role as part of a liberal education, and of the necessity of sustaining practice by scientific theory.[1] Turner, Professor of Chemistry, who had been trained in Germany, lectured on civil engineering and the practical applications of chemistry and mechanics. Finally, the medical school, to which University College owed its early success, was developed by Charles Bell of Edinburgh, one of the most outstanding medical men of his day, who held the post of Professor of Anatomy, Surgery and Physiology. Under the guidance of such men, University College acted as a focus for much that was most advanced in contemporary educational theory and practice.

At first students were taken from the age of fourteen but in 1831 the age of entry was raised to fifteen. A regular course of four years was planned, allowing some latitude for students' options. The compulsory core of the curriculum was made up of the classical languages, mathematics, logic and philosophy, chemistry, physics and applied mathematics, law, political economy, moral and political philosophy. Optional courses included English, foreign languages, history and science.[2] Though these requirements were to be revised later, the

[1] Rev. Dionysus Lardner, *A Discourse on the Advantages of Natural Philosophy and Astronomy as a part of a general and professional education* (1828).

[2] Bellot, *op. cit.*, 79.

general conception of a broad liberal education was maintained in the formative years of development. At the same time the college pioneered new teaching methods. The chemical laboratory, for instance, was "one of the first, if not the first open to students" for practical work.[1] Lardner's models and apparatus formed the basis of a museum to assist the teaching of physics and applied mathematics. The first engineering courses at university level began in 1833, and by 1846 there were three professors of engineering. With this development, the contribution made by such men as Watt and Stephenson, who gained their knowledge and experience in the workshops, was transformed into a subject of disciplined study.[2]

In bringing together higher studies in science and technology, medicine and law, the traditional and modern arts subjects, University College met the insistent needs of the time. While its founders had looked to Edinburgh, the founders of succeeding decades were to look to London; in fact University College was the prototype for the modern universities initiated in the industrial cities in the latter half of the century. Equally, as we shall see later, this example affected ideas about the whole character and purpose of university education; so that University College had not a little to do with the ultimate reform of Oxford and Cambridge in a variety of ways.

Inevitably, therefore, Oxford and Cambridge are to be found making every effort to prevent its establishment. It was largely this opposition, backed by that of the medical schools of London hospitals who saw their monopoly threatened, which prevented the grant of a charter in 1830. Meanwhile, King's College, London, under Royal patronage and with the Archbishop of Canterbury as Visitor, had received a charter without trouble in 1828, and two more ecclesiastical foundations, St. David's, Lampeter, and Durham University, were also to gain their charters before University College finally obtained recognition. After the passage of the Reform Act, the Church's opposition to the "Godless" College hardened to such an extent that "the last three years of the conflict were the most strenuous of all, and the creation of a university became a matter of practical political moment."[3] It was not until 1836 that the final solution was found, and University College gained its Charter as a constituent College of the newly created University of London. With this success

---

[1] W. P. Ker, *Notes and Materials for the History of University College, London*, 1898, 71.
[2] Bellot, *op. cit.*, 206.
[3] *Ibid.*, 227. See Ch. 7, *passim*, for a description of the struggle for incorporation.

the middle class put the crown on their own, independent system of education.

In the 1830s, as Thomas Wyse pointed out, two different systems of education stood opposed: "the education of the past age, and the education of the coming age: one with the object of holding back, or keeping still, the eternally moving man; the other of moving onward with him, of accompanying, and in some instances of moving beyond him in the course". The old instruments are clumsy, "the old systems limp and lag behind us". "Everywhere is rising up the '*new education*', in contrast, . . . in successful rivalry with the old . . . in no country is the strife between the new and the old education more vehement" than in England. "In no country are there greater anomalies—greater differences, not merely on the means, but the end of education." The merchant, the artisan, the mechanic are "conspicuous elements of our modern organisations", they "require their respectively fitting educations".[1]

This is how the situation appeared to a partisan of educational change. The next urgent task was to bring about a fundamental reform of the ancient universities, the endowed public and grammar schools. But the time was not yet ripe for the final, decisive steps. In spite of Parliamentary Reform, in spite of the new Poor Law and the Municipal Corporations Act, Melbourne's government was still predominantly Whiggish in character, its aristocratic leadership concerned chiefly to prevent more fundamental social changes by a tactic of procrastination. The more outspoken Radicals—Roebuck, Hume, Grote and others—were in a minority, and were conceded little say in the progress of events. Another two decades were to pass, decades of sharp political struggle, rapid economic development and social change, before the middle class could set on foot a basic transformation of the educational scene as a whole—through the use of the final weapon, the apparatus of the state and the full force of the law.

[1] Wyse, *op. cit.*, 46-7, 59.

CHAPTER III

THE MIDDLE CLASS AND THE EDUCATION OF THE WORKERS, 1800-1850

THE philosophic radicals, it has been suggested, were the most active propagators of new forms of secondary and higher education for the middle class. Such activity was a necessary concomitant of the struggle for power. But, in addition, it was precisely this grouping who were among the first to put forward the idea of universal education. Indeed they worked actively in the cause of the enlightenment of the masses on rational and unsectarian lines and advocated compulsory elementary education for all.

Was this, as the textbooks usually suggest, pure, distinterested benevolence? Were Mill and Bentham concerned with education "for its own sake", with extending to the people the fundamental means to cultural development? Did they conceive of education for the workers in the same terms as for the middle class—as a factor in their political and economic emancipation?

The answer to these questions is to be found in their political philosophy. The greatest happiness of the greatest number could only be achieved through harmonising the interests of governors and governed. This necessitated a wide extension of the franchise, if not universally, as Bentham suggested, at least for the middle class with its extension at a later stage, which was Mill's position. This extension of the franchise was absolutely necessary in order to prevent selfish government carried on purely in the interests of a class (the aristocracy and landed interest). Good government could only be government by consent; hence the people must be allowed to elect their representatives.

To the argument advanced against this standpoint by the aristocracy, that the people were incapable of understanding where their true interests lay, and could not, therefore, be allowed any part in electing governments, Mill had a ready reply. Certainly the common people, given a voice, might readily mistake their true interests. But this only underlined what must be the central point of all political philosophy— the need to enlighten the people. Education was the essential concomitant of an enlarged suffrage.[1]

[1] Article on "Government", *Supplement to Encyclopaedia Britannica* (1820); Alexander Bain, *James Mill, a Biography* (1882), 215-21.

But, while arguing on these lines, Mill and his colleagues did not for a moment envisage that working-class members would be returned to Parliament. On the contrary, convinced of the superior moral and intellectual attributes of the middle class, they had no doubt that a Parliament elected on an extended franchise would, and should, be composed predominantly of members of the middle class. Mill specifically underlined that only the rich are in a position to develop "the high mental qualities, which fit men for the discharge of public duties".

"Our opinion, therefore, is that the business of government, is properly the business of the rich; and that they will always obtain it, either by bad means or good. Upon this everything depends. If they obtain it by bad means, the government is bad. If they obtain it by good means, the government is sure to be good. The only good means of obtaining it are, the free suffrage of the people."[1]

The aristocracy obtained power by corrupt means and governed badly in the selfish interests of the landowning class. The utilitarians looked to a transformation of society and its institutions into an enlightened democracy under the political and economic leadership of the middle class who, according to Mill's theory, would exercise their power in the interests of all. It remained to convince the people that it was in their interests to be so governed. How could this be done? By enlightening them as to middle-class virtues and values in economic and political affairs. The workers must come to understand that their interests coincided with those of the industrial capitalist; that their prosperity, like that of the middle class, was dependent on the institution of private property and the free play of capital. Such appreciation of the harmony of interests would be the inevitable outcome of the spread of "enlightenment".

It was in this context that the utilitarians sought universal education. Their policy, then, had a double aspect. On the one hand they sought the transformation of the state's institutions to allow for the political and economic expression of capitalist interests. On the other hand they attempted to free the people from ignorance and dependence upon the aristocracy and the Church; to mould the outlook of the propertyless masses to willing co-operation within the new forms of social relations, then so rapidly developing. Though this policy had its positive aspects, fundamentally the utilitarians saw the education of the working class

[1] Bain, *op. cit.*, 352.

as a necessary means to the emancipation of capital—of the middle class, not of labour, of the working class itself.

It is this policy that underlies the changing attitude of the middle class to working-class education in the early decades of the nineteenth century. But, if the utilitarians had no thought of real enfranchisement for the masses, this attitude was not shared by the working class who immediately dubbed the measure of reform introduced in 1832 as "the Humbug Bill". The workers had lent full support to the middle class in the struggle for Parliamentary reform but, strongly resentful of their exclusion from the franchise—which, after all their efforts, was still confined only to the propertied—they now began to understand what government by the middle class implied. Not only did the factory owners make a strong stand against limitation of the working day (in the eyes of the workers the essential prerequisite to extended education), but also the new Poor Law (1834)—the essence of Benthamism in action—was a measure of harsh inhumanity. The advocacy of alternative policies in the interests of the people, was, moreover, stifled by persecution of the working-class press.

In other words, just as, at an earlier stage, fundamental differences between the interests of the aristocracy and the manufacturers had come to the forefront after a period of apparent harmony, so now after a joint struggle of capitalist and worker—even in the course of it —there came to the fore new and more fundamental divergences. The sharpening struggle between these two classes was an important factor not only in the economic and political but also in the educational field.

In fact, throughout this period, the industrial middle class were engaged in a fight on two fronts. First and foremost they fought to oust the aristocracy from power and clear the road for the development of a capitalist order. This could only be done by a wide propagation of democratic ideas to win the support of the mass of the people and the development of intensive political agitation and action. By these means the Reform Act of 1832 was carried, but another fourteen years were to pass before the repeal of the Corn Laws marked a decisive defeat for the landowners, both politically and economically. During this latter period, indeed from 1820 onwards, it became progressively more important to damp down political activities of the working class which threatened to take an independent direction. The chief opponent had been brought low, but the development of a working-class political movement threatened to bring into being another, even more dangerous; one which, by raising fundamental objections to the institution of property in the name of the mass of the people, threatened capitalism itself.

It is the nature of this fight on two fronts which provides the key to an understanding of the educational proposals and activities of the utilitarians in the first decades of the nineteenth century.

1. THE CHALLENGE OF THE WORKING CLASS

"Why", Thomas Walker had asked, after the defeat of the libera democratic movement of the 1790s, "are the mass of the people, the poorer class, the swinish multitude, as Mr. Burke contumeliously calls them, so generally adverse to their friends, and so blindly the dupes of their oppressors?"[1] At this period the poorer classes could be rallied by the cry "for Church and King" to burn down Joseph Priestley's house and scatter the forces of leading reformers. By 1815, however, all this was changed.

Already in the 1790s the Corresponding Societies had begun to spread the ideas of the French revolution among the artisans and smaller tradesmen of towns which were awakening to the effects of economic change. Political activity, coupled with thorough discussions at Sunday "class" meetings, in which each member participated in an organised way, provided a new form of political education, much deeper than had ever been available before.[2] Moreover the thirst for knowledge began to be met with a literature propagating the most radical political views, a popular literature addressed to the common man which was read in ever widening circles.

Tom Paine's *Rights of Man* (1791-2), with an estimated sale running into hundreds of thousands, spread the idea of human equality among all sections of the population. His *Age of Reason* (1794-5), regarded (wrongly) as an atheist tract, was widely read and equally influential. The radical press, stung into action by Burke's *Reflections* and especially by his reference to the masses as the "swinish multitude", poured out publications. Typical of this literature, often produced locally, were such pamphlets as *The Rights of Swine* from Stockport; the *Political Glossary* from Birmingham; *A Rod for the Burkites . . . by one of the 'Swinish Multitude'* from Manchester; *Twopence Worth of Hogs' Bristles, for the Use of the Rabble*, a collection of political songs from Edinburgh; *Church and King Morality*, a 1d. pamphlet from London,

[1] Thomas Walker, *Review of some of the Political Events in Manchester* (1794), 127
[2] Cf. G. Wallas, *The Life of Francis Place* (4th edn, 1951), 22. This development is discussed in greater detail in the next chapter, p. 181.

sold by Ballard "bookseller to . . . the Swine of Westminster"; and Daniel Isaac Eaton's publication *Hog's Wash*;[1] publications, as the Bishop of London described them, "of the most impious and indecent nature . . . distributed with infinite activity and industry" not only in towns and obscure villages but even in "the very bowels of the earth, among the miners of Cornwall and the colliers of Newcastle, some of whom are said to have sold their Bibles in order to purchase the *Age of Reason*".[2]

Regular readers of such literature could no longer be numbered among the unthinking supporters of Church and King. Nor could the government's repressive measures halt the spread of radical ideas. If, then, Wordsworth, Coleridge and others of the middle strata renounced liberalism, disillusioned with developments in France, the period of the Napoleonic wars saw the maturing of new political attitudes among other sections of the population. Economic and industrial developments constantly prepared the soil for their growth. Indeed, from time to time, in different parts of the country, the popular movement against intolerable conditions burst out with the urgency of desperation, as in the Luddite actions of 1811-12. When peace came in 1815, it was only to bring more acute and widespread distress. This climax to the bitter experience of the war years saw many more turn to political radicalism, decisively rejecting the established authorities who had so signally failed to solve economic problems. Among them were men who had equipped themselves to lead the mass struggles of succeeding years which reached a climax in 1819.

The period 1816-20 is the period of Wooler's *Black Dwarf*, of Carlile's *Republican*, of Cobbett's 2d. *Register*, of *The Medusa's Head*, *The Cap of Liberty*, "and many more of the same stamp".[3] Popular journals, explaining political and economic issues and reporting working-class activities, these both reflected and helped to develop further the new political consciousness among the mass of the population.

It was, as we have seen, the year 1815 which also marked the beginning of organised political opposition to Tory policies among the manufacturers. Two issues united both masters and men at this time. The cry for "Liberty" and the reform of Parliament, carried on the banners of the handloom weavers at Peterloo, was also raised by the

[1] R. K. Webb, *The British Working Class Reader* (1955), 39.

[2] Bishop of London's Charge, quoted in the *Anti-Jacobin Review*, 1799, Vol. IV, 284.

[3] C. Knight, *Passages of a Working Life* (1864), Vol. I, 234.

industrial middle class; and had, too, the support of such men as Shelley, Byron and Leigh Hunt, who exposed in most searing terms the administration of Sidmouth and Castlereagh. The second issue was specifically economic. The Corn Laws had been passed through Parliament in 1815, an evident example of class legislation against the interest both of the capitalist and the workers. A certain unity of action was inevitable. In the words of a contemporary pamphlet: "Dustmen and porters read and discuss politics; and labourers, journeymen, and masters, speak *one language of disaffection and defiance*".[1]

But beneath this unity there developed the consciousness of a deeper opposition. In the north, industry was being transformed by the introduction of steam power and factory production. These new and powerful technological forces, under no social control, were transforming social relations. The industrial capitalist sought to maximise his profits and to clear the way for more rapid development. But labourers who had lived on the land for centuries, eking out a living by spinning and weaving, found it impossible to win a livelihood in the old way. The average wage for handloom weavers in Lancashire dropped from 18s. a week in 1814 to 8s. in 1818, a starvation wage.[2]

Many sections of workers saw the introduction of machinery, whether agricultural or industrial, as the real cause of pauperisation and distress. Hence the smashing of threshing-machines, which spread throughout the country in 1816; the destruction of shearing-frames, hosiers' frames, power looms, and the firing of textile mills. But others were delving more deeply in the search for causes and cures. This was the period of the Hampden Clubs and the Political Protestants, whose struggle for political and social change was fed by the radical press. In 1817, a Secret Committee of the House of Lords called attention to the unprecedented circulation of "publications of the most seditious and inflammatory nature, marked with a peculiar character of irreligion and blasphemy, and tending not only to overturn the existing form of government and order of society, but to root out those principles upon which alone any government or any society can be supported".[3] The most dangerous of these ideas were those of Thomas Spence, proposing the common ownership of the land.

For the industrial middle class these ideas and actions were anathema. Mass, popular political activity, while desirable when linked with

[1] Quoted by Webb, *op. cit.*, 47.
[2] G. D. H. Cole and R. Postgate, *The Common People 1746-1946* (4th edn, 1946), 141-2.
[3] *Annual Register* for 1817 (1818), 11.

middle-class purposes, might if undirected, sow the seeds of a more dangerous disaffection. A battle of ideas was under way, one on which the future of society, of capitalism itself seemed to depend. Above all it was necessary to control and direct the thoughts and actions of the workers—to win them as allies in the task of establishing a capitalist order. "There is a *new power* in society", wrote Charles Knight in 1819, and the popular journals "have combined to give that power a direction. The work must be taken out of their hands."[1]

The Radical representatives of the middle class, then, saw mass education as a political necessity, and it was for this reason that Mill, Wakefield, Francis Place and others of the philosophic radicals were early active in the promotion of elementary schools through the Lancasterian Society (later the British and Foreign Schools Society). But this was to act in direct opposition to the policy of the Tory administration whose answer to social discontent at this stage took the form of outright suppression.

Tory opposition to the spread of education among the people was of long standing. It had been put with great clarity by Davies Giddy in the debates leading to the defeat of the bill for the establishment of parish schools brought in to the House of Commons by Samuel Whitbread, the liberal-Whig leader, in 1807. "However specious in theory the project might be", he declared, "of giving education to the labouring classes of the poor, it would, in effect, be found to be prejudicial to their morals and happiness; it would teach them to despise their lot in life, instead of making them good servants in agriculture, and other laborious employments to which their rank in society had destined them; instead of teaching them subordination, it would render them factious and refractory, as was evident in the manufacturing counties; it would enable them to read seditious pamphlets, vicious books, and publications against Christianity; it would render them insolent to their superiors; and, in a few years, the result would be, that the legislature would find it necessary to direct the strong arm of power towards them."[2]

This was certainly the orthodox view. So strongly was it held that even Hannah More, whose loyalty to Church, King and the established order could hardly be questioned, had come under sharp attack for establishing her Sunday schools in the Mendips mining area in

---

[1] Knight, *op. cit.*, Vol. I, 235. Charles Knight was to become the leading figure in the production of popular literature reflecting the outlook of the capitalist class.

[2] *Parliamentary Debates* (Hansard) Vol. IX, 798, July 13th, 1807

the late 1790s, schools which had the clear political purpose of inculcating a state of resignation in the labouring class. "Beautiful is the order of society", she wrote, "when each, according to his place, pays willing honour to his superiors—when servants are prompt to obey their masters, and masters deal kindly with their servants;—when high, low, rich and poor—when landlord and tenant, master and workmen, minister and people, . . . sit down satisfied with his own place."[1] Only such education as would contribute to this end should be made available to the workers. "My plan of instruction is extremely simple and limited", she wrote in defending her schools against charges made against them, "they learn, on weekdays, such coarse works as may fit them for servants. I allow of no writing for the poor. My object is not to make them fanatics, but to train up the lower classes in habits of industry and piety."[2] To achieve this, the inculcation of religious beliefs was essential, and this was the function of her schools: "The political value of religion can never be too firmly believed, or too carefully kept in view. . . ."[3] This approach had been reiterated by Andrew Bell, the moving force behind the "National Society for Promoting the Education of the Poor in the Principles of the Established Church throughout England and Wales", the organisation set up by the Church of England in 1811 in opposition to the Lancasterian Society: "It is not proposed", he wrote, "that the children of the poor be educated in an expensive manner, or even taught to write and to cypher. . . . It may suffice to teach the generality, on an economical plan, to read their bible and understand the doctrines of our holy religion."[4]

Far from seeing the wide diffusion of education as the answer to the political crisis following 1815, then, Castlereagh, Sidmouth, Eldon and the rest of the Tory government of the time, unyielding upholders of the policy of no concession, met the popular demands and actions of the people with the suspension of Habeas Corpus, the employment of spies, convictions for treason, the "Gagging Act" (1817), the "Six Acts" (1819), and the use of the yeomanry as at Peterloo. Inevitably the Tory party was also obsessed with the idea that education would be turned to revolutionary ends. "A permanent state of siege", write J. L. and B. Hammond,

[1] Quoted in M. T. Hodgen, *Workers' Education in England and the United States* (1925), 30.

[2] R. Brimley Johnson (ed), *The Letters of Hannah More* (1925), 183.

[3] Cadell and Davies, *Collected Works of Hannah More* (1818), Vol. IX, 293.

[4] A. Bell, *Experiment in Education* (2nd edn, 1805), 62.

"was the vision of English society that inspired men like Castle-reagh and Sidmouth. In their view, the problem, though formidable in extent, was in character simple enough. A small class was set to defend its own property and that of a larger class against the tur-bulence of a huge unpropertied population. This mass of people was liable to be infected with Jacobin doctrines, and if the State was to be made safe from revolutionary agitation, it was essential that the proletariat should be excluded from all opportunity of discussion, association, education, and remonstrance. The more the ignorant masses seemed tempted by dangerous and seductive principles, the more necessary it was to drive out that temptation by terror."[1]

The Whig party, while opposing Tory policy, itself had no real solution to offer to mitigate growing discontent. But the Whigs, traditionally the upholders of "Liberty", were, after a long period of opposition, seeking to return to power; concerned to appear as a popular party fighting for the interests of the people they were dis-posed to countenance some concessions. Hence the tolerance accorded during this period to a liberal grouping within the Whig party, the "mountain", which included men such as Romilly, Brougham and Whitbread, who were prepared to work closely with the Radicals on certain issues.

In particular the Whigs could afford to be liberal in their attitude to education. Already in 1807, Whitbread, seconded by William Roscoe of Liverpool, had introduced his Bill based on the Poor Laws for the provision of parish schools. This, as we have seen, met the sharpest opposition in the Commons and was rejected by the Lords. But subsequently prominent members of the Whig party were pre-pared to lend their names in support of Joseph Lancaster's projects for extending elementary education, and later to the British and Foreign School Society. The two Royal Dukes closely allied to the Whigs, Kent and Sussex, also supported this movement.

The Whig attitude to popular education must be differentiated from that of the Radicals. Whig aristocrats and their spokesmen, though prepared to work for a measure of educational advance, neces-sarily saw it as a means of habituating the people to the existing social order and the dominance of the landed aristocracy rather than, in the Radical sense, of consolidating support for the middle class. This is nowhere more clearly illustrated than in their energetic propagation of the educational schemes of a Swiss aristocrat, de Fellenberg, who

[1] J. I and B. Hammond, *The Town Labourer 1760-1832* (1917), 321.

had established on a large agricultural estate at Hofwyl, model schools for the rich and the poor.

In the latter, under an undoubtedly brilliant and devoted master, manual labour was combined with "enlightened" instruction; effecting so great a change in the children, that Brougham, who had recently visited the school, described it to the Parliamentary Committee of 1818 as "one of the most extraordinary and affecting sights that can be imagined".[1] The *Edinburgh Review*, referring to the fatal consequence of the indiscriminate reading of common newspapers by the poor, underlined the value of the education in the school for the poor at Hofwyl where "the boys never see a newspaper, and scarcely a book (and) are taught, *viva voce*, a few matters of fact, and rules of common application. The rest of their education consists in inculcating habits of industry, frugality, veracity, docility, and mutual kindness".[2] The school for the rich, meanwhile, taught essential lessons of a different kind, for "they have evidently more to learn. . . . It is for them to understand the true tenure of power, and especially of hereditary power, legitimate because of its public utility; and feel the justice and necessity of securing the end so well, and making it so evident and plain that no one may be tempted to question the means".[3] Here the Whig organ admirably summed up the Whig view of education.

Fellenberg's plans enjoyed a great popularity in England throughout this period,[4] and proposals were made for basing the education of the poor on industry in much the same way as Fellenberg based education on agriculture. Seeking to promote an education which habituated the labouring poor to the prevailing social order, the liberal Whigs could make common cause with the Radicals—indeed, Brougham acted as their mouthpiece within the Whig party and in Parliament. The Radicals also gained support from wealthy dissenters, men such as the Quaker, William Allen and the Baptist, Joseph Fox. It was these three elements which made up the driving force behind the propaganda and activity of the Lancasterian Association from 1808 to 1815.

In the provinces, it was industrialists and professional men, many of them Unitarian, who provided the main impetus in promoting Lancasterian schools during the first decades of the century. The

[1] *Select Committee on Education of the Lower Orders, Third Report* (1818), 195.

[2] *Edinburgh Review*, Vol. XXXII, No. 64, October 1819, 492.   [3] *Ibid.*, 506.

[4] An article in the *Edinburgh Review* of December 1818 (Vol. XXXI, No. 61, 150–65), is devoted to five pamphlets and reports on Hofwyl. A further article in October 1819 (Vol. XXXII, No. 64, 487–508), lists thirteen tracts and reports in different languages on the same subject at its head. Both these articles were written by Brougham.

Royal Lancasterian Free School in Manchester, which opened in 1809, accommodated 1,000 children taught under the monitorial system, and was administered by a committee of which William Neild, a Quaker business man, was Chairman, while John Owens, Unitarian and later founder of Owens College, and the Quaker scientist, John Dalton, were members.[1] Others belonging to scientific and literary societies in the northern towns were similarly active; William Roscoe in Liverpool, Samuel Galton in Birmingham, Joseph Strutt in Derby. Robert Owen, an active member of the Manchester Literary and Philosophical Society in the 1790s,[2] set up his schools in New Lanark before 1813. David Ricardo, economist and wealthy broker, was also interested in the matter: "Except in establishing schools for the poor", he wrote to his mentor, James Mill, in 1817, "I do not know what good we have done here (in Gloucestershire) which should deserve to be well-spoken of by Lady Romilly"; while, in a letter to a friend who feared the "senseless and mischievous spirit now abroad" which "seems to threaten danger to all", he replied that the people were improved in morals. "I am in hopes too that as they increase in knowledge they will more clearly perceive that the destruction of property aggravates and never relieves their difficulties."[3]

Though others were concerned with education, the Radicals alone held the view that if the workers were turbulent and even revolutionary, it was because no appeal had been made to their reason. Rejecting the Tory tactic of suppression combined with religious indoctrination as well as the Whig desire to use education to establish more firmly the existing social order, they maintained that the workers, once informed of the realities which underlay temporary dislocation and difficulties, would understand that it was in their best interests to become calm, orderly and acquiescent. Education, in their view, was the most powerful instrument for changing men's minds and outlook; it was through education alone that the working class could be brought within the orbit of civilisation and led to assist, rather than obstruct, the establishment of a new order. This was the Radical perspective at this stage. It led directly to the promotion of various forms of popular education.

[1] S. D. Simon, *A Century of City Government* (1938), 214.

[2] F. Podmore, *Robert Owen* (1906), 57ff.

[3] P. Sraffa (ed), *The Works of David Ricardo*, Vol. VII (1952), 206, 45, 49. In 1821, Maria Edgeworth, in a letter to her stepmother from Ricardo's country seat, writes: ". . . we are going out to see Mrs. Ricardo's school, she has 130 children there, and takes as much pains as Lovell" (*Ibid.*, X, 169). This school was run on the Lancasterian system.

2. THE RADICAL THEORY OF UNIVERSAL ENLIGHTENMENT

The Radicals were not, of course, the first to advocate universal education. This conception had been advanced before. But the specific approach of the early nineteenth century must be differentiated from earlier ideas. Mass education has a different content at different times.

The idea stems essentially from the Reformation—the first of the great social and political upheavals which marked the close of the Middle Ages and the birth of the modern world. It was basic to the Protestant creed that all should learn to read the Bible for themselves; here, also, was an attempt to change men's minds—to free mankind from the blind dependence on authority implicit in the tenets of the mediaeval Church, though Luther's appeal to the German towns to promote education was also clearly linked to the interest of the burghers in ensuring the "stability of all our institutions, temporal and spiritual alike". The Reformation led to a development of education throughout Northern Europe, especially in those areas where it had a pre-eminently revolutionary significance—for instance, in Germany, Scandinavia and Scotland. The parish school system of Scotland was essentially the product of this movement, and it was to this system that reformers turned when the idea was once more brought forward towards the close of the eighteenth century.

But the idea of education as a fundamental human right in which all should share first found expression during the English Revolution of the 1640s, when for a brief period, a section of the middle class—supported by popular forces—spoke for all men. It found expression again in this sense during the early period of the French revolution. Condorcet's plan, accepted by the Convention, included proposals for universal education with free access from the parish school to the university. In England, this approach was reflected in the attitude of Tom Paine, who, in his *Rights of Man*, put forward a practical scheme for the education of all to the age of fourteen. More particularly John Thelwall proposed, with Condorcet, that all children should be educated so that "if they should have the virtue and the talent" they should be able "to improve their condition and mount to their intellectual level, though it should be from the lowest to the very highest station of society".[1]

---

[1] C. Cestre, *John Thelwall* (1906), 186-7 (quoted from "The Rights of Nature", Part II, Letter III).

(i) *Political Economy and Mass Instruction*

This was not, as has been suggested, the spirit in which the utilitarians approached the question. In fact, their proposals derived primarily from the work of the political economists, whose analysis revealed to some extent the clash of class interests and the conditions necessary for the development of capitalism.[1] It was the doyen of political economy, Adam Smith, who first advanced the demand for popular education as the essential concomitant of the growth of factory production in *The Wealth of Nations* (1776). Some measure of the influence of his argument may be gauged from the fact that it is summarised in James Mill's article on education in the *Encyclopaedia Britannica* (1818) and in Dr. J. Kay's *The Moral and Physical Condition of the Working Classes in Manchester in 1832*, both works of seminal importance which were widely read. It also formed the basis for the educational policy advocated by Malthus in his *Essay on the Principle of Population* (1798).

Living at a period when an expanding market and the early development of factory production was resulting in a rapid increase in the division of labour, Adam Smith saw specialisation as the chief means to industrial prosperity and the community of interests:

"It is the great multiplication of the productions of all the different arts, in consequence of the division of labour," he writes, "which occasions, in a well-governed society, that universal opulence which extends itself to the lowest ranks of the people."[2]

Nevertheless, this gain in prosperity was achieved at a cost. The individual craftsman, capable of carrying out every process in the manufacture of a product, still formed a large proportion of the working or artisan class during Adam Smith's lifetime. He was, therefore, in a position to evaluate the human results of the division of labour as exemplified in the simple, repetitive operations required of the workers, for instance, in the factory he describes for the manufacture of pins.

Concentration on "a few simple operations", he observes, makes the labourer "as stupid and ignorant as it is possible for a human creature to become"; "his dexterity in his own particular trade seems, in this manner, to be acquired at the expense of his intellectual, social and martial virtues . . ." In short, the individual becomes incapable

[1] E. Halévy, *The Growth of Philosophic Radicalism* (2nd edn, 1934), 243-4, 247-8.
[2] Adam Smith, *An Inquiry into the Nature and Causes of the Wealth of Nations* (1838 edn), Bk. I, Ch. 1, 5.

of understanding what are the interests of his country, or of being aroused to defend it. This, Adam Smith underlines, is the price of civilisation, the debased "state into which the labouring poor, that is, the great body of the people, must necessarily fall, unless government take some pains to prevent it". This state of affairs can be mitigated by education. The more the workers are instructed,

> "the less liable they are to the delusions of enthusiasm and super-stition, which, among ignorant nations, frequently occasion the most dreadful disorders. . . . They are more disposed to examine, and more capable of seeing through the interested complaints of faction and sedition, and they are, upon that account, less apt to be misled into any wanton or unnecessary opposition to the measures of government."[1]

Having thus frankly outlined the political function of education, Adam Smith is in a position to advocate "prodigal" expenditure on education by the state in its own interests. He proposes the establishment in every parish or district of "a little school", similar to the Scottish parish schools, where children should be taught to "read, write and account". If instruction were also given in "the elementary parts of geometry and mechanics, the literary education of this rank of people would, perhaps, be as complete as can be", the principles of mechanics being applicable to most trades. This degree of education could be imposed "by obliging every man to undergo an examination, or probation . . . before he can obtain the freedom in any corporation, or be allowed to set up any trade, either in a village or town corporate".[2]

It is important to note that Adam Smith's argument for education violates his main principle, that of the natural identity of interests of all sections of society. In general he treats the division of labour as an expression of the unity of interest of all individuals in society; since each contributes in his own field to provide the sum of goods and services the community needs, all are dependent on each other and have a community of interest in the society of which they are an essential part. Yet considering the effect on the factory worker he is bound to advocate a system of popular education specifically in order to counter the adverse effect of the division of labour. A similar inconsistency is to be found in his economic analysis when, at certain points, he also contradicts his main supposition by pointing out that

[1] Adam Smith, *op. cit.*, Bk. V, Ch. i, Art. ii, 350-3.
[2] *Ibid.*, Bk. V, Ch. i, Art. ii, 352.

the interests of capitalist, landlord and labourers can be divergent.[1] At this period, the economic basis for such a divergence of interest could hardly be analysed with the same acuteness as was to be shown by Ricardo, when analysing the relations of landlord and capitalist in 1817, and, later still, by Hodgskin, Thompson and Bray in analysing the relations between capitalist and worker. But if the full extent of the contradictions was, as yet, obscure, Adam Smith recognised the opposition between labour on the one hand, and capital and land on the other, sufficiently clearly to advocate education as a necessary step for ensuring the internal and external stability of the "state". He is the first to advance the idea that the labourers can be convinced that their "true" interests are bound up with the accumulation of capital and the introduction of machinery, even though this development *appears* to be detrimental to their interests, by an injection of education.

Adam Smith's warnings were reiterated with a new urgency by Malthus at the turn of the century, but in the new context of more general industrial development and growing social unrest. It was precisely this period that saw a great enhancement of the prestige of political economy, whose newly formulated laws were elevated by the middle class almost to the status of a religion. Since these appeared to provide unanswerable arguments for the unrestricted sway of capital, they were profoundly congenial to the industrial middle class, providing a firm ideological basis not only for political action but also for a moral outlook consistent with the requirements of capitalist development.[2] The significance, from this standpoint, of the economic theories of Malthus and Ricardo, of Mill and McCulloch, was ironically but sufficiently accurately summarised in the Tory *Quarterly* in 1831:

> "In their theory of *rent*, they have insisted that landlords can thrive only at the expense of the public at large, and especially of the capitalists: in their theory of *profit*, they have declared that capitalists

[1] For instance, in discussing the "Causes of the Prosperity of New Colonies", he states: "In other countries, rent and profits eat up wages, and the two superior orders of people oppress the inferior one. But in new colonies, the interest of the two superior orders obliges them to treat the inferior one with more generosity and humanity; at least where the inferior one is not in a state of slavery." *Ibid.*, Bk. IV, Ch. 7, 253. An acute analysis of the contradictions inherent in Adam Smith's economic thought is to be found in Halévy's *The Growth of Philosophic Radicalism*, 88-107.

[2] In their brilliant chapter, "The Mind of the Rich" (*Town Labourer*, Ch. 10), J. L. and B. Hammond analyse the use made by the middle class in their own interests of the ideas of the political economists.

can only improve their circumstances by depressing those of the labouring and most numerous class: in their theory of *wages*, they have maintained that the condition of the labourers can only be bettered by depriving them of their greatest happiness and their only consolation under trouble, the feelings of the husband and the father: in their theory of *population*, they have absolved government from all responsibility for the misery of the people committed to their care: and in their theory of *morals*, they have impressed on the poor that the legitimate indulgence of their natural appetites is the greatest of all crimes—on the rich that the abandonment of the poor to destitution is the most sacred of all duties."[1]

Certainly Mill and Ricardo had a tendency to accept the "laws" of political economy as if they were laws of nature. Though they ridiculed Tory policies to ameliorate conditions, they were themselves rigorously opposed to any action which might interfere with the working of these laws in the economic field; content to advocate that the poor save themselves from starvation by limiting their own numbers. The year 1816 brought weather which threatened the harvest. "There must now of necessity be a very deficient crop", writes Mill to Ricardo, "and very high prices."

"These with an unexampled scarcity of work will produce a degree of misery, the thought of which makes the flesh creep in one's bones—one third of the people must die—it would be a blessing to take them into the streets and high ways, and cut their throats as we do with pigs. Church-and-State, at the London tavern, where Church-and-State was nicely served, recommends subscription—a whole people to be fed by subscription!"[2]

Ricardo, replying from his country seat to a suggestion from Brougham, relayed by Mill, that he contribute to the setting up of a model infant school in London, writes:

"If it is part of the plan of the establishment . . . , to feed as well as to take care of and educate the children of three years of age, and and upwards, belonging to the poor, I see the most serious objections to the plan, and I should be exceedingly inconsistent if I gave my countenance to it. I have invariably objected to the poor laws, and to every system which should give encouragement to an excess of population. If you are to feed, clothe, and educate all the children

[1] Quoted by H. L. Beales "Was there an Industrial Revolution?", *The Listener* February 21st, 1957.

[2] Sraffa, *op. cit.*, Vol. VII, 61-2.

of the poor, you will be giving a great stimulus to a principle already too active."[1]

It was, above all, Malthus's theory of population that allowed the middle class to regard the misery of the workers as the latter's own responsibility, and the accumulation and profitable investment of capital as a moral and ethical necessity. Equally this theory demanded an end to all charity towards the poor. In his attack on the doctrine of the "right to assistance", embodied in the surviving Elizabethan Poor Law and reiterated in a new context by Godwin,[2] Malthus laid the theoretical basis for the New Poor Law of 1834; in so doing he played a large part in sweeping away ideas and practices which restricted the free development of capitalist enterprise and accumulation. If, as Malthus forcibly argued, the only path to an improvement in the condition of the masses lay through the exercise of sexual restraint on their part, it followed logically that the working class, in their own interests, must be convinced that they are the cause of their own destitution and that their salvation lay in their own hands. This, as the utilitarians were to establish, they manifestly were not. "Why is it not felt by the labouring men to be infamous to live upon the labour of others?" wrote Mill, referring to the provisions of the existing Poor Laws. "If it were so, a numerous brood, sprung from the engendering of a base couple unable to support them, would be as rare a phenomenon in the immoral world as robbery and murder."[3]

The people could, however, be apprised of these truths by education. Malthus himself strongly advocated a system of parish schools where, in addition to those subjects suggested by Adam Smith, the poor could be taught the Malthusian principle of population and the virtues of restraint.[4] He also, significantly, advocates that "if . . . a few of the simplest principles of political economy were also taught, the benefit to society would be almost incalculable . . . a knowledge of these truths so obviously tends to promote peace and quietness, to weaken the effect of inflammatory writings and to prevent all unreasonable and ill-directed opposition to the constituted authorities".[5]

These arguments are, in part, formulated in answer to those who

[1] Sraffa, op. cit., Vol. VII, 359-60.

[2] To whose Political Justice (1793), Malthus's Essay on the Principle of Population (1798) was a reply.

[3] "The State of the Nation", Westminster Review, Vol. VI, No. 12, October 1826, 263.

[4] T. R. Malthus, An Essay on the Principle of Population as it affects the Future Improvement of Society (1878 edn), Bk. IV, Ch. 9, 436-41.

[5] Ibid., Bk. IV, Ch. 9, 439-40.

feared that popular instruction would lead to wider disaffection. Citing the experience of Scotland, Malthus claimed that education would make "the common people . . . bear with patience the evils which they suffer, from being aware of the folly and inefficacy of turbulence." Parish schools will "have the fairest chance of training up the rising generation in habits of sobriety, industry, independence and prudence, and in a proper discharge of their religious duties. . . ."[1] It is clear, then, why Malthus gave public support to Whitbread's Bill of 1807.[2] Like Adam Smith twenty years earlier, he was deeply concerned to teach the working class the difference between their "apparent" and their "true" interests. His influence was far-reaching; in so far as it concerns the education of the poor, "the radical theory of popular instruction is Malthusian in origin".[3]

But if the education of the poor was already being strongly urged as a political measure by the turn of the century, it was left to the utilitarians to work out a theory of mass education as the cornerstone of a political philosophy which aimed to rebuild the whole structure of government and social affairs.

(ii) *James Mill on Education*

Before their first meeting in 1808, both Mill and Bentham had expressed characteristic views on the role and importance of education. In 1806, in an article on Colquhoun's *System of Education for the Labouring Poor*, Mill, emphasising the overriding importance of education in the formation of character, had stated the essentials of the educational policy he was to propagate throughout his life—that the necessity of enlightening the people as to their true interest was the basis of all good government. For Bentham, the problem of identifying the egoism of individuals with the "general" interest remained the major political issue. Initially he produced a scheme for industry houses, where paupers would be put to work, which covered measures for the education of pauper children where they "would be submitted to the most effective 'plastic power' which could be thought of".[4] But since the divorce between the "true" and the "apparent" interests

---

[1] T. R. Malthus, *op. cit.*, Bk. IV, Ch. 9, 439-40.

[2] "You already know how ardently I wish you success in your plan of extending the benefits of education to the poor. There are at this time, I believe, few countries in Europe in which the peasantry are so ignorant as in England and Ireland." *Letter to Samuel Whitbread* (2nd edn, 1807), 34-5.

[3] Halévy, *op. cit.*, 244.

[4] Halévy, *op. cit.*, 234. Cf. *Outline of a Work to be called Pauper Management Improved* (1797); J. Bowring (ed), *The Works of Jeremy Bentham* (1838-43), Vol. VIII, 369-439.

of the poor had been demonstrated by Malthus's principle of population, it followed logically that the 'plastic power' of education should be fully brought to bear on all the children of the poor. This was the basis of what Halévy describes as Bentham's "pedagogic despotism".[1]

It was in 1818 that James Mill gave complete expression to the Radical theory of education in his article on the subject in the *Encyclopaedia Britannica*; "the first attempt", as a modern critic has put it, "at a completely scientific treatment of education".[2] But this article must not be seen in isolation. Not only was it written at a crucial moment in educational development—that of the struggle for a secular system of education open to all, in which Mill and Bentham played a most active part—but also it was one of a number of articles contributed by Mill to the encyclopaedia; the others dealing with the liberty of the press, prisons and prison discipline, jurisprudence, the laws of nations, and including the epoch-making article on government, which provided the basis of the whole Radical agitation for an extension of the franchise. These articles appeared at the time when the tacit alliance between the landed aristocracy and the manufacturers was breaking up, a process hastened by the events of 1815; when, therefore, the Radicals were beginning to see themselves as leaders of a genuinely popular struggle.

The utilitarians stood, in theory, for a rational, secular, scientific education for all. It is to this view that Mill gives expression in his article. Profoundly convinced of the power of reason, he was certain that it was only necessary to put the facts of political economy before the labouring class for them to understand that their interests lay in giving their support to the institution of property and to the middle class generally. Indeed, he added,

"I should have little fear of the propagation among the common people of any doctrines hostile to property, because I have seldom met with a labouring man (and I have tried the experiment upon many of them) whom I could not make to see that the existence of property was not only good for the labouring men, but of infinitely more importance to the labourers as a class, than to any other."[3]

Education, therefore, was essentially a matter of enlightenment.

[1] Halévy, *op. cit.*, 234.

[2] F. A. Cavenagh, *James and John Stuart Mill on Education* (*1931*), xi. Mill's article was published in the *Supplement* to the Fifth Edition of the *Encyclopaedia Britannica* in 1818. It was reprinted by Roebuck in 1836 in his series "Pamphlets for the People," price 4*d*.

[3] Letter to Brougham, September 3rd, 1832; Bain, *op. cit.*, 365.

Properly directed, it could determine the thoughts and so the character and disposition of men.

The central position of education in the political doctrine of utilitarianism is based on the theory of the association of ideas. "It is astonishing", wrote Mill of Hartley, "how many of the mental phenomena he has clearly resolved; how little, in truth, he has left about which any doubt can remain."[1] According to associationist theory, the developed mind was the resultant of successive sense impressions, which built up a pattern (or sequence) of associated ideas determining the individual's thoughts and feelings. "All simple ideas are copies of impressions; . . . all complex ideas are only simple ideas united by the principle of association."[2] If "the character of the human mind consists in the sequences of its ideas", then the object of an enlightened education must be "to provide for the constant production of certain sequences, rather than others".[3] This can be done by "applying the prospect of pleasure and pain to render beneficent trains (of ideas) perpetual in the mind".[4] All this constitutes the "plastic power" of education recognised by Bentham. Hence the importance of education in the political philosophy of utilitarianism.

Though not committing himself fully to Helvétius's view that all normal beings are "equally susceptible of mental excellence", Mill, as a thoroughgoing associationist, had much sympathy with this standpoint, and clearly believed in the power of education (conceived of in its widest sense) to lift the mass of the people to a high intellectual level. In his view it was of little importance to determine whether the differences between men are wholly due to environmental influences or partly to "original peculiarities". Enough is known, he writes, "to prove that if education does not perform everything, there is hardly anything it does not perform: that nothing can be more fatal than the error of those who relax in the vigilance of education, because nature is powerful, and either renders it impossible for them to accomplish much, or accomplishes a great deal without them". It was far more in accordance with experience, "and much more conformable to utility", to ascribe everything to education and so carry "the motive for vigilance and industry, in that great concern, to its highest pitch. This much, at any rate, is ascertained, that all the

---

[1] Cavenagh, *op. cit.*, 17. Mill undertook to resolve these remaining doubts in his *Analysis of the Phenomena of the Human Mind* (1829), which became the basis of the psychological theories of the philosophic radicals. The book was edited and re-issued by John Stuart Mill in 1869.

[2] *Ibid.*, 15.   [3] *Ibid.*, 17.   [4] *Ibid.*, 19.

difference which exists, or can ever be made to exist, between one *class* of men, and another, is wholly owing to education".[1]

Here Mill tends to ascribe to education the role which Adam Smith assigned to "habit, custom and education"—to the division of labour as a whole. Thereby the way was opened for an unlimited optimism and he saw education not so much as a panacea for the down-trodden as a lever to raise them to any height. "Whatever is made of any *class* of men," he writes elsewhere, "we may then be sure is possible to be made of the whole human race. What a field for exertion! What a prize to be won!"[2] In theory, then, all are capable of improvement; all should have the benefit of enlightenment which will conduce to happiness—the end and aim of education.

But it is when this theory is applied that we approach the contradiction at the heart of utilitarian educational philosophy. This becomes clear when Mill poses and answers the question—"What is the sort of education required for the different classes of society and what should be the difference in the training provided for each?"[3] He approaches this question from the point of view of the qualities of mind education should develop.

Mill's professed object is "to render the Individual as an instrument of happiness, first to himself, and next to other beings". The qualities of mind necessary for this are Intelligence (comprising both Knowledge and Sagacity—the ability effectively to utilise knowledge), Temperance, Generosity and Justice. "These qualities", he writes, "are desirable in all men; and if it were possible to get them all in the highest possible degree in all men, so much the more would human nature be exalted."[4] Circumstances, however, make this impracticable—it cannot even be held out as an ideal aim. Certainly, equal care should be taken with all classes so far as the qualities of Temperance and Benevolence are concerned, and this is possible since the associations on which they depend can be "fixed" without the expenditure of much time; such trains of associations "may go on while other things are attended to, and amid the whole of the business of life".[5] As regards "Intelligence", however, the case is different.

Mill argues strongly against those who hold "that the human race ought to consist of two classes—one that of the oppressors, another that of the oppressed". On the contrary, the question whether the people "should have more or less of intelligence, is merely the question, whether they should have more or less of misery, when happiness

[1] Cavenagh, *op. cit.*, 29.   [2] *Ibid.*, 12.   [3] *Ibid.*, 58.   [4] *Ibid.*, 59.   [5] *Ibid.*, 62.

might be given in its stead".[1] Theoretically, therefore, all classes should have "an equal degree of intelligence". But there is "a preventing cause" which is this, that "a large proportion of mankind" is required for labour, and therefore has not the necessary time for the acquisition of "intelligence". "There are degrees of command over knowledge to which the whole period of human life is not more than sufficient"; it follows that "there are degrees . . . of intelligence, which must be reserved to those who are not obliged to labour".[2]

So Mill, while denying that the human race should be divided in two classes, in fact acquiesces in existing class relations and proposes to perpetuate them. A higher degree of education (of intelligence) is reserved for those who are not obliged to labour—since they live on the labour of others. As Halévy points out, Mill neither enquires how this division came into being, questions its justice, nor envisages its future disappearance.[3]

In spite of this "preventing cause", Mill protests that "a very high degree of intelligence" is attainable by "the most numerous class". If children are "bound close to labour" before the age of fifteen or sixteen, there results a loss of productive powers, but "if those years are skilfully employed in the acquisition of knowledge, in rendering all those trains habitual on which intelligence depends, it may easily be shown that a very high degree of intellectual acquirements may be gained; that a firm foundation may be laid for a life of mental action, a life of wisdom, and reflection, and ingenuity, even in those by whom the most ordinary labour will fall to be performed". In "proof" of this, he cites Bentham's plan, outlined in *Chrestomathia*, since "of the practicability of the scheme no competent judge has ever doubted".[4]

A more revealing insight into what he had in mind as a practical possibility is given in a note on a scheme drawn up by Baptist missionaries in India, which he mentions with "extraordinary satisfaction" as being "hardly less extensive than what is here alluded to". The scheme is to teach the Indian peasantry and artificers, by means of "simple axioms, delivered in short and perspicuous sentences", an

---

[1] Cavenagh, *op. cit.*, 60.   [2] *Ibid.*, 61-2.

[3] Godwin, in *Political Justice*, did precisely this, envisaging the final disappearance of the division of labour with the development of machinery and man's consequent control over nature, and so the ending of the division between mental and manual labour in a society where each works according to his ability and receives according to his needs. In ignoring these fundamental questions, as Halévy points out, Mill reflects the final separation of "philosophic radicalism" from revolutionary or Utopian radicalism.

[4] Cavenagh, *op. cit.*, 63.

account of the solar system, the laws of motion, attraction and gravity, a "compendious view of geography," "a number of popular truths and facts relative to natural philosophy," "a compendium of history and chronology united" and another on "Ethics and Morality," all of which would be written from dictation "and even committed to memory". "Why", asks Mill, "should not the same idea be pursued in England, and as much knowledge conveyed to the youth of all classes at school, as the knowledge of the age, and the allotted period of schooling will admit?"[1]

We may note here the profound difference between this approach to the educational process and the education which Mill gave to his own son, John Stuart. This aimed, above all, at developing the analytical and reasoning powers of the mind. "Striving, even in an exaggerated degree, to call forth the activity of my faculties", writes John Stuart, "by making me find out everything for myself, he gave his explanations not before, but after, I had felt the full force of the difficulties", so making him a thinker in both logic and political economy.[2] It was because the monitorial method, which Bentham and Mill espoused, did not develop the powers of reasoning but made for passive rote learning, that Robert Owen and other socialist educators rejected it.

In spite of the glowing phrases about universal enlightenment, the references to education as a means to the elevation of the whole human race, Mill in practice envisaged a system restricted on class lines. In so doing, he expresses clearly the dilemma of the Radicals, desirous of speaking for all men, but tied to the chariot wheels of one class whose interests could only be met by the sacrifice of the many. In this sense his *Essay* is the classic exposition of the utilitarian theory of education and of the contradiction at its heart.

3. EDUCATIONAL ACTIVITIES OF THE RADICALS

(i) *Secular Schooling for the Masses*

To turn from theory to practice is to find the Radicals in the forefront of the struggle for a genuinely secular system of education for the mass of the people. This issue was being fought out between 1808 and 1820, just at the period when Radicalism was given cohesion and a definite middle-class political orientation based on respect for private property by the support of Bentham, Mill, Place, Wakefield and others

---

[1] Cavenagh, *op. cit.*, 63-6n.   [2] John Stuart Mill, *Autobiography* (1873), 29.

Lancaster's original school at Borough Road (1798), and the educational movement which derived from it, at first attracted influential support but later became the centre of a storm of controversy. Initially the Royal Lancasterian Institution, established in 1809, was not only supported by dissenters and Radicals, but gained the patronage of the King, the Prince of Wales, the Dukes of Kent and Sussex and many members of the aristocracy; accordingly it adopted the title "Royal British System of Education." "It was the alarming progress of Lancaster's operations", writes Bain, "that made the Church dignitaries turn to Bell as the convenient instrument of their rival organisation."[1] Andrew Bell, a Church of England parson, was also an advocate of the large school, taught by a single teacher with the aid of older pupils, or monitors. Not without some difficulty, the Church party succeeded in 1811 in setting up the "National Society" as a counterpart to the non-sectarian Lancasterian Society, on the basis that education must be conducted according to the tenets of the Church of England. The King and other patrons were persuaded to transfer their allegiance, and the new Society proceeded with the establishment of schools.

James Mill, who—together with Brougham, Place, Wakefield and Hume—played a leading part in the work of the Lancasterian Society (re-established as the British and Foreign School Society in 1813), entered the struggle for a secular education with tremendous energy, becoming the Society's leading polemicist in its attack on the Church of England party—the "Bellites". His long articles in the *Philanthropist* and the *Edinburgh Review*, his pamphlet *Schools for All, Not Schools for Churchmen only* (1812), proclaimed that popular education was an urgent necessity, and that, since it must be universal, it must be unsectarian.[2]

Bentham, though at this time working on *Chrestomathia*, also turned his attention to an exposure of the claims of the Church. His *Church of Englandism and Its Catechism Examined* (1818), was preceded by *Strictures on the Exclusionary System, as pursued in the National Society's Schools*. "The work is written", noted Romilly, "against the National School Society, whose aim is to proscribe all education of the poor, except that in which the religion of the Church of England forms an essential part; and the work, therefore, undertakes to prove, that

[1] Bain, *op. cit.*, 84.

[2] The articles are primarily an attack on the tactics of the Church of England for "thwarting the education of the poor". In general they expose the inaction of the Church in education, reject the argument that if poor children are taught to read and write without being taught the creed they will renounce Christianity

Church of Englandism is wholly different from true Christianity, as it is to be learned from the gospel."[1] So outspoken was the book, that Romilly had tried to persuade Bentham against publication, for fear of persecution. But not content with this, Bentham delivered a second broadside, this time anonymously, under the title *Not Paul but Jesus* (1823), where he set out to show the founder of Anglican doctrine as Anti-Christ.[2]

Apart from polemical work of this character, the Radical grouping took an active part in the day-to-day work of the Society, especially in the activities of its offshoot, the West London Lancasterian Association, set up in 1813, which took as its motto the slogan "Schools for All". "Few men did more for the Society in 1814-15 than did Place", writes the historian of the movement; he "represents that notable group of free-thinking Radicals which contributed more to the framing of the society's policy during these critical years than is usually remembered."[3] In fact, the aim of this group was "nothing less than the organisation of a complete system of primary and secondary education, at any rate for London".[4] To this end a practical plan was carefully worked out, based on the division of London into school districts, each controlled by independent committees. The Chrestomathic plan was an integral part of this scheme. For a short time things went well, but the plan, indeed this branch of the society itself, foundered on the crucial issue of secular education.

In the main it was wealthy dissenters, particularly Quakers, who provided the funds. Place, on the other hand, frankly described himself as an infidel. Differences eventually arose as to whether all reading lessons should be taken solely from the Bible; a rule of the parent society which Place and Mill succeeded in dropping in the case of the West London Association, together with the rule that all children should be taken to a place of worship on Sundays.[5] Joseph Fox, who was secretary of both societies, began to take things into his own hands and there began a campaign of denigration against Place which was finally successful in driving him out of the West London Association, and eventually out of the parent society. Once the evangelical

[1] Bain, *op. cit.*, 151.

[2] In 1822 Bentham had published, again anonymously, a further anti-religious work, entitled *Analysis of the influence of the natural religion on the temporal happiness of mankind*.

[3] H. B. Binns, *A Century of Education* (1908), 82-3.   [4] Wallas, *op, cit.*, 96.

[5] Binns, *op. cit.*, 95; Wallas, *op. cit.*, 105-6; Place's attempts to develop rational forms of education in these schools, and the opposition he encountered from the representatives of the different sects, is fully described in his evidence to the Select Committee on Education (1838).

section of the dissenters had gained the upper hand in this way there was no further possibility of winning the association for a policy of promoting secular education.

It was at this point that Brougham took up the cause of education in Parliament with his customary energy. A liberal Whig, Brougham followed a political path peculiar to himself (his tendency to "Whiggism" was bemoaned by Mill), but he worked closely with the Radicals in the British and Foreign School Society and at this stage gave Parliamentary expression to Radical educational policy.[1] Spurred on by the rising temper of the people and, outwardly at least, convinced of the necessity for universal instruction, he had succeeded in 1816 in persuading Parliament to set up a Select Committee on the Education of the Lower Orders in the Metropolis.[2]

This Committee, as we have seen, exposed the widespread misuse of endowment funds, often by the clergy, and also spotlighted the lack of educational facilities, particularly in London. It led directly to the appointment of Charity Commissioners, with the task of investigating the administration of nearly all the charitable trusts in the country. It was Brougham's contention that educational endowments included under this head, and amounting to £500,000 a year, could be used to finance a wide development of schools for the people. This was the purpose of his famous Bill "For the better education of the Poor in England and Wales", introduced in 1820.

Although Brougham's Bill made great concessions to the Church of England, so rousing the opposition of dissenters and liberals, it must be regarded as a product of the Radical case for popular education; his speech introducing it has been described as "the direct result of Benthamite propaganda".[3] This was the first measure to be brought before Parliament which advocated a system of universal compulsory elementary education, provided by the state. It incorporated measures to set up the necessary schools and appoint schoolmasters to teach reading, writing and arithmetic and to give religious instruction to all children. When he buttressed his arguments by quoting from the Pope's letter to the Irish Catholics in 1819, Brougham was stating the

[1] In 1812 Brougham had come close to accepting the complete Radical programme in order to render himself acceptable as Parliamentary candidate for Westminster, one of the few constituencies with many working-class voters. A. Aspinall, *Lord Brougham and the Whig Party* (1939), 69.

[2] An honourable expression, said Brougham, in his speech in Parliament in 1820, for "what would be the rich without the poor? Where would be the pyramid without its base?"

[3] Halévy, *op. cit.*, 296. As Halévy notes, Brougham "owed all his ideas to Mill".

classical Radical argument for education in a different context: "In order to avoid the snares of the tempter, I beseech the holy brotherhood, through the bowels of Christ, to work day and night in the establishment of Catholic schools, in order to prevent the dissemination of improper doctrines". Brougham's comment is significant: "no man seemed to have a better knowledge of the use of schools; no man saw more fully the necessity of instructing the ignorant".[1]

Brougham's initiative was doomed to failure. This was not merely because of opposition organised by the Church, which feared that state provision meant secular control, and from the Dissenters, who shared this fear while also resenting the preponderance given the Church of England, nor because of the lukewarm attitude of the aristocracy. The real cause of failure lay elsewhere. There could be no question of establishing a system of compulsory popular education when the new factory system was insistently demanding child labour. The battle for education was to be fought out on what might appear to be a different issue altogether, the reduction of the working day and the Factory Acts. Without such legislation, schools might be provided, but they would not be filled. Robert Owen had pointed this out four years earlier, in his evidence before the Select Committee "On the State of the Children employed in the Manufactories of the United Kingdom" (1816). "When I was in Manchester last year", he said, "there was more school room than children to fill it, and upon enquiring the reason, I found that there was such strong inducements held out from the different manufactories of the town and neighbourhood to the parents to send the children early to work, that it counterbalanced any inclination such people had to send them to school: therefore the schools were not filled, not nearly so."[2]

(ii) The Instruction of the Artisan

The comparative failure of their early efforts to promote elementary education did not deter the Radicals. In fact, with the defeat of the Tory administration in 1823 and the advent of the Liberal-Tory government of Canning and Huskisson there was a definite political turn which favoured new developments.

Economic conditions improved and the new government conceded some of the main demands of the capitalists and even of the workers,

[1] J. E. G. De Montmorency, State Intervention in English Education (1902), 256-7.

[2] Quoted by S. E. Maltby, Manchester and the Movement for National Elementary Education (1918), 25.

repealing the obnoxious Orders in Council as well as the Combination Laws directed against trade union organisation; in general moving from a policy of oppression to one of concession, while the extreme Tories (Eldon, Wellington and the High Church Party) held aloof. It was in this situation that a new sphere of educational activity opened out. This time it was with the adult worker that the Radicals were primarily concerned; the institutions they concentrated upon were Mechanics' Institutes and the association they now brought into action was the Society for the Diffusion of Useful Knowledge.

In these activities there was, once more, an alliance between Radicals and liberal Whigs, supported locally by the industrialists of the northern cities. The object was to exercise a more immediate and direct influence on the working class than could be achieved by the foundation of schools. The economic, technical, and especially the political developments of the last thirty years had led to the growth of an upper stratum of artisans, or mechanics, among the working class; men who were not only avid for scientific knowledge but also politically informed and seeking to extend their knowledge of economics and politics. As will be shown more fully in the next chapter, working-class organisations were becoming consolidated; they had already developed their own press, sponsored educational activities and were beginning to embark on independent political action. To give a suitable direction to working-class thinking and action had, therefore, become urgent. This was no longer in any sense an academic question. Behind the working-class organisations there loomed the mass of the working people, open to disaffection, only too prone to be misled. It was the "spectacle of an incalculable and vaguely threatening multitude, which so greatly alarmed the employing and governing classes",[1] and which spurred on their initiative in this movement.

The story of the London Mechanics Institution, founded in 1823, provides an instructive example of the way in which Radicals, industrialists and Whig politicians combined to turn what originated chiefly as a working-class institution to their own purposes. The initial impetus had come from Thomas Hodgskin and J. C. Robertson, editors of the *Mechanic's Magazine*, who wanted an Institute under workers' control, which would provide an education not only in science and mechanics but also in politics and economics.

Hodgskin and Robertson, the original secretaries of the Institute, received their main support from a group of radical working men

[1] M. Tylecote, *The Mechanics' Institutes of Lancashire and Yorkshire before 1851* (1957), 53.

"consisting of working mechanics, tradesmen, and the radical reformers of that day", including some "who had suffered for political offences"; these were already members of a small society which "assembled nightly at Lunn's Coffee House, Clerkenwell, devoting two evenings to reading, two for discussion, and one for music . . ."[1] After proposing the establishment of the Institute, Hodgskin approached the astute Radical politician, Francis Place, for assistance.

From this point, control of the Institute gradually but inevitably passed out of the hands of the mechanics themselves, in spite of a strong attempt by Robertson and a section of the mechanics to prevent it. "Place quickly explained to Hodgskin and Robertson the impossibility of founding a stable institution simply on the subscriptions of working men; he overcame their opposition and obtained their consent to opening a subscription list along with all the notable members of the radical group."[2] Thereafter he concerned himself intimately with the Institute's affairs. "Place is the main promoter," wrote Mrs. Grote at this time, "and is devoting his whole time just now to its establishment."[3] By February 1825, a fund of £2,000 had been raised of which Place himself had collected £1,500.[4] Birkbeck, who had taught workers science in Glasgow and was now living in London, had accepted the Presidency of the Institute, and subsequently loaned £3,000 of his own money. Radical and Whig politicians, such as Brougham and Lambton (later Lord Durham), were also eager and ready to put themselves at the head of the movement.

The workers, realising that such men would control the Institute in their own interest and resenting the idea of patronage and dependence, countered by passing a resolution opposing any request for donations to the building fund. They were outmanœuvred and outfinanced. Hodgskin and Robertson, the last of whom had remained on the workers' side and fought actively for independence, were not re-elected as secretaries in December 1823, when the Institute was finally established. A paid official was appointed "and the Institute of which they were the true originators slipped from their control".[5]

As Birkbeck's biographer remarks, the London Mechanics' Institution, and many others too, came largely "under the control of the moneyed classes, and became props of orthodoxy and respectability instead of independent working-class organisations". In London the

[1] J. W. Hudson, *History of Adult Education* (1851), 49.

[2] Halévy, *Thomas Hodgskin* (1956), 87 (published in France in 1904).

[3] Bain, *op. cit.*, 214.   [4] Wallas, *op. cit.*, 112.   [5] Halévy, *op. cit.*, 88.

primary responsibility for this rested with Place who, in what was a long conflict over the government of the institution, packed the management committee, issued anonymous pamphlets, defamed the character of working-class representatives—in short, used every means in his power in order to wrest control from the workers themselves.[1]

It was symptomatic of the resulting transformation that, when a new lecture theatre was opened in 1825, the ceremony was performed by the Duke of Sussex (the King's brother) supported by a bevy of Whig magnates and other notabilities. At this stage the London Mechanics' Institution bore every mark of success. "The sight of eight or nine hundred artificers, thus collecting, after their daily toils are over, to listen to the voice of science, is something new in this metropolis", commented the *Morning Chronicle* of the first set of chemistry lectures. It was also a welcome sight to the Radical beholder; Place confided to Burdett his joy at seeing "from 800 to 900 clean, respectable-looking mechanics paying most marked attention" to a lecture on chemistry.[2] Mr. Brougham "is almost always present, encouraging, by his own deep attention to the lectures, the attention of others", runs another report.[3]

The real issue at stake in the battle for control of this and similar institutions was, however, still to be highlighted in London. Thomas Hodgskin, who had broken with Robertson and remained on friendly terms with Place and Birkbeck, published in 1825 *Labour Defended against the Claims of Capital*; one of the first books to challenge the political economy of the middle class from the standpoint of the working class. In the same year he offered to give a course in political economy at the institute and, though Place at first succeeded in getting the offer turned down, a year later it was accepted.[4]

The significance of this book was that it revived Ricardo's analysis of the contradiction between the interests of land and capital on the one hand, and labour on the other, and took it a stage further. Mill, McCulloch and others, imbued with the idea of the identity of interest of capitalist and worker, had vulgarised Ricardo's theory and overlaid its crucial point, holding out the prospect of united advance along a road which offered continuous and indefinite progress. But Hodgskin, after submitting aspects of Ricardo's analysis to radical criticism, restated the economic grounds for a fundamental divergence of interest

---

[1] T. Kelly, *George Birkbeck* (1957), 88. Kelly deals very leniently with Place and does not mention the most decisive of his manœuvres.

[2] Wallas, *op. cit.*, 112-13.   [3] *Mechanic's Magazine*, Vol. II, 125 (May 1st, 1824).

[4] Kelly, *op. cit.*, 98-9, 116-18; Halévy, *Thomas Hodgskin* ,91.

between labour and capital, and advanced a serious argument for the claim of labour to the full value of its product.

The lectures eventually delivered embodied a similar economic analysis, "conceived from the standpoint of the interest of the people— the working class, or, as one might say today, a proletarian political economy".[1] Attended by "a numerous and attentive audience", including probably William Lovett and other working-class leaders in London, these lectures clearly pointed to the conclusion that the capitalist exploited the worker by depriving him of the full fruits of his labour. In short, the political economy Thomas Hodgskin taught challenged that of the Radicals at the most crucial point. Francis Place, "influential as ever, protested and the experiment was not repeated".[2] This, however, did not quell Hodgskin, who had the lectures published under the title *Popular Political Economy, from Lectures delivered at the London Mechanics' Institute* (1827), and went on to take every opportunity to popularise his views among the working people.[3]

By the early 1830s, Hodgskin's theories had spread widely. "Those who were disappointed in Mr. Owen's promises and prediction", wrote Place, fell "as it were into the snare of Mr. Thomas Hodgskin, who by his lecturing and publishing induced thousands to believe that every thing produced belonged to the individual producers each in his own right".[4] That such ideas aroused anguish and fury among the Radicals goes without saying, and is illustrated by a letter to Place in 1834 from James Mill. Who, he asks, is at the bottom of the deputation from the working class which has been preaching communism to the editor of the *Morning Chronicle*? "Their notions about property look ugly. . . . Rascals, I have no doubt, are at work among them." Place duly replied that the deleterious influence of Hodgskin was the cause of the trouble.[5] Later Mill informed Brougham: "The nonsense to which your lordship alludes about the rights of the labourer to the whole produce of the country, wages, profits, and rent, all included, is the mad nonsense of our friend Hodgskin, which he has

---

[1] Halévy, *Thomas Hodgskin* ,92.   [2] *Ibid.*, 91.

[3] The *Mechanic's Magazine*, now under the control of "that enlightened and indefatigable Friend of the Working Class, Henry Brougham", as it proclaimed, immediately condemned the book as visionary and impracticable and decried the value of a knowledge of political economy to the working class: "Working men have so much to learn that may be of *real use* to them in their journey through life, and such ample employment for every minute they can spare in acquiring this sort of learning, that it is sheer folly in them to trouble their heads about anything else". *Mechanic's Magazine*, Vol. VII, June 16th, 1827, 378.

[4] Halévy, *Thomas Hodgskin*, 128.   [5] Wallas, *op. cit.*, 274n.

published as a system and propagates with the zeal of perfect fanaticism. . . . These opinions, if they were to spread, would be the subversion of civilised society; worse than the overwhelming deluge of Huns and Tartars".[1] "Such doctrines", wrote Charles Knight in a publication specifically intended to refute Hodgskin, "may begin in the lecture room, and there look harmless enough as abstract propositions; but they end in the maddening passion, the drunken frenzy, the unappeasable tumult—the plunder, the fire, and the blood".[2]

At the Mechanics' Institute Hodgskin's place as a lecturer in political economy was later filled by a more suitable candidate. "Last night to Wilmot Horton's second lecture at the Mechanic's Institute", noted Greville in his diary in 1830, "I could not go to the first. He deserves great credit for his exertions, the object of which is to explain to the labouring classes some of the truths of political economy, the folly of thinking that the breaking of machinery will better their condition, and of course the efficacy of his own plan for emigration. The company was respectful enough, and they heard him with great attention. He is full of zeal and animation, but so totally without method and arrangement that he is hardly intelligible."[3]

After 1823 the movement to establish Mechanics' Institutes developed with extraordinary impetus. But elsewhere the lesson had been learned, and, where possible, the middle class assumed full control.[4] In Manchester, a group of bankers and business men advanced £6,000 at five per cent to found a Mechanics' Institute in 1825.[5] Typically, one of their number, Sir Benjamin Heywood, suggested as the first topic for "plain and popular lectures" in 1830 "That security of property is indispensable to the welfare and advancement of society and that difference in the fortunes and conditions of individuals must necessarily exist in every community".[6]

---

[1] Bain, op. cit., 364.

[2] The Rights of Industry, Vol. II, "Capital and Labour", 152-3. (Halévy, op. cit., 129). It is interesting to note that Thomas Cooper, the Manchester democrat of the 1790s, domiciled for thirty years in America, was among those who set out to refute Hodgskin. (Halévy, op. cit., 128; cf. Cooper's Lessons in Political Economy (1830), ch. xxxi.)

[3] C. C. F. Greville, Journal of the Reign of George IV and William IV (1874 edn), Vol. II, 97-8.

[4] Though there were some exceptions, both Kelly and Tylecote agree that the majority of these Institutes were set up and supported by "the employing class", the "well-to-do middle classes. The manufacturers, merchants and bankers of London, Manchester, Liverpool, Leeds, Huddersfield, and many smaller centres . . ."; cf. Tylecote, op. cit., 57-8; Kelly, op. cit., 212-13.

[5] This group consisted mostly of Unitarians, centred on Cross Street Chapel, the direct descendants of the group surrounding Percival discussed earlier.

[6] B. Heywood. Addresses delivered at the Manchester Mechanics' Institution (1843), 38.

In Manchester, as elsewhere, the workers themselves were originally allowed no representation whatsoever in the government of the Institute; political and religious discussions, even newspapers, were banned. The purpose of such foundations is clearly expressed by J. W. Hudson, an early historian of the movement, who summarised the objects of the founders of Mechanics' Institutes as:

(i) "The rapid promotion of general science by the greater number of persons engaged in the observation of its phenomena. The lower ranks, who are chiefly engaged in manual labour, have frequent opportunities of making observations on certain peculiarities in the processes of art, which often escape the notice of a superior rank, and thus the labouring classes of society would be rendered mutually useful, in uniting and concentrating the scattered rays of genius, which might otherwise be dissipated and lost to the scientific world."

(ii) "An extensive diffusion of rational information among the general mass of society."

(iii) "The creation of intellectual pleasures and refined amusements, tending to the general elevation of character."[1]

It is a far cry from Mill's eulogies of the middle-class contribution to scientific advance, and the consequent demand for a full scientific education, to this statement of the working-class role; that of bringing to the attention of their superiors isolated observations which, co-ordinated by their betters, might add to scientific knowledge. Shorn of the fine phraseology, the underlying aims are clearly to exploit the workers' technical and inventive powers; to instruct them in the "right" political and economic theories (in 1840 Heywood expressed appreciation that the mass of the people had shown "comparatively little sympathy" with "the wild schemes of political agitators"); and to provide suitable distractions to divert their minds from independent political activity.

Industrialists, such as Heywood, tended to concentrate on the first of these objectives, constantly citing such men as Watt and Murdock as examples worthy of emulation. But in his *Practical Observations upon the Education of the People* (1825) Brougham stresses the two latter aspects. This influential pamphlet was in effect a plea to the wealthy classes to assist in the formation of Mechanics' Institutes and, too, in the dissemination of cheap literature. The case of a "common cutler" who amused himself in his leisure hours with entomology "strongly

[1] Hudson, *op. cit.*, 54-5.

confirmed" Brougham in his opinion "that a high degree of intellectual refinement and a taste for the pleasures of speculation, without any view to a particular employment, may be united with a life of hard labour, even in its most humble branches, and may prove both its solace and its guide".[1] Stressing the necessity for a careful selection of the best authors, he writes: "That history, the nature of the constitution, the doctrines of political economy, may be safely disseminated in this shape, no man now-a-days will be hardy enough to deny. Popular tracts, indeed, on the latter subject, ought to be much more extensively circulated for the good of the working classes, as well as of their superiors."

In Brougham's view, much good could come from expounding "the true principles and mutual relations of population and wages"; indeed, without this necessary economic instruction, the opposition of employers and employees might well come to a crisis. Convinced of the necessity for political discussion as a safety valve, Brougham went so far as to advocate that the working men should have "the principal share in the management" of Mechanics' Institutes. But these institutions inevitably only reached a few workers. The most effective way of ensuring liberty and "good order", of securing "the peace of the country, and the stability of the government" was "the universal diffusion of this kind of knowledge".[2] To this end, another kind of society had been formed.

(iii) *The Diffusion of Useful Knowledge*

In 1821, Charles Knight, deploring the influence of the popular press in misleading working-class opinion, had stated the Radical alternative:

> "If the firmness of the Government, and, what is better, the good sense of the upper and middle classes who have property at stake, can succeed for a few years in preserving tranquillity, the ignorant disseminators of sedition and discontent will be beaten out of the field by opponents of better principles, who will direct the secret of popular writing to a useful and righteous purpose."[3]

The instrument devised by men of principle to further righteous purposes was, appropriately, the Society for the Diffusion of Useful Knowledge, launched by Henry Brougham with the help of Matthew

[1] H. Brougham, *Practical Observations upon the Education of the People* (1825), 27.
[2] *Ibid.*, 4-5, 15-17.   [3] Knight, *op. cit.*, Vol. I. 261.

Davenport Hill in 1826. Knight became the main publisher to the society shortly after its foundation, under the patronage of Brougham, Lord John Russell, and other leading liberal-Whigs.

At this stage the diffusion of knowledge was seen as the great panacea by both Radical and Whig. Knight refers to Brougham's unremitting activity at this period, citing a letter from Hill from Ambleside: "I came here with Mr. Brougham, from Lancaster, today. Scenery glorious of course. But I fear we talked more about diffusion of knowledge than anything else. Mr. B. is delighted with all you have done."[1] "Diffusion is now the most important thing to be done for knowledge", wrote James Mill to McCulloch in 1825, urging him to write a popular essay on wages and another on the Corn Laws.[2] In particular, instruction must be given in the science of political economy. "The road to happiness is discovered—no groping, no perplexing research, no hopeless, thankless toil is required—all that remains to be done is, to remove the obstacles which conceal that road from the view of those who are less fortunate than ourselves."[3] The political economists, as Francis Place put it, "are the great enlighteners of the people".

But though the Radicals expected this society to become another channel for the propagation of their political and economic theories among the workers, they were at first disappointed. Treatises on morals, politics and political economy were promised in the original prospectus. But the Society's early publications were a *Library of Useful Knowledge* and a *Library of Entertaining Knowledge* appearing in monthly numbers. Filled with miscellaneous scientific and cultural information, ranging from Lepidoptera to "Autumnal Customs in Kardofan", these set out to meet the requirements of men like the cutler, admired by Brougham; to provide intellectual fare of a kind to solace those whose lives were given to manual labour.

It was not until the economic crisis of 1830, accompanied by serious outbreaks of rick-burning and machine breaking, that the S.D.U.K. set out directly to tackle the crucial economic issues. By this time not only Hodgskin's economic theories but also Robert Owen's socialist ideas had penetrated deeply among the people. There was a deep-seated fear, expressed by Place and others, of a "convulsion" in which the middle classes "will be swept away—no matter which party conquers" unless they "at once go among the people" and instruct them.[4] In April 1831, a sharp attack in the *Westminster Review*, organ of the

---

[1] Knight, *op. cit.*, Vol. II, 113.   [2] Bain, *op. cit.*, 292.
[3] *Westminster Review*, Vol. IV, No. 7, July 1825, 89.   [4] Webb, *op. cit.*, 93.

Radicals, appealed for a fundamental change of policy. What did the Society do, it asked, when faced with riotous assemblies, forcible raising of wages, open attacks on private property, machine breaking and the firing of ricks and barns in 1827? It produced a lot of irrelevant and obscure treatises in science and promised: "To a people ignorant of every thing most intimately connected with their welfare . . . two treatises, . . . on the Polarisation of Light, and another on the Rigidity of Cordage!"[1]

By the time this article appeared, however, the S.D.U.K. had finally moved into the field of political economy. First came *An Address to the Labourers on the Subject of Destroying Machinery* (1830), a penny pamphlet which showed the importance of machinery for future wellbeing; then the famous *Results of Machinery, Namely, Cheap Production and Increased Employment Exhibited: being an Address to the Working-Men of the United Kingdom*, written by Charles Knight, though published anonymously. It was the ignorance of the peasantry, leading to what he calls "a servile insurrection" in the southern agricultural counties, which spurred Knight on to write this work; of the "unparalleled success" of which, he was later to note, "it would scarcely become me to speak".[2] The book, which sold at a shilling, became a by-word in the working-class movement for the advice it tendered to the workers if wages fell:

> "When there is too much labour in the market, and wages are too low, do not combine to raise the wages; do not combine with the vain hope of compelling the employer to pay more for labour than there are funds for the maintenance of labour; but go out of the market. . . . You have, in too many cases, nothing but your labour for your support. We say to you, get something else; acquire something to fall back upon. When there is a glut of labour go at once out of the market; become yourselves capitalists."[3]

Knight followed this up, in 1831, with *Capital and Labour* "especially addressed to working men, to exhibit their rights in connection with

[1] *Westminster Review*, Vol. XIV, No. 28, April 1831, 322. The article specifically attacks Brougham, for his "unworthy ambition" which has led him to link himself with an aristocratic party. He is pictured as "quailing with fear" before the "vile and interested clamour" of clergy and aristocracy, and hence avoiding the publication of any matter of real importance.

[2] Knight, *op. cit.*, Vol. II, 158, 160. In 1844 Brougham paid tribute to the effect of this work which, he said, at a time of great public excitement, was "eminently conducive to allaying the reckless spirit which . . . was leading multitudes to destroy property and break up machines." *Ibid.*, Vol. II, 310.

[3] *Results of Machinery* (2nd ed., 1831), 197-8.

their duties by proving that the interests of every member of society properly understood, are one and the same". It has become a matter of grave necessity, he adds, "that from some influential source, such as that of the Useful Knowledge Society, should go forth a popular exposition of the cardinal points of political economy, as far as related to the production of wealth". A further volume on the distribution of wealth was projected, since "pretended teachers of political economy . . . were ranting in popular assemblies about the unequal allotment of riches and proposing schemes for the 'division of property' whose absurdity rendered them in some degree more dangerous at a time when many of the uneducated were moved rather by passion than by reason". Such might fall victims to teachers like Thomas Hodgskin, referred to in *Capital and Labour* as "these ministers of desolation" who if they had their way "would be able to sing their triumphal song of 'Labour defended against the claims of Capital' amid the shriek of the jackal and the howl of the wolf".[1]

These publications, to which in 1831 was added the *Short Address to Workmen on Combinations to Raise Wages*, were inevitably written in a doctrinaire, theoretical and patronising way, apart from the fact that the content of the arguments advanced was unpalatable. "When labour offered for sale is plentiful its price will be low," preached this pamphlet, "when it is scarce it will be high. This is a law of nature against which it is vain to contend"; only "forbearance, management and economy" could alleviate the inevitable lot of human life, as revealed in the iron law of wages. Active protest was out of place. "Your complaints are sometimes exaggerated and were they better founded than they are, you have not chosen the remedy to remove them."[2] In all this lecturing, then, the S.D.U.K. drew heavily on the doctrines of political economy to stifle the demands of the workers. Though Knight himself realised that no scheme for popular instruction could be effective if it depended on "gratuitous, and therefore suspicious distribution" by the superiors of those to whom the works were addressed, yet his own organisation "was entirely dependent on upper class support, both financially and administratively". Still worse, the bias of his publications was such as to defeat their purpose. Francis Place, who really knew the workers, clearly saw the danger. Bitterly attacking a publication of Knight's, as so one-sided in its regarding all employers as wise, and all workers as fools, as to be productive of civil

[1] Quoted in *Ibid.*, Vol. II, 168-71.
[2] *A Short Address to Workmen, etc.* (1831), 10-11.

war. "Every such essay as this", he wrote "makes it more and more difficult to drum sound doctrine into the people."[1]

Here the utilitarian perspective of moulding minds "like wet clay in a plastic hand"[2] is less discreetly expressed. Undoubtedly the main aim of the Radicals in supporting the S.D.U.K. and the Mechanics' Institutes was "to drum sound doctrine into the people", first and foremost the doctrine of the unity of interest of employer and employee, the latter having the duty to follow where the former led. This was an overtly political aim and generally assessed as such, not only by the working class—as will be seen more fully later—but also by the Church and Tory party. This is no place to assess the effectiveness of the Institutes, which depended not so much on the purposes of their promoters as on the attitude of the workers; nor does space allow for further detailing of the S.D.U.K.'s propaganda. It is sufficient to note that these two forms of organisation were the concrete embodiment of Radical educational aims at this particular stage; that is, during the decade which preceded the introduction of the Reform Bill.

4. AFTER THE REFORM ACT

(i) The Education Bill of 1833

The Reform Act, carried under the threat of revolution, granted the middle class of the industrial towns, for so long disfranchised, a voice in government. But, at the same, by insisting on a property qualification, it swept away such working-class rights to vote as had existed; for instance, in the relatively democratic constituencies of Westminster and Preston. This pointed the inequity of a measure which, while granting the middle class full political rights, specifically excluded the working class from any part in electing representatives to Parliament. From this point dates the first clear-cut political divergence between workers and capitalists, a divergence that widened rapidly between 1833 and 1837 when the Whig government, if somewhat reluctantly, passed a series of measures wholly in the interests of the newly-enfranchised middle classes, utilised the Tory laws of 1819 against the unstamped (popular) press and rejected working-class demands for a wide extension of the franchise—this in the famous statement that earned Lord John Russell the title of Finality Jack.

[1] Webb, op. cit., 159, 142-3.

[2] The phrase is Brougham's in a speech in the House of Lords, in May 1835 (de Montmorency, op. cit., 300).

Several Radicals were returned to Parliament for the first time after 1832. Bentham had died in this same year; Mill had only four more years of life. But, though lacking former guides, the Radicals were able to exercise a consistent pressure on the predominantly aristocratic government of Lord Melbourne. In the mid-1830s, at the time of their greatest strength, there was even a possibility that a Radical party would be formed, capable of taking the reins of government, with Lord Durham as a leader. The party drew its strength partly from political associations, and from the backing of a key section of the industrial middle class. But they were also the only group which had any close relations with the mass of the working class which was still politically submerged and denied any direct expression in Parliament; for men such as Roebuck, Hume, Bowring, Hindley and, of course, Francis Place still had contacts with working-class organisations and, to some extent, their confidence.

It was in these circumstances that the Radical educational programme was once more advanced in the Commons. In the first year of the reformed Parliament Roebuck made a new appeal for "the universal and national education of the whole people". He found little support for his scheme to establish infant schools, technical schools and normal schools for the training of teachers, controlled by a Minister of Cabinet rank and administered by local committees.

Indeed, a few months earlier, Brougham had announced in the Lords that he no longer favoured the principle of compulsory education but was in favour of leaving the matter to voluntary bodies, principally the Church. But Roebuck's speech is of interest as a new expression of Radical aims at this period, stressing the more despotic attitude to which utilitarian philosophy inevitably gave rise in conditions of increased conflict between middle and working class. "The business of government is not," he warned,

"and can no longer be, the affair of a few. Within these few years a new element has arisen, which now ought to enter into all political calculations. The multitude—the hitherto inert and submissive multitude—are filled with a new spirit—their attention is intently directed towards the affairs of State—they take an active part in their own social concerns, and however unwilling persons may be to contemplate the fact, anyone who will calmly and carefully watch the signs of the times, will discover, and if he be really honest and wise, will at once allow, that the hitherto subject many are about to become paramount in the State."

"I therefore cast about me to learn", he continues, "in what way this new force may be made efficient to purposes of good, and how any of its probable mischievous results may be prevented." Inevitably education is given the vital role, since it offers not merely the "necessary means and instruments for the acquiring of knowledge, but . . . also the so training or fashioning the intellectual and moral qualities of the individual, that he may be able and willing to acquire knowledge, and to turn it to its right use".[1]   True to the teaching of his friend, James Mill, Roebuck is careful to point out that an extension of the suffrage and of education would not remove control from safe hands:

> "As the leisure class must, of necessity, be the most instructed, and as we should wish the most instructed to undertake the office of instructors, it is this leisure class that would in a good Government—always indeed subject to the control of the mass of the population—be the guides to the rest of the people in the business of education, as also of Government."[2]

This speech clearly expresses, once more, the abstract desire to spread enlightenment to all, elbowed out by concrete concern to drum only the right doctrines into the people. Roebuck's encomium on the Prussian system of education, chiefly remarkable at this time of political reaction in Germany for its disciplinary intent, revealed where lay his major preoccupation.

In the outcome, it was the view to which Brougham had come round that prevailed. In the following month, August 1833, by a vote of 50 to 26 taken in an empty House, the Commons approved the expenditure of not more than £20,000 to aid voluntary societies to build "School Houses for the Education of the Children of the Poorer Classes in Great Britain".

(ii) The Condition of the Working Class

Once the middle class felt itself to be in the saddle, the task of teaching the working class to recognise its claims seemed much less urgent. Industrialists, in particular, had many more pressing concerns. Such men as Bentham, Mill and Place, far removed from the realities of factory production and conditions of life in the mills and huddled streets of northern towns, could reasonably envisage and plan for universal education. If Place could not bring himself to contemplate

---

[1] Speech of J. A. Roebuck in the House of Commons, July 30, 1833, de Montmorency, *op. cit.*, 327, 330.
[2] *Ibid.*, 336.

industrial conditions, while Bentham's connection with cotton manufacture was confined to shareholding in Owen's New Lanark mills,
both could see clearly the ultimate necessity of education in the interests
of the capitalist class. Their propaganda won adherents but few practising industrialists took the proposition seriously; so far as they were
concerned, children were first and foremost an indispensable adjunct
of the labour force. Moreover, most manufacturers were far too
closely engaged in amassing wealth, in internecine struggle and
consequent exploitation of the worker, to have time even for schemes
with a more immediate end. In 1828, Charles Knight found little
but lip-service in support of the S.D.U.K.'s efforts during a tour of
the industrial north. "It was not always very easy", he writes of
Manchester, "to interest the busy mill-owners in the object for which
I came amongst them. Some were too absorbed in their ledgers to
hear long explanations; others were wholly indifferent to matters
which had no relation to the business of their lives."[1]

But not everyone remained unconcerned. In the northern industrial
cities the actual living and working conditions of the mass of the
operatives was driving them desperate. It is in this situation that a
significantly new note appears in the Radical propaganda for education.
It was stated with the utmost clarity by Dr. Kay, officer in charge of
public health in the chief industrial city of Lancashire.[2] His book,
published under the title *The Moral and Physical Condition of the
Working Classes in Manchester in 1832*, constituted the first real exposure
of the conditions of the factory proletariat.

A stranger visiting Manchester, writes Kay, cannot but be struck
when, after acquainting himself with the great capitalists,

"he contemplates the fearful strength of that multitude of the
labouring population, which lies like a slumbering giant at their
feet. He has heard of the turbulent riots of the people—of machine
breaking—of the secret and sullen organisation which has suddenly
lit the torch of incendiarism, or well nigh uplifted the arm of rebellion in the land. He remembers that political desperadoes have ever
loved to tempt this population to the hazards of the swindling game
of revolution, and have scarcely failed."[3]

Many other passages similarly reflect a deeply felt dread of social

[1] Knight, *op. cit.*, Vol. II, 83.
[2] Later Sir James Kay-Shuttleworth, the leading civil servant concerned with education
in the mid-nineteenth century.
[3] J. Kay, *The Moral and Physical Condition of the Working Class in Manchester in 1832*,
republished in *Four Periods of Public Education* (1862), 48-9.

disintegration and rebellion, as a consequence of intolerable pressures. To drive the point home Kay draws a vivid picture of Manchester's working class. At home they are "crowded into one dense mass, in cottages separated by narrow, unpaved, and almost pestilential streets, in an atmosphere loaded with the smoke and exhalations of a large manufacturing city".[1] At work they are daily subject to "the dull routine of a ceaseless drudgery, in which the same mechanical process is incessantly repeated, (resembling) the torment of Sisyphus—the toil, like the rock, recoils perpetually on the wearied operative".[2] It is such people "rendered reckless by dissipation and want—misled by secret intrigues, and excited by the inflammatory harangues of demagogues", who have "frequently committed daring assaults on the liberty of the more peaceful portions of the working classes, and the most frightful devastations on the property of their masters". Machines have been broken, factories gutted and burned in broad daylight, while the insufficient body of police have been unable to quell the disturbances.[3] What, then, was the solution?

Kay's political and economic standpoint is exactly that of the Radicals, especially in its reflection of the growing optimism of the capitalist class in spite of the social chaos and appalling living conditions consequent on the growth of factory production. The capitalist system, he says, "which promotes the advance of civilisation, and diffuses it over the world—which promises to maintain the peace of nations by establishing a permanent international law, founded on the benefits of commercial association, cannot be inconsistent with the happiness of the *great mass of the people*".[4] The development of factory production in cotton manufacture had already inspired the new generation of "political economists"—Babbage, Ure and others—to write their paeans of praise in its favour. The scientific analysis of Ricardo, developed by Hodgskin, Gray and Thompson, which laid bare the divergence of interest between employer and employed, was simply ignored. A mystical optimism had taken the place of science.[5] The

[1] J. Kay, *op. cit.*, 8.   [2] *Ibid.*, 7.   [3] *Ibid.*, 22.   [4] *Ibid.*, 49.

[5] Halévy discusses the crucial change of direction that overcame political economy when McCulloch, James Mill and others vulgarised Ricardo's teaching, ignoring his analysis of the opposition of interest of land, capital and labour. The merchants wanted to believe in the identity of interests of different classes, and in the theory of indefinite progress: "Consequently it mattered little that certain economic forces brought serious restrictions to bear on the harmony of interests, or set a limit to the progress of the human race: the theorists were not free to keep their attention on considerations of this kind. In spite of them, optimism tended to prevail in their doctrine over pessimism. The industrial revolution, like the political revolution in France thirty years earlier, was demanding its principles." (*Philosophic Radicalism*, 370.)

defects of capitalism were not inherent, but due to "foreign and accidental" causes, to a faulty fiscal policy, to that old enemy, a false conception of charity. Kay fully accepts this analysis. Repeal the Corn Laws, pass a new Poor Law, above all, educate the masses. "The preservation of *internal peace*, not less than the improvement of our national institutions, depends on the education of the working classes."[1] Particularly impressed by the power of the co-operative unions of the late 1820s and early 30s to "create disorder", Kay reiterates the classic solution: "The radical remedy for these evils is such an education as shall teach the people in what consists their true happiness, and how their interests may be best promoted."[2]

His more detailed proposals are also sufficiently familiar. The education of the workers "must be substantial", including not only reading and writing but "such branches of general knowledge as would prove sources of rational amusement". The exact sciences connected with the worker's occupations "should be familiarly explained to him, by popular lectures and cheap treatises". Mechanics' Institutes "should be multiplied by the patrons of education"; here "the ascertained truths of political science should be early taught to the labouring classes, and *correct* political information should be constantly and industriously disseminated amongst them". Thereby the poor might also "be made to understand their political position in society, and the duties that belong to it—'that they are in a great measure the architects of their own fortune; that what others can do for them is trifling indeed, compared with what they can do for themselves; that they are infinitely more interested in the preservation of public tranquillity than any other class of society; that mechanical inventions and discoveries are always supremely advantageous to them; and that their real interests can only be effectually promoted by their displaying greater prudence and forethought' ".[3]

Such instruction should extend to cover family life and social relations. "The evils which imprudent marriages entail on those who contract them, on their unhappy offspring, and on society at large, should be exhibited in the strongest light. The consequence of idleness, improvidence, and moral deviations should be made the subjects of daily admonition; so that a young man might enter the world, not, as at present, without chart or compass, blown hither and thither by

[1] Kay, *op. cit.*, 61.   [2] *Ibid.*, 74.
[3] *Ibid.*, 63-4; the quotation is from McCulloch's article "On the Rise, Progress, Present State and Prospects of the British Cotton Manufacture", *Edinburgh Review*, Vol. XLVI, No. 91, June 1827, 38.

every gust of passion, but, with a knowledge of the dangers to which he is exposed, and of the way to escape them."[1]

So, far, then, Kay advances the normal Radical solution for the major social and political problem of the time. But in the new conditions he makes a very significant addition, specifically excluded both by Bentham and Mill. Religion must be closely linked to education, if this is to fulfil its social function. "Religious observances", he says, "are exceedingly neglected." "With pure religion and undefiled, flourish frugality, forethought, and industry." Without religious and moral training "crime, diseases, pestilence, intestine discord, famine, or foreign war—those agencies which repress the rank overgrowth of a meagre and restless race—will, by a natural law, desolate a people devoid of prudence and principle, whose numbers constantly press on the limits of the means of subsistence." Let us then, says Kay in effect, ensure that the "vast masses of our operative population" at present exposed to every vice and "the emissaries of every faction", are also "acted on by the ministers of an ennobling faith".[2]

It was to economic indoctrination of the working class that the utilitarians had looked for the defence of property. Their disciple, up against the realities of the factory system, adds to this the demand for religious indoctrination as a necessary insurance for the monopoly of wealth—and frames his argument to underline the point:

"The increase of intelligence and virtue amongst the mass of the people will prove our surest safeguard, in the absence of which, the possessions of the higher orders might be, to an ignorant and brutal populace, like the fair plains of Italy to the destroying Vandal. The wealth and splendour, the refinement and luxury of the superior classes, might provoke the wild inroads of a marauding force, before whose desolating invasion every institution which science has erected, or humanity devised, might fall, and beneath whose feet all the arts and ornaments of civilised life might be trampled."[3]

No doubt Kay was out to frighten the middle and upper classes into action. Yet despite the urgency of his appeal he did not succeed, and for a good enough reason. "Ministers and men in power," wrote Francis Place in 1833, "with nearly the whole body of those who are rich, dread the consequences of teaching the people more than they dread the effects of their ignorance".[4]

Meanwhile conditions continued to deteriorate. It was, of course, precisely in the industrial districts—those areas where capitalism was

[1] Kay, *op cit.*, 64.   [2] *Ibid.*, 39-40.   [3] *Ibid.*, 62.   [4] Wallas, *op. cit.*, 338-9.

free to develop without hindrance and should, according to utilitarian theory, have had the most beneficial effect—that the position was the worst. A Select Committee of the House of Commons, appointed in 1837 "to consider the best means of providing useful education for the children of the Poorer Classes in large towns throughout England and Wales", surveyed the position. They reported that an effective educational system should result in an eighth of the population attending school, but found "in Leeds, only one in 41; in Birmingham, one in 38; in Manchester, one in 35" receiving an education "likely to be useful." "The kind of education given to the children of the working classes", they concluded, "is lamentably deficient, . . . it extends (bad as it is) to but a small proportion of those who ought to receive it."[1] In 1842 there was not a single public day school for poor children in the 32 square miles comprising Oldham and Ashton and housing a population of 105,000.[2] The Children's Employment Commission report issued in this same year made clear that the position was little better in other industrial towns.

Young Frederick Engels, already a socialist when he joined a Manchester business house at the age of twenty-two, summed up the position as he saw it in 1844. The working class was vouchsafed "only so much education as lies in the interest of the bourgeoisie; and that, in truth, is not much. . . . The few day schools at the command of the working class are available only for the smallest minority, and are bad besides". The lack of attention accorded to Kay's arguments is indicated in the conclusion: "So short-sighted, so stupidly narrow-minded is the English bourgeoisie in its egotism, that it does not even take the trouble to impress upon the workers the morality of the day, which the bourgeoisie has patched together in its own interest for its own protection."[3]

(iii) *The Factory Acts*

Why, even at this late stage, had the Radicals achieved so little? In the last analysis they failed because their approach to education was profoundly doctrinaire, because the very society whose economic "laws" they propagated with such zeal depended on the exploitation of the working class, and so could bring neither "happiness" nor the

[1] *Report from the Select Committee on Education of the Poorer Classes in England and Wales* (1838), vii-viii.

[2] J. L. and B. Hammond, *Town Labourer* (1917), 55.

[3] F. Engels, *The Condition of the Working Class in England in 1844* (1892, Trans. F. K. Wischnewetzky), 110, 114.

means of enlightenment. The real struggle for the very possibility of education for the working class had to be fought out by the workers themselves on another issue altogether, that of the working day; and fought out against the determined opposition of the Radicals, and those who espoused their cause.

It is here that the contradiction at the heart of Mill's philosophy—that of "degrees of intelligence"—takes on a real and a very concrete significance. With a few exceptions, the factory owners were most strongly opposed to any legislation which shortened the working day. To this stand the Benthamites gave full support in the sacred name of the "free" contract between the buyer and seller of labour power. Of the Ten Hours Bill, Place wrote:

> "All legislative interference must be pernicious. Men must be left themselves to make their own bargains; the law must compel the observance of compacts, the fulfilment of contracts. There it should end. So long as the supply of labour exceeds the demand for labour, the labourer will under-sell his fellows, and produce poverty, misery, vice and crime."[1]

Yet, as Marx was later to show when analysing the history of the long struggle to shorten the working day, it was the worker who was the victim, "the isolated labourer, the labourer as 'free' vendor of his labour power, when capitalist production has once attained a certain stage, succumbs without any power of resistance". Since freedom of this kind was in the interests only of employers, the workers necessarily combined forces to fight the matter out; indeed "the creation of a normal working day is . . . the product of a protracted civil war, more or less dissembled, between the capitalist class and the working class".[2]

In this war the philosophic radicals, spokesmen of capital, and the workers inevitably took opposing sides. Despite the passage of five labour laws between 1802 and 1833, adult hours remained entirely unregulated, while the Cotton Factories Act of 1819 was disregarded and children from the age of five or six were worked to the point of exhaustion in the factories and mines, including at night. "We are un-acquainted with any nation, ancient or modern," wrote Robert Owen in the same year that Mill published his article on education, "that has suffered its hundreds of thousands of children of seven to twelve years of age to work incessantly for 15 hours per day, in an overheated unhealthy atmosphere, allowing them only 40 minutes out of that

---

[1] Wallas, op. cit., 174.   [2] K. Marx, Capital, Vol. I (ed Dona Torr, 1946), 285.

time for dinner and change of air, which they breathe often in damp
cellars or in garretts, in confined streets or dirty lanes."[1] Under these
conditions, to talk of the diffusion of knowledge, of universal education, was little more than self-deception if a little less than hypocrisy.

Even after the first limitation of hours, the situation of factory
workers remained intolerable. "I am at a loss to understand", wrote a
contributor to *The Champion* in 1849, "what a factory master can think
of himself, or what he really expects will result from his conduct when
he boasts of running his mill, meal-times included, between fourteen
and fifteen hours a day, and also boasts, that he has secured the patronage and support of the Bishop of Manchester to the Mechanics' Institution of which he is one of the active directors."[2] The *Ashton Chronicle*
added its voice, "Labour so protracted, incessant and fatiguing as that
of the cotton factory unfits a man for mental application and study";
and the article continued roundly: "These short cuts to knowledge are
a gross delusion and imposture . . . it is sheer cruelty to volunteer these
professions of assistance and patronage, when, at the same time, we are
aware, or ought to be, that we are either deceiving ourselves or them.
. . . I have not seen a single Mechanics' Institution accomplish the object
avowedly contemplated by its projectors."[3]

Meanwhile a mass movement for the reduction of hours of labour
developed in the 1830s around the 10 Hours Bill, when the working
class significantly broke with the liberals (except those few who, like
Fielden, supported their demands) and, led by the Tories Oastler,
Sadler and later Ashley, carried through a nation-wide agitation. In
1833, as a result of the new influence of employers in the Commons,
who hoped thereby to prevent legislation, a Royal Commission to
investigate working conditions was appointed, almost all of whom
"had drunk deeply of the distilled waters of Philosophic Radicalism."[4]

The Commissioners went out in groups of three to make their
enquiries; only to be met by organised obstruction and hostile demons-
trations (at which they saw themselves burned in effigy) by workers

[1] R. Owen, "On the Employment of Children in Manufactures" (1818), *A New View
of Society and Other Writings* (ed. G. D. H. Cole, 1927), 135.

[2] Quoted by Tylecote, *op. cit.*, 253-4.

[3] Quoted by M. Phythian, "The Mechanics' Institute Movement in Lancashire and
Yorkshire, 1824 to 1850, with special reference to the Institutions at Manchester, Ashton-
under-Lyne and Huddersfield". Ph.D. thesis, Manchester University (1930), Vol. II, 341.
This thesis has since been rewritten and published as M. Tylecote, *The Mechanics' Institutes
of Lancashire and Yorkshire before 1851* (1957).

[4] Cecil Driver, *Tory Radical, the Life of Richard Oastler* (1946), 226. Edwin Chadwick
and Southwood Smith, the "dominating personalities" of the Commission, had been
personal friends of Jeremy Bentham.

deeply suspicious of their motives. The eventual outcome was an Act which did not include the ten hours clause, but instead limited the working day for children under thirteen in textile industries to eight hours, laying down also that they must have two hours education a day. These clauses were in line with the Benthamite theory that although the state should not interfere in the case of adults, children were not in a position to make a "free" contract, and so should be "protected" and, of course, educated. For the first time provision was made for inspection, but no funds at all were allotted for the education required.

Nevertheless, the principle of compulsory education had, for the first time, been conceded, and this was welcomed as a first victory by the Radicals. Analysing the reasons for this and later concessions Marx writes, in terms which recall Adam Smith's original analysis of the effect of the division of labour:

> "The intellectual desolation, artificially produced by converting immature human beings into mere machines for the fabrication of surplus-value, a state of mind clearly distinguishable from that natural ignorance which keeps the mind fallow without destroying its capacity for development, . . . this desolation finally compelled even the English Parliament to make elementary education a compulsory condition to the 'productive' employment of children under 14 years, in every industry subject to the Factory Acts."

But Marx goes on to point out that, even in the 1850s, the educational measures were theoretical concessions untranslated into practice because of the absence of administrative machinery, "an absence that again makes the compulsion illusory"; while the whole spirit of capitalist production is clearly evinced "in the opposition of the manufacturers themselves to these education clauses, and in the tricks and dodges they put in practice for evading them".[1]

The latter point is substantiated with a quotation from Leonard Horner, the first Warden of University College, London, and one of the Factory Inspectors appointed under the Act of 1833:

> "For this the legislature is alone to blame, by having passed a delusive law, which, while it would seem to provide that the children employed in factories shall be *educated*, contains no enactment by which that professed end can be secured. It provides nothing more than that the children shall on certain days of the week, and for a certain number of hours (three) in each day, be inclosed within the four walls of a place called a school, and that the employer of the

[1] Marx, *op. cit.*,, Vol. I, 397.

child shall receive weekly a certificate to that effect signed by a person designated by the subscriber as a schoolmaster or schoolmistress."[1]

The educational clauses of this typically Radical measure constituted, then, a hollow victory. Nor were the other educational measures passed by the reformed Parliament any more effective. In 1833 the first small grant of public money was divided between the two religious bodies which were also contending for the children's minds, the British and Foreign Schools Society and the Anglican National Society; if this again marked a precedent, in practice the gesture was too restricted to influence events. The educational clauses of the new Poor Law of 1834 were equally limited.

In spite of Kay's warnings and adjurations, educational provision in the manufacturing towns during the late 1830s and 40s was, if anything, deteriorating; for if there were increased numbers in school by comparison with previous decades, there was also an increase in population. By 1838 there was little further pressure from the Radical group in the Commons; it had disintegrated and virtually disappeared.

The Radicals had lost much of the workers' support since 1833. Now the working-class movement had turned to Chartism, to an independent political struggle for the enfranchisement of the common man. While the Radicals drew back in face of the determined demand for the People's Charter, working-class leaders finally realised that they had nothing to gain from such allies. It was at this point that the Radical group in Parliament broke up, a process hastened by the unexpected death of their potential leader, the immensely popular Lord Durham. Some moved into the Whig camp, others aligned themselves with the Tories; there were those, like Grote, who retired from politics while a number were to lose their seats. Francis Place, in a letter to the son of his old associate—John Stuart Mill, who had latterly done much to unify the Radicals—wrote the epitaph of this incipient party. He would waste no more time, he said, "with men who are infirm of purpose". John Stuart, showing this letter to a friend, remarked, "I shall keep it as a memorial of the spiritless heartless imbecility of the English Radicals".[2]

Indeed, having played its part in bringing about the Reform Act which firmly established the middle class on the road to power, the Radical movement had fulfilled its essential role. Henceforth, instead

---

[1] Marx, *op cit.*, Vol. I, 397, quoted from *Reports of Inspectors of Factories for 30th June 1857*, 17.

[2] M. St. J. Packe, *John Stuart Mill* (1954), 235.

of writing polemics and leading revolts, former Radicals were to accommodate themselves to new political tasks, to seek an established status, to become respectable; even, in defiance of the shades of Jeremy Bentham and James Mill, to give their adherence to the Church of England. It was a more mature, and less aggressive John Stuart Mill who was eventually to promulgate for the next generation the modern doctrine of liberalism.

With this eclipse of Radical politics utilitarian educational theory also drops into the background, especially its concern for the spread of scientific, secular education for the working class. Mill had set no limits to the possible intellectual development of the people except those of necessity; this aspect of educational theory was no longer mentioned. But when, with the developing mass support for Chartism and socialist aims in the 1840s, the Commons turned once more to education it was to give support to the main point that the utilitarians had endeavoured to drive home, that "an ignorant populace was a dangerous populace."[1]

It is not, however, so much James Mill as James Kay's adjurations that are recalled by Sir John Graham's speech in the House in March 1843. "I am informed that the turbulent masses who, in the course of last autumn, threatened the safety of property . . . were remarkable for the youth of the parties comprising them", he observed. "If I had entertained any doubt on the subject . . . the events of last autumn would have convinced me that not a moment should be lost in endeavouring to impart the blessings of a sound education to the rising generation in the manufacturing districts."[2]

What was now meant by a "sound" education was soon to become clear; discipline, mass instruction in the three Rs and, last but by no means least, religious instruction. Eighty years earlier Adam Smith had advocated comparatively enlightened teaching; even the clergyman Malthus, though concerned with moral and religious training, had advocated the teaching of technical subjects and economics. James Mill had once looked to the improvement of all men, out of all knowledge, as the great prize to be won; and had spared no effort in denouncing religious indoctrination as an invitation to intellectual slavery. Yet he, also, had been the first to postulate that capitalism demands an educational system divided according to social class and designed to inculcate the "right" ideas. This, according to their lights, in a new situation,

---

[1] J. L. and B. Hammond, *Age of the Chartists* (1930), 191.
[2] E. Halévy, *The Age of Peel and Cobden*, (1947), 54n.

was exactly what his successors were to plan and provide. So the early aim of universal enlightenment, advanced at a period when the middle class were themselves struggling for rights and recognition with the support of the working class—when there was a united onslaught and a common enemy—necessarily turned into its opposite. This contradiction had, however, been inherent in the whole theory of the philosophic radicals.

CHAPTER IV

THE WORKERS' MOVEMENT AND EDUCATION (I),
1790–1832

THE last two chapters have dealt with middle-class criticisms of established schools and demands for a new, scientifically based education for those destined for the professions and the task of directing economic and political affairs. With these activities were coupled projects for the instruction of the masses, at least in the elementary principles of science and on secular lines, both in schools and adult institutions and by means of the dissemination of cheap literature. This last matter was also approached entirely from the standpoint of the middle class who had a specific interest in loosening the hold of Church and aristocracy and, at the same time, in weaning the workers from the reading of inflammatory literature and study of political and economic theories hostile to capitalism. In the decades before 1832, the philosophic radicals consciously aimed to substitute for such activities inculcation of the truths of bourgeois political economy, the reading of sober and useful tracts, and the acquisition of technical knowledge which might serve to increase the usefulness of workers to their employers.

It is now necessary to examine, in more detail, what were the political activities which gave rise to fears and suspicions among all the propertied classes; how the workers were educating themselves and what kind of education they looked for. They, too, were interested in universal enlightenment and the diffusion of knowledge, but of a kind and in ways which would express and further the interests of the working class. Inevitably, therefore, they came to see through the pretensions, to understand the motives, of aristocratic Whigs, Radical educationists and industrialists as they found expression in the Mechanics' Institutes, the S.D.U.K. and plans relating to the poor and the schools.

But this took time. Before the workers could free themselves from dependency and from ideas thrust upon them, political understanding had to be gained in a number of ways. It was gained, above all, in the course of participation in the mass popular movements of the 1790s, and again, in the period 1815-19 when the cessation of war brought economic crisis and acute distress.

The ideas which chiefly promoted radical political views at this time were those advanced by Tom Paine in his *Rights of Man*, which gained general currency in the upheavals accompanying the French Revolution. In this work, Paine, drawing on the experience of the American and the French Revolutions, stressed that all men are born equal and free, and that all power must be derived from the people; in so doing he laid the foundations of a new democratic outlook. In his *Age of Reason* he followed this up with a trenchant criticism of prevailing religious beliefs. Here was one of the major influences in freeing the workers from respect for the Church and aristocracy, in opening their eyes to the ways in which religious and political indoctrination and control were used to bar the way to social change. This was so far understood by governments of the day that publication of Paine's book in England was, in effect, banned for twenty years.

The ideas which inspired Priestley and his colleagues, which brought Thomas Walker to trial and lost Frend and Beddoes their university posts, did, then, penetrate to the workers; the fervent belief in the power of reason, the significance of science, the need for freedom of thought, was shared by working men who studied not only Paine but also the works of the philosophers of the Enlightenment.

Throughout this period the popular press was the chief means of promoting and diffusing such views among the people; indeed it was in the fight for a free press, in the teeth of continuous persecution, that the workers' demand for access to knowledge on their own terms was mainly expressed. But there was also organised education in clubs and societies while individuals studied extensively in order to extend their knowledge. There was, then, a well-established tradition of self-education before 1820 when the theories of Robert Owen began to exercise a powerful influence on the growing working-class movement.

At this time many workers, as we have seen, reacted violently against industrial developments which dislocated the whole pattern of work and life. Small producers and employees of small masters lost their means of earning or employment as a result of the extension of factory production; tradesmen, artisans, agricultural labourers found their livelihood threatened by economic and technological change. In these circumstances, men looked back to the past and saw it in a rosy light, while attributing all the evils of the present to the machine and the factory. Formerly they had owned their instruments of production; it was the present monopoly of these by the factory owners and large landowners which seemed to them the root of present oppression. This instinctive reaction was reinforced by such publicists as Cobbett, who argued that the monopoly of property was itself the result of corrupt government and financial policies; that, with political reform, a democratic government, property could be divided and a return made to a simpler society.

It was at this point that Owen advanced his scheme for co-operative communities. His ideas fell on fertile ground. Not only did they appeal to the working class but also to many professional men who, in an increasingly commercialised world, welcomed the new conception of service to the community.

But, as the working-class movement began to translate Owen's plans into practice, other aspects of his teaching came to the fore. His criticism of all religion as an obstacle to human progress chimed in both with the direct experience of the working class and with rationalist, anti-clerical ideas acquired from Paine. Above all, his assertion that it is labour that creates all wealth and that the whole product of labour should rightly come to the worker in one form or another evoked a wide response. This argument was to be taken furthei by John Gray and William Thompson who began to show that it was not the monopoly of property but the institution of private property itself that was responsible for the exploitation, misery and degradation of the workers; that, accordingly, the workers must take political power from the property owners if a just society was to be established.

So there began the dissemination of embryonic socialist ideas, ideas which extended to cover the theory and practice of education. One strand of thought took its inception from Bentham's political philosophy in the light of which a new kind of demand for universal education was framed; this by men who, though not themselves of the working class, approached social problems from the angle of labour, of the workers' rights and interests. But working-class leaders, on the basis of their own direct experience, and armed with writings which not only criticised but also saw through and beyond the capitalist order, could begin to advance towards an independent social and political outlook; to formulate their own criticisms of existing education and envisage an altogether new approach.

We may now turn back to the 1790s and see how the workers educated themselves, what plans they advanced for their children, and what was the educational outlook they absorbed in the decades before 1832.

1. THE SELF-EDUCATION OF THE WORKERS, 1790-1820

(i) *The Corresponding Societies*

One outcome of the mass political agitations in the 1790s was that artisans, small tradesmen and labourers began to study and learn. They learned through direct participation in political struggles, by reading the radical press which now emerged for the first time, and by attending the popular agitational lectures of such propagandists as John Thelwall, Gale Jones and Horne Tooke. But the more serious benefited particularly from the disciplined study provided in the class organisation of the Corresponding Societies.

The workers, organised in these societies, soon realised the necessity of extending social and political knowledge among the people. Thus the Sheffield Society originated from a group of five or six mechanics who, concerned with the "enormous high price of provisions, the unbounded authority of the monopolists of all ranks . . . the waste of public property by placemen, pensioners, luxury and debauchery, together with the mock representation of the people, concluded that nothing but ignorance in the people could suffer the natural rights of every free man to be thus violated".[1] Asked, at a treason trial in 1794, what was the object of the meetings of this society, one of the strongest in the provinces, a member replied: "To enlighten the people, to show the people the reason, the ground of all their complaints and sufferings; when a man works hard for thirteen and fourteen hours of the day, the week through, and is not able to maintain his family; that is what I understood of it; to show the people the ground of this; why they were not able."[2] "Instruction is the want of all", declared a publication of the London Corresponding Society in the same year, and "the Society ought to favour with all its powers the progress of human reason, and to place instruction within the reach of every citizen."[3] This, then, was the main object of the class meetings organised by such societies in London and in the provinces.

This process of self-education was of great significance. It helped

---

[1] *Second Report from the Committee of Secrecy of the House of Commons respecting Seditious Practices; Parliamentary History of England,* Vol. XXXI (1818), Col. 717.

[2] Quoted by P. A. Brown, *The French Revolution in English History* (1918), 62-3.

[3] *The Voice of Truth against Corruption in Church and State* (1794), Sect. 22; quoted in N. Hans, *New Trends in Education in the 18th Century* (1951), 178.

materially to develop, from among the rank and file of the workers, men who were able to comprehend and master the most advanced political and social thinking of the time; men capable of acting on and communicating their knowledge and so of leading the nascent working-class movement at both a local and a national level.

The activities of the London Corresponding Society, which was composed largely of artisans and mechanics, were, from the outset, designed to promote systematic education. Francis Place, at that time a poor journeyman tailor, gives a full description of the methods used at the Covent Garden division in 1794, where, he writes:

"I met with many inquisitive upright men and among them I greatly inlarged my acquaintance. They were in most if not all respects superior to any with whom I had hitherto been acquainted. We had book subscriptions . . . (and) the books for which anyone subscribed were read by all the members in rotation who chose to read them before they were finally consigned to the subscriber. We had Sunday evening parties at the residence of those who could accommodate a number of persons. At these meetings we had readings, conversations, and discussions."

Besides these parties, there were weekly meetings with regular proceedings, each member taking his turn in the chair.

"The chairman read from some book a chapter or part of a chapter, which as many as could read the chapter at their homes, the book passing from one to the other, had done, and at the next meeting a portion of the chapter was again read and the persons present were invited to make remarks thereon; as many as chose did so, but without rising. Then another portion was read and a second invitation was given—then the remainder was read and a third invitation was given when they who had not before spoken were expected to say something. Then there was a general discussion. No one was permitted to speak more than once during the reading. The same rule was observed in the general discussions, no one could speak a second time until everyone who chose had spoken once, then any one might speak again, and so on till the subject was exhausted. . . ."[1]

Here were methods, devised by a workers' society, of a kind to encourage self-confidence, clear thinking, and the capacity for self-expression. They were to be found, in one form or another, in most

[1] Quoted in R. K. Webb, *The British Working Class Reader* (1955), 36-7.

of the Corresponding Societies. That they spread even to the country-side is confirmed by Samuel Bamford, a Lancashire weaver, who describes the activities of a "small band . . . of readers and enquirers after truth" in Middleton which included his father and uncle, and was made up of weavers, shoemakers, druggists and other "Painites." "They met at each other's houses to read such of the current publications as their small means allowed them to obtain, and to converse on the affairs of the nation, and other political subjects." These activities laid them open to attacks by thugs "armed with thick cudgels and bludgeons" who passed by the meeting place in groups, "swearing and threatening what they would do at the 'Painites' when they returned", and, as an outcome of the resultant rioting, to trials for creating disorder.[1]

In Birmingham, Manchester, Leeds, Sheffield, Norwich and elsewhere, there were similar organisations; here also books were purchased and discussions held. The Sheffield Constitutional Society, which is said to have numbered 2,000 "well-behaved men, most of them of the lower sort of workmen", met regularly for class discussions, republished *The Rights of Man* "at the low price of 6d. per copy." and formed branches in neighbouring districts in order "to extend useful knowledge from town to village, and from village to town, until the whole nation be sufficiently enlightened. . . ."[2] Thomas Walker of Manchester opened his doors to members of the Reformation Society which again was largely composed of artisans. Counsel for the prosecution, at Walker's trial for treason in 1794, summed up the activities of the society from the angle of the ruling class:

"they assembled, night after night, in numbers, to an amount which you will hear from the witnesses. Sometimes, I believe the extended number of such assemblies amounting to more than a hundred persons. There were three considerable rooms allotted for their reception. In the lower part of the house, where they were first admitted, they sat upon business of less moment, and requiring the presence of smaller numbers; in the upper part, they assembled in greater multitudes, and read, as in a school, and as it were to fashion and perfect themselves in everything that is seditious and mischievous, those writings which have been already reprobated by other juries sitting in this and other places, by the courts of law, and, in effect, by the united voice of both houses of parliament. They read, amongst other works, particularly the works of an author whose

[1] Samuel Bamford, *Early Days* (ed Henry Dunckley 1893), 53-4.
[2] *Parliamentary History of England*, Vol. XXXI, 717-19, 840-2.

name is on the mouth of everybody in this country; I mean the works of Thomas Paine."[1]

The importance of combining systematic education with mass political agitation was, then, understood among a section of the working class from the early 1790s. Nor was the significance of this combination lost on the government of the day. Section 15 of the Act of 1799 "for the more effectual suppression of Societies for seditious purposes" was specifically directed against educational activity of the kind described.[2] Under this Act the Corresponding Societies were suppressed.

(ii) *Individual Study*

That the lessons learned were not forgotten is shown by the adoption of similar plans for organised education in the clubs and associations which were to spring up after 1815. Meanwhile, it is possible to trace how the men who led the mass agitations of succeeding years obtained the grounding in education necessary for political activity and built upon this foundation; to look at the available schools from the point of view of what they offered to the working class.

Sunday schools were first established in the late 1780s to educate the poor in the principles of religion and the duties of their lowly station in life. But they sometimes had an opposite effect. Bamford, describing the labourers' meetings in the Hampden Clubs of 1816-17, writes: "Nor were there wanting men of their own class, to encourage and direct the new converts; the Sunday schools of the preceding thirty years had produced many working men of sufficient talent to become readers, writers and speakers in the village meetings for Parliamentary reform."[3] So also, an historian of Manchester notes how the Sunday school teachers "with the single undeviating purpose of promoting the eternal welfare of their pupils", were in fact "preparing them for the fit discharge of their social and public duties. They were creating *thought* among the hitherto unthinking masses".[4]

[1] *The Whole Proceedings in the Trial of an Indictment against Thomas Walker* (1794), 3.

[2] "Whereas divers places have of late been used for delivering lectures or discourses and of holding debates . . . which lectures, discourses and debates have in many instances been of a seditious or immoral nature . . . be it . . . enacted that any house, room, field or other place, at or in which any lecture or discourse shall be publicly delivered, or any public debate shall be held on any subject whatever . . . to which any person shall be admitted by the payment of money, shall be deemed a disorderly house within the intent and meaning of the said Act . . . unless the same shall have been previously licensed in the manner hereinafter mentioned." F. Podmore, *Robert Owen* (1906), 522-3.

[3] Samuel Bamford, *Passages in the Life of a Radical* (ed Henry Dunckley 1893), 12.

[4] A. Prentice, *Historical Sketches and Personal Recollections of Manchester* (1851), 116.

Besides Sunday schools there were local "dame schools", usually run by old women who looked after children for a small sum but taught little or nothing. Charity schools, endowed or "free" schools, and small private schools which charged a fee, made up the sum of educational facilities available to the poor. Often a combination of these provided little enough education, but at least it was possible to learn to read and write.

William Lovett, later the leader of the London artisan wing of the Chartist movement, describes his own progress from one school to another. Born in 1800 at Newlyn, a fishing village in Cornwall, after his father's death, he "was sent to all the dame-schools in the town" before he mastered the alphabet and eventually had to be taught to read by his great-grandmother. "I was then sent to a boys' school", he writes, "to learn 'to write and cipher', thought at that time to be all the education required for poor people. . . . Having made but little progress at this school, . . . I was sent to another. . . . Here I learned to write tolerably well, and to know a little arithmetic and the catechism, and this formed the extent of my scholastic acquirements."[1] Lovett was apprenticed to a rope-maker at an early age.

Thomas Cooper of Gainsborough, later the colourful leader of the Leicester Chartists, whose father, a dyer by trade, died when he was four, had a more regular education. Born in 1805, he learned to read at a local dame's school kept by "Old Gatty" in the lower room of her two-storied cottage. Later he became a Bluecoat scholar in a charity school, where teaching was on the monitorial system, and later still attended a private school "chiefly patronised by tradesmen and better-paid workmen", where he assisted in teaching the younger children, and remained until he was fifteen.[2] Among others, Richard Carlile, whose father (originally a cobbler, but later successively exciseman, schoolmaster and soldier) also died when he was four, learned the alphabet from local schoolmistresses, and later attended at the free school at Ashburton; here he learned writing, arithmetic and even some Latin, before leaving at the age of twelve to be apprenticed to a tin-smith for seven years—often working fifteen or sixteen hours a day.[3] George Julian Harney, born in 1817, received only a dame school education.[4] Ebenezer Elliott, the working-class poet and Corn

---

[1] William Lovett, The Life and Struggles of William Lovett (1876), 3-5.
[2] Thomas Cooper, The Life of Thomas Cooper (2nd edn 1872), 7, 13, 32-3.
[3] T. C. Campbell, The Battle of the Press, as told in the Life of Richard Carlile (1899), 10-11.
[4] A. R. Schoyen, The Chartist Challenge (1958), 2.

Law rhymer "picked up some kind of education at a small Presbyterian school in Rotherham", while Rowland Detrosier, the Lancashire working-class educator, "learned to read and write at a Sunday school".[1] James Watson, who owed to his mother ("poor but intelligent", a teacher at a Sunday school) his taste for reading and what little education he received, was apprenticed as a labourer in a clergyman's employ at the age of twelve; an occupation, as he wrote later, "not very favourable to mental development". By this time, however, he "could read well, write indifferently, and had a very imperfect knowledge of arithmetic".[2]

Some of the workers, then, managed to achieve the essential elements of literacy before being thrust into a working life which, as Adam Smith so clearly saw, was anything but conducive to mental activity. But it is not only by study that men learn and are led to seek further knowledge. When the young Lovett, Cooper and the rest began to work it was in an era of economic dislocation and widespread political agitation. "I shared the general distress of 1816," wrote Carlile later, "and it was this that opened my eyes. Having my attention drawn to politics I began to read anything I could get at upon the subject with avidity, and I soon saw what was the importance of the free press. . . . In the manufactories nothing was talked of but revolution, and I soon became so far fired as to begin to build castles in the air."[3] So Carlile, drawn into political activity, began to write. At this period he opened a bookshop in London, where he was later assisted by James Watson, who had also been drawn into active political work. Watson had arrived in Leeds in 1817 and found employment as a warehouseman. Here he came into contact with a group of radical reformers who read Wooler's *Black Dwarf*, Carlile's *Republican* and Cobbett's *Register*, and found "a great many good things" in these journals. After four years' activity "spreading the liberal and free-thinking literature, and, by meetings and discussions, endeavouring to obtain the right of free discussion", he volunteered to take Carlile's place at his bookshop, and so came to London in 1822.[4] William Lovett took the same road to knowledge. Shortly after his arrival in London in 1823, he was accidentally introduced to an association known as the "Liberals", "composed chiefly of working men", who met two evenings a week

[1] J. L. and B. Hammond, *The Town Labourer* (1917), 249.

[2] W. J. Linton, *James Watson. A Memoir* (1880), 15-16.

[3] G. A. Aldred, *Richard Carlile, agitator, his life and times* (3rd edn 1941), 60; cf. Campbell, *op. cit.*, 12.

[4] Linton, *op. cit.*, 17-18.

for "literary, political or metaphysical discussions". Under this intellectual stimulus and the impact of political action, he wrote later, "my mind seemed to be awakened to a new mental existence, new feelings, hopes and aspirations sprang up within me, and every spare moment was devoted to the acquisition of some kind of useful knowledge".[1]

The ardour with which such men sought education sometimes carried them to extraordinary lengths. Thomas Cooper normally rose at 3 or 4 a.m. winter and summer, reading till work, at work (when possible), and again in the evening. His reading covered a very wide field in history, literature, metaphysics, while he also mastered Latin, Greek, some Hebrew, and committed whole plays of Shakespeare to memory.[2] Carlile, while imprisoned in Dorchester Gaol, "perfected himself in grammar and handwriting", securing a writing master to instruct him; he also studied theology, political economy, history, phrenology and literature.[3] When James Watson was likewise sentenced, he spent his time reading Gibbon, Hume, and similar authors. "I endeavoured to make the best use of the opportunity for study and investigation," he wrote, "and the more I read and learned the more I felt my own deficiency".[4]

The tradition of working-class self-education may be said to have begun with the heroic efforts of Francis Place and William Cobbett in the 1790s.[5] It continued unabated, with the result that many working men were very widely read not only in contemporary radical literature, but also in the political and social writings of the eighteenth-century Enlightenment. Studied against a background of social and political struggle, these works stimulated fresh efforts to achieve elementary political rights and, not least, to claim the right to knowledge.

(iii) *Hampden Clubs and Secular Sunday Schools*

After 1815, new clubs sprang up, in London and the provinces. In the north, in particular, the agitation for Parliamentary reform in 1816-17 resulted in the formation of the so-called Hampden Clubs—inspired directly by Major Cartwright—which, like the Corresponding Societies, promoted discussion in organised classes side by side with political activity. "Cobbett's books were printed in a cheap form", wrote Bamford, referring to the "weekly readings and discussions of

[1] Lovett, *op. cit.*, 34-5.   [2] Cooper, *op. cit.*, 53-66.
[3] Campbell, *op. cit.*, 57-8   [4] Linton, *op. cit.*, 19.
[5] Wallas, *The Life of Francis Place* (4th edn 1951), 17-19; G. D. H. Cole, *The Life of William Cobbett* (3rd edn 1947), 29-30.

the Hampden Clubs" in Lancashire villages, "the labourers read them and thenceforward became deliberate and systematic in their proceedings."[1] This description is confirmed by a witness of another kind. "Instead of attending divine service," reported a Lancashire magistrate's spy of the same villages, "the Sundays of the people were occupied in reading the works of Cobbett and Paine and other similar publications, that were industriously circulated among them." The same witness noted that Parliamentary reform "took hold of the minds of the people and spread among them astonishingly, assisted by a great flow of political pamphlets at the same time into the houses of the lower orders of society".[2]

The close link between education and political action is brought out particularly clearly in the later development of the Lancashire democratic movement. Following the failure of the plans which culminated in the march of the Blanketeers, the Lancashire leaders immediately concentrated on setting up political Sunday schools and, according to the same informer, "went . . . up and down the country explaining the plan which they had adopted, as being the same as that of the Methodists, who had so greatly spread their doctrines". They succeeded in establishing Sunday schools "in all parts . . . each place being anxious who should first establish one".

The intention and significance of this move will be better understood when it is recalled that the working class and democratic reformers of this period saw the Church as the main obstacle to political reform, its ideological influence as the chief means whereby the people were held back from action. Thus the magistrate's spy found that the group in Royton which took the lead in forming Hampden Clubs, "laid it down as a maxim, which they often repeated, that to root out iniquity and corruption from a nation, they must begin with the priesthood, as they had the most influence over the people; and they said that a more liberal form of government was not to be hoped for, so long as the priests had the power of awing them by the fears of being damned to all Eternity".

Just as the reformers took their anti-religious propaganda throughout Lancashire in the course of setting up the Hampden Clubs, so also they endeavoured to replace the religious indoctrination of children with a

[1] Samuel Bamford, *op. cit.*, 12.

[2] These and succeeding quotations are taken from the MS. narrative of a Lancashire magistrate's spy, in the Manchester Reference Library (MS f363 D1). I am indebted for my knowledge of the existence of this manuscript to Donald Read's article "The Hampden Clubs", *Manchester Guardian*, October 2nd, 1956.

rational education in the Sunday schools they promoted, as part of the Union movement for Parliamentary reform from 1817 onwards. This clearly emerges from the report of the magistrate's spy, who attended the original meeting which determined on this course of action. The reformers argued, as did the philosophers of the Enlightenment, that experience shows education to be all-powerful in the formation of opinions, and second:

"That one of the chiefest evils under which the Nations of Europe laboured was that of suffering the children to be educated and instructed in the doctrine of a Religion which was so ambiguous, doubtful and contradictory, that it almost always cramped their understandings and baffled their judgments:—whereas on the contrary, if they were instructed in the principles of Government, and the right use of reason, they would be enabled to know their own worth in Society—to distinguish between right and wrong—to know the real object of worship—and what value to set upon the ceremonial and idolatrous worship of the Christians.—That it would be impossible for any King or Government to tyrannize over a people educated in such a manner and that if every other effort to reform the State and banish superstition failed, this of education would effect it. For . . . only conceive that if schools were to be established to the extent of the Methodists what would be the consequence? Why the soldiers and sailors and almost all the constables and lower officers in the Nation would be educated in this manner, and then what chance would either Government or priesthood have of tyrannizing over them. Corruption and all its attendant evils would be banished from such a society. That it was the duty of every good man to attend to the right directing of young minds as the welfare of the next generation depended on it."

Here, a year before James Mill enlarged upon the subject of education in the *Encyclopaedia Britannica*, is a clear demand for a rational, secular education for all as the necessary foundation for good government, as an essential aspect of the struggle for radical reform.

Many of the schools established opened in the evenings as well as on Sundays, and included both adults and children. The adults came to "read the news or hear it read" from opposition pamphlets and newspapers bought by subscription, or engaged in political and religious discussions; in the larger towns, such as Manchester, "the school rooms in a short time became so crowded," that adults and children were divided "in order to separate the scholars from the news readers". In the school rooms also, reports the informer, whose main task was to uncover seditious political activity, "all secret despatches were written—the resolutions for public meetings drawn up—the Unions classed—the leaders of the sections appointed—and all other business that came under the consideration of the committee of the district, transacted". Seldom can the process of education have been more closely linked with politics.

(iv) Political Protestants and the "Black Dwarf"

This movement was, of course, by no means confined to Lancashire but covered the north-east, Yorkshire and the Midlands. In 1818 the Political Protestant Unions for Parliamentary Reform, the title of the radical movement in the north-east, were organised into classes of twenty, each class meeting once a week and each member subscribing a penny to "purchase such means of instruction as may be required". "Political ignorance has been the cause of all our national misery and degradation", they wrote. T. J. Wooler, replying in the Black Dwarf to the Society of Political Protestants at York, commends the members on their "desire for political information . . . the means you have adopted are some of the most efficient. Nothing can be accomplished but by Union. . . . Men must meet each other, unite their knowledge and their powers, compare their sentiments, weigh together the force of opposite statements, and draw the pure gold of truth from the dross of the inferior ore with which it is generally combined".[1]

With such co-ordination and guidance the movement constantly spread. A letter from the Hull Political Protestants Union reports: "We have formed ourselves into an institution of political protestants, which we most earnestly recommend to be adopted in every town and village in the nation. We divide ourselves into classes of twenty each, and each class meets once a week, and reads Cobbett, and Sherwin's Register, Wooler's Black Dwarf, and other works, calculated to diffuse political knowledge; the leaders of each class hold a meeting on the first Monday in every month, to report the progress of the institution to the Chairman."[2] Of Tyneside it was reported in 1819 that "the majority of the workmen of almost every colliery on both rivers are formed into classes of twenty, with a leader to each class".[3]

An insight into the procedure at these meetings can be obtained from

[1] Black Dwarf, April 21st, 1819.
[2] R. F. Wearmouth, Some Working Class Movements of the Nineteenth Century (1948), 35.
[3] Ibid., 43.

the rules of the Newcastle Political Protestants. Every week the class leaders were expected to "read or cause to be read interesting extracts from papers and political publications," to "encourage the members to make remarks," to "repress any violent or improper expression". "The class leaders", the rules ran, "shall determine what papers and books shall be purchased ... the works recommended are Cartwright's *Bill of Rights*, which ought to be had in all classes—also the *Black Dwarf* —Bentham's *Reform Catechism* and other works—Ensor's *Works*— Cobbett's *Paper against Gold*, and his weekly *Register*—also the publications of Wooler, Sherwin, etc."[1]

At Stockport, the first of the Lancashire Union Societies which followed the decline of the Hampden Clubs, the classes met weekly "for the purpose of reading any political or other books, papers, etc." Here the Society had acquired rooms which were open on Wednesday evenings for reading, on other weekdays for "instruction in reading, writing, arithmetic, grammar," and on Saturday for reciting political pieces learned by the younger members; on Sunday mornings and afternoons reading, writing, arithmetic, grammar were taught to both sexes.[2] The aim of this activity, according to the rules, was to ensure that every member would be adequately trained "to promote by all just means in his power, a radical reform of Parliament, by means of suffrage in all male persons of mature age and sane minds, ... of Parliaments having a duration not exceeding one year, and of elections by ballot".[3]

The link between popular education of this kind and political action comes out clearly in contemporary comments. Thus a correspondent from Manchester, writing to the *Black Dwarf* about the Manchester Union Sunday School, refers to the thirst for knowledge among the "lower orders" and to the increasing success of the school. "The public mind has already undergone a complete *revolution*. The ranks of reform have . . . been swelled beyond *all expectation*. . . . It is satisfactory to see that *misery* has had one good effect—that of stimulating the mind to enquire into its cause." The Manchester Sunday School, he adds, "is one of the levers which will one day act with considerable effect; and the numbers that throng there for instruction, are the best proofs of its necessity and advantage."[4]

"We are endeavouring most assiduously to inform ourselves by all

---

[1] Wearmouth, *op. cit.*, 49.   [2] *Ibid.*, 49.

[3] *Manchester Observer*, May 8th, 1819; quoted in Donald Read, *Peterloo* (1958), 48.

[4] *Black Dwarf*, April 6th, 1819.

means in our power," writes another correspondent from Oldham in the same year, "that when called upon by circumstances we may be able to act as lovers of our country, and of mankind. The stagnation of trade, though the greatest evil to our families, gives us ample time for reflexion, while it forces consideration on our minds. Our distresses have caused us to reason upon the causes of them." Here the participants had opened a room for political debates, having been driven from the public houses by threats that their presence would lead to loss of licences. Here also they had set up a school for their children with 200 scholars.[1] Female Societies were also organised, particularly in the Lancashire area; their purpose being partly, in the words of the Blackburn Female Union rules, "to instil into the minds of our children a deep and rooted hatred of our corrupt and tyrannical rulers".[2]

The class meetings of this period, then, were "schools of education in affairs . . . whether judged in regard to organisation, education, finance, or all three, the meetings of the weekly classes were of very high importance in the techniques, development, expression and direction of working-class agitation".[3] Fundamental to this movement was the conviction, to be reiterated time and again in the following thirty years, that if once the working class could gain a full understanding of the functioning of society (both political and economic), and of their own rights and duties, they would have the strength to enforce their demands.

It was to ensure that this knowledge should be made available that Cobbett, and more particularly Wooler, Hone, Carlile, Watson and many others led a militant struggle for the freedom of the press. The radical journals and other cheap publications were, as has been shown, the essential reading matter of workers. In 1816, Cobbett reduced the price of his *Political Register* from 1s. 0½d. to 2d., excluding news in order to evade the stamp tax. The first number at this new price, dignified by the name of "two-penny trash" in Parliament, sold 44,000 copies within a month.[4]

It was primarily such widely popular journals, characterised by

---

[1] "Your readers and yourself will learn with pleasure that a room has been opened at Oldham with forms, desks, and etc., for the purpose of instructing the young in reading, writing and accounts. Nearly 200 scholars have been enrolled, in a few weeks, and an abundance of gratuitous teachers have come forward . . ." *Black Dwarf*, June 2nd, 1819.

[2] *Manchester Observer*, June 26th, 1819; quoted in Read, *op. cit.*, 53.

[3] Wearmouth, *op. cit.*, 49.

[4] W. H. Wickwar, *The Struggle for the Freedom of the Press* (1928), 54.

Sidmouth as "the worst description of poison",[1] that the government of the day was concerned to silence; one of the notorious Six Acts of 1819 being directed against "pamphlets and printed papers containing observations on public events and occurrences, tending to excite hatred and contempt of the Government and Constitution of these realms as by law established, and also vilifying our holy religion".[2] Before this, Habeas Corpus had been suspended, and in the spring of 1817 Cobbett fled to America "in fear of the Government and of his creditors". More intrepid spirits carried on the work at home. But in the same year Hone and Wooler were tried for blasphemous and defamatory libel,[3] and Carlile gaoled for selling Hone's *Parodies on the Book of Common Prayer*.[4]

In 1819 Carlile was sentenced afresh to what amounted to six years' imprisonment, for the crime of selling Paine's *Age of Reason* and Elihu Palmer's *Principles of Nature*. During the course of this struggle, editors, printers and publishers, as well as hundreds of sellers of unstamped publications were gaoled time and again. But the pamphlets and papers continued to appear. Hone characteristically satirised the consternation they caused in his parody of a speech from the throne at the opening of Parliament:

> But pray, My L—ds and G—tl—n,
> don't shrink
> From exercising all your care
> and skill,
> Here, and at home,
> TO CHECK THE CIRCULATION

(Cut of an execution of a printing press—personified as a woman. Three men approach with chains, rope, axe and dagger.)

> OF LITTLE BOOKS,
> Whose very looks—
> Vile '*two-p'nny trash*,'
> bespeak abomination.
> Oh! They are full of blasphemies
> and libels,
> And people read them
> oftener than their bibles.[5]

---

[1] A. Aspinall, *Politics and the Press* (1949), 54.
[2] C. D. Collett, *History of the Taxes on Knowledge* (1899), Vol. I, 17; Wickwar, *op. cit.*, 138.
[3] Wickwar, *op. cit.*, 56, 57-9.   [4] Campbell, *op. cit.*, App. iv, 320.
[5] *The Man in the Moon* (1820). See illustration opposite p. 177.

The production and sale of cheap journals and books, organised study in class meetings, these—always coupled with active political campaigning—formed the core of educational efforts in the years from 1816 to 1823. Not only had self-education become an integral aspect of working-class political activity, the chief means whereby local leaders emerged from the ranks of the workers, but also there was a new departure. Efforts were made to educate children with the clear purpose of bringing up the coming generation with a new set of moral values, as harbingers of a new society. There were, then, two aspects of the struggle for education and knowledge which were closely linked.

This development was to have a new impetus with the dissemination of Robert Owen's *New View of Society*. To seek the theory which from now on informed this movement it is necessary to turn to the teaching of Owen and his circle, for the education of both child and adult was a central point in the plans they advanced for social re-generation.

2. EDUCATION AND THE NEW SOCIETY

(i) *Robert Owen and the New Lanark Schools*

Robert Owen, born the son of a saddler, started work at the age of ten but had become a wealthy master by the time he reached his majority. In the 1790s, as we have seen, he was an active member of the Literary and Philosophical Society in Manchester, where he was then working, and so in contact with leading scientists and indus-trialists interested in educational matters. By 1800 he had become manager of a large textile concern in Scotland—the New Lanark Mills—and there he attempted, singlehanded, to put into practice radical educational ideas.

In 1813 Owen published his *New View of Society*, in the framing of which he had the active assistance of James Mill and Francis Place. This was the period when Whig aristocrats, wealthy dissenters, philo-sophic radicals, were all engaged in promoting the affairs of the British and Foreign Schools Society and other philanthropic ends. Indeed, Owen himself had supported Whitbread's bill in 1807 and contributed to Lancaster's schemes. It was to these circles, as well as to Parliament, that he first addressed his proposals, which aroused a certain tolerant interest.

Like the philosophic radicals, Owen was chiefly concerned to find the solution to the problem of pauperism. But his approach was, by comparison with that of Bentham and Mill, not merely rational within the limits of the iron laws of political economy, but broadly humanist. It was his argument that industry could be rendered efficient and profitable by humane treatment of the workers and by an education designed to develop potentialities of all kinds. The force of his appeal lay in the fact that he seemed to have proved his thesis at New Lanark. To the school he established there, and the mills themselves, there flocked an unending procession of notabilities and visitors from this country and from overseas, and Owen's name was soon widely known.

Fundamental to Owen's educational approach is the conviction that "Man's character is formed *for* him, and not *by* him". In the past, he asserts, this simple truth has been overlooked. People have been treated as if they were responsible for their own characters and in consequence have been "vilified and savagely treated" which has only increased evil. But "man is the creature of circumstances", his character is formed by his environment, particularly at an early age. "Any character, from the best to the worst, from the most ignorant to the most enlightened, may be given to any community, even to the world at large, by applying certain means";[1] and, Owen affirmed, those means are known and under our control.

It followed that any error in the formation of character was the fault, not of the child but of his teachers and the conditions under which he lived. By changing these conditions, by providing the right kind of teaching, the character of the whole population might be changed within the foreseeable future. The right kind of education, in Owen's view, is a rational education directed to an understanding of the external world and which aims to develop reason so that error and superstition may be rooted out. The method of changing conditions he advocated is the establishment of co-operative communities. Within these the minute division of labour, with all its evil effects, can be overcome and science, instead of acting as a hostile force causing unemployment and poverty, can provide the condition for human advance; thus new mechanical inventions, instead of displacing the labourer, will serve to shorten his hours of work while opposing interests will disappear because members of the community will have equal rights and an identical interest in improving the process of production. Such would be truly educative communities; envy, strife

[1] From the title page of the first edition of *A New View of Society* (1813).

and all vicious propensities would inevitably be superseded by social qualities, by reason, tolerance, friendship and love.

Owen enunciated his educational theory as if he had discovered it for himself.[1] But the conviction that "circumstances make man," was not, of course, new. It was this theory that Joseph Priestley had developed, that Godwin held, that James Mill explained in detail in his famous article. In this sense, Owen gives expression to the materialist view stemming originally from Hobbes and Locke, developed by Hartley and the French sensationalists Helvétius and Condillac, and perfected in the late eighteenth century primarily by the French *philosophes*.

But what was new in Owen's contribution, in the strictly educational field, was the humanism with which he applied this theory. He was not concerned to use education to inculcate particular beliefs or theories, nor with happiness conceived of in an abstract way, but sought rather to educate children as human beings capable of applying their reason to nature and society and of enjoying all aspects of life. In the New Lanark schools these ideas were translated into practice.

Owen's predecessor, Dale, had already provided a modicum of education for the pauper children and others employed in the mills, but only at the close of a thirteen-hour day when they were too exhausted to profit from it. Though at first restricted by his partners, who intended to build up a profitable enterprise, Owen had put an end to the practice of employing pauper child labour and had also withdrawn all children under ten from work. In December 1814, he succeeded in forming a new partnership, including such men as Jeremy Bentham, William Allen and Joseph Fox, who were more sympathetic to his plans. He was now able to limit the hours of adults to twelve (including meals), to go ahead with his plans for education and his efforts to improve the home life and surroundings of the younger generation.[2]

On January 1st, 1816, Owen opened a new building at New Lanark known as the Institution for the Formation of Character. It was in this building that the famous day school for ʳchildren and the evening schools for young workers and adults were carried on. Mechanical learning by rote, on a monitorial system, Owen would have none of;

---

[1] Owen's educational theory is fully expressed in the third essay of *A New View of Society*; later statements added little of significance.

[2] Podmore, *op. cit.*, 92-7.

lessons must be made interesting, questions and discussion encouraged. Besides the normal subjects, Owen insisted on the teaching of geography, history and the natural sciences. The latter were taught from natural objects and specimens brought in from the countryside, and with the help of models, charts and pictures of animals, shells and minerals that hung round the schoolroom; large maps were used for the teaching of geography while charts illustrating the "Stream of Time" formed the means of teaching ancient and modern history. In addition, Owen introduced music, dancing and elementary military drill. The children were to be governed solely by kindness and affection; no punishments were permitted, nor any prizes encouraging individual emulation; instead, there should be a co-operative search for knowledge which would be its own reward.[1]

Among the hundreds of visitors to the school was the liberal Unitarian, W. J. Fox, who was there in 1823. "The children of this factory", he wrote to a friend,

> "have every provision for amusement and instruction that could be coveted by the wealthiest, and when they get to the working age . . . the fewer hours than others, the cleanliness, the reading-rooms, lectures, concerts, dances, the comfortable dwellings, and all this in one of the most beautiful spots in Scotland, make one astonished that such a paradise could be made out of a cotton manufactory even by the talent, benevolence and perseverance of Mr. Owen. The examinations of the children proved that about the school at least there was no quacking. I believe the pupils of few boarding schools in England could have stood such an examination so well."[2]

Such was the character of the New Lanark school between 1816 and 1824. At the latter date, Owen's nonconformist partners insisted on certain changes which—to some extent—transformed the character of the school. A year later, Owen left for America to attempt to establish there the ideal co-operative community he had in mind, taking with him his famous "boatload of knowledge", including two teachers who had taught at Pestalozzi's school at Yverdun.[3] He

[1] Podmore, op. cit., 142-50. In 1824 Owen's eldest son, Robert Dale Owen, published An Outline of the System of Education at New Lanark, which contains a full description of the school including the content of education and the teaching methods.

[2] E. Garnett, The Life of W. J. Fox (1910), 48-9.

[3] Podmore, op. cit., 299-300; a description of the Owenite community at New Harmony, giving special attention to the role of education in the community, can be found in A. E. Bestor, Backwoods Utopias (1950); here, Owen's "boatload of knowledge" is described as "one of the significant intellectual migrations of history" (p. 133); see also Mark Holloway, Heavens on Earth (1951), Ch. 4.

returned in 1828, after the failure of this project, to find that workers in many parts of England had already begun to set up co-operative societies.

(ii) *Owenism and the Co-operative Community*

It was in 1816, at the height of the economic crisis following the end of the Napoleonic Wars, that Owen had come forward with a practical plan for the immediate establishment of co-operative communities to remedy unemployment; a plan which he laid before prominent men, in the attempt to gain funds for the establishment of model villages. He met with little response. Subsequently, elaborating this plan, he first proclaimed his belief that labour creates all wealth and that it is to the workers that the whole product of labour should come.

In canvassing his ideas, Owen argued that co-operative communities might be set up in a variety of ways—by landed proprietors or wealthy capitalists, by established companies, by parishes or counties "and by associations of the middle and working classes of farmers, mechanics, and tradesmen, to relieve themselves from the evils of the present system".[1]

It was these last alone who were to respond. A way had been suggested of contracting out of the system which brought poverty and unemployment, or long hours at work where there could be no joy in labour. To establish a community which could use the surplus gained from the work of its members to provide civilised living and working conditions seemed to many both a practicable and an ideal solution. In such a community, Owen told them, "the best habits and dispositions" would be imperceptibly created, for members would "be trained to fill every office and to perform every duty that the well-being of their associates and the establishments require." All this was, in itself, education. "It is only by education", Owen affirmed, "that communities of men can ever be well governed, and by means of such education every object of human society will be attained with the least labour and the most satisfaction."[2]

Since it was in the interests of all to educate and train every member and make him an efficient producer, ignorance could not exist in such a society. Here Owen's preoccupation with the problem which had struck Adam Smith is shown, even as he proposes its solution:

[1] "Report of the County of New Lanark" (1820), reprinted in *A New View of Society, etc.* (ed G. D. H. Cole 1927), 285.
[2] *Ibid.*, 283.

"Instead of the unhealthy pointer of a pin,—header of a nail,—piecer of a thread,—or clodhopper, senselessly gazing at the soil around him, without understanding or rational reflection, there would spring up a working class full of activity and useful knowledge, with habits, information, manners, and dispositions that would place the lowest in the scale many degrees above the best of any class which has yet been formed by the circumstances of past or present society."[1]

This was to approach contemporary problems from the angle of the working class, to advance perspectives which could not but exercise the strongest appeal. Within ten years of the publication of Owen's scheme, men had begun to band together with the aim of contracting out of a society where they were robbed of the full value of their labour, and of establishing working communities in the countryside; here they could carry on their trades, live like human beings and ensure their children an enlightened education. Such communities, many felt, must inevitably succeed, and, by their gradual extension, would bring about a complete transformation of human society.

In 1821, working printers and their friends formed a "Co-operative and Economic Society" in London, started the *Economist* as their propaganda journal and ran a small settlement on co-operative lines —here the education of the children was made the first duty of the whole community.[2] Other projects included the Edinburgh "Practical Society," founded by Abram Combe in the same year and including at one time as many as 500 to 600 families; these not only opened a co-operative store, but also met regularly for mutual instruction and entertainment, and opened a school for their 120 children on the New Lanark model.[3] The ambitious Orbiston scheme, initiated by Combe in 1825, involved a huge building with accommodation for 1,000, including dormitories for children who were educated at common nurseries and schools.[4]

When these more ambitious schemes failed through lack of funds, workers began to set up new forms of co-operative societies, usually associations of men engaged in the same trade. In the first place they often collected a small capital to buy materials for the use of unemployed members, then developed further as means allowed. Initially products were disposed of locally, but later an exchange of co-operative products was established and attempts made to provide a labour

---

[1] "Report to the County of Lanark" (1820), reprinted in *A New View of Society, etc.* (ed G. D. H. Cole 1927), 284.

[2] Podmore, *op. cit.*, 350-1.   [3] *Ibid.*, 357.   [4] *Ibid.*, 352, 368-9.

currency. These societies multiplied; by 1830 there were some 300 local co-operative societies and the number increased to 500 in the next year or two. In many cases, the importance of providing education for the children of the co-operators was seen as an essential part of the plan. So there developed the early co-operative movement, many years before the days of the Rochdale pioneers whose co-operative shop, set up in 1844, is often taken as the inception of co-operation in this country. This early movement was to exercise an important influence in the educational field after 1830.

By this time Owen had become identified with the working-class movement, with socialism and atheism, and the wealthy had long since washed their hands of his schemes. Indeed, his sturdy rationalism, which he proclaimed at Sunday lectures in London, even caused dissension within the co-operative movement itself. But he had gathered other adherents who, in turn, helped to spread socialist ideas among other sections of the workers. William Thompson, an Irish landowner, much concerned with the poverty and squalor of the peasantry, and, as already mentioned, profoundly interested in education, saw in co-operation not only an immediate means of rescuing the masses from present distress but also the prospect of building a just society on earth. Richard Carlile, fervent follower of Tom Paine, who believed that once reason triumphed over superstition the way would be open for representative government and great social advances, found much that was congenial in Owen's message. So also did Thomas Hodgskin, who believed that the working class must wrest the true value of their labour from the capitalists before they would achieve emancipation.

Through their lectures, in journals and books, such men won first the interest and then the enthusiastic support of future leaders of the working-class movement; of William Lovett, Cleave, Watson, Hetherington (who remained all his life a confirmed Owenite) as well as Bronterre O'Brien, George Julian Harney and others who were to figure among the Chartist leaders in the late 1830s and 40s. With the message that labour could be directed by science to the end of improving human welfare went also the message that education was the key to understanding science and social change; and, too, the means whereby the coming generation might be prepared for a new kind of life and to complete the establishment of a world fit to form the lives of men.

That the way had been prepared for these ideas is evident from the programme of the Lancashire reformers of 1817. They had already come to realise, from their own experience and their reading of Paine, that through the control of education church and state had for centuries moulded the people's minds and so preserved their power. All existing schools inculcated sectarian dogmas and superstitious ideas, giving children a false view of society, of man's rights and duties, of the universe as a whole; this was to mislead and disarm the people. Now came Owen and his associates to insist that education should be concerned only with what is true, that it should free the mind from error and uphold the primacy of reason. These ideas the developing working-class movement was to make its own.

(iii) *Richard Carlile's "Address to Men of Science"*

Already in the early 1820s the idea that truth and reason could be spread through education was being pressed on the workers with passionate conviction by those to whom they looked for intellectual leadership. One of the most striking expressions of this outlook is to be found in the *Address to Men of Science* (1821),[1] written, printed and published by Carlile while serving his six years' imprisonment in Dorchester gaol. In this pamphlet Carlile expresses the standpoint of the most advanced free-thinkers of the time, who saw in the advance of science and a scientific education the means to moral and material improvement. These views Carlile had acquired above all from the *Age of Reason*, from Paine, of whom he was a passionate admirer and follower; indeed, it was for publishing this book in defiance of the ban that he was sentenced.

A good idea of the intellectual influences to which Carlile—and indeed most of the early radicals—were subject can be gained from those to whom toasts were proposed at the public dinner held to celebrate Paine's birthday ("in the most public manner") on Carlile's release from gaol in 1826. Besides Thomas Paine, these were to Robert Owen ("We admire his perseverance in his career of humanity and generosity"—proposed by Carlile), to the memory of Rousseau and Voltaire, of Diderot and d'Holbach, of Benjamin Franklin and Elihu Palmer, of Tindal, Toland and Annett, of Tillotson and Dr. Conyers

[1] The full title reads: "*An Address to Men of Science: calling upon them to stand forward and vindicate the Truth from the foul grasp and persecution of Superstition; and obtain for the Island of Great Britain the noble appellation of the Focus of Truth; whence mankind shall be illuminated, and the black and pestiferous clouds of persecution and Superstition be banished from the face of the earth; as the only sure prelude to Universal Peace and Harmony among the Human Race. In which a sketch of a Proper System for the Education of Youth is submitted to their judgment.*"

Middleton, of Byron and Shelley and "all Englishmen who have written to the end of human improvement".[1]

The rationalist influence is paramount, and this is also the case with the *Address*, in which Carlile takes up a materialist position, in particular in relation to science. In the *Age of Reason* Paine had demanded the teaching of science in place of the dead languages; attacking also the advocates of Christianity who, seeing that "the continually progressive knowledge" of man "would militate against, and call into question, the truth of their system of faith, . . . not only rejected the study of science out of the Christian schools, but they persecuted it".[2] Paine argued that a true scientific knowledge of the universe and its laws exposed the errors of Christian mysticism and made clear that its interpretations were against all reason. Christian myths about the creation, based on error, were morally wrong. "It is the moral duty of man to obtain every possible evidence that the structure of the universe, or any other part of creation affords with respect to systems of religion. But this the supporters or partisans of the Christian system, as if dreading the result, incessantly opposed."[3] It is this view that Carlile develops.

The first part of the *Address* is specifically directed to scientists, especially to chemists and astronomers. It is an appeal that scientists should make the philosophical implications of their discoveries known to mankind. Chemistry, for instance, shows that "Creation is an improper word when applied to matter. Matter never was created—matter never can be destroyed. There is no superior power: it has no rival. It is eternal both as to the past and the future. It is subject to a continual chemical analysis, and as continual a new composition."[4] So also astronomy exposes the futility of all religious cosmologies. Scientists, however, have not made their conclusions known. Instead, most have countenanced error and imposture. But, says Carlile, "superstition corrupts and deteriorates all the human passions; science alone is qualified to amend and moralise them".[5] Hence his appeal to scientists "to stand forward and support me. . . . It is certain that superstition would not linger another year, if the philosophers of the country would stand forward and make war upon it". If they did so and advanced the truths of science, the money now extorted by the priesthood (£6 million) "would be willingly given for the

---

[1] *The Republican*, Vol. XIII, No. 5, February 1826.
[2] The *Age of Reason*, reprinted in *Works by Thomas Paine* (ed Mrs. Bonner 1908), 19.
[3] *Ibid.*, 20.   [4] Carlile, *op. cit.*, (2nd ed 1822), 19-20.   [5] *Ibid.*, 15.

erection of Temples of Science, and the support of competent professors in the Arts and Sciences"; for individuals, for society itself "mutual instruction in everything that can benefit a society, would be the first and last object in view".[1]

Of equal importance was the establishment of an entirely new type of education. "All existing systems", wrote Carlile, "are imperfect and improper." Half a boy's time in school is spent in religious in-doctrination, and while this makes no impression, constant repetitions stupefy the will and blunt the mind; these "are viewed but as a matter of school discipline, and the youth returns to them with a loathing". No aspect of education is designed "to kindle the fire of genius, or to cherish the aspiring spirit of youth". But if education is exclusively concerned with scientific subjects "so as to leave the mind in a continual state of exercise upon the subject of science, and that alone," all this can be changed and a new purpose provided. Science will "employ, amuse, and delight . . . expand their minds in the knowledge and comprehension of those objects which are above all things conducive to the interests of society, and which relate to the progressive improvement and advancing state of the Arts and Sciences."[2]

With religion Carlile would also banish other contemporary subjects on the grounds of their immoral tendencies; for instance, all classical works which allude to the mythologies of Greece and Rome, as well as history which, as taught, displayed mainly the ignorance and brutality of the past. The content of education, apart from reading and writing and the use of figures, should include "the elements of astronomy, of geography, of natural history and of chemistry", so that the children may "at an early period of life form correct notions of organised and inert matter, instead of torturing their minds with metaphysical and incomprehensible dogmas about religion".[3]

In outlining the scientific subjects to be taught Carlile once more takes his start from the classical materialist standpoint. "As matter and motion comprise every thing we can behold or can conceive, and as Chemistry is an investigation of the properties of matter, with the causes and effects of its various combinations, it is evidently the most important part of science"; within its scope come many practical applications—the cultivation of the earth, the preservation of health, the preparation of clothing, cookery, all these are chemical

[1] Carlile, *op. cit.*, (2nd ed 1822), 27.   [2] *Ibid.*, 28-9, 33.   [3] *Ibid.*, 3-4.

operations. The elements of chemistry should, then, be made comprehensible to children who should be encouraged to undertake their own experiments.[1]

Children should also study every branch of Natural Philosophy by means of observation and experiment; everything in the animal and vegetable world can be described and classified in school books, and the Linnæan system of classification taught. The teaching of astronomy should extend to cover all recent discoveries, while new discoveries should be rapidly passed on in the schools. Geography should be concerned solely with the present divisions of the earth, and the "present customs, manners and distinctions of its inhabitants".[2] Arithmetic, geometry, algebra and mechanics, complete Carlile's curriculum, and he appeals once more to "Men of Science", this time to produce textbooks which would enable enlightened teaching "free from allusion to mythologies and superstition". So the child will learn man's place in nature, be humbled, and become enlightened.

Carlile also makes his proposals regarding methods of teaching in the light of a materialist understanding of psychology. "The materiality of the mind being now conceded by all who have ventured to think, . . . the necessity for an entire new system of educating youth unfolds itself." Instead of repetition and superstition, there must be free discussion and a positive morality, taught by example rather than precept. Carlile here once more rejects religious principles and practice, claiming that "scientific pursuits, or a scientific education, must naturally lead to the extension of moral virtue". So long as children are taught that this life is only a probation for the next, "the mind can never have a free range on the beautiful and enchanting scenery of nature. To make this life, and there is no other, a scene of happiness, all those dogmas of the priest must be expelled from the mind." In their place must be put "a study of nature and her laws", which "alone forms any substantial faith or religion".[3]

Science, then, is the key both to knowledge and freedom, freedom to form one's own morality and reject imposed beliefs. "Man does not naturally delight in ignorance and credulity, but he naturally strives to free himself from those vices. . . . All tyranny, oppression, and delusion, have been founded upon the ignorance and credulity of mankind. . . . Knowledge, scientific knowledge, is the power that must be opposed to those evils."[4] Every schoolmaster, then, "ought

[1] Carlile, op. cit., (2nd ed 1822), 30.   [2] Ibid., 34.
[3] Ibid., 31, 36-7.   [4] Ibid., 41.

to be a Man of Science, and not a parish priest, as Mr. Brougham would have".[1]

"Let our youth", Carlile concludes, "be educated upon this basis, let even grown persons re-educate themselves in the same manner, and we shall soon see mankind in its proper character. That character will be the opposite of what it is at present. The Representative System of Government will be found to be the only necessary Government amongst them and the chief part of legislation will consist in an advancement of the Arts and Sciences."[2]

Here, at the last, the demand for an enlightened education is inseparably linked with the task of securing the reform of Parliament which was increasingly to engage the attention of the popular movement in succeeding years.

(iv) *William Thompson on the Diffusion of Knowledge*

Just as Carlile saw a scientific education as the necessary prelude to the establishment of a just society, so also William Thompson gave education a central significance in his scheme for the transformation of society through co-operation. Thompson's books and lectures had a very considerable influence on working-class thought in the formative period of the late 1820s and early 30s. His *Inquiry into the Principles of the Distribution of Wealth most conducive to Human Happiness* (1824), a direct challenge to orthodox political economy, had a particular effect; it was followed by *Appeal of one half of the Human Race* (1825), a defence of women's rights, and *Labour Rewarded* (1827), in which he stressed the importance of trade unions as the means of achieving a new order of society based on co-operative production and distribution. Finally, in *Practical Directions for the Establishment of Communities*, he gave clearer and more concrete directions for the organisation of co-operative societies than Owen had done, so greatly influencing the character of the early co-operative movement.[3]

Born in Ireland in 1775, and originally a follower of Bentham, William Thompson first came to England in 1822 to study educational developments—this being, at the time, his main interest. In his *Inquiry*, which marked an advance from Benthamite thought towards socialism, he devoted a long chapter specifically to education.

With Robert Owen and Hodgskin, Thompson held that the worker was entitled to the full value of his product, but was at present

[1] Carlile, *op. cit.*, (2nd ed 1822), 4. This is a reference to Brougham's Education Bill of 1820.

[2] *Ibid.*, 39.   [3] R. K. P. Pankhurst, *William Thompson* (1954), *passim*.

defrauded of most of it. But he went beyond Owen's utopian conception that a just society would evolve from the progressive expansion of co-operative communities. His *Inquiry* is concerned to establish what he regarded as "the natural laws of distribution," the operations of which are the condition for a rational society and maximal happiness. Such a state of society, he argued, could be gained through co-operation but only if this was coupled with the attainment of political power. "Labourers must become capitalists," he wrote later in *Labour Rewarded*, "and must acquire knowledge to regulate their labour on a large united scale, before they will be able to do more than dream of enjoying the whole products of their labour. Added to knowledge, the Industrious Classes must also acquire *power*, the whole power of the social machine in their own hands, in order to render their knowledge available, on a national scale, and with an immediate effect, for promoting the impartial and equal happiness of all."[1]

In the co-operative society, the natural laws of distribution must be permanently secured through the acquisition and diffusion of knowledge. This becomes possible once knowledge and labour, originally integrated in the process of production but later separated, are again reunited. In co-operative production knowledge, instead of standing in opposition to labour "not only concealing its treasures from the labourers, but systematically deluding them and leading them astray," will "once more re-unite with labour, which, informed by science, would cease to be entirely muscular, mechanical and obedient." Thereby the division between mental and manual labour would be overcome both "because the happiness of all demands it; and because the very progress and development of the social art has enforced the *means*". Such a society would "be wise enough to diffuse and perpetuate, through all its members, that knowledge, which is essential to its support".[2] It would do so first, by a complete change in the character of social institutions, second, by instructing adults by every possible means in truth, science and rationality through the press and free discussion, and finally, through the education of children.

Thompson held strictly to the materialist view of the mind, asserting that "The feeling and the judgment are equally a cerebral operation",[3] and fully accepted the view that education and environment determined the formation of human qualities. For this reason, like

---

[1] *Labour Rewarded* (1827), 73.
[2] W. Thompson, *An Inquiry into the Principles of the Distribution of Wealth*, (ed W. Pare 1850), 199-200.
[3] *Ibid.*, 234.

a true Benthamite, he directed attention first, to the immense influence of social institutions in the formation of character. Existing institutions, he claimed, do not develop the essential human qualities of industry, truth, fortitude, temperance, prudence, beneficence and mental cultivation (qualities much the same as those the Lunar educators desired to impart). Instead they implant diametrically opposite habits. The first step, then, must be to replace existing institutions and methods of government. The extension of the franchise would, for example, be a "most powerful instrument for the diffusion of knowledge"; the highest of human qualities, the ability to take a comprehensive view of social affairs, can only be developed by promoting its exercise.

In general, Thompson held, the age of mental darkness among the masses, perpetuated by governments in their own interest, had come to an end, though "there are still those who openly maintain, and many more who secretly strive for, the perpetuating of this ignorance".[1] During this long period the people's minds, left without exercise, had atrophied; they had never been taught to doubt and so to think, their poverty had denied them the means to knowledge, free discussion had been suppressed. But now, the use of reason and the acquisition of knowledge was becoming widespread. Men everywhere are "found ready to yield whatever blood and torments, political, legal, or religious persecution may still demand, till moral science shall be as unshackled as physical science, till *nothing* shall be esteemed too sacred for the uncompromising scrutiny of reason, and till all support shall be withdrawn from all institutions, old or new, but their *perceived utility*".[2] The many obstacles still to be overcome, for instance the taxes on knowledge—on books and the political press—these will soon be pushed aside. The time is not far distant when human beings will begin to be "educated to truth alone, according to the evidence, without any pre-excited partialities for any opinions". Once this is achieved, the education of adults will be so rapid and have so profound and extensive an influence as is "hardly now to be conceived".[3]

Like Carlile and Owen, Thompson was sharply critical of existing schools, from those for the upper to those for the labouring classes. As for the intellectual education of the former, little progress had been made, first because little real knowledge existed either about the physical world or about morals, and second, because of ignorance

---

[1] Thompson, *op. cit.*, 223   [2] *Ibid.*, 228.   [3] *Ibid.*, 231-2.

as to the communication of knowledge. Therefore, what was taught, "or professed to be taught, at schools," necessarily consisted of "mere words, or idle speculations, or empty precepts, impotent even when tending to good".[1]

In education generally, nothing of any significance had been achieved. All attention is "directed to the exclusive advantage of the privileged . . . who could provide for their own education". Ninety-nine out of a hundred people are shut out from the universities, whose aim is "the support of certain prescribed opinions and institutions". There "all doubt and examination were denounced as *vices*, and deserving of horror and punishment." In short, the universities are "establishments, to drill the unproductive, at the expense of the productive classes, into interested and zealous machines for perpetuating the institutions, however pernicious, under which they originated, and *keeping down* for ever from knowledge and consequently from comfort the great mass of the community, by monopolising the little real, or supposed knowledge of the times".[2]

Thompson advances the claim that the universities be turned to the improvement of the whole of society. Further, the masses must be educated, but not according to the present approved methods of mass instruction. Here, after referring to the long period when any spread of education was opposed "as a most alarming evil" by those with a vested interest in the preservation of existing institutions, Thompson sharply criticises the "failure" of the monitorial schools derived from Bell and Lancaster:

> "The reasons for the failure are obvious. Its partisans were too sanguine, and expected too much from it as a *single* instrument of good. Many of them were *viciously* determined to make use of the new instrument, to diffuse, *without enquiry*, their peculiar views on moral subjects, particularly theological, as were their opponents; hence the contest was, who should have the drilling of the machines by the new mode; whether to truth or error, they were still, and equally, to be drilled; the object was not to give the people knowledge for their *own sakes*, but to swell the numbers of the future partisans of some unimportant dogma."

The "radical defect in the systems of Bell and Lancaster", Thompson underlines, is "that the understanding is by them altogether sacrificed to the memory". As a consequence, what little effect school

---

[1] Thompson, *op. cit.*, 235.   [2] *Ibid.*, 235-6.

education has had up to now, has been "to co-operate with existing institutions in forming passive habits of blind obedience".[1] To leave education in the hands of sects and parties would, then, be to connive at the inculcation of sectarian views and the upholding of exclusive interests.

In opposition to this approach, Thompson advances the interest of the community as a whole and the right of all men to a truly enlightened education. It is in the interests of all that truth should prevail. National education must be founded on the whole community, and, instead of transmitting mere opinions, must diffuse truth.

> "The members of every community of sentient rational beings, and of course the majority of those members, should be educated for their own sakes, with a view to their own happiness, and not to increase the number of the followers of the opinions, physical or metaphysical, theological or anti-theological, or to be made instrumental to the interests of any class or classes of men whatsoever; they should be educated for *their own sakes alone*. And it is clearly the interest of every community, in order to form right judgments, to see things as they really are, the real qualities and relations of physical objects, real facts and the real consequences of actions, it is their interest to be taught *nothing but the truth*; the truth meaning nothing more than this."[2]

How is this to be done?

> "First, by discarding at once about nine-tenths of the utterly useless matter now taught, or pretended to be taught, to the richer classes; second, by retaining the one-tenth of useful matter; and third, by substituting highly useful and interesting matter from the lately investigated experimental and practical sciences, entirely adapted to the minds of youth, for the parrot-memory work of grammars and foreign words now practised."[3]

By these means the majority of the community can become as intelligent, moral and happy as are already the best of men. National education of this kind will increase the productive power of labour and ensure that all the talent in the community is developed "and brought forward for the public service"; thereby the sciences and the arts "would be everywhere advancing and improving".[4] The children of the poorer classes, because they are not cossetted like those

---

[1] Thompson, *op. cit.*, 232-3.   [2] *Ibid.*, 239.   [3] *Ibid.*, 240.   [4] *Ibid.*, 245.

of the rich and do things for themselves instead of being constantly watched over, develop qualities of initiative and a greater aptitude to profit from intellectual instruction than the child of wealthy parents. When they reach school age, however, they are neglected while the rich are educated; yet "the excitement to a poor child when put into a theatre of education, is greater than to a rich child. To the poor 'tis a gain, a source of hope, a novelty, an introduction to those above him; to the rich child, it is a loss of liberty, a source of dread because of restraint, nothing novel but everything less comfortable than at home, and no honour in the introduction to poorer children or to a dreaded schoolmaster, nor any indefinite hope of future advantage".[1] Thompson concludes with the outline of a scheme for raising the necessary money to finance a universal system of education covering the whole country.

(v) Thomas Hodgskin and the Understanding of Society

The same faith in the power of knowledge to bring about social change inspired Thomas Hodgskin, even though he did not accept the co-operative "vision". It was his primary aim to make clear to the working class the fundamental nature of the conflict of interest between worker and capitalist; to explain that the latter took from the worker, the producer of all value, the greater part of what was his due. It is, Hodgskin affirms, in order to preserve this state of affairs that the capitalist "prevents the labourer from knowing on what *natural* laws his existence and happiness depends".

Labour Defended against the Claims of Capital (1825) incorporates a powerful attack on contemporary political economy, in particular on James Mill's theory of profits and interest.[2] Hodgskin framed his argument to win public opinion to the side of the labourers, but was concerned, above all, to convince the workers of the justice of their case and their right to pitch their claims high and combine against the capitalist class to win them.

"The manual labourers," he wrote, "oppressed by the capitalist, have never been paid high enough, and even now are more disposed to estimate their own deserts rather by what they have hitherto received than by what they produce. This sort of prejudice makes it,

---

[1] Thompson *op. cit.*, 247.

[2] "Mr. Mill's account of these effects, though not so precise, is still more astounding. 'The labourer,' he says, 'has neither raw materials nor tools. These are *provided* for him by the capitalist. For *making this provision* the capitalist of course *expects a reward*!' " *Labour Defended against the Claims of Capital* (1922 edn), 34.

and will long make it, difficult even for labourers themselves to apportion with justice the social reward or wages of each individual labourer." On the other hand, the capitalists, who live by profit and interest, "have no just claim but custom to any share of the national produce".[1] In fact, contemporary workers, descended from bondsmen and serfs, still suffer from the bondage of their ancestors; their claim to a proper reward has never been tried on the principles of justice.

All this can be changed now that, for the first time in history, the workers are becoming educated and so beginning to understand the truth, "to probe all things to the bottom". It is impossible to suppose that they can much longer be kept in ignorance of the principles on which societies are formed and governed. "No Holy Alliance can put down the quiet insurrection by which knowledge will subvert whatever is not founded in justice and truth"; the workers will not "stop short in their career of enquiry. They may care nothing about the curious researches of the geologist or the elaborate classification of the botanist, but they will assuredly ascertain *why* they only of all classes of society have always been involved in poverty and distress." In this process "as the labourers acquire knowledge, the foundations of the social edifice will be dug up from the deep beds into which they were laid in times past, they will be curiously handled and closely examined, and they will not be restored unless they were originally laid in justice, and unless justice commands their preservation".[2]

To spread a true understanding of the nature of society—this was the main aim of Hodgskin's economic writings and of his public lectures, including those delivered at the London Mechanics' Institution, later printed under the title *Popular Political Economy* (1827). In these lectures and writings, Hodgskin tirelessly transmitted his message: that the workers had but to discover the truth, to apply the basic principles of justice to existing institutions, for evils to be eliminated and give place to a just social order.

Owen, Carlile, Hodgskin and Thompson provided important theoretical guidance within the working-class movement in the decade before the Reform Act. They taught the principles of co-operation and the justice of combination to wrest from the capitalist what was the worker's due. Alongside the small producers' co-operative societies the trade unions also made rapid progress, following the repeal

[1] T. Hodgskin, *Labour defended against the Claims of Capital* (1922 edn), 89-90.
[2] *Ibid.*, 100.

of the Combination Acts in 1825, when workers began to combine in an organised way on a much larger scale to defend their rights. All the theorists linked with the need for such social and political action the need for education, regarding this as the necessary accompaniment, if not prerequisite, of a transformation of society.

In the late 1820s and early 30s the demand for a new kind of education became a central theme, not only advanced in the press and at meetings, but also finding a practical outlet in the establishment of new institutions and schools.

3. THE MOVEMENT FOR AN INDEPENDENT EDUCATION

(i) *Educational Activities of the Early Co-operative Societies*

In 1825, the London Co-operative Society, preparing for the "formation of a community on Principles of Mutual Co-operation" outside London, drew up its articles of agreement. In Article XII is to be found a clear expression of the educational aims of the growing body of co-operators:

"To all the children entering the Community, or born within it, we guarantee the best physical and intellectual education that the present state of human knowledge affords, *an advantage for which our peculiar arrangements afford facilities not to be obtained by any exertion of toil, or sacrifice of wealth, in the present state of society*. To maintain uninterrupted health during the longest possible life, and to render that life the most happy, diversified by all the innocent pleasures of sense, of active exertion, of knowledge, of sympathy, and mutual benevolence, with every variety and combination of these enjoyments will be the great objects of the general education of the whole Community. The *mode* of education, combining always practice with theory, the Community will hereafter determine. To individual parents, and those teachers in whom they confide, the teaching of their peculiar religious tenets is assured: with religious instruction the general teachers are forbidden to interfere."[1]

This was to generalise the experience of co-operative communities which had succeeded in establishing schools for the children of members. But the London scheme, like those at Edinburgh and Orbiston, failed through lack of funds, and subsequently co-operators turned to less ambitious plans; primarily to the formation of smaller producers' co-operatives and trading communities which spread rapidly

[1] John Gray, *A Lecture on Human Happiness* (1931 edn), Appendix, 7-8.

in succeeding years. Prominent among these was the society founded at Brighton in 1827.[1]

Composed almost entirely of working men,[2] the society ran a journal, *The Co-operator*, edited by Dr. William King, from 1828-30, which exercised a leading influence at this crucial period when the principles of co-operation were first translated into practice. So much is this so, that King has often been regarded as the founder of this early phase of the co-operative movement.

The model rules for such societies, published in *The Co-operator*, once more show the emphasis given to the education of both old and young:

"Those members who have leisure, should meet at the room and form themselves into classes for mutual instruction. As the societies will consider labour to be the source of all wealth, and therefore be called Working Unions, so they will perceive that labour must be directed by *Knowledge* and therefore they will acquire all the useful knowledge they possibly can."

The same principle applied to children. Members, it is said, will

"pay particular attention to the education of their children. They should select the best school the neighbourhood affords; and agree to send their children to the same, on condition that the members of the society may visit the school and notice the progress of the children. But a still more desirable plan would be, to have a school of their own, and employ a master, at a salary."[3]

In fact, the Brighton Society established its own school, appointing one of the members to act as schoolmaster and librarian. The need for education was early brought home to co-operators who had set themselves the aim of establishing self-governing productive communities. If they were to accumulate sufficient capital out of the surplus produced by trading, to purchase the necessary land and machinery, and to make the community a going concern, then knowledge of various kinds was essential. Once the community was firmly established, there would be a possibility of immensely increasing the

---

[1] Podmore, *op. cit.*, 385.

[2] "Agricultural labourers, carpenters, bricklayers, printers, cabinet-makers, turners, painters, gardeners, dressmakers, bakers, tailors, tinmen, coppersmiths, shoe-makers, bookbinders, grocers, domestic servants, etc." *Ibid.*, 385.

[3] *The Co-operator*, No. 6, October 1st, 1828, 21. The original journal is reprinted in *Dr. William King and the Co-operator, 1828-30* (1922).

range of their knowledge; this, following Owen, was the perspective which King held out, insisting on the untapped abilities of the mass of the workers. With command of their own machinery and labour, the members of a co-operative community could shorten the working day and have leisure for the acquisition of knowledge.

"Their minds are as capable of acquiring knowledge as those of other people. Almost all men of science have risen out of workmen. They only want leisure and opportunity. Capital will give them both, and labour will give them capital: therefore they have everything in their own hands—labour, capital and knowledge, and therefore independence, virtue and happiness."[1]

Here is an idea contrasting strongly with that of the philosophic radicals who, assuming the dependence of the workers on the capitalist, suggested that they might develop the qualities of benevolence and tolerance but could not attain to the heights of intelligence and independence.

With the development of the co-operative movement, the linking together of hundreds of societies took place in a number of ways. In 1829 the British Association for Promoting Co-operative Knowledge was founded, of which Lovett acted as secretary for a time. By 1831, at the second co-operative congress, the movement could speak with an authoritative voice on education and is found urging all societies to found schools. The resolution calls for the establishment of "Schools of Industry for the formation of a superior physical, moral and intellectual character" in the children "at the least expense to their parents". Societies are advised to apply a portion of subscriptions and trading profits "to the maintenance of proper teachers", and also to make schoolrooms available on Sundays and other days for members "to hear Lectures on Co-operation and other subjects, to hold Discussions and read co-operative works and Newspapers— forming a school of Mutual Instruction, and discontinuing their attendance at Public Houses as places of meeting or amusement".[2]

There is evidence that many societies followed this plan. Speaking at the third national congress of the movement in 1832, a Lancashire representative said that the members of local societies believed that "the power of producing wealth was not sufficient, without knowledge to teach them how to distribute their wealth"; all co-operative

---

[1] *The Co-operator*, No. 8, December 1st, 1828.
[2] *Report of Proceedings of Second Co-operative Congress*, October 1831, 24.

establishments in Lancashire, therefore, had "attached schools of know-ledge and industry, which served not only for their own and their children's instruction, but as places of meeting".[1]

There were also attempts to promote socialist schools independently of co-operative societies. There were at least three in London by the mid-1830s; an infant school in Charlotte Street, a Free School for "children of the disciples of Robert Owen" in Golden Square and the "Westminster National School and General Scientific Institution".[2] Owenite schools were also to be found particularly in the industrial north, at Bolton, Bradford, Runcorn, Salford, Worsley, Newark and other population centres.[3] At Salford, in 1832, a Sunday and evening school successfully provided for up to 200 children, despite strong opposition from the local clergy, one of whom is said to have "stated from the pulpit that the parents would go to hell if they sent their children there".[4]

In the late 1820s and early 30s, then, co-operative societies regarded the establishment of schools and the organisation of educative dis-cussions as an integral aspect of their life and work. Later, there began the establishment of schools alone in some centres of population, and this was to be followed by more ambitious projects to provide meeting-places for adult workers. Such were in the air in the Manchester dis-trict before 1832. Owen's biographer, Lloyd Jones, describes how the more active propagandists set about extending their work. When the Salford co-operative store closed its doors in 1831,

"we set to work in a different fashion. We had counters and shelves' and a few tables and chairs, so we took a couple of large rooms ... and opened a school for the instruction of boys and girls and such adults as might think it worth while to learn what we had to teach."

[1] *The Crisis*, ed R. Owen, Vol. I, No. 4, April 28th, 1832, 15.

[2] *Ibid.*, Vol. II, No. 34, August 24th, 1833; Vol. III, No. 19, January 4th, 1834; Vol. III, No. 20, January 11th, 1834. The constitution of the Charlotte Street school includes the following points:

  1 Every child shall be encouraged to express his or her opinion.
  2 No creed or dogma shall be imposed on any.
  3 Admitted facts alone shall be placed before the pupils, from which they shall be allowed to draw their own deductions.
  4 No distinctions shall exist, but all shall be treated with equal kindness.
  5 Neither praise nor blame, merit nor de-merit, rewards nor punishments, shall be awarded to any; kindness and love to be the only ruling powers.
  6 Both sexes shall have equal opportunities of acquiring useful knowledge.

[3] *Proceedings of the Third Co-operative Congress* (April 23rd, 1832). Ed W. Carpenter (1832); *Proceedings of the Fourth Co-operative Congress* (October 1st, 1832). Ed W. Pare (1832), Statistical Tables.

[4] *The Crisis*, Vol. I, No. 29, September 22nd, 1832, 116.

Among their number were two carpenters who transformed shelves and counters into desks and forms and soon a house-to-house canvass had drawn pupils of all ages, from twelve to forty.[1] School was held in the evenings and all day Sunday, adults and children being to some extent taught together. The subjects taught included the three Rs, drawing, singing, music and dancing, as well as mathematics, science (geology, astronomy, chemistry) and political economy. This school, which had as many as 170 scholars, was to continue in being for six years, acting as an intellectual, social and propaganda centre for the Owenite movement in the Manchester district; and, also, as an inspiration to other educational ventures, such as the Hulme Sunday School and the Co-operative Industrial School at Worsley. When, in the late 1830s, it was transformed into one of the first Owenite "Co-operative and Scientific Institutions" or Halls of Science, a new phase of educational activity had begun.[2]

(ii) *New Mechanics' Institutes*

If the co-operative societies could establish their own schools without outside interference, once they had succeeded in organising a self-sufficient community or obtaining their own premises, elsewhere there must be action of another kind to secure workers' control of educational institutions.

In London, as we have seen, there was a long struggle before the Radicals and Whigs finally managed to wrest control of the Mechanics' Institute from the workers and their allies, and assume direction. At the outset, Thomas Hodgskin and his friend Robertson had urged that if the institution "was to be of real service to the workers" it must be entirely under their control; for, as they saw it, to be of use to the workers education must have the aim of equipping them for the struggle against capital. "Men had better be without education", they wrote in the article which first proposed the establishment of the institution, "than be educated by their rulers; for then education is but the mere breaking in of the steer to the yoke; the mere discipline of a hunting dog, which, by dint of severity, is made to forego the strongest impulse of his nature, and instead of devouring his prey, to hasten with it to the feet of his master".[3]

[1] Lloyd Jones, *The Life, Times and Labours of Robert Owen* (ed W. C. Jones 1890), Vol. II, 47.

[2] *Proceedings of the Third Co-operative Congress; Proceedings of the Fourth Co-operative Congress; The Crisis*, Vol. III, Nos. 7 and 8, October 19th, 1833, 58-9.

[3] *Mechanic's Magazine*, No. 7, October 11th, 1823, 100.

It is small wonder that Francis Place stopped at nothing to discredit such promoters and to divert the project to other ends; ends which were, in fact, not far removed from those which Hodgskin and Robertson so vividly expose.

Elsewhere, for instance at Manchester, Leeds and Birmingham, business men who had themselves taken the initiative in establishing Mechanics' Institutes firmly kept control in their own hands from the start. Their aim was to use their powers to instil their own doctrines of the freedom of industry and the security of property, and to ensure this they banned all political and religious controversy and any form of free discussion; normally not even allowing newspapers on the premises. At the same time, their dealings with the workers inevitably had an air of patronage and condescension which repelled the very people whose minds and attitudes they wished to influence.

It was at the Andersonian Institute at Glasgow, the prototype of all Mechanics' Institutes, that the first decisive reaction to treatment of this kind took place. It was sparked off by interference in the management of the library and equipment which had been under the workers' control. The final outcome was that a large proportion of the workers seceded from the institute and formed the independent "Glasgow Mechanics' Institution" in 1823. The breakaway body enrolled 374 members, and the question of maintaining its financial and therefore its educational independence was to the fore from the start, the new body forthwith resolving "that, as the Institution had been begun without the assistance of the wealthy and influential citizens of Glasgow, it should continue without asking for their support, and that such property as it might acquire should belong to the Mechanics of Glasgow for ever".[1]

Brougham, in his *Practical Observations*, had warned that it might be as well not to ride the workers on too tight a rein; to allow them a considerable degree of control, even political discussion, might be an advantage. Clearly, if the object was to win skilled workers to the support of capital, it could not be achieved by treatment likely to keep all self-respecting workers away. But this lesson was not learned. In Manchester in particular, Heywood and his fellow industrialists would make no concession in spite of continued protests and refused to allow the workers even a share in the government of the Institute.

[1] J. W. Hudson, *The History of Adult Education* (1851), 43; M. Tylecote, *The Mechanics' Institutes of Lancashire and Yorkshire before 1851* (1957), 17; *Mechanic's Magazine*, No. 7, October 11th, 1823, 100-1.

When the reaction came here, it was not a response to minor irritations, but once more in the form of a challenge to the very conception that the middle class should monopolise and control the workers' education in their own interests. The moving spirit behind the establishment of independent Mechanics' Institutes in Lancashire—first in Hulme and Salford and then in Manchester itself—was Rowland Detrosier, who firmly believed that "knowledge to the people is the true basis of their political power"; and that to gain the necessary knowledge the workers must found and administer their own educational centres.[1]

This time it was a self-educated worker, born and bred in the heart of the Lancashire cotton industry, who took up the ideas of the theoreticians and translated them into practice. In 1829 Detrosier became the first president of the breakaway Manchester Institute. Two years later he was appealing for a further development.

In his lecture, *On the Advantages of the Intended Mechanics' Hall of Science* (1831), Detrosier, taking up the theme that man is the creature of his education and circumstances, argues forcibly that the degradation of the working class is not of their own making. His straightforward statement of working-class experience contrasts strongly with the detached analysis of the philosophic radicals, who so often succeeded in placing all the blame for the evils of advancing capitalism on the workers themselves; and, too, with that of James Kay which saw in the miseries of the workers cause, not so much for sympathy as for fear. "Are there not", asks Detrosier,

"thousands in this enlightened country, whose circumstances bequeath to them little beside rising to labour and lying down to rest? Are there not thousands in this humane country with whom labour commences almost before infancy has passed? Thousands, the whole of whose education presents to them scarcely anything more edifying than the examples of ignorance and brutality"?

If the workers were no longer serfs, they were yet

"the slaves of commerce, and the victims of bad government. Urged to exertion by the powerful stimulus of recurring wants, the imperious demands of their necessitous situation, the whole of their energies are directed to the attainment of one all-engrossing object,

[1] Tylecote, *op. cit.*, 137; G. J. Holyoake, *History of Co-operation* (1875), Vol. I, 361. Detrosier's foundation of Mechanics' Institutes in Hulme and Salford is referred to in the "Memoir of the late Rowland Detrosier" by his friend, Alderman John Shuttleworth, which appeared in the *Manchester Times*, December 1834.

sustenance for the body; and this necessity has been taken advantage of, to push their powers of production to the greatest extent."[1]

If they are to free themselves from this exploitation, the working class must achieve political power; in order to do so they must acquire political and moral knowledge. This, affirms Detrosier, will never be provided by their betters; they will gain it only in educational centres of a new kind under their own control.

"How can the working men of this country become intelligent, submitted as they are to an education which is the veriest mockery that ever insulted the human understanding? When shall they find time to devote themselves to study, who have scarcely time to swallow their food from one week's end to another? To the first enquiry I answer, become yourselves the founders and supporters of Institutions where the governing principle shall be the greatest possible knowledge to each, that all may enjoy the greatest possible happiness. Where the business of youthful education shall be to form the character of the future man; where the highest honours shall be reserved for those who are best prepared to perform their civil and political duties; where, in short, education shall be rationally conducted, and where your daughters shall be taught to become good wives and good mothers, and your sons good citizens, husbands and fathers."[2]

It is not only the right upbringing of youth but the political and educational organisation of workers that Detrosier has in view. There are, he goes on, many political and economic issues which the workers must discuss together before they can decide on the measures to be adopted for the cure of their ills. But suppose they do unite to "devise means to protect the value of . . . labour", where can they go to discuss their plans? To the public house? "Still are your meetings in the camp of your enemies . . . The little you earn is made less by a fruitless and criminal expenditure, and your opponents become more sure of their victims." There is an easy remedy. "You have no room that you can call your own—why not build one? Why not erect for yourselves a hall which . . . you may truly term your own, in which you may meet, not only for the protection of the value of your labour, and for existing political purposes, but also to celebrate the anniversaries of

[1] Rowland Detrosier, *Address on the Necessity of an Extension of Moral and Political Instruction among the Working Class* (1831), 13.

[2] Rowland Detrosier, *An Address on the Advantages of the Intended Mechanics' Hall of Science delivered at the New Mechanics' Institution, December 31, 1831.*

those great political events by which a greater degree of freedom and prosperity has been obtained and secured for mankind?"[1]

So Detrosier adjures the workers to build a reading room, a coffee room, a theatre where they can discuss the great questions of "capital, population, supply and demand; and last, not least, the subjects which occupy so much of the working man's attention at the present time, the wages of labour and co-operative unions". Here also, their children could receive an education comparatively cheap and "superior . . . to any at present within reach of the poor"; an education which would prepare them to build a new society.

> "You sigh for reform—you pant for the establishment of cheap and efficient government—you demand an attention to the interests of the many: one short twenty years of such a general moral and political education would give to this country a youthful host so firm in moral principle, so schooled in true political justice, and so *prepared to establish and support it*, that the expression of their wills would be omnipotent to effect all that humanity can hope for or desire."[2]

Here, in the main centre of factory production in the north, is a clear expression of the working-class demand for education and enlightenment; not in any abstract terms, but as part of a live movement for political and industrial action, inspired by the Owenite vision of the good society based on reason and justice.

Detrosier's initiative was to gain immediate support from John Doherty, leader and organiser of the Lancashire cotton operatives, the most influential trade unionist of his time. In a forthright leader in his journal *The Poor Man's Advocate and People's Library*, Doherty praises this spirited attempt "to erect a building which shall be the property, as well as the school-house, of the artisans and mechanics of Manchester, and in which every branch of human knowledge may be cheaply communicated to those who have hitherto been kept ignorant, that they might be the more easily duped".

He goes on to underline that while many institutions have been established "professing to be for the exclusive use of the working class—mechanics' institutions—not one of them has ventured to teach or communicate that species of knowledge which, of all others, is the most closely connected with, and essential to, their social happiness, and moral regeneration, *political* knowledge, or the mode of

---

[1] Detrosier, *ibid.*, 4.   [2] *Ibid.*, 5, 6.

managing their affairs as a community". The teachers in these institutions, Doherty observes ironically, "seem to imagine, that it is of much more consequence to the working man to understand 'the theory of the winds', which it is impossible he can control, than the theory of government, which can render him either happy or miserable; thus adding insult to injury". First, "we are stripped of the produce of our own industry", then "those who are enjoying it endeavour to divert our attention from the system which beggars us, in order that the work of plunder may go safely on".

To found an independent Mechanics' Hall of Science is the very answer needed. "Let us reject, with disdain, the stunted lessons which aristocratic pride would have us be grateful for, and provide for ourselves the abundant and unrestrained feast for our mental and hungry appetites." It is clear that the intentions of the Radicals have not passed Doherty by, for he continues: "Let the huxtering owners of the misnamed Mechanics' Institutions, and the would-be rulers of mechanics' minds, see that the day is gone by when the millions will be satisfied with the puny morsel of mental food which aristocratic pride and pampered cunning have been wont to deal out to them. Let them see, in reality, that 'the schoolmaster is abroad'."

"Once a Manchester Hall of Science has been erected, the example will be too good, too glorious, not to spread with the rapidity of contagion."[1] And the work had already begun and begun bravely, with over 800 £1 shares taken up. Finally Doherty draws attention to Detrosier's appeal:

"Working men of Manchester and this district, aid us in carrying this humane plan into execution; lay the foundation-stone of your children's emancipation; be partakers in the glorious work of humanity which we are seeking to effect, and leave to your successors a monument of your sincerity in the advocacy of human happiness. You owe it to yourselves, you owe it to your children, you owe it to your country and to posterity. Abandon the public-house, which adds strength to the chain that binds you to poverty and to political degradation, and become yourselves the fabricators of your own independence."[2]

In Birmingham also a similar project was in the air and in 1833 the Builders' Union resolved to erect a Guild Hall. This decision was

[1] *The Poor Man's Advocate and People's Library*, No. 6, February 25th, 1832, 43-4.
[2] Detrosier, *Address on the Advantages of the Intended Mechanics' Hall of Science*, 8.

taken in the heat of a battle with the employers, who had set out to smash the Union with the weapon of "the document". Robert Owen attended the annual delegate meeting held at Manchester in September of that year, when he spoke on the theme that labour is the source of all wealth; there is little doubt that the delegates were greatly influenced by his policies. The Guild Hall was to comprise not only offices and a meeting place, but also schools for adults and children. This project was reported in *The Pioneer*: "One of the most important and highly desirable objects, connected with the present great movement of the working mass, is about to be achieved by the united builders of Birmingham: namely, the erection of a Union Hall or Operative Builders Institution." There would be a hall to hold a thousand, or three times this number standing, and a suite of committee rooms. "This, we believe, will be the first successful attempt on the part of the operatives of England to possess their own place of Assembly. We say THEIR OWN: for the Mechanics' Institutes already established in this country are anything but such: though we are willing to admit, that in many instances they have been productive of good."[1]

Thus, by the early 1830s, working-class leaders had become convinced of the imperative need for knowledge as a means to effective political action and eventual social transformation. First in the Corresponding societies, and later in the mass movements of 1815-19, they had begun to link systematic education with political agitation designed to bring about social and economic change. In the latter period, the education of children was seen as an essential part of this movement—an education in science and reason as opposed to the inculcation of particular religious creeds and dogmas.

It was at this period that the political economists who developed Ricardo's teaching from the point of view of the working class began to provide a theoretical foundation for working-class activity. Just as Place and Mill set out to propagate those economic laws which, if diffused and accepted, would facilitate the development of capitalism, so the political economists who, in effect, supported the working class, popularised their own analysis and plans. These, together with the rationalist outlook derived from Paine, found a widespread response. In the 1820s and early 30s, the struggle between these opposing views, concretised in the actual experiences of the workers, resulted in a growing understanding of the need for a new kind of education,

[1] *The Pioneer*, November 2nd, 1833; see also R. W. Postgate, *The Builders' History* n.d.), 100-10.

involving a conscious opposition to the forms of education the employers and others had seen fit to provide. Hence the moves to found independent institutes and schools for the true enlightenment of the workers.

By 1832, the principles at stake were becoming clear. New institutions were already being set up, forms of independent working-class activity already established. In that year the Reform Act was passed, the Whigs remaining in power with Brougham again as Lord Chancellor. The workers had gained nothing from their joint agitation with the middle class for the extension of the franchise and the reform of Parliament. From this point a new stage opens in the relations between these two classes; for the first time the working class began to emerge as an independent political force.

CHAPTER V

THE WORKERS' MOVEMENT AND EDUCATION (II),
1832–1850

"THIS Brougham was always a great stickler for popular education", wrote the *Northern Star*, organ of the Chartist movement,
in the revolutionary year of 1848. "Indeed the whole batch of Malthusian conspirators signalised, and still signalise themselves, by an
affected regard for the 'mental culture' of the people"; though it was
plain to see that the object of the new Poor Law (which had Brougham's
wholehearted support) was the prostration of the masses to the classes
above them. No wonder Cobbett had "held in the utmost abhorrence,
the wretches who, mouthing 'education', tried to make them slaves.
In our day, the Educationists are still what they were in Cobbett's
time—the pretended friends, but the real enemies of the people. . . .
Ah gentlemen, we see through your craft. . . . You would educate us,
not, as you sometimes pretend, to fit us for the exercise of political
rights, but to make us indifferent to these rights. And you call yourselves 'Philosophical Radicals'."[1]

This uncomprising statement epitomises the reaction of the most
advanced section of the working class to the educational tactics of the
bourgeoisie. Already before 1832, as we have seen, such men as
Doherty, who were directly engaged in the struggle with the employers and the establishment of trade union organisation, grasped
the point and consciously promoted independent educational institutions. Equally, in 1831, Hetherington's the *Poor Man's Guardian* was
consistently warning that, notwithstanding the wooing of the workers
in the political field, the intention was to exclude them from the
franchise, that the Reform Bill was a "Humbug Bill" to be exposed
and opposed as such.

With the advent of the Reformed Parliament these warnings and
policies were much more widely appreciated and understood. The
government of which Brougham was Lord Chancellor persecuted the
working-class press even more viciously than had the Tory administration of 1819.[2] Moreover, while paying lip service to the need **to**

---

[1] *Northern Star*, January 29th, 1848.
[2] A. Aspinall, *Politics and the Press, 1780–1850* (1949), 60.

extend the franchise and promote education, Radicals connived at policies in the industrial field which made increased education for the workers and their children impossible. While opposing the limitation of adult hours of labour they gave outright support to the new Poor Law which epitomised the Benthamite approach to social problems, sweeping away old practices and safeguards in the interests of efficiency and treating the poor in the way Malthus had advocated. As, at a time of economic upheaval, the majority of the working class ran the risk of going on relief, the new provisions aroused the deepest resentment and mass protest.

This movement, based on the industrial north, was to merge in 1838 with the continuing campaign of London artisans and others for freedom of the press, a campaign which itself developed into a wider movement for electoral and governmental reform as set out in the People's Charter. So the struggle for economic demands, for the 10 Hours Bill, for repeal of the Poor Law, for freedom of speech and the extension of the franchise fused together in the Chartist movement, aimed first and foremost at the winning of political rights as the means to power. This movement dominated political events in the decade 1838-48. It was inspired not only by the radical tradition derived from Paine and the Owenite vision, but also by the example of the proletarian movement under Babeuf in revolutionary France. It was Bronterre O'Brien, whose influence gained him the title of "schoolmaster of Chartism," who applied the lessons of the French Revolution to argue that the English middle class, having achieved their own ends in 1832, were beginning a counter-revolution against their former allies the working class. In this situation it was imperative for the working class to take the revolution to its logical conclusion by destroying the power of this new class of oppressors. Only in this way could their demands be won.

It is, then, on the eve of the Reform Act that independent working-class policies begin to be advanced covering political, economic and educational demands. In 1831 the paper chiefly expressing them is founded, the *Poor Man's Guardian*. Though some working-class leaders are still influenced by middle-class Radicals and social reformers, others increasingly develop a distinctive approach to the great issues of the day. Moreover, steps are taken to organise, and to co-ordinate, different sections of the workers' movement with the aim of conducting a united struggle for political rights.

At this period attention shifts to the different sections within the working-class movement which, though pursuing broadly similar educational aims of the kind already outlined—promoting their own halls and schools—differ on vital questions of political strategy and tactics. Initially the Owenites turn from co-operative and trade union organisations to exclusively educational propaganda. As the struggle sharpens in 1839 and 1840 there is a growing division within the Chartist movement itself. One section, representing the artisans rather than the factory workers, turns to the elaboration of broadly educational projects, and attempts to realise them, while the active movement concentrates on the political struggle for the franchise as the only means of winning universal education. It is, therefore, in the plans advanced by the former, led by William Lovett, that we find the fullest exposition of the educational outlook of this age as it is applied to methods of school organisation and teaching; while it is in the speeches of leading Chartists, and in articles in the chief Chartist journal the *Northern Star*, that the working-class attitude to the political issues of the day which touch on education—to Factory Acts, Education Bills and in general the educational attitudes of the middle class—is most fully expressed.

1. AN ORGANISED WORKING-CLASS MOVEMENT

In 1830 John Doherty had succeeded in forming in Lancashire the "National Association for the Protection of Labour", an attempt at an all-embracing national trade union organisation. The same year saw the birth in London of the Metropolitan Political Union, an association formed to exercise pressure for Parliamentary Reform under middle-class domination. By 1831 the London workers had broken away to found the National Union of the Working Classes and Others, one of the first independent working-class political organisations. The members of this union were generally known as the Rotundists from the place of their meeting—the "Rotunda"—a hall owned by Richard Carlile and developed as a centre of free discussion.

The new workers' organisation was most bitterly attacked by both Whigs and Tories,[1] but it throve and developed links with similar organisations throughout the country, while its mouthpiece, the *Poor Man's Guardian*, exposed and condemned the Whig Reform Bill for its failure to introduce universal suffrage and the ballot. The leaders were William Lovett and Henry Hetherington, a compositor by trade

[1] W. Lovett, *The Life and Struggles of William Lovett* (1876), 72.

who became publisher and editor of succeeding organs of the working-class press. Others were James Watson and John Cleave, a bookseller who also turned publisher and agitator for a free press. In May 1831, this organisation issued a "Declaration of Rights" including a demand that society and government "ought . . . to do all in their power to favour the progress of reason and truth, and to place instruction within the reach of all".[1] From the first, the National Union of the Working Classes and Others provided for the education of its members.

It was organised, writes Lovett, "on the plan of the Methodist Connexion. *Class-leaders* were appointed at public meetings of the members in the proportion of one for about every thirty or forty members; the class-leaders mostly meeting with their classes weekly at their own houses." At meetings "political subjects were discussed, and articles from the newspapers and portions of standard political works read and commented on."[2]

Branches of the union were established in various parts of London and weekly public meetings held. After the advent of the reformed Parliament and the introduction of a measure which permitted much stronger action against the 1d. press, the union was very active. Something of the spirit of the time can be caught from the many notices of meetings appearing in issues of the *Poor Man's Guardian*. That for January 12th, 1833, carries, among others, the following notice:

National Union of the Working Classes

Public Meetings of the Union will be held during the week at the following places:

Monday—Finsbury Forum, Helmet Row, St. Lukes.
        Messrs. Fowler, Cleave, Bailey, Mee and others.

        Three Jolly Gardeners, end of Lambeth Walk.
        Messrs. Young, Peck and others.

        Chapel, Chapel Court, High Street, Borough.
        Messrs. Plummer, Lynch, Petrie and Cast.

        Palmer's School Room, 2, Lower Chapman Street, St. George's in the East.
        Messrs. Wagget, Preston, Ferguson and Watts.

[1] "The National Union of the Working Classes and Others," *Carpenter's Monthly Political Magazine*, January 1832, 178ff.

[2] Lovett, *op. cit.*, 68.

Subject for discussion

"That the sublime effect which knowledge has had in the advancement of the progress of civilisation demonstrates the necessity of its unshackled and unrestrained diffusion to all ranks of society."

J. Watson requests the attendance of the members of his class (the 73rd) on Sunday afternoon, January 13th, at half-past Two o'clock, and every succeeding Sunday until further notice, at the same hour, at the Finsbury Forum, Helmet Row, St. Lukes.

The 41st, 78th and 106th classes are requested to meet at the Painted Red Lion, Islington Green, on Special business. Every member is particularly requested to attend. T. Preston. T. Cooper. A. Watts. Leaders.

TAXES ON KNOWLEDGE

A GENERAL GRAND MEETING will be held, in a few days, to devise the most efficient and immediate method of resistance to the detestable and unjustifiable Taxes on Knowledge; and to direct public execration against the Whigs, who, when out of office, were the most clamourous advocates for a Free Press, but now (eternal shame on the shirks!) are its most eager persecutors.

The case of citizen HETHERINGTON, confined in Clerkenwell Bastille, for publishing the POOR MAN'S GUARDIAN, will be especially considered.

The *Poor Man's Guardian* was, of course, an unstamped paper. It stated in bold type on the front page: "Established contrary to the Law, to try the power of 'Might' against 'Right'. Price 1*d*."; and its slogan was "Knowledge is Power". "Repeatedly convicted," wrote W. J. Linton later of his friend Hetherington, "hunted like a wild beast, imprisoned, stripped of his property, he gallantly maintained the contest to a successful ending."[1] At this time the sellers of the *Poor Man's Guardian* were unmercifully persecuted up and down the country; James Watson was jailed with Hetherington, Cleave and his wife seized, Heywood of Manchester, Guest of Birmingham, Hobson and Mrs. Mann of Leeds, and about 500 others suffered imprisonment, as sellers of the unstamped press. Yet at the same time prominent members of the government unctuously promoted the activities of the S.D.U.K. whose *Penny Magazine*, which had been

[1] W. J. Linton, *James Watson. A Memoir of the days of the Fight for a Free Press in England and of the Agitation for the People's Charter* (1880), 32.

launched in 1832 as part of the policy of providing innocent amusement for the workers, but which should equally have been stamped, circulated unchallenged.[1]

The reaction of the workers was sharp. Typical is that reported in a letter from the Leicester Branch of the National Union to the *Poor Man's Guardian*:[2]

"Sir,

At a meeting of the National Union of the Working Classes and Others, held at the Crown and Cushion, Church Gate, Leicester, January 14th, the following resolutions were put and carried unanimously:—

Moved by Mr. Jackson and seconded by Mr. Harrison:

That we look with the greatest detestation and abhorrence on the base spite, and vindictive malice, which could induce the vilest and most traitorous tyrants in office that ever cursed any country, to single out Mr. Hetherington, the publisher of the *Poor Man's Guardian*, for persecution; a man (as he is) of more political honesty and patriotic virtue, than the English government, individually or collectively, have possessed for the last hundred and twenty years; and this, too, whilst Brougham, and a whole host of *lying* editors, proprietors, and publishers of the *Penny Magazines*, *Omnibus*, and others too numerous to mention, all equally offending against the *damnable and detestable taxes on knowledge*, are suffered to go on with impunity, and even rewarded with honour, expressly because they either basely abuse and deceive the people, or attempt to divert their attention from their true state, and the cause of their distress, instead of showing these, and the Whig impostors, in their true colours, as the patriotic editor of the *Guardian* does; and we further resolve never to cease our exertions till we see tyrants and tyranny of every description overthrown, and 'Equal Rights' and 'Equal Laws' established.

Moved by Mr. Hughes and seconded by Mr. Cobley:

[1] Lord John Russell, Lord Auckland, Lord Althorp, Mr. (later Lord) Denman, Mr. Spring Rice (later Lord Monteagle), Sir Henry Parnell, "were always ready to work as members of our committee, even after they had been called to the highest offices of state", wrote Charles Knight. "After the Reform era I have sat at the monthly dinner with five Cabinet Ministers, to whom it appeared that their duty was to carry forward that advancing intelligence of the people which had conducted them to power. . . ." Charles Knight, *Passages of a Working Life* (1864), Vol. II, 131. (C. D. Collett shows conclusively that the *Penny Magazine* should have been prohibited as an unstamped paper, if the relevant Act had been equally implemented. *History of the Taxes on Knowledge*, (1899), Vol. I, 27-30.)

[2] *Poor Man's Guardian*, No. 86, January 26th, 1833, 31.

That the foregoing resolution be sent to the brave editor of the
Poor Man's Guardian for insertion.

> Mr. Weeks, Chairman. D. Brook, Secretary".

It seems clear, from this and much other evidence, that Francis
Place was right when he wrote that the Unionists "will read nothing
which the Diffusion Society meddles with. They call the members
of it Whigs, and the word whig with them, means a treacherous
rascal, a bitter, implacable enemy".[1]

Certainly contempt for the activities of the S.D.U.K. was expressed
at the Co-operative Congresses where the same men were active as
in the National Union. William Lovett opened the proceedings of
the 1832 Congress with a sharp attack on bourgeois political economy,
and subsequently Charles Knight's most recent publication, *The Results
of Machinery*, was held up to ridicule by one of the delegates, William
Pare:

" 'There is a glut of labourers,' says the Society, 'in the market.
If you (the labourers) continue in the market of labour during this
glut, your wages must fall. What is the remedy? To go out of the
market.' (Loud laughter.) 'When wheat falls five shillings at Mark
Lane,' continues the Society, 'the farmer receives a hint that the
supply is beyond the demand; he holds back for a few weeks, and
prices regain their former level. What enables the farmer to hold
back his corn? He has something to fall back upon; he is not compelled to sell his corn that week, or that month;—he is a capitalist.
Endeavour to acquire the same power yourselves. Become
capitalists.' (Laughter.)"

But how, asks Pare, can this advice be followed when wages are
so low?

"Upon this fallacious reasoning I will make but one remark:—
it is a gross delusion; and a greater insult could not be offered to the
working classes than the offer of such a remedy. (Loud cheers.)"[2]

Was the knowledge offered by the S.D.U.K. and its *Penny Magazine*
of any real use to the working class, asked James Watson, making
a criticism that was to be very generally levelled at the S.D.U.K.
in the next few years:

"Had it any tendency to improve their condition, by giving them
more of the fruits of their own labour? Would it lead them any

[1] Quoted by R. K. Webb, *The British Working Class Reader*, (1955), 144.
[2] *The Crisis*, Vol. I, Nos. 3 and 4, April 28th, 1832.

better to understand their rights, or to comprehend and act upon the principles of co-operation? No. They had been amusing the people with the fruit of their antiquarian researches about Charing Cross, and the fruit of their natural researches in descriptions of the Zoological Gardens. That was all very well and very useful in its place; but while he and others—tens and thousands of others—felt degraded in the land of their birth, having no participation in their political and social rights, and carrying about the brand of a slave on their foreheads, they were not in a condition to sit down coolly and philosophically to such investigations."[1]

With this outright rejection of the reading matter and forms of education sponsored by the middle class, went new efforts to provide independent meeting places and libraries. The National Union of Working Classes and Others was concerned with agitation and education on a whole number of political issues, if especially, at this period, with the struggle for the freedom of the press. But its leaders also sought to extend educational activities outside their own organisation, for instance through the establishment of coffee houses, which served as centres of radical thought and discussion outside the public house and where all the contemporary literature was made available.[2]

Thus John Doherty, after abandoning trade union organisation in the mid-1830s, turned to political education and bookselling, opening a coffee house where ninety-six newspapers and periodicals were taken each week. The reading fee was 1d. "Those who came—as scores did daily to keep abreast of news and opinions—could have a cup of coffee for 2d., a cup of tea for 2½d. or a boiled egg for a penny as they read their way through the journalism of the time."[3] In London Cleave kept a coffee house, while William Lovett—who had himself first heard Gale Jones, Robert Taylor, Richard Carlile and others speak at coffee houses when he came to London in 1823—opened "Lovett's Coffee and Conversation Rooms", with a library of several hundred volumes, in 1834.[4] An advertisement in the *Poor Man's Guardian* publicised this venture.[5] It lists twenty-eight journals, including *The Mechanic's Magazine*, *Westminster Review*, *Cobbett's Register*, *The Moral World*, and asks

[1] *Proceedings of the third Co-operative Congress*, April 23rd, 1832 (1832), Ed W. Carpenter, 70-1.
[2] See L. C. Wright, *Scottish Chartism* (1953), 179, for a reference to Chartist Coffee Houses in Scotland.
[3] Francis Williams, *Dangerous Estate*, (1957), 101; A. Aspinall, *op. cit.*, 26.
[4] Lovett, *op. cit.*, 36, 60, 88-9.
[5] *Poor Man's Guardian*, Vol. V, No. 195 February 28th, 1835, 448.

"Do you wish to read of the Contentions of the Whigs and Tories for Places and Emoluments? Do you wish to hear the opinions and speculations of the proppers, patchers, and repairers of Church and State? And do you wish to know what the Radicals, Destructives, and Republicans think of all those parties? Consult the following list of Mr. Lovett's publications:

(List of periodicals)

"Are you anxious to acquire correct information on leading political questions, to possess a knowledge of Political Economy, of the Social System, of the Science of Morality?—In fact, if you wish to know the best opinions of the best men who ever existed, on the most important subjects, W. L. begs to inform you that he has a Library of several hundred Volumes for the use of his customers gratuitously.

"Do you doubt the correctness of your own opinions? Come to *Lovett's Conversation Rooms*, and submit them to the test of Free Discussion. . . .

"W. L. further invites the Landholders to come and submit their reasons for holding an absolute right in land.

"Also the Fundholders, to show cause why the people should pay the interest, and respect the principal of a debt which was contracted for a purpose inimical to their interests.

"Also all Placemen, Sinecurists, and Pensioners of both sexes are invited to render an account of those services for which they are so handsomely paid.

"Also the Bishops, Parsons, and Preachers of all denominations are politely invited to preach to W. L.'s customers, provided they allow themselves to be asked questions.

"The Malthusians, Political Economists, Co-operators, and Anti-Co-operators, Believers, and Unbelievers, are specially invited; as they all profess to have knowledge to impart, and to be the advocates of the Truth. . . .

Coffee, per pint   ..   .. $3d.$
Egg ..   .. $1\frac{1}{2}d.$"

These coffee houses abounded—there were over 1,600 in London in 1840—and the majority of their customers were artisans.[1] Many had a clear educational purpose; so also, if at a humbler level, did the mutual improvement societies and the public readings which took place in inns and workshops.[2] All these activities helped to create

---

[1] Aspinall, *op. cit.*, 28.   [2] Webb, *op. cit.*, 34.

political consciousness and stimulated the desire of the workers to extend their knowledge.

To some it seemed that this was the most important work to be done. But this was, in large part, due to the failure of the more active trade union movement and renewed suppression of working-class attempts to organise in the struggle to maintain the level of wages and shorten the working day. Robert Owen's appearance at the congress of the newly founded Operative Builders' Union in 1833 and the influence of his ideas on the delegates, has already been referred to. Later in the same year Owen addressed a congress of representatives of trades unions and co-operative societies who were considering amalgamation. With the return of the delegates to their own organisations there began an intensive campaign to extend trade union organisation which brought immediate results in the form of the recruitment of thousands of workers up and down the country. This success, in turn, led to the establishment in February 1834, under Owenite leadership, of the Grand National Consolidated Trades Union which had as its immediate aim "to raise the wages of the workmen, or prevent any further reduction therein, and to diminish the hours of labour," and as its final purpose "to establish the paramount rights of Industry and Humanity, by . . . bringing about A DIFFERENT ORDER OF THINGS, in which the really useful and intelligent part of society only shall have the direction of its affairs".[1]

With the rapid accession of workers in all industries to the ranks of the Grand National it soon numbered half a million; while other organisations, such as the National Union of the Working Classes and Others, fell away. Members of the new Union, inspired by a new sense of purpose and strength, were almost immediately involved in strikes and lockouts over questions of wages, hours of work and the right to trade union organisation.

"You have heard, I doubt not," wrote Dr. Thomas Arnold of Rugby to a friend, "of the Trades' Unions; a fearful engine of mischief, ready to riot or to assassinate . . . and I see no counteracting power."[2] Inevitably there was to be no sympathy for the claims of the workers among those who believed themselves to be "the only really useful and intelligent part of society". But if Dr. Arnold could see no counteracting power the Whigs were ready with the weapon of

[1] Quoted by A. Hutt, *British Trade Unionism* (3rd edn 1945), 18.

[2] A. P. Stanley, *Life and Letters of Thomas Arnold* (1890 edn), 227 (letter dated September 29th, 1834).

repression, whose use by the Tories they had previously condemned, and they struck at the weakest link in the chain of organisation—the agricultural labourers. So, in 1834, the Loveless brothers and their associates stood trial and suffered transportation; and, while the middle-class social reformers averted their eyes, the first mass working-class demonstration of protest took place in Copenhagen Fields, near King's Cross, when well over 100,000 demonstrators expressed solidarity with the Tolpuddle Martyrs.

Nevertheless, the Grand National, partly as a result of internal struggle on the whole direction of policy, had disintegrated within a year and its Owenite leaders, who had emerged victorious and neither wished to nor were capable of leading strikes and action on this scale, once more turned all their attention to education and socialist propaganda as the means to realising "a different order of things." In this they were concerned with the regeneration of the working class through the inculcation of temperance and the pursuit of suitable forms of recreation, as well as the acquisition of knowledge and socialist ideas.

On the other hand, Lovett, Hetherington, Cleave, Watson and their associates founded in 1836 the London Working Men's Association, primarily to continue the political struggle for the workers' press. A small and select body consisting exclusively of the "intelligent and influential portion" of the workers, it proclaimed its purpose as the achievement of the "political and social rights" of the working class by every legal means but particularly through the dissemination of knowledge. In 1837, this organisation issued its famous *Address on Education* which reiterated the political argument for independent organisation and education.

"Think you a corrupt Government could perpetuate its exclusive and demoralising influence amid a people thus united and instructed? Could a vicious aristocracy find its servile slaves to render homage to idleness and idolatry to the wealth too often fraudulently exacted from industry? Could the present gambling influences of money perpetuate the slavery of millions, for the gains or dissipation of the few? Could corruption sit in the judgment seat—empty-headed importance in the senate-house—money-getting hypocrisy in the pulpit—and debauchery, fanaticism, poverty and crime stalk triumphantly through the land—if the millions were educated in a knowledge of their rights? No, no, friends; and hence the efforts of the exclusive few to keep the people ignorant and divided. Be ours the task, then, to unite and instruct them; for be assured the good that is to be must be begun by ourselves."[1]

It was in the same year that Lovett and his associates, in consultation with Francis Place, Roebuck and other middle-class Radicals, drew up a Bill embodying the demand for an extension of the franchise, the reform of electoral procedure, abolition of the property qualification and annual Parliaments. Inevitably this was not to be accepted by Parliament but it was published in May 1838, as the "People's Charter". Thereafter the Working Men's Association entered into the political field and established active branches to campaign for the Charter.

Meanwhile there had developed in the preceding years the violent campaigns of protest against the implementation of the new Poor Law and for shorter working hours, particularly in the north; a movement first led by the two Tory-Radicals, Richard Oastler and J. R. Stephens. It was in the course of this campaign that the term "Malthusian" became "the supremely abusive epithet for all enemies of the popular cause".[2] It swept into action men who had formerly been active in the Hampden Clubs and the march of the Blanketeers, and drew mass support. One of those who rose to leadership in this movement was Feargus O'Connor, an impoverished Irish landowner who was to become prominent in Chartist activities.

In London, Bronterre O'Brien's pupil George Julian Harney turned from the Working Men's Association, rejecting its leaders' policy of maintaining relations with the Radical middle class, and founded the London Democratic Association in 1838. His object was to organise the poorer sections of London workers—the Spitalfields weavers, the dockers, the Irish labourers—and to advance the condition of the working class "by disseminating the principles propagated by that great philosopher and redeemer of mankind, the Immortal Thomas Paine."[3]

All these different strands merged into the Chartist movement, launched on a national scale with a petition for the Charter issued in August 1838. But, leaving aside for the moment differing political aims among different strata of the movement, those who supported it were engaged up and down the country in efforts to provide their own meeting places, as also were the Owenites. In the decade after

[1] Lovett, op. cit., 97.   [2] Mark Hovell, The Chartist Movement (2nd ed 1925), 91.
[3] A. R. Schoyen, The Chartist Challenge (1958), 14.

1838, therefore, a new stage in the development of independent working-class institutions opened with concerted efforts to provide and maintain whole networks of halls and schools for the extension of working-class organisation and education. We may first consider the movement initiated by the Owenites after 1834 before going on to assess Chartist achievements in this field.

2. THE PROVISION OF INDEPENDENT EDUCATION

(i) Owenite Halls of Science

In May 1835, Robert Owen founded a new organisation—"The Association of all Classes of all Nations to effect an entire change in the character and conditions of the human race." Although the intentions were apocalyptic, the methods adopted were quite practical. Two years later an annual Congress was held in Manchester, and the publishing office of Owen's journal the New Moral World was transferred there. The society advanced rapidly and set up a further organisation—the "National Community Friendly Society"; this was "for the mutual assistance, maintenance and education of the members, their wives and husbands, children and nominees" and funds were raised to acquire buildings where the children might be educated. Finally, in 1838, the two bodies amalgamated as "The Universal Community Society of Rational Religionists".[1]

This Owenite body was the spearhead of Socialist educational and propaganda activities of the early 1840s. "Educate! Educate!! Educate!!!" was the slogan of this movement. "Let every institution forthwith have its Sunday and Day school, distribute tracts and works explanatory of the Social System with unsparing liberality," wrote the New Moral World in 1840, "let the lecture rooms be made as attractive as possible, and be as seldom empty and unused. Commence, where possible, private classes, lyceums, reading rooms and other means of instruction and innocent recreation. Let us not be outstripped in the endeavour."[2] Ten missionaries were forthwith appointed who toured the country lecturing and holding discussions to propagate Owenite ideas and organisation.

From 1839, also, dates the establishment of the Halls of Science which proliferated, especially in the north of England, in the following years. These varied from the magnificent building in Camp Fields,

---

[1] F. Podmore, Robert Owen (1906), 463-8.
[2] New Moral World (3rd Series), Vol. I, No. 17, October 24th, 1840, 265

Manchester, which cost £6,000, to the efforts of the Worcester Socialists later described rather disparagingly by Holyoake:

"English socialists expected to improve society by showing the superior reasonableness of the changes they sought. A small branch of these propagandists existed in Worcester. An enthusiastic carpenter had enlarged and fitted up an oblong workshop as a lecture-room, some sympathisers—who never appeared in the hall— furnished means of purchasing materials. These humble lecture rooms were called 'Halls of Science,' not that we had much science— merely a preference for it."

Holyoake himself was first employed at this hall, at a salary of sixteen shillings a week. After six months he became an accredited lecturer of the Socialist movement, moving to Sheffield, where the "branch wanted a lecturer who was willing also to teach a day school." To conduct the school more effectually, said Holyoake, "I provided an assistant at my own cost, as I approved of branches having good schools".[1]

The link between the propagandist and the educational activities of the Socialists is clear even in this small society. This was still more the case in larger centres. The Manchester Hall was a very considerable undertaking. Known as a "Temple of Science", it is described by a contemporary as

"an immense building in Camp Field, raised exclusively by the savings of the mechanics and artisans, at a cost of £7,000 (sic), and which contains a lecture-hall—the finest and most spacious in the town. It is tenanted by the disciples of Mr. Owen. In addition to Sunday lectures upon the doctrines of Socialism, they possess a day and Sunday school, and increase the number of their adherents by oratorios and festivals—by rural exursions, and by providing cheap and innocent recreation for the working classes. They are mostly advocates of temperance societies, and never allow fermented liquors to be drunk at any of their festivals. They were among the first to introduce tea-parties at a low rate of admission; and the popularity they have obtained by these endeavours to improve the habits of their fellow-townsmen, is one great cause of their success in the propagation of their system. The large sums of money they raise, prove that they belong to the wealthier portion of the working classes. Their audiences on Sunday evenings are generally crowded."[2]

[1] G. J. Holyoake, *Sixty Years of an Agitator's Life*, Vol. I, 133-5.
[2] L. Faucher, *A History of Manchester, its present condition and future prospects* (1844), 25 (translator's note).

This Hall was opened by Robert Owen in January 1840, the chair being taken by the radical bookseller, Abel Heywood. A full description of the opening ceremony, together with a verbatim account of Owen's speech, is given in the *Northern Star* for January 13th, 1840. The Hall is there described as containing a lofty room for 1,500 to 2,000 people on the first (ground) floor and an even more spacious room on the second floor with galleries on three sides; there were also smaller libraries and reading rooms.

Here, in subsequent years, lectures on scientific, economic and political subjects were given by full-time lecturers, concerts and parties were organised, while evening classes provided instruction in the three Rs. A Sunday school giving scientific teaching was added in 1841 (by May 1842, there were more than 250 pupils in attendance), and a few months later a day school with over 100 scholars.[1] As the Hall became an important centre of working-class and socialist activity it caused considerable consternation among the more orthodox citizens and evoked a violent reaction. At the end of April 1840, according to Owen's biographer, "a deliberate attempt was made to burn the building, fires consisting of shavings dipped in turpentine having been kindled in three separate places simultaneously. Fortunately the attempt was discovered, but the perpetrators were never brought to justice".[2] The existence of the Hall also brought into being a committee of churchmen and employers to suppress "that hideous form of infidelity which assumes the name of Socialism." Their solution was to set up a school specifically to counter this heathen propaganda, in which scientific lectures were provided as an attraction, while various warning pamphlets, written in unmeasured language, were distributed more widely among the people. A series of legal actions was also instituted by Church of England parsons against the Socialist lecturers and missionaries.[3]

The infant school educationist, Wilderspin, descanting on the necessity of orthodox religion as part of education, pays tribute to the influence of Owen at this time even while perverting his philosophy and decrying his adherents among ordinary people. "If such men as Mr. Owen address them under the specious pretext of making them

[1] *New Moral World* (3rd Series), Vol. II, 248, 355, 346; Vol. III, 370.

[2] Podmore, *op. cit.*, 518.

[3] *Ibid.*, 522ff. This incident, together with the history of the Manchester Hall of Science generally, is described in detail by Aubrey Black in an unpublished dissertation, "Owenite Education, 1839-1851, with particular reference to the Manchester Hall of Science" (this may be consulted by arrangement with the Education Department, Manchester University).

all happy, by merely uniting them together, like a flock of sheep, to eat and drink together, to sleep together, if they think fit, and to enjoy all the propensities of the natural man just as *mere animals* would do, they will listen to him, set him down as a wonderful philosopher, and collect money to build what they call 'a Hall of Science,' in such a thickly populated place as Manchester, look upon him as little less than a God, and give him credit for things which he himself would never claim; and, in short, go so far as to say that all men are irrational, and *never did know how to live*, nor ever will know how to live, until they can swallow all down as gospel which he chooses to assert."[1]

In spite of persecution the movement to found Halls of Science developed very rapidly in 1839 and 1840. In 1841, the Central Board of the Society of Rational Religionists allocated funds in the following order of priority: (1) for the general advancement of Owenite opinion, (2) for the building of Halls of Science, Lyceums and Schools, (3) for establishing Communities of United Interests.[2] Education was therefore paramount, linked always with Owenite propaganda, for the term Science covered not only the generally accepted meaning of the word, but also the science of society, as set out by Owen and his followers. By this time, the Society had invested £32,000 in Halls of Science, capable of holding 22,000 people. For a largely working-class organisation this was a very considerable sum, a proportion of which had been subscribed by active Chartists and other reformers.[3] This effort "had been greatly stimulated by the refusal of the local authorities and others to lend Town Halls and other public rooms for the purpose of Socialist meetings".[4] But another factor was the determination of working-class leaders and especially Socialists to find a place to meet outside the public house—a cause that had been particularly dear to the heart of Rowland Detrosier.

Temperate social meetings, festivals, tea-parties, combined with social instruction, were an essential aspect of Socialist activities, and many such functions, combining amusement with instruction, are described in the columns of the *Northern Star* as well as in Socialist journals. The workers' disillusion with the Mechanics' Institutes was, of course, the background against which the Halls of Science were supported. Mechanics' Institutes, said the *New Moral World* in 1840,

[1] S. Wilderspin, *A System of Education for the Young* (1840), 310-11.

[2] *New Moral World* (3rd Series), Vol. III, No. 2, July 10th, 1841, 12.

[3] Podmore, *op cit.*, 455n.   [4] *Ibid.*, 470.

echoing previous criticisms, were willing to educate the working people only in so far as the instruction given squared with "the interests of the clergy and the wealthy classes";[1] they were nothing more than "half-way houses to the attainment of social knowledge";[2] by contrast, Owenites were not concerned to produce capable machine minders, but fully developed men and women able to take their part in building a new society. It was for this reason that, to the physical and natural sciences, they added instruction in the social and political sciences; that they erected Halls of Science, and financed their own lecturers (or missionaries).

Halls similar to that at Manchester, if not quite so grand, were erected in other industrial centres, often under conditions of great difficulty.[3] The energetic Joseph Smith, who had been involved in earlier Owenite educational ventures, took the lead in the erection of the first Hall of Science (or "Social Institution" as it was called) which was opened in Salford in 1836; "a pleasant structure," writes Holyoake, "costing £850, and capable of holding six hundred persons."[4] The Liverpool Hall of Science (1840), costing £5,000, contained a lecture hall seating 1,500, a library, schoolrooms, observatory, and a kitchen capable of serving 1,500 meals. Other Halls were at Huddersfield (1839), Sheffield (1839), Stockport (1841), Halifax (1841), and Bristol (1841) which had a hall seating 3,000; while in 1842 it was decided to build a hall holding 2,000 to 3,000 in London, at Lambeth. Another Hall in London was situated in John Street, off Tottenham Court Road, built, according to Holyoake, at a cost of

[1] *New Moral World* (3rd Series), Vol. I, No. 23, December 5th, 1840, 360.

[2] *Ibid.*, Vol. I, No. 3, July 18th, 1840, 41. This remark is made in connection with the secession, from the Coventry Mechanics' Institute, of some sixty to seventy socialists, "many of its most talented, intelligent and active members". The cause of this secession, according to the *New Moral World*, was that the workers wished to obtain a wider knowledge than that available; they wished also "to apply that knowledge to practical purposes"; but "the clergy, and other obstructives, stood in the way and so the parties differed and separated". This, the article goes on, "is the history of many other institutions besides that of Coventry".

[3] Some idea of the sacrifices involved in building these Halls may be gained from a letter from the Radcliffe Bridge socialists asking Owen to perform the opening ceremony at their Hall of Science in 1839. "Our village has suffered a great deal from the ravages of the present system, so much so that families who were comparatively comfortable when we began our new Hall are now actually in a state of misery beyond description. It is enough to make one give up in despair if we did not see a brighter and glorious era springing out of the present dark and bewildered state of Ignorance and Selfishness." Quoted by A. Black "The Owenites and the Halls of Science", *Co-operative Review*, Vol. XXIX, No. 2, February 1955.

[4] Holyoake, *op. cit.*, Vol. I, 296. The Salford Social Institution closed in 1839 with the erection of the Manchester Hall of Science.

£3,000. Sometimes existing buildings were taken over as at Birmingham (1841), where local Owenites acquired a chapel from the Southcottians for £800. At Glasgow there were great difficulties in finding premises as a result of anti-socialist feeling, but eventually an old parish church was bought capable of holding 1,000, and re-christened the Hall of Science (1840). Among smaller halls were those at Yarmouth, Macclesfield and Radcliffe Bridge.[1]

The workers, by attending the organised public meetings, lectures, readings, debates and discussions, were able to acquire education of a kind which it was impossible to get elsewhere. But if this was the main purpose of the Halls of Science, many of them also provided, at least for a time, an education for children. Such was the case at Sheffield, where the school was at one time run by Holyoake; a man who, in addition to his other multifarious activities, produced a number of text-books on grammar, arithmetic, logic, for adults and children. There were also day schools at Huddersfield, Glasgow, Yarmouth, Lambeth, Birmingham, Manchester and Liverpool.[2]

At this stage the Owenites regarded such schools as the necessary first step in bringing about a complete change in the character of the human race. "The great aim of Rational Religion or Socialism (which includes not only the science of education, but all the other great duties incumbent upon man in relation to his fellows)," writes the *Herald of the Future*, "is to form a superior race of human beings to any the world has hitherto known . . ."

"What the people of this country are most in need of, is enlightened education, and healthy and well remunerated employment: to the securing of which, all changes in the institutions of society should be directed. The Social, or Co-operative system, alone promises these things in abundance, and hence is denounced as a dangerous innovation. But it recommends, and enforces education in positive knowledge, and not in mystical faith—education in the works of nature, and therefore it is *Atheistical* and *Blasphemous* in the eyes of Bishops and Priests, who trade and fatten on the credulity of the people."

In fact, for God the Socialists substituted the natural world and,

[1] A. Black, "The Owenites and the Halls of Science", *Co-operative Review*, Vol. XXIX, No. 2, February 1955, 42-4; F. Podmore, *op. cit.*, 470. Podmore mentions further Halls at Coventry, Bradford and Leeds.

[2] A. Black, *op. cit.*, see also A. Black, "Education before Rochdale", *Co-operative Review*, Vol. XXVII, No. 6, June 1954, 130-1.

as described, their aim was primarily to give a scientific education; to ensure

> "that the rising generation should be well read in the book of God, displayed in brightest characters in the visible world;—that youth should be trained in a knowledge of the laws of nature, as manifested in the human structure, and the various external objects which bear a relation to mankind, so that they might acquire accurate knowledge of the properties of all existence cognizant to the senses, the mechanism and functions of the human organisation, and the laws of health and disease, . . . and to apply all this useful knowledge for the general purposes of life, that happiness might be the result."[1]

It was to promote a positive education of this kind that "a number of the thinking and well-disposed of the working classes, together with others of the middle classes in Liverpool" formed the Liverpool Rational School Society in 1839 "for the purpose of giving a superior education to their children", and agreed on a resolution, address and laws setting out their standpoint.[2] The failure of the government to carry out a plan for a non-sectarian training college as a result of the implacable opposition of Church and Dissent is cited as the immediate cause of this action: "Seeing therefore that the State cannot, and that the Church and the priesthood will not, educate the people, nothing now remains for them but either to remain for ever in a state of ignorance and superstition, or to unite to burst their bonds asunder, and to educate themselves".

A clear statement of the rationalist educational outlook is incorporated in the laws of the Society. Facts and useful knowledge alone are to be taught, together with the "Rational Religion" which consists in "promoting to the utmost extent in our power the happiness of every man, woman and child without the least regard to sect, party, class, country or colour". In conformity with the principle that "the character of man is formed for him, and not by him," the children are to be governed "in the spirit of kindness and love, without praise or blame, rewards or punishments". The aim of the school will be to promote the "full development and temperate exercise of

---

[1] *Herald of the Future*, No. 6, March 1840. (The editor was the Manchester Owenite, G. F. Mandley.)

[2] These are to be found among the Owen Correspondence at Holyoake House, Manchester, with a letter from John Finch and James Spurr, asking Owen to make any alterations he wished before publication (Letter No. 1135 dated July 31st, 1839); for John Finch, see R. B. Rose, "John Finch, 1784–1857: a Liverpool Disciple of Robert Owen", *Transactions of the Historic Society of Lancashire and Cheshire*, Vol. 104 (1957).

all the physical, intellectual and moral powers" of all the children. "All will be trained in the same manner and to the same extent without any distinction except what is rendered necessary from the peculiar natural organisation of each child,"—so they will learn both by principle and practice that "all mankind are by nature equal" and that no human being has any right to exploit another. The curriculum suggested, apart from the three Rs, includes science, the social and political sciences, and music, singing and dancing. It is added that "Practical experiment, object teaching, familiar conversation and oral instruction will be the general mode of teaching".

The Society expressed the view that such schools should, as soon as practicable, become boarding schools "for the purpose of removing the rising generation altogether from the vicious and degrading circumstances, by which they are everywhere surrounded". Here is fresh evidence of the extent to which the aim of establishing ideal communities still dominated the socialist movement. Its essentially Utopian character is made clear by the subsequent history of the Liverpool school. Opening in February 1841 in the Hall of Science with fifty scholars, it reached a maximum of 150 before closing down in the following year. Financial resources were too slender to maintain it in the face of bad trade, reduced wages and the intimidation of its supporters.[1]

In default of detailed local research it is difficult to say how widespread the rational school movement was, how many schools were started and how many successfully maintained. Beset, as these schools were, not only with financial difficulties but also with religious and political obstruction amounting often to persecution, their path was not an easy one. Nevertheless, day schools imbued with these principles did exist, both in connection with the Halls of Science and independently,[2] and they were supplemented by more numerous Socialist Sunday schools, particularly in the North of England.[3] All these propagated among the rising generation an outlook which derived

[1] New Moral World (3rd Series), Vol. II, No. 8, February 20th, 1841, 118; Vol. III, No. 47, May 21st, 1842, 370; Vol. II, No. 15, April 10th, 1841, 232.

[2] For instance, at Hyde, where John Ellis, author of an Owenite school textbook, taught a school of over 100 scholars in 1841-2, in spite of the efforts of religious bodies "to bring it into disrepute." New Moral World (3rd Series), Vol. II, No. 16, April 17th, 1841, 248; Vol. III, No. 26, December 25th, 1841, 208; Vol. III, No. 39, March 26th, 1842, 311.

[3] The New Moral World (3rd Series, 1840-2) contains references to Socialist Sunday schools at: Honley (Yorks), Oldham, Rochdale, Bradford, Hyde, Failsworth, Congleton, Ashton, Padiham, London, Sheffield, Leicester.

from the teaching of the French Encyclopaedists and their English counterparts, and more immediately from that of Owen, and the work of Thompson, Carlile and many others.

With the decline of the Socialist movement in the mid-1840s, the rational tradition developed in these Socialist schools and halls merged into the great secularist movement in which, in the latter half of the century, Holyoake was prominent and, more particularly, Charles Bradlaugh. Bradlaugh, who in his youth had been taken in and cared for by Carlile's second "wife" Isis, termed himself an iconoclast in religion, but was a strong opponent of socialism. In the new form which it now took on, however, the secularist outlook remained an important force in English education.

(ii) Chartist Halls and Schools

The Chartist Halls came into being after 1838, initially once more as a product of a political movement similar to that which had preceded the Reform Bill and inspired the efforts of Detrosier and Doherty in Manchester. In fact, this earlier drive to establish independent working-class meeting-places and forms of education naturally merged into the Chartist movement which crowned the political and industrial struggles of the post-1832 era. It forms one element, and an essential one, of the diverse strands which went to make up Chartism.

The publication of the People's Charter in 1838 was preceded by the *Address on Education*, the first statement on the theory and practice of education to be issued by a working-class organisation in Britain. At this period, there was already a much wider realisation among the working class not only of rigid Tory and clerical opposition to any real educational advance but also of the aims of the Whigs and aristocracy. As Lovett was later to characterise the position with bitter irony:

> "while a large portion of the hawks and owls of society were seeking to perpetuate that state of mental darkness most favourable to the securing of their prey, another portion, with more cunning, were for admitting a sufficient amount of mental glimmer to cause the multitude to walk quietly and contentedly in the paths they in their wisdom had prescribed for them."[1]

After the Bull Ring riots in Birmingham in 1839, which was a culminating point in the first stage of Chartist agitation, Lovett was

[1] Lovett, *op. cit.*, 134.

gaoled and, with his fellow prisoner John Collins, turned his attention to elaborating the educational proposals of the *Address*. Meanwhile active upholders of the movement were facing the problem of finding places to meet and carry on their political work and education.

"We are called ignorant," said a Chartist lecturer in the course of an impassioned plea for Trades Halls where workers could meet freely,

> "We are called *ignorant*, however, by the scions of a purse-proud aristocracy; by those who, by a see-saw game at political power, happen to be uppermost; be it so, we will remove that ignorance by teaching one another, by discussing politics day after day, and by an interchange of thoughts and sympathy (loud cheers). But they tell us also that we are ignorant, at the very time when a tool-cutter and a cabinet maker are engaged, even in the dungeon to which those tyrants had unjustly consigned them, in writing a system of education, before which all their modish plans, and 'abstract theories', and 'histories of birds and fishes' sink into insignificance."[1]

Halls were provided, the money once more being raised by the workers. One of the most successful, used as an educational centre during the first few years of the Chartist movement, was again in Manchester. This was the great Carpenters' Hall, erected by the operative carpenters and joiners Union at a cost of £4,500 and completed in 1838, "a glorious establishment," wrote O'Connor in 1844, "a great intellectual hotbed".[2] The building had "a spacious hall, calculated to hold between five and six thousand persons"[3] as well as a library and later a Sunday school. In Manchester, then, besides the Owenite Hall of Science, there was a second centre of working-class political and educational activity. Here the local Chartists met monthly and there was also a Carpenters' Hall locality (or organised branch) whose members were joiners, painters and carpenters. This hall, writes a contemporary, is

> "the Sunday resort of the Chartists. They open and close their meetings with the singing of democratic hymns, and their sermons are political discourses on the justice of democracy and the necessity for obtaining a charter."[4]

Later Carpenters' Hall slipped from Chartist control, but a new hall was built known as the People's Institute, in Heyrod Street, a

---

[1] *Northern Star*, October 17th, 1840.   [2] *Ibid.*, April 13th, 1844.
[3] *Ibid.*, February 10th, 1838.   [4] Faucher, *op. cit.*, 25.

building which took only three months to erect. "Bear in mind," said O'Connor at its opening in 1846, exhorting his audience to lend financial support, "that this hall has been erected by the zeal, the confidence, and the pence of working men alone."[1] Throughout the north, and also in other parts of the country, workers had expressed their zeal and confidence in the same way. The *Northern Star* and other Chartist journals are full of references to such halls and rooms.

Besides that at Manchester, the most successful halls, according to O'Connor in 1848, were in Oldham, Leeds and Birmingham. That at Oldham, built in 1845, because the Town Hall was refused to the Chartists, was financed by 700 shareholders to the tune of about £1,000. Here educational activities were to the fore, including "Lectures and discussions on Science, Literature, the Fine Arts, Theology, Morals, Social and Political Economy, etc.," and "schools for children of all parties and denominations." As well as a room seating 500, there was a school-room, newsroom, library and a "depot" for books, tracts and newspapers.[2] At Leeds, a building seating 1,500 was acquired in 1843 and renamed the "New Chartists Hall", while similar premises acquired by Birmingham Chartists were called "People's Hall".[3]

It was not only in the large population centres that meeting places were provided. Among those mentioned in the *Northern Star* as early as 1838, for instance, are the rooms taken by the Radical Association near Huddersfield, where readings and meetings were held on Mondays, and discussions on Tuesday evening; the association rooms of the Radical reformers at Dukinfield, where various publications and periodicals were taken; the "spacious room" taken by the Wakefield Working Men's Association, where lectures were given on Anatomy and Physiology with the use of models and where there was also, according to Richard Carlile, "a good library".[4] In this year also a large Working Man's Institution was built at Hyde, where, so the report runs, "the working classes . . . are making a noble effort to free themselves from the thraldom of servile and religious despotism"; here the Institute was opened with two sermons by J. R. Stephens and three lectures by Robert Owen.[5] In 1839 a People's Institute was founded by Stalybridge Chartists, where a Sunday and

---

[1] *Northern Star*, July 25th, 1846.   [2] *Ibid.*, April 13th, 1844; March 29th, 1845.

[3] *Ibid.*, November 25th, 1843; April 24th, 1841; February 6th, 1847.

[4] *Ibid.*, March 17th, 1838; March 24th, 1838; March 31st, 1838; T. C. Campbell, *The Battle of the Press, as told in the Life of Richard Carlile* (1899), 213.

[5] *Northern Star*, September 1st, 1838; M. Tylecote, *The Mechanics' Institutes of Lancashire and Yorkshire before 1851* (1957), 125.

246 STUDIES IN THE HISTORY OF EDUCATION, 1780-1870

a day school were also housed.[1] In 1841, apart from places mentioned as having National Charter Association Rooms, there is reference in the *Northern Star* to reading rooms or lecture halls at Newcastle, Congleton and Halifax (where a hall was eventually built in 1847). Other meeting places were also used. The Chartist leader and temperance campaigner Vincent writes in a letter from Nottingham: "This is a famous radical town. Reading rooms and libraries abound, though some of them are unfortunately held at public houses."[2]

From now on the references multiply. In 1842, a Chartist Hall is opened in Mile End Road; Colonel Thompson presents his works to the Bradford Chartist Library; the Newcastle Chartists meet at their "Hall" at the Goat Inn. Nottingham Chartists meet at the "Democratic Chapel".[3] Early in 1843 there is a commemoration of the opening of the City of London Political and Scientific Institute in Skinner Lane—an institution which included a day school. This depended to some extent on middle-class support and was more expressive of the policy of the "Knowledge Chartists"—as Lovett's wing of the movement became known—than that of the main body. Here, Cleave and Duncombe spoke, and the event was celebrated with a long poem beginning:

> "Hail, sons of freedom! with a heart-felt cheer,
> Rejoice, in friendship, as are those met here;
> Like bonded brethren in the holy cause
> By Temp'rance guided, and by reason's laws,
> By calm discussion, truth shall shed her light,
> And ignorance vanish, like the shades of night.
> Here may we utter with a freeman's tone,
> *Sound truths* for why?—*the building is our own*."[4]

In succeeding years Hamilton, Kipponden, Wednesbury, Macclesfield, Ashton-under-Lyne find mention. In 1845, Hanley and Shelton Chartists propose the erection of a Working Men's Hall where workmen may meet to discuss their grievances, where lectures in science, history and politics will be given, and where, as soon as practicable, an elementary day school will be held.[5] The connection between education, propaganda and political activity is still very much in

---

[1] Tylecote, *op. cit.*, 241.

[2] *Northern Star*, February 6th, 1841; March 27th, 1841; April 10th, 1841.

[3] *Ibid.*, September 10th, 1842; September 17th, 1842; October 1st, 1842; April 15th 1843.

[4] *Ibid.*, February 25th, 1843.   [5] *Ibid.*, January 25th, 1845.

evidence in 1847 and 1848. By this time many Chartist groupings are developing their own libraries; the Derby Land and Charter Society, for instance, decides to establish a library, reading room and discussion class as "essential to the progress of Chartist principles in this town". In the same year a Marylebone grouping of working men, meeting weekly, decides to purchase "a handsome new bookcase" holding 2,000 volumes, while the Rochdale Chartists, meeting in their room in Yorkshire Street, open a library, feeling confident "that the friends of liberty and education in Radical Rochdale will lend their kindly assistance to the good work by presenting them with useful books or rendering them pecuniary assistance".

Preston Chartists, after establishing a Chartist Association, take a large room holding 1,000, for reading and discussion, while Chartist libraries are opened at Greenwich, Deptford and Heywood. Mutual Improvement Societies attached to the Chartist movement were also in evidence, at places as far apart as Westminster and Aberdeen where lectures were given and a magazine started. Indeed, a delegate meeting at Birmingham in September 1848 suggested to the Chartist Executive "the establishment of mutual instruction societies throughout the Chartist ranks, as the dispelling of ignorance is the only means of obtaining the Charter".[1]

In December 1848, Samuel Kydd, Secretary of the Executive, undertook a lecture tour, putting up *en route* as the Chartist candidate (at the hustings only) in a West Riding by-election. Passing through Daventry on his way to Yorkshire he experienced to the full the bitter realisation of the work that was still to do. "The old and barbarous practice of cock-fighting", he wrote to the *Northern Star*, "is still common in this district. Monday was set apart for such purpose. It being seven o'clock in the evening before I arrived, I cannot describe the actual scene, but in the evening almost every public house was crowded with drunken men—the topics of conversation were cock-fighting, dog-fighting and man-fighting, and all the gross bestiality I ever heard from the lips of men stands unequalled, compared with the brutal coarseness and obscenity I here listened to."[2]

In the light of this the Owenite stress on regeneration falls into place and the political significance of the temperance campaign becomes clear. But in Yorkshire Kydd found a different type of working man.

[1] *Northern Star*, October 2nd, 1847; October 16th, 1847; October 30th, 1847; November 6th, 1847; July 3rd, 1847; September 30th, 1848.
[2] *Ibid.*, December 2nd, 1848.

Nowhere in England, he reports, does Chartism stand higher than in Keighley. "The hall—which is an excellent and substantial building —is their own property, to which belongs a committee room and library; they teach a Sunday school; hold their mutual instruction and reading classes; also classes for instruction in grammar and logic; their orchestra consists of vocal and instrumental music; all their leaders are sober men of known respectability—some of them men of property." The Keighley Chartists, he says, bear "every outward sign of mental and moral elevation". They have an interest in their own institute, which is the germ of a genuine People's College, and they are at the same time the most intelligent, most respectable and the most influential body in the district. What a reproach is the example of Keighley to London, where the promised Chartist Hall has never materialised. "Men of London," writes Kydd, "will Chartism never have a local habitation and a name among you? Will it never step out into daylight from the dark rooms of beer shops, and the corrupting influences of gin palaces?" If all would do like the Keighley Chartists, "next Christmas you would celebrate the anniversary of the People's Charter".[1]

That Kydd's complaints against the London Chartists for meeting in beer shops have some justification is suggested by a number of references in the *Northern Star* to public houses as "Chartist houses" in 1848. Nevertheless, there were Chartist institutions in London, if none of them measured up to the requirements of the metropolis as a whole. In 1843, for instance, the Chartists had taken over the old "Rotunda", which Carlile first made famous as a centre of working-class agitation and free discussion in the early 1830s when the National Union of the Working Classes and Others met there. This was first re-christened the South London Hall of Science and later, the South London Chartist Hall, indicating a change of emphasis. In addition there was a City Chartist Hall in Turnagain Lane, and, at least for a time, a Chartist Church in Regent Street in addition to the coffee-houses and smaller meeting places. London, then, was not without Chartist Halls. Their establishment on a more ambitious scale in the north of England is a simple reflection of the fact that it was from this area that Chartism derived its main strength.[2]

Among the more energetic of Chartist educationists who made use of the halls and rooms for teaching purposes was George Julian

[1] *Northern Star*, December 23rd, 1848.
[2] *Ibid.*, July 1st, 1848; July 29th, 1843; January 2nd, 1847.

Harney, who made the meeting-place at Sheffield (in Fig Tree Lane) "the centre of intellectual life for the members". Here discussion meetings took place weekly, Harney and others lecturing on such topics as the history of the working class. "On the walls hung home-made banners inscribed with the names of working-class heroes, ranging from Wat Tyler to Byron and Shelley; a small library was started." Dinners and teas were provided for the families of Chartists—including the children—and the hall became a centre of social as well as political activity.[1]

In Leicester, Thomas Cooper, the exponent of physical force Chartism, was also active. His autobiography gives a vivid description of contemporary events and conditions in Leicester, in particular of his own educational efforts. These he combined with political agitation with an *élan* which won him wide support. Cooper's intensive reading and study have already been referred to. He was well-fitted, as an orator, to pass on his knowledge, and found occasion during a lull in directly political agitation after the elections of 1842. Looking back on this period he recalls:

"I began now to turn my thoughts to something more worthy of men's earnestness. As soon as the Shakespearean Room was secured, I formed an adult Sunday-school, for men and boys who were at work on the week-days. All the more intelligent in our ranks gladly assisted as teachers; and we soon had the room filled on Sunday mornings and afternoons. The Old and New Testaments, Channing's 'Self-Culture,' and other tracts, of which I do not remember the names, formed our class-books. And we, fancifully, named our classes, not first, second, third, etc., but the 'Algernon Sydney Class,' 'Andrew Marvel Class,' 'John Hampden Class,' 'John Milton Class,' 'William Tell Class,' 'George Washington Class,' 'Major Cartwright Class,' 'William Cobbett Class,' and so on."

Later, meetings were held on weekday evenings as well as Sunday, and

"unless there were some stirring local and political topics, I lectured on Milton, and repeated portions of 'Paradise Lost', or on Shakespeare, and repeated portions of 'Hamlet', or on Burns, and repeated 'Tam o' Shanter', or I recited the history of England, and set the portraits of great Englishmen before young Chartists, who listened with intense interest; or I took up Geology, or even Phrenology,

[1] Schoyen, *op. cit.*, 123.

and made the young men acquainted, elementally, with the knowledge of the time."[1]

This adult school had to be given up later, when, according to Cooper, times became very bad and the people utterly wretched.[2] "If events had not broken up the system I was forming," he writes, "how much good I might have effected in Leicester!" The background of economic crisis, which brought misery and destitution to thousands of working-class families, together with the long hours of work in normal times, must not be forgotten when assessing what Chartists and Socialists achieved at this period.

Though Cooper was not typical, it would be wrong to underestimate the degree of knowledge, scientific, cultural and political, made available to the Chartists in their Halls and lecture rooms, and in the class meetings which developed widely at certain stages of the movement.[3] Though immediate political issues necessarily predominate in Chartist literature, the journals also contain much cultural and scientific material which provided matter for reflection and discussion. Papers like the *Northern Star* (edited for a long period by Harney), and later those edited by Ernest Jones, Bronterre O'Brien and others, were fully in the tradition of earlier working-class literature in devoting a great deal of space to educative articles on economic, cultural and scientific subjects; O'Brien's letters and articles in the early period of the *Northern Star*, for instance, went to the heart of political and economic theory. A great deal of Socialist writing, also essentially educative, appeared in most Chartist as well as in Socialist journals—one example is the series of twenty-four articles by W. Gilpin on socialist theory and practice in the *Northern Star* in 1842-3.

There were full reports of the hard-fought political debates between Owenites and Chartists, or between the Owenites and J. R. Stephens on religion, which often continued for several evenings in front of huge audiences. These were a feature of working-class politics for a long period, not to mention the great political meetings addressed by leading Chartists literally all over the country at this time. At certain periods, the *Northern Star* devoted almost an entire page

[1] T. Cooper, *The Life of Thomas Cooper* (2nd edn 1872), 164, 169.

[2] Although the Leicester Chartists produced *Hamlet* in 1843, with Cooper in the title role. *Northern Star*, January 14th, 1843.

[3] In many areas the National Charter Association was organised in class meetings, like the radical clubs of 1818 to 1823. Here political education and discussion was carried on —on a large scale; see R. F. Wearmouth, *Methodism and the Working Class Movement of England, 1800-1850* (1937), 113-29, for a full analysis of the Chartist class meetings.

(roughly the present size of *The Times*) to literature. Byron was an especial favourite, but Burns, Shelley, Whittier, Clare, Mackay, were also represented, as well as Chartist verse written by working-class poets and such men as Thomas Cooper and Ernest Jones.[1] Whole pages were often devoted to foreign news, to reports of Parliament and of Parliamentary Commissions. Small wonder that the Chartists indignantly rebutted the taunt of "ignorance", flung at the workers as reason for refusing them the vote. There is no doubt that the general cultural standard maintained by their press was extremely high, and this must have had its effect on the discussions and debates held in the Chartist meeting rooms and halls.

More difficult to assess is the provision Chartists were able to make for the education of their children; here again local research is needed. Probably most of the organised education was in Sunday schools. The Rev. William Hill, first editor of the *Northern Star* and himself a schoolmaster, refers in an early number to his Sunday school and frequently advertises thereafter his *Rational School Grammar and Entertaining Class Book*.[2] In 1842, "lectures, instruction groups, and Sunday schools flourished throughout the winter" at Leeds and the proposal was made for a National Charter Association Sunday School Union "to co-ordinate Sunday schools for adults and children".[3] In 1844, the radical booksellers were selling a new monthly children's magazine: *The Rational Day and Sunday School Magazine*, which dealt with "Morals, Science and Natural Things", and received a long review in the *Northern Star*; all schools and fathers of families were recommended to buy it to enable them to instruct their children in "*real* knowledge" which cannot be got elsewhere. "For Chartist Sunday schools," the reviewer goes on, "now so rife" the journal will be very useful; teachers of these should get the magazine and circulate it among their pupils.[4]

One of the most successful Chartist Sunday schools was held in the Carpenters' Hall in Manchester. Here, in 1844, O'Connor made a point of appearing at the quarterly examinations. The *Northern Star* reports that the spacious hall was cheerfully thronged with parents and friends of children's education in this "democratic academy".

[1] Many of the poems by Chartist poets, which originally appeared in the *Northern Star* and other Chartist journals, have been republished in *An Anthology of Chartist Literature* (ed Y. V. Kovalev, Moscow, 1956).

[2] *Northern Star*, January 6th, 1838.

[3] J. F. C. Harrison, "Chartism in Leeds", in *Chartist Studies* (ed Asa Briggs, 1959), 81-2n, 90.

[4] *Northern Star*, March 23rd, 1844.

The proceedings opened with the singing of Chartist hymns, while the forcible and clear answers of the children to the questions put by their teacher evoked applause. Later, the children recited poems reflecting democratic aspirations, such as "The Downfall of Poland", "Byron's Dream", "The Factory Slave's Last Day", "The Charm of Freedom", "The Democratic Working Man", and so on. It was gratifying to know, said O'Connor in his address, that there was a little army coming up who would take the field and finish the work that their fathers had so nobly begun.[1]

Indications of Chartist schools elsewhere may be briefly given. At Elland, in 1838, a radical school opened with 104 scholars—young men and women "as anxious in the affairs of politics as that of writing and accounts". At Yew Green the Chartists, about to open a school, write that they

"hope this undertaking will receive the support of the Chartist body, for most desirable it is that the rising generation should receive instruction (afforded to them by no sect or party under the present system) which will bring them up in the nurture and love of the principles of liberty, and fit them in after years to 'know their rights, and knowing dare maintain them'".

In 1843 the Ashton Chartists started a school in their reading room, appealing to the editor of the *Northern Star* for his "influence and talent in support of this newly adopted mode of educating the rising generation in the true progress of democracy, and without religious sectarian compulsion of any kind".[2] Two years later, the "Shaksperean" Chartist locality in Birmingham announces a school for adults and children, to be held on Sunday, and appeals for a few of "our best educated members" to "join us in teaching the 'young idea how to shoot'". By 1845, Leicester Chartists are once more running a school for the instruction of adults and children on Sunday, and on Tuesday and Thursday evenings.[3]

It has already been no d that the Chartist Halls at Oldham, Keighley and Hanley included schools. In 1847 the Chartist Hall at Mottram was being used as a Sunday and day school, the latter apparently catering for 500 working-class children who were taught reading and spelling, and were soon to be taught grammar and arithmetic.

[1] *Northern Star*, April 20th, 1844; August 24th, 1844; December 14th, 1844.
[2] *Ibid.*, April 14th, 1838; August 15th, 1842; December 9th, 1843.
[3] *Ibid.*, January 25th, 1845; March 22nd, 1845.

According to one report this venture was meeting with some opposition. "Our *very amiable* vicar . . . has been at no little trouble to denounce the whole fraternity as infidels"; he goes from house to house trying to get parents to withdraw their children.[1] There is, in addition, evidence of a number of day schools set up by Chartists in Scotland, described by the historian of Scottish Chartism as "a bold experiment in positive Radicalism".[2] The *Chartist Circular*, a Scottish journal, devoted considerable space to education and to Chartist schools. Finally mention may be made of O'Connor's ill-fated Chartist land colonies set up between 1846 and 1848. At least three of these included schools for the children as well as cottages and allotments for the settlers.[3]

No doubt instances of concerted efforts to promote education could be multiplied. But enough has been said to suggest that, the pressures of economic difficulties and the demand for political action notwithstanding, many Chartist supporters were very actively engaged in providing organised classes for adult workers and schools where children, besides learning the elements, might also acquire a love of liberty, a knowledge of their rights and the courage to fight for their convictions.

(iii) *The Extent and Character of Working-class Education*

It was also in the 1840s, as we have seen earlier, that the middle class were actively engaged in establishing the first boarding proprietary schools where their children might receive the right kind of education in the right surroundings. The working class could not, of course, command the funds to found boarding schools, though the Liverpool Owenites held this out as an ideal to aim for. But the better paid artisans could, and did, make use of private schools—and the local endowed schools which still offered a free or cheap education. In Manchester, in 1834, 4,070 children were attending free or partially assisted schools; but another 13,108 were to be found in common day schools or in dame schools, which were entirely supported by fees ranging from 3*d*. to 9*d*. a week. At about the same period, working-class parents in Bristol, which had a population of 120,000, were paying over £15,000 a year for their children's education; a sum over half

---

[1] *Northern Star*, February 6th, 1847.

[2] Wright, *op. cit.*, 102. Schools were set up at Leven, Greenock, Aberdeen, Partick, Arbroath, Paisley and Kilbarachan.

[3] W. H. G. Armytage, "The Chartist Land Colonies 1846-1848," *Agricultural History*, Vol. XXXII, No. 4 (1958), 87-96.

that reluctantly granted by Parliament in 1833 to aid the building of schools throughout England and Wales.[1] This gives a glimpse of the extent to which the working class supported schools out of their own pockets.

Meanwhile the halls and schools built and maintained by the more politically active workers provided educational centres for men who might formerly have attended the Mechanics' Institutes fostered by industrialists. Already in 1840, the Yorkshire Union of Mechanics' Institutes stated that it is "universally acknowledged" that the members of Mechanics' Institutes

"are nineteen-twentieths of them, not of the class of mechanics, but are connected with the higher branches of handicraft trades, or are clerks in offices, and, in many instances, young men connected with liberal professions".[2]

By this time it was recognised that the policy of preventing free discussion had, in fact, driven the workers out of the original Institutes; and that, while these emptied, the Socialist and Chartist Halls were full. Reporting to the S.D.U.K. on "The State of Literary, Scientific and Mechanics' Institutes," Thomas Coates does not spare his hearers; indeed he makes it clear that it is only the working-class institutions which provide a liberal and general education in any real sense of the term.

"The Chartist and the Socialist zealously diffuse their opinions far and wide; they have erected halls, and established places of meeting in which they discourse to thousands; they invite persons of adverse opinions to listen to and freely discuss the exposition of their principles: the Socialists, especially, comprise in the plan of their societies some of the most useful and attractive objects of the Mechanics' Institutions; they have lectures on the sciences, they have music, and in some cases other classes, and they add to these the occasional attraction of tea-parties, accompanied by dancing."

Coates notes that, though the actual members of socialist institutions in London numbered far less than those of Mechanics' Institutes,

[1] From contemporary calculations by the Manchester and Bristol Statistical Societies; J. L. and B. Hammond, *The Age of the Chartists*, (1930), 179-80.
[2] "Report of Central Committee of Yorkshire Union of Mechanics' Institutes, 1840"; quoted in James Hole, *An Essay on the History and Management of Literary, Scientific and Mechanics' Institutions* (1853), 21. The general conclusion that the Mechanics' Institutes failed in their original purpose to attract working men is contested by Kelly (*George Birkbeck*); but all the contemporary observers (James Hole, J. W. Hudson, Thomas Coates), themselves sympathetic to the Mechanics' Institutes, are unanimous on this point.

attendance at their "lectures, discussions and festive meetings" was very much greater. "This", he writes, "is believed to arise principally from the fact that the rival institution offers to the workman those things the exclusion of which from Mechanics' Institutions (especially the right kind of free enquiry) renders them, if not distasteful, at least uninteresting to him." Several years later, James Hole, Secretary of the Yorkshire Union of Mechanics' Institutions, made the same point: "No teacher in this country will gain the ear of the working-man, unless he is willing to have his opinions and statements canvassed, to invite the utterance of conflicting opinion, and to give truth 'a fair field and no favour'. This course has not been, and cannot be, adopted in mechanics' institutes, and, therefore, any attempt to convey econo-mical doctrine, 'sound or unsound', through their media must prove a failure."[1] In Coates' view, unless these matters were discussed, the men would resort to the tavern and the political club where their prejudices would be reinforced; ironically summing up the attitude of Mechanics' Institutes to the working-men who sought such knowledge, Coates wrote:

"We explain to you the physical sciences; we demonstrate to you the atomic theory; we show you the orbit of the planets, but the nature and advantages of our political Constitution, a question which every newspaper more or less raises, and which is obtruded upon you and made a motive for your conduct at every election, shall not be taught or discussed here—nevertheless, the Chartists in the next street handle it quite freely, and will spare no pains to induce you to adopt their opinions."[2]

This testimony, the more valuable since it comes from one who has the cause of the orthodox Mechanics' Institute at heart, is upheld by the observations of Frederick Engels, a frequent visitor to the Man-chester Hall of Science and warm partisan of the workers. The Mechanics' Institutes, he writes in 1844, are

"organs for the dissemination of the sciences useful to the bourgeoisie. Here the natural sciences are now taught, which may draw the working-man away from opposition to the bourgeoisie. . . . Here Political Economy is preached. . . . Here all education is tame, flabby, subservient to the ruling politics and religion, so that for the

[1] Hole, op. cit., 66.
[2] Thomas Coates, Report of the State of Literary, Scientific and Mechanics' Institutions in England (1841), 29-31; see also Kelly, op. cit., 235-6.

working-man it is merely a constant sermon upon quiet obedience, passivity, and resignation to his fate. The mass of the working-men naturally have nothing to do with these institutes, and betake themselves to the proletarian reading-rooms and to the discussion of matters which directly concern their own interests."[1]

Engels remarks on the number of these. "Schools and reading rooms for the advancement of education" have been founded by "different sections of working-men, often united, often separated, Trade Unionists, Chartists and Socialists."

"Every Socialist, and almost every Chartist institution, has such a place, and so too have many trades. Here the children receive a purely proletarian education, free from all the influences of the bourgeoisie; and, in the reading rooms, proletarian journals and books alone, or almost alone, are to be found."

He can also report at first hand on the popularity of lectures and discussions.

"That ... the working-men appreciate solid education when they can get it unmixed with the interested cant of the bourgeoisie, the frequent lectures upon scientific, aesthetic, and economic subjects prove which are delivered especially in the Socialist institutes, and very well attended."

Engels gives a straight answer to those who condemned the working class as ignorant, claiming that, by their own efforts, they often surpass the so-called educated classes and have absorbed the heritage of European philosophy and science.

"I have often heard working-men, whose fustian jackets scarcely hold together, speak upon geological, astronomical, and other subjects, with more knowledge than most 'cultivated' bourgeois in Germany possess. And in how great a measure the English prole-tariat has succeeded in attaining an independent education is shown especially by the fact that the epoch-making products of modern philosophical, political, and poetical literature are read by working-men almost exclusively."

[1] F. Engels, *The Condition of the Working Class in England in 1844* (1892 edn), 238-9. This testimony is upheld by Coates: "It is worthy of remark, that whilst the mechanic zealously bestirs himself to attach his fellow-workmen to provident societies, trade societies, temperance societies, and the various political clubs that from time to time agitate the country, there is no evidence to show any of this spirit of proselytism in favour of the Mechanics' Institutions." T. Coates, *op. cit.*, 22.

Here Engels pays particular tribute to the Socialists who "have done wonders for the education of the proletariat". They have translated and disseminated in cheap editions the works of the French materialists —of Helvétius, Holbach, Diderot; Proudhon's *Property* and Strauss's *Life of Jesus*—one of the first rational critiques of Christianity—also circulate only among working-men. So also with English philosophy:

> "The two great practical philosophers . . . Bentham and Godwin, are, especially the latter, almost exclusively the property of the proletariat; for though Bentham has a school within the Radical bourgeoisie, it is only the proletariat and the Socialists who have succeeded in developing his teachings a step forward."

In literature, it is above all the poets who appeal:

> "Shelley, the genius, the prophet, Shelley, and Byron with his glowing sensuality and his bitter satire upon our existing society, find most of their readers in the proletariat."

Such works, often available only in journals and pamphlets, make up the reading of the workers who have thus provided for themselves a literature which "is far in advance of the whole bourgeois literature in intrinsic worth".[1]

Engels lived in the centre of the Chartist movement, at Manchester, which was also one of the greatest educational centres for both Chartists and Socialists. But much the same is heard of more remote areas where Chartist influence spread to revive earlier interest in politics and education. In 1847 Samuel Kydd wrote to the *Northern Star* of his experiences in Ayrshire.

> "The inhabitants of the weaving villages are the most intelligent men with whom I ever conversed; they are readers and thinkers. In those districts is many a well-thumbed pile of pamphlets— Cobbett's *Register*, the *Black Dwarf*, and twopenny *Dispatch* being the text-books of the old politicians; the *Northern Star* the book of political life read by the younger of the schools of political and social regeneration. Literature, too, is a favourite pursuit with the weaving population. . . . Those who speak of the ignorance of the working classes would do well to visit Ayrshire."[2]

It has been for generations, he adds, the seat of political and religious revolt.

[1] Engels, *op. cit.*, 238-40.   [2] *Northern Star*, December 25th, 1847.

3. WILLIAM LOVETT ON EDUCATION

The general ideas which inspired working-class education have already been discussed. These were constantly disseminated through the press and by lectures, while Chartist and Socialist journals co-ordinated and guided local efforts and consolidated the organisation of new ventures initiated by the missionaries of the Rational Religionists and the regular "lecturers" maintained by the Chartist organisation.

There were also various school texts and books, of which little is yet known. But in 1841 there appeared a more specific contribution to the theory and practice of education, a work which went into much greater detail on questions of educational content and method than those of other educationists—Thompson, Carlile and Owen himself not excepted. This was *Chartism*, written under conditions of great difficulty by William Lovett and John Collins during their confinement in Warwick gaol in 1839-40.

In the *Address on Education*, issued in 1837 when the People's Charter was also formulated, Lovett had proclaimed a humanist approach to popular education. It was not "a boon to be sparingly conferred upon the multitude" but a "universal instrument for advancing the dignity of man, and for gladdening his existence".[1] In *Chartism* full body is given to the conception of a broad, general education—equally concerned with physical, intellectual and moral development—which should be freely available to all as a right, scientific and unsectarian in character, and under democratic local control. The system Lovett envisages has much in common with that advanced by the great Czech reformer, Comenius, two centuries before and by the advocates of a national system of education during the English Revolution. Education should be given in a series of common schools organised in ascending stages. Its foundation should be infant schools for children aged three to six; thereafter all children should go to preparatory schools until the age of nine and subsequently to high schools. A system of free colleges "for the higher branches of learning" and of normal colleges to train teachers crowns the system.

(i) *The Purpose and Methods of Education*

In his general approach, Lovett takes up and develops the prevailing educational ideas of the "practical philosophers" of the age. The

---

[1] The "Address on Education" issued by the Working Men's Association is reprinted in Lovett, *op. cit.*, 135-46.

ultimate aim of education is the happiness of the individual. But individual happiness depends not only on the full development of mental and physical powers but also on moral training and guidance. Everyone, "unless they are malformed or diseased", can profit from such an education; if this fact has been obscured it is because the majority have not yet been subject to any positive teaching or guidance.

"All men are not gifted with great strength of body or powers of intellect, but all are so wisely and wonderfully endowed, that all have capacities for becoming intelligent, moral, and happy members of society; and if they are not, it is *for want of their capacities being so properly cultivated*, as to cause them to live in accordance with the physical laws of their nature, the social institutions of man, and the moral laws of God. Education will cause every latent seed of the mind to germinate and spring up into useful life, which otherwise might have lain buried in ignorance, and died in the corruptions of its own nature; thousands of our countrymen, endowed with all the capabilities for becoming the *guides* and *lights* of society, from want of this glorious blessing, are doomed to grovel in vice and ignorance, to pine in obscurity and want."

All this can be changed, men can control the world instead of being victims of their environment, once they are armed with knowledge and aware how to put it to good use.

"Give to a man knowledge, and you give him a light to perceive and enjoy beauty, variety, surpassing ingenuity, and majestic grandeur, which his mental darkness previously concealed from him —enrich his mind and strengthen his understanding, and you give him powers to render all art and nature subservient to his purposes— call forth his moral excellence in union with his intellect, and he will apply every power of thought and force of action to enlighten ignorance, alleviate misfortune, remove misery, and banish vice; and, as far as his abilities permit, to prepare a highway to the world's happiness."[1]

The individual's happiness does not, of course, depend only on his own education; it depends also on the character and political organisation of society. But social evils, which may corrupt a child however well he has been educated, themselves originate in ignorance. Therefore not only individual happiness, but also social reformation, depend on

[1] *Chartism; a New Organisation of the People*. Written in Warwick Gaol by William Lovett, Cabinet-maker, and John Collins, Tool-maker (2nd ed 1841), 75-6.

getting *"at the root of the evil"*, on "establishing a just and wise system of education".[1] As an example, Lovett cites those excluded from the franchise who submit to this injustice because of ignorance. "Whether . . . we view man individually, socially, or politically," he concludes, "there is no situation he can be placed in, in which his happiness will not be marred by ignorance, and in which it would not be promoted by the spread of knowledge and wisdom."[2]

Education, then, must be given to all for its own sake—not only to the few who use it to rise in the social scale and who, therefore, deny it to the mass of the people; nor should it be designed for the purpose of "moulding the infant mind upon the principles of church and state" or according to the morality of particular sects. Education for all must be education in "the great principles of human nature, social morality, and political justice". For this reason education must be unsectarian, and, to prevent it being used to enhance the power of a despotic central government, it must be under the control of directly elected local representatives.[3]

Perhaps the keynote of Lovett's educational theory is the linking of theory and practice—of the child's activity with his physical, intellectual and moral development. In the infant school, fresh air, physical exercise and games are given a particular importance. But Lovett's general conception of physical education extends much more widely than this. The child must not only experience physical activity but must be led to understand *why* and *how* fresh air and exercise are essential to health. Mere precepts, the inculcation of purely mechanical habits, are useless; the aim must be to develop a rational understanding, based on knowledge of the bodily functions and leading to "a blending of habit and conviction in the very nature of the child". Teaching therefore, must include not only the rules of health, but human physiology generally.[4] Indeed, Lovett felt this normally neglected subject to be so important that he later wrote a text-book on human physiology which was used in a number of schools.[5]

Of equal, if not greater importance is moral education to predispose the child "to a love of justice, truth, benevolence, firmness and respect for whatever is great and good". That these abstractions, which bring to mind the eighteenth-century educators, had a very positive content is made clear in the *Address*, where the need for moral training is

---

[1] *Chartism*, 79.   [2] *Ibid.*, 80.   [3] *Ibid.*, 79-83.   [4] *Ibid.*, 87-8.
[5] *Life and Struggles*, 363-4. The book is entitled *Elementary Anatomy and Physiology (for schools and private instructors)*. It is extremely well illustrated, with large coloured plates showing the structure of the nervous system and of the human organs generally.

closely linked to the teacher's duty "familiarly to acquaint them with the *social* and *political* relations that exist between them and their fellow beings". Just as the purpose of physical education, as Lovett later expressed it, was to enable children "to acquire some knowledge of their own nature", so the purpose of moral education was to give "a knowledge of the conditions of social and political life, and the rules of conduct on which their well-being chiefly depends".[1] For the Chartist "justice, truth, benevolence and firmness" meant a specific attitude and mode of conduct, a morality which arose out of the needs of the working people, and which contained its own justification. Moral education in this sense was a necessary and integral part of the ill-round development of the individual.

In this sphere also, Lovett emphasises, mere advice and precepts are ineffective; to form the child's moral outlook, a positive moral education is essential. Conceptions of moral behaviour can only be formed by the children if they are concretised, "made evident to their senses", and arise from the children's activities themselves. In the playground, for instance, "the teacher should incite (the children) to amusement and activity, in order to develop their characters"; in the case of misbehaviour, she should not attempt coercion—which must surely fail—her object must be to convince the child, "she should put forward her *reasons* rather than her authority". All rewards and distinctions should be avoided since these excite "envy, hatred and hypocrisy"; "all corporal punishments should be dispensed with, . . . as they serve to call forth revengeful propensities in some, and cow others into slavish subjection". Children should be brought up to "love one another"—while the essential educative task is to develop in each child "a high sense of duty" based on a conscious understanding that "he who cultivates his powers, and employs them to promote *the happiness of society*, is sure to meet with the approval of all good men, independently of his own conscientious satisfaction".[2]

The same concern for the unity of theory and practice underlies Lovett's proposals for intellectual education. Basing himself firmly on the classical tradition of philosophic materialism, he saw the observation of reality as the foundation for the formation of ideas and concepts; since knowledge of the external world is derived from the evidence of the senses, the capacity for "clear and consecutive reasoning" and for gaining an accurate knowledge of all phenomena can only result from the analysis of reality. It is in the light of this approach that

---

[1] *Life and Struggles*, 431.   [2] *Chartism*, 98-9, 48-9.

methods of teaching are defined. The teacher must proceed systematic-ally "step by step"—this is the condition for developing the child's understanding; otherwise the children will merely "*imbibe her explana-tions by rote*, without understanding them," becoming the victims of mere verbalism.

"The child", writes Lovett, in a passage which recalls Milton, Dury, Petty and other educational writers of the 1640s,

> "may be burthened with a multitude of words—mere barren sym-bols of realities of which it has no cognizance, with imaginary notions of every description—mere treasured phrases, imbibed from every source, without inquiry or knowledge of the reality,—it may be furnished with rules, figures, facts, and problems by rote without examination, and consequently valueless for practical purposes;—these acquisitions failing to produce *clear ideas*, and forming no *real basis* for reflection or judgment, cannot, therefore, be properly designated *real knowledge*."

Yet, as things are, this kind of learning passes as the best:

> "this word-teaching, rote-learning, memory-loading system is still dignified with the name of 'education'; and those who are stored with the greatest lumber are frequently esteemed the greatest 'scholars'. Seeing this, need we wonder that many scholars have so little practical or useful knowledge—are superficial in reasoning, defective in judgment, and wanting in their moral duties? or that the greatest block-heads at school often make brighter men than those whose intellects have been injured by much cramming?"[1]

At a time when such men as James Mill advocated the acquisition of knowledge in the form of gobbets of information, repeated unt learned by heart, when rote-learning was as rife in the grammar schoo. as in the monitorial schools, Lovett is emphasising the prime import-ance of educational method. He describes an apparatus of his own invention for teaching reading, which is designed to ensure the forma-tion of firm associations between words and phrases and the actual objects and qualities designated. Similar concrete methods, invented by Wilderspin, are proposed for the formation of elementary number concepts. But it is above all when discussing the teaching of science and mathematics that Lovett stresses the need to promote the child's self-activity, while also using every possible teaching aid and model

[1] *Chartism*, 89-90.

which can represent real phenomena in a way easily comprehensible to the human mind.

On this last subject he has many suggestions. The infants' classroom should be ornamented with coloured prints or drawings "in natural history, zoology, astronomy and machinery", together with models and specimens of minerals and fossils. Geometrical relationships should be taught with the aid of models, while weights and measures must be mastered by practice and experiment. In the preparatory schoolroom, which should be furnished with tables instead of desks, maps, drawings, diagrams and models of the various branches of knowledge should be available. Among these should be relief maps of the home county, prints or drawings of the human skeleton, muscular system and internal organs, geological and mineralogical maps of the earth's strata, diagrams illustrating the solar system, the operation of the laws of mechanics, perspective, and so on.

Every school should have a pair of globes, a quadrant, thermometer, compass, geometrical models, and a model or cast of the human brain. Such apparatus, together with the teacher's explanations and the children's own activity and experiments, form the means to education; it is a primary task of the teacher to use all this apparatus in such a way as to develop a clear understanding in the minds of the children.

Further evidence that Lovett fully appreciates the creative aspect of education is to be found in the importance he attaches to developing the capacity for self-expression. Writing and composition must be linked to the children's experiences. The younger ones can be set to describe "places, scenes and occurrences" witnessed during walks with the teacher outside the school; elder children should give short talks to the class on subjects selected by themselves and answer questions put by the class. This will also encourage the acquisition of knowledge and improve the children's mastery of speech.

Lovett's ideas about the subjects which should be taught in school are already apparent from the description of teaching aids and methods. Heir to the age of Enlightenment, an eager student of the Encyclopaedists, of Paine, Owen and Carlile, Lovett lays the greatest emphasis on the teaching of science; particularly geology, zoology and astronomy, which he saw as the great liberating studies of the time.[1]

[1] This conception comes out clearly in his later remarks on astronomy: "A science that I think all should know something about, at least of its great outlines. For in contemplating the heavens of gorgeous grandeur and boundless extent—filled with suns and worlds innumerable—the mind is filled with the most delightful imaginings regarding their nature, origin, and extent; and is lifted far above all superstitious grovelling on

Physics and chemistry are, however, the basis for understanding the laws of nature. Other subjects border on to man's control over nature. Theory and practice should be linked by teaching mathematics in relation to its practical applications; the same is true of horticulture and botany which, based on practical work in the school gardens, should lead on to agriculture. Thereby the children, already impressed with the moral value of labour, will learn the use of tools and the instruments of labour; they should also learn about the functioning and use of such "machinery, manual and scientific operations" as they can have access to.[1]

The same outlook characterises Lovett's approach to other subjects. Geography should give an understanding of the physical formation, trade and manufactures of the pupil's own country. His comments on history recall Carlile's strictures about current teaching. It should be taught, he says, so that the child can "strip sophistry of its speciousness, interest of its panegyric, and heroes of their hollow fame; and, as far as possible, . . . extract wisdom from the black record of our species in their advance from barbarism *towards* civilisation".[2] Further, politics and political economy are essential if the child is to become familiar with his "rights and duties, his moral and social relations".

But all this knowledge was to be imparted in such a way that the children came to love learning. The classroom should be a place of "lively and interesting enjoyments", the teachers affectionate and cheerful, singing and dancing should form part of each day's activities, particularly for the younger children, and there should be special efforts to develop the child's imaginative powers. The stress on the glory of nature, so prominent in Owenite teaching, finds expression in Lovett's wish that children should learn to appreciate the "beauty, grandeur and sublimity" of "the glowing landscape, the flowing stream, the raging storm, the brilliant sunshine, and the fragile flower; and, above all, the radiant glory of a star-light night". Such lessons, he

becoming acquainted with the great facts the science of the heavens unfolds. It has been in this region of enquiry above all others that the human mind has been expanded to the achievement of its grandest and proudest triumphs; for in striving to grasp the mighty magnitudes, the rapid motions, the unfathomed distances, and the laws that govern the majestic movement of the orbs above him, man has not only unravelled thread by thread the veil of mystery and error, but has made his knowledge of the heavens his noblest guide on earth; enabling him to push his fearless course across the trackless ocean, to spread his bounties, extend his knowledge, improve and bless his brethren, and finally, let us hope, to link the whole world together in amity." *Life and Struggles*, 376-7; see also the succeeding passage on geology. Lovett later wrote elementary text-books on both these subjects.

[1] *Chartism*, 104.   [2] *Ibid.*, 102.

added, "will teach them to soar beyond the grovelling pursuits of vice and sordid meanness".[1]

Lovett, then, expressed in the most definite terms the belief that education is a science. Use of the correct methods could develop people with an accurate knowledge of the real world and of social relations; with a capacity for rational thought, a specific moral outlook based on an inner awareness of moral values, judgment and the ability to communicate ideas. These methods should be applied in the teaching of a wide range of subjects which would introduce children to every aspect of the natural world and society; to labour and recreation, to an understanding of their own bodies and minds, to the appreciation of beauty and to joy in achievement and well-doing.

It could only be, at this period, a man who had experienced the creativeness of labour and untiringly sought knowledge on his own account who could so blend the two to formulate a coherent method of education; one which united theory and practice and envisaged the educational process as an active one, whether for pupil or teacher, leading to something new. Carlile had written glowingly of the powers of reason and the promise of science. Owen had given concrete form at New Lanark to the belief that children must be educated in body and mind and that the classroom should be a place of joy offering stimulation and aids to learning in the form of pictures, models, books. All the Owenite educators stressed the importance of learning about society and, too, the extent to which society forms man. But it is Lovett alone who grasps the contradiction and indicates, though he is not himself altogether aware of doing so, that man makes himself; that by his activity, by making skills and knowledge his own, man can change his nature.

While, therefore, the "practical philosophers" of the age were still approaching education externally, emphasising, as did Bentham, its "plastic power" when administered from above, Lovett sees education as a great creative power. This is the key to his whole approach to methods of teaching, and this is where his greatest contribution lies. The teacher must see his task, not as that of imposing knowledge and habits on the children, but of assisting them to acquire knowledge and habits through their own activity, so exercising their reason and moral judgment that they come to understand for themselves and to know aright.

Such an approach was completely foreign to men who saw education

[1] *Chartism*, 98.

as a means of moulding society to serve the interests of a class or sect; inevitably Mill and the Churchmen of the day laid stress on the need to teach only the "right" ideas. But while the Mechanics' Institutes taught only the accepted truths of bourgeois political economy, the Church only an accepted creed, to the Chartist Halls were invited men "of adverse opinions" so that the workers could "freely discuss" the exposition of their principles. This attitude expressed the interests of a class which had nothing to lose and everything to gain from the spread of scientific ideas about the natural world, society and man. It is essentially, however much he may draw on the experience and ideas of others, the interests and aspirations of the working class that find expression in Lovett's educational writings and that give these their distinctive character and worth.

(ii) *"Knowledge Chartism"*

It is easy to understand why Lovett became preoccupied with the question of education. To read his book is to see only the importance and potentialities of education for the workers and to forget the obstacles that stood in the way of establishing an organised, and rational, system of schooling; of translating these educational ideas into practice.

In both the *Address* and in *Chartism* it is proposed that a system of common schools—infant, preparatory and high schools—should be provided by the state. But these should be organised, administered and maintained by local committees elected annually on a universal franchise; these committees having the power to levy a rate and responsibility for appointing and paying teachers, indeed for the whole management of the school even down to the choice of textbooks.

But in *Chartism* more immediate plans are advanced for the establishment and financing of schools, based on the developing experience of the Chartist movement. Lovett and Collins propose to establish a National Association and, through this, to provide district halls where adults and children can be educated. A plan of a district hall is given which includes an infant, preparatory and high school for boys and girls, situated in the midst of a recreation ground and flower beds. The school itself includes a museum, laboratory and workshop, cloak-rooms and baths for the children and apartments for the teachers.

Institutions of this kind, once established, would ensure the achievement of the political demands of the working class in a comparatively short time; of this, imbued with his faith in education, Lovett was convinced.

> "The spark once struck is inextinguishable, and will go on extending and radiating with increasing power; thought will generate thought; and each illumined mind will become a centre for the enlightenment of thousands, till the effulgent blaze penetrates every cranny of corruption, and scares selfishness and injustice from their seats of power."

This could not but be so for Chartism spoke for all men. Its aims, wrote Lovett, are "the regeneration of all, the subjugation of none"; its objects, "to place our institutions on the basis of justice, to secure labour its reward, merit its fruits, to purify the heart and rectify the conduct of all, by knowledge, morality and love of freedom."[1]

Lovett himself had initially been active in the early co-operative movement, eventually parting with the Owenites because of their failure to appreciate the need for political action. But when he subsequently became one of the leaders during the first stage of Chartism, he brought with him into this political movement much that he had learned from Owen, in particular a passionate belief in the power of education to effect fundamental social change. This was reinforced by the working out of his educational method. On his release from gaol in 1840 the most important step seemed to him to be the formation of a special organisation to promote child and adult education, and this he immediately set out to do.

Francis Place, telling Lovett that he would "never have even one school",[2] attempted to discourage these plans and engage his support for the campaign led by industrialists against the Corn Laws. But Lovett published his book and turned his energies to education. One school was, in fact, founded with the help of a middle-class friend. No doubt, also, some of the Chartist halls and schools were inspired by Lovett's ideas, though they necessarily did not begin to approach his ideal plan. But in general, the formation of the National Association brought to a head what had long been differences between Lovett and the more radical Chartist leaders.

The beginnings of what was a fundamental divergence of view are to be discerned already in 1837 with the secession of George Julian Harney and his associates from the London Working Men's Association. Differences arose over Lovett's desire to collaborate with middle-class Radicals, and to limit activities in order to retain their support,

[1] *Chartism*, 9.   [2] G. Wallas, *The Life of Francis Place* (1951 edn), 378-9.

while also directing his main efforts into educational rather than directly political channels. Harney's letter explaining the reasons for his secession sets out the arguments which continued to be put by Chartist leaders in succeeding years, both in answer to men of Lovett's stamp and to the Owenites:

> "We fully appreciate the advantages resulting from education, and we would earnestly wish to see the principles of a sound educational system widely disseminated; but we cannot but consider all the ideas of amelioration from this source alone, to be chimerical, perfectly illusory. Depend upon it, fellow Democrats, that that which your enemies will not give to justice, they will not yield to *moral* persuasion. No, we must act upon their fears, if we cannot upon their sympathies. Nor can we subscribe to the notion that, under present circumstances, the adoption of a sound educational system, one, the principal feature of which shall be to teach the people their rights, and not merely, as now, their duties, is practicable. Men, interested in the continuance of the present robber-like system of society—the lordly aristocrat—the monied vampire and the prostituted priest—in a word the enemies to the rights, the liberties, and the happiness of millions, will pretendedly acquiesce in the propriety of *educating*—of *moralising* the people; and it will ever be found that so long as the people's political rights are withheld from them, any system of education which meets with the acquiescence of their foes, will have for its object the perpetuation of the people's slavery."

The Working Men's Association, Harney goes on, have

> "uniformly and pertinaciously inculcated the belief of the possibility of the establishment of a system of education, by and through which we shall acquire our rights. They have repeatedly scouted the idea that their rights are to be attained by any other means than *educating* the people; nay more, they have calumniated those who have entertained and expressed a contrary belief . . ."

At the same time, in order to further specific educational plans, Harney charged, the association courted the support of the "respectables"—Hume, Grote, and others of the Philosophic Radicals. It was the workers alone who could secure their own emancipation.[1]

Subsequently, Lovett fully participated in the struggle for the Charter; his imprisonment resulted from political activities in 1839 which saw Chartist agitations rising to a peak. But with the mass

[1] *Northern Star*, March 24th, 1838.

imprisonments and repression of that year there followed a lull and a period of relative consolidation. In 1840 the National Charter Association was set up, financed by contributions from local associations which served to maintain regular "lecturers". Harney held such a post and toured continuously in the north and Scotland organising and promoting local organisations which, in turn, went on to found libraries and halls.

The leaders of the main Chartist movement strongly opposed Lovett's attempt, in 1841, to set up a new association for a specifically educational purpose. Feargus O'Connor and his supporters contemptuously termed this approach "Knowledge Chartism" which, with "Church Chartism" and "Teetotal Chartism" they regarded as diversions (even treacherous diversions) from the main objective of all true Chartists—the political struggle for Universal Suffrage. By the end of 1842, William Lovett had dropped out of the mainstream of the movement to devote himself to particular educational projects. But it was, nevertheless, the political wing of Chartism which effectively conducted the main struggle for educational reform.

4. THE PEOPLE'S CHARTER AND A NATIONAL SYSTEM OF EDUCATION

One of the most influential of the Chartist leaders was Bronterre O'Brien, who had once been a star pupil at the school at Edgeworthstown, run by Richard Lovell, Edgeworth's son. Subsequently he had gone on to university and studied for the law before throwing in his lot with the working-class movement. As early as 1833 he is found taking issue with Cobbett in the matter of the first Parliamentary grant for education.

Cobbett, member for Oldham, opposed the grant, arguing that schools were not improving the condition of the country. Education was increasing, but men still became more and more immoral; there was then no justification for taxing the people to impose more of it—this was a French, a doctrinaire, plan which he would always oppose.[1]

Earlier, as we have seen, Priestley and his associates, including Godwin, had opposed the conception of a state system of education

[1] J. E. G. De Montmorency, *State Intervention in English Education* (1902), 239; Cobbett's attacks on "Headikashun", which he believed would be used to indoctrinate the poor with the ideas of Malthus and Ricardo, were developed in the *Political Register*, September 21st and December 7th, 1833, April 19th, 1834, May 9th and June 6th, 1835.

on the grounds that it would be used as a means of oppression. This attitude persisted strongly, but O'Brien was not disposed to question state aid for schools and sharply attacked Cobbett's attitude in the *Poor Man's Guardian.*

Cobbett, he writes, does not care whether the workers are educated or not, provided they can plough and make hurdles and have plenty of home-brewed ale and bacon. In Cobbett's view, the workers' millennium is where they work well and feed well. This, O'Brien charges, is to hold that the millions are born to toil for the few, that education is good for those who can get it, but not for those who cannot. O'Brien's opinion is the antipodes of this, and he regrets that Cobbett has lost his powers, and is now opposed to the cause of humanity. Elementary education, says Cobbett, will generate idleness and vice. If this is so, counters O'Brien, why all Cobbett's own efforts to educate himself and others—his *Grammar*, the *Register*, and so on? There is no rational cause for his present objections. Education is a stimulant to virtue and public spirit. If it is widely diffused it will do nothing but good.[1]

This approach, in the first place that of O'Brien and his pupil Harney, finds expression in the chief Chartist paper, *Northern Star*, and other periodicals after 1838, always in conjunction with political and economic demands. The attitude towards education is throughout positive. Even elementary education in reading and writing is the key to the sciences. It is, therefore, "a matter of high moment to seize every opportunity of extending to the masses the possession of a key to that intellectual improvement which can scarcely fail to be the vestibule or hall of entrance to the fane of freedom".[2] "Every child has a claim to be taught," writes the *Northern Star*, discussing the Factory Bill of 1843, "the children of the poor are enveloped in gross ignorance and mental darkness." But the Sunday schools must be superseded by a system of day schools:

> "The *necessity* that exists for Sunday schools at all, is a strong condemnation of all our fiscal, political and social arrangements. The Sabbath should be a day of REST. But there is no rest for the children of the poor. . . . The working day is the time for the schoolmaster to pursue his avocation."

The Sunday schools have certainly taught hundreds of thousands

[1] *Poor Man's Guardian*, August 24th, 1833; September 14th, 1833; October 19th, 1833; November 12th, 1833; November 26th, 1833.
[2] *Northern Star*, April 15th, 1843.

to read. When children, so taught, "have been cast abroad into the wide world, to battle with the stern realities of life", thought has been awakened and "man's injustice has taken a firm hold on minds". Nevertheless, on a Sunday the children should be out on the greens, not incarcerated within the four walls of a school.[1]

Again and again the *Northern Star* returns to the main point: that there can be no short cut, the problem must be tackled at the roots. The conditions of life of the people are appalling, wages low, hours of work long, children flung into employment "just when the mind should be receiving instruction".[2] The first essential step towards education is, then, the amelioration of the condition of the people. In other words, since nothing can be expected from the "Malthusians", the "Philosophic Radicals", the working class must gain representation in Parliament; they must win the Charter, and everything else will follow. The "Education-mongers" are seeking to extinguish Chartism by the diffusion of "knowledge", wrote the *Northern Star* in 1839. "Those gentlemen denounce all who will not join in the admonition to abandon politics for the more profitable pursuit of literature and the arts." And again, towards the close of 1840,

> "Let the people have their rights, and those comforts to which they are so justly entitled, and they will instruct themselves. Let their hours of labour be diminished, and they will have time and inclination for intellectual pursuits. Let them receive their due wages, and they will have the means. Above all, let each have a share in the state by Universal Suffrage, and they will have a grand object for the improvement of themselves and their children in every way. . . . The true and profitable education, will be that which is voluntarily sought by men rendered peaceful in mind and free in action."[3]

A truly human education, wrote the *Northern Star*, returning to this question in 1846, "can only be attained when the people are all politically equal". Hence "the political enfranchisement of the whole male adult population, is an indispensable preliminary to every kind of educational, social and physical improvement".[4] "Education will follow the suffrage as sure as day succeeds night."[5] The argument that the people were too ignorant to exercise the vote was inevitably denounced. "The ignorance of the people is the tyrant's title to power",

[1] *Northern Star*, May 6th, 1843.   [2] *Ibid.*, August 29th, 1840.
[3] *Ibid.*, June 22nd, 1839; December 26th, 1840.
[4] *Ibid.*, July 11th, 1846.   [5] *Ibid.*, September 12th, 1846.

wrote O'Connor, and an accompanying leader succinctly demonstrates that the state sets out to keep the people in ignorance by refusing leisure for education, and keeping children's noses to the grindstone.

Throughout the decade of Chartist activity (1838-48), its leaders constantly hammered home the point that all general talk about the need for education, all general schemes for the establishment of schools, evaded the main issue—the overriding necessity to withdraw child labour from the factories so that children might have time for education, as well as the need to reduce the adult working day to allow for recreation and leisure. At the same time there is the realisation that labour is an essential aspect of education. "All the *work* that a child or youth should perform before the age of fourteen", wrote the *Northern Star* in 1843, "should be only such as is needful for *educational* purposes."[1]

Meanwhile the fullest publicity was given to the Report of the Children's Employment Commission in Mines and Manufactories, the *Northern Star* devoting considerable space to quotations exposing the conditions of work of the children, and focusing attention on the lack of education and understanding that the Commissioners brought out so clearly.[2] Equally, full support is given to Sir James Graham's Bill in 1843, except for the clause providing for a reduction of the legal age of employment from nine to eight; the proposal to reduce hours of labour for children in mills from 8 to $6\frac{1}{2}$ is welcomed as "a great step"—especially since there is also a schooling clause which should allow for "properly conducted" schools instead of the makeshift arrangements exposed by the Commissioners where " 'the school' has . . . been the 'fire-hole' and the 'schoolmaster' the 'firer-up' ".[3]

During the spring of 1843, leader after leader in the *Northern Star* returns to Graham's Bill, supporting Lord John Russell's amendments against the gathering attacks by the nonconformists; not least those of Edward Baines, representative of the dissenting manufacturers of the north, who, it was claimed, although attacking the Bill openly on religious grounds, were using this as a cover for their real aim: to prevent the government carrying the protective clauses.[4] So urgent was the need for education—so tragic the condition of the children exposed by the Children's Employment Commission—that the complaints of Church and Dissent against the clauses of the Act are of

[1] *Northern Star*, March 11th, 1843.   [2] *Ibid.*, May 26th, 1842.
[3] *Ibid.*, March 11th, 1843.   [4] *Ibid.*, April 22nd, 1843.

little importance "when weighed against the great comprehensive principle of national instruction". "We say, therefore, by all means let the Education Bill pass."[1] But the Bill was shelved, the government giving way to the opposition. This withdrawal, the *Northern Star* characterised as one of the most disgraceful acts of the government.[2]

In general, the political struggle for education was inseparably linked with continuing action to secure a shortening of the working day. Whereas in the mid-1830s the main object of attack had been the hated Poor Law, a decade later the working-class movement was in the thick of the battle for the Ten Hour Bill. Here again, the main opponents were the "enlightened" representatives of the industrial middle class—Bright, for instance, strongly opposing state limitation of the hours of adult labour, while at the same time claiming that no man was more strongly in favour of the diffusion of education than himself.

At meetings in support of the Ten Hour Bill (and the Eight Hour Bill) speaker after speaker stressed the same essential point. The miners, it was said, at Bolton, "had to toil 12 or 14 hours a day, so that they had no opportunity of enjoying rational amusement, or of cultivating their minds". A Warrington meeting passed a resolution supporting the Bill, whereby "the domestic comfort of the operatives would be increased, and they would have more frequent opportunities for moral and intellectual improvement". At Manchester it was said that fathers and children worked in the same factories; but the workers, deeply impressed with the duty they owed their children, deplored conditions which prevented them from instructing their children in moral and domestic duties. The *Northern Star*, welcoming this renewed agitation, claimed that "the hours spared from slave labour would be bestowed upon mental culture and the discovery of the value of free labour—rather than wasted on the GIN PALACE and PEEP SHOW", as was claimed by the Bill's opponents.[3] "The masses are awake to the value of education," wrote a correspondent to the Lancashire *Ten Hours' Advocate* in 1847, "it is for this they desire the leisure to promote it. Education is to the mind what knives and forks are to the stomach, the instrument for supplying each with their proper food."

This lesson is once more applied to educational policies. "The educational reform that Lord John Russell will doubtlessly propound, according to his political creed," argued the *Northern Star* in 1847,

---

1 *Northern Star*, April 15th, 1843.   2 *Ibid.*, June 17th, 1843.
3 *Ibid.*, January 18th, 1845; January 31st, 1846; November 14th, 1846.

"will be more advanced by a Ten Hour Bill than by the mere establishment of schools, which, under the present system, the working
man's child has not much leisure to attend—even though an education grant should equal that for Her Majesty's stables."[1] At the same
time, while exposing the policies of Whigs and middle-class Radicals,
Chartist leaders held that it was the duty of the state to provide for
the education of the people. Since education must be an affair of the
state and be national, wrote the *Northern Star* in April 1847, it should
exclude all theology and dogma and confine itself to secular instruction. A national system of schools would increase the power of the
people, since it would increase knowledge. Thereby the dangers of
state control can be avoided, for the power of public opinion will
prevent the system from leading to the despotism typical of the
Continent.[2]

Whereas the industrial middle class held to, and incorporated in
the Poor Law, the principle that no man had the right to any support out of another man's pocket, Chartists argued that those who
exploited the workers had a duty to educate their children. "We
affirm the right of every child to be educated is as binding as its right
to be fed when hungry", wrote Samuel Kydd in *The Labourer* in
the same year. "If the low wages and inadequate means of parents
be such as prevent them from educating their children, it is the duty
of those parties who profit by their labour to provide the necessary
education." The government must take the necessary steps to enforce
this. In the meantime, Kydd continues,

> "the people continue to educate themselves; knowledge progresses;
> and the direction of the increasing intelligence will, at no distant
> day, be manifested, in forcing the rich few to contribute for the
> mental support of the poor many, by establishing a system of educa-
> tion wisely arranged in details, efficient and honest in principle,
> educating Jew and Gentile, Catholic, Protestant and Freethinker,
> without distinction, and leaving the bubbling ocean of creeds and
> faiths to be quelled by increased reasoning powers, teaching all to
> discriminate between truth and error for themselves, having no
> fear, but much hope, in the result."[3]

At the close of the Chartist period, then, the demand for universal,
secular education is advanced as strongly as ever, combined with a

---

[1] *Northern Star,* January 30th, 1847.   [2] *Ibid.,* April 24th, 1847.

[3] "Education and the Russell Cabinet", *The Labourer,* (ed Feargus O'Connor and Ernest
Jones), Vol. II, 1847, 6, 11-12.

sharp rebuttal of the interested claims of Church and Dissent, Whigs and Radicals. Sometimes it seems a nebulous rather than a clear demand for a national system. The third point in Ernest Jones' election address to the electors and non-electors at Halifax (July 1847) is for a "Voluntary system of education, enabling every section of the community to give their children religious and secular instruction, in accordance with their own convictions, without any Government interference or control".[1] But Ernest Jones, one of the outstanding leaders after 1845, is stressing freedom of religion against the claims of the Church to inculcate its dogma in the schools. Chartism, wrote McDouall, another of the more militant leaders of the final stage of Chartism, in 1848, "conceives that each family has a right to instruct its members in the faith it has adopted, and that from public, free and national schools all sectarianism should be banished, and the children of all sects meet on common ground without having their minds biased from the creed of their parents".[2]

Such men carried on with political agitation after the presentation of the great petition of 1848 which marked the culminating point of the Chartist movement, in face now of widespread arrests and intimidation. But a forecast of the fact that, in future, it was the trade unionists who took up the demand for education is to be found in the Appeal of the London Trades Delegates to the Trades of Great Britain and Ireland in November 1848, which claims the duty of government to be "to secure a real practical, scientific and secular education for the people, as the only means of fully developing the genius and intellect of the nation, and rendering it subservient to the interests of the whole community".[3]

Chartist demands for education, however, continued to be advanced under the able and determined leadership of Ernest Jones. As late as 1851, when the Chartist Convention met in London, the third point on the programme presented, which was introduced by Ernest Jones, concerns education; the first calling for the nationalisation of the land, and the second for the separation of church and state. "As every man has the right to the means of physical life," runs the proposal, "so he has to the means of mental activity. It is as unjust to withhold aliment from the mind, as it is to deny food to the body. Education should, therefore, be national, universal, gratuitous and, to a certain extent, compulsory." Schools, colleges, and universities, supported by

[1] *Northern Star*, July 3rd, 1847.   [2] *Ibid.*, July 1st, 1848.
[3] *Ibid.*, November 18th, 1848.

the state, should be free, and it should be compulsory for all parents "to have their children educated in the common branches of learning". Higher education should be free but optional, while the system of apprenticeship, long outmoded, should be replaced by a system of industrial (technical) schools where "the young may be taught the various trades and professions".[1]

By 1850, therefore, the establishment of a national system of education could figure as part of a working-class political programme, as one of a number of indispensable political reforms. At first the way to achieving a scientific, secular education for all children had been seen largely in terms of establishing independent institutions under working-class control, closely allied with active political organisations. Later, while some adhered to this view, indeed concentrated on education to the exclusion of politics, the Chartist movement led the struggle for political rights as the essential prerequisite to any real educational reform; though, meanwhile, any extension of education in the direction of a national system, any step to free the children from slavery in the factories, was upheld and pressed.

This marked a new stage in so far as the winning of the right to education was seen as an aspect of winning the battle in the political field, in the last analysis winning political power. From this new vantage point the leaders of the working-class movement foresaw the lines on which education must develop; and in propagating their view, in opposition to Whigs, Tories, and the religious bodies which pursued the interests of a single class or creed, spoke in the interests of all.

[1] John Saville, *Ernest Jones: Chartist*, (1952), 260. Jones defended these proposals in detail, especially the demand for compulsory education, in his journal *Notes to the People*. See Vol. I, No. 6, 120; No. 7, 131-2.

CHAPTER VI

THE STATE AND EDUCATION (I), ESTABLISHING AN EDUCATIONAL SYSTEM

THE last four chapters have considered educational developments in the light of the relations and antagonisms between the three main class groupings of the early nineteenth century. If, at this period, the main struggle lay between the capitalist class and landed aristocracy, each side attempted—with varying success—to win the workers as allies. The workers, in their turn, were able to take advantage of this situation to develop their own political activity; with the Radicals for Parliamentary Reform (from 1815), but with the Tories (Oastler, Sadler, Ashley, Stephens) for shorter hours and factory legislation. From 1832, the working class began to play an independent political role; the National Charter Association may be regarded as the first working-class political party.

But, after reaching a climax in 1848, the Chartist movement was suppressed and gradually disintegrated, and the organised working-class movement turned from political action to the economic front. Efforts were chiefly concentrated on building up the unions, on winning a legal status for trade union organisation and activity and so, through accepted forms of bargaining and conciliation, securing a greater place for the skilled worker within the capitalist order. In place, then, of the fight for a new and just social order, the leaders of the new amalgamated unions held out a perspective of co-operation with capital to extend and improve production and to ameliorate the conditions of key sections of the working class.

This attitude reflected also a changed approach on the part of an important section of industrialists towards the workers, a readiness, if only under considerable pressure, to raise the wages of the skilled workers in leading industries, even to countenance factory legislation which had earlier been hotly opposed. Such concessions could now be made, for the economic crisis of 1846 was followed by a trade revival which heralded an era of apparently limitless opportunity. Britain's huge colonial possessions provided raw materials in plenty, while the opening up of new markets in China and elsewhere fostered rapid industrial development at home. With other predominantly agricultural countries crying out for manufactured goods, and new means of communication making this potential world market actual, Britain's industrialists entered on twenty years of unexampled prosperity.

Full advantage could be taken of new opportunities for, with the repeal of the Corn Laws, the long struggle of the capitalist class to dominate the landed interest had ended in victory. The massive agitation carried out by the Anti-Corn Law League, led by the Lancashire manufacturers Cobden and Bright, had in the end forced the Tory government to give way. This defection, under the leadership of Peel— himself, significantly, a member of a leading Lancashire manufacturing family—split the Tory party and left the way open for two decades of what was effectively Whig-Liberal rule. It is from this moment that there dates the great expansionist epoch of free trade (the Manchester gospel) involving a "readjustment of the whole home and foreign, commercial and financial policy of England in accordance with the interests of the manufacturing capitalist—the class which now represented the nation".[1] And, just as this class now "mercilessly removed every obstacle" to industrial production, so also it was determined to remove obstacles which had hindered educational development, to remodel the educational system in its own image.

At an earlier stage, as we have seen, the philosophic radicals—spokesmen of the capitalist class—had advanced a distinctive theory of education and envisaged far-reaching reform. Schools and colleges of a new type were established, as models of what was required, and there was a constant and outspoken criticism of established institutions dominated by the Church and associated with Toryism or devoted to cultivating an effete and amoral aristocracy. After 1832 criticism was replaced by an insistent demand for Parliamentary action to enforce reform on closed corporations outside the reach of normal pressures.

So long as the old régime remained entrenched this demand was ignored. But after 1846 it could no longer be denied, and the first breach was made in 1850 with the appointment of Royal Commissions to enquire into Oxford and Cambridge. In 1861 the Clarendon Commission began its examination of the nine chief "public" schools, and three years later the Taunton Commission was requested to investigate all other endowed schools. Subsequently, in each case, Acts were passed enforcing the most essential reforms.

[1] F. Engels, Preface to the English edition of *The Condition of the Working Class in England in 1844*, (1892), xii.

The measures adopted, however, hardly followed the lines envisaged by James Mill and his colleagues, who had pressed exclusively the outlook and educational needs of the enlightened middle class of an earlier age—not least the claims of science—as against aristocratic culture and pretensions. However great divergencies might be on particular policies, there was no longer the same fundamental opposition of interest and outlook. The easy access to great wealth, and growing power, rapidly tamed men who had once rebelled against an aristocracy which appeared as the stumbling block to middleclass initiative, a millstone round the neck of the nation. The immense prosperity of the '50s and '60s not only permitted concessions to key sections of the working class, but could be shared also by the landowners; agriculture, in fact, contrary to what had been feared, also prospered at this time, for it was not until the American wheatlands were opened up that England was to be flooded with cheap corn. Hence, in place of former conflict, there was a new conjunction of interest, even a fusion, between former opponents. So the wealthier industrialists of this age cease to scorn aristocratic pretensions; individuals seek rather to learn the arts and graces of social superiority to add to the realities of political power, to climb into the ranks of the aristocracy themselves.

The outcome is the Victorian upper middle class. No longer "revolutionary", radical, secularist, the representatives of this class must be differentiated from the Manchester liberals who led the Anti-Corn Law League in the 1840s and from the new Radicalism centred on Birmingham, which began to develop in the late 1860s under the leadership of Joseph Chamberlain. In fact, the Parliamentary scene at this period was marked by a complex shifting of alignments. The old solid phalanxes of Whigs and Tories were breaking up and groups reformed in temporary coalitions; Radical and Irish M.Ps. introduced a new flexibility and made the situation even more fluid. In Liberal administrations Whig aristocrats still held most of the reins of office, and such men as Gladstone began to reflect the outlook of the aspiring industrialists and manufacturers—it was not, however, until 1869 that the old Radical leader, John Bright, was to gain a seat in the Cabinet, to be followed by Chamberlain himself in 1880. As Frederick Engels was to remark in 1892, looking back on this period:

"In England, the bourgeoisie never held undivided sway. Even the victory of 1832 left the landed aristocracy in almost exclusive possession of all the leading Government offices. The meekness with which the wealthy middle class submitted to this remained inconceivable to me until the great Liberal manufacturer, Mr. W. E. Forster, in a public speech implored the young men of Bradford to learn French, as a means to get on in the world, and quoted from his own experience how sheepish he looked when, as a Cabinet Minister, he had to move in society where French was at least as necessary as English!"

The fact was, Engels concluded,

"the English middle class of that time were, as a rule, quite uneducated upstarts, and could not help leaving to the aristocracy those superior Government places where other qualifications were required than mere insular narrowness and insular conceit, seasoned by business sharpness. . . . Thus, even after the repeal of the Corn Laws, it appeared a matter of course that the men who had carried the day, the Cobdens, Brights, Forsters, etc., should remain excluded from a share in the official government of the country, until twenty years afterwards a new Reform Act opened to them the door of the Cabinet."[1]

When, therefore, the demand for reform of the ancient universities and schools was taken up in the 1850s, it was in a new spirit of compromise. In seeking entry to institutions hitherto dominated by the Church of England and the aristocracy, the middle class of this age were ready to make a devastating exposure of deficiencies. But when it came to reform there was not so much a desire to build on radically new lines as to take over and remodel institutions with a recognised status in order, while removing the most glaring faults, to secure a share in the benefits they could confer. For their part, Whig aristocrats were not slow to join in overcoming Tory and Anglican opposition to change, in realising that some reform of the strongholds of aristocratic education was expedient if these were to be preserved and to retain a pre-eminent social role.

But in the outcome, whatever the limitations set on reform, state intervention brought about a fundamental transformation in the structure of the educational system. When it is recalled that, in 1870, there followed an Act establishing a system of elementary schooling it becomes clear that the period 1850-70 marks a crucial moment of change in English education. During these two decades the affairs of Oxford and Cambridge and of the chief "public" schools were enquired

[1] F. Engels, Introduction to the English edition of *Socialism: Utopian and Scientific*; K. Marx and F. Engels, *Selected Works* (1950), Vol. II, 102-3.

into in minute detail, their shortcomings laid bare and the direction of future development determined; hundreds of small schools throughout the country were also placed under the microscope and their affairs rigorously reordered. We may now examine the procedure adopted and some of the chief findings of the Royal Commissions which dealt so sweepingly with educational institutions, from the sacrosanct universities to the meanest of local endowed schools, consider the legislation which resulted and attempt to assess the nature of the transformation which took place.

I. REORGANISING THE UNIVERSITIES

(i) *Internal Politics*

It would be an oversimplification to interpret the eventual reform of the universities and public schools as due only to external intervention—to the imposition of new regulations by Parliament. The reform of an institution is a complex process—particularly that of a university; new regulations may be useless unless they are operated in the spirit intended, and this implies the existence of a section or party within the institutions themselves who are determined on reform. Two hundred years earlier, during and after the civil war, commissioners appointed by Parliament had purged colleges of recalcitrant dons and placed as heads and fellows men "well-affected" to the new power in the state. In 1850 less drastic steps were necessary. A reform party existed, even at Oxford. For years it had carried on a sharp ideological struggle within the university, the repercussions of which had been felt outside. Here was an instrument ready to hand when the time for action came. The man appointed as secretary of the Oxford University Commission in 1850 was A. P. Stanley, star pupil and follower of the leader of liberal thought at Oxford, Thomas Arnold.

The struggle between reformers and traditionalists in the university world is epitomised in the persons of two men—Arnold, whose influence remained strong even when head of Rugby School from 1828-42, and J. H. Newman, later Cardinal Newman. Both were, in the mid-1820s, fellows of Oriel, the only Oxford college at which all the fellows were elected on merit alone; a college which became noted, in Newman's words, for a "wide liberality of thought".[1] It had even received recognition in the *Edinburgh Review* as "the school of speculative philosophy in England". Here, and in two or three other colleges, the university reformers were concentrated.

[1] J. H. Newman, *Apologia Pro Vita Sua* (1909 edn), 46.

The two young fellows of Oriel were, however, destined to take different directions. Faced with the industrial changes and political upheavals of his age, Arnold sought a synthesis between established beliefs and modern knowledge and social developments; and, in so doing, developed a broad, liberal outlook both in religion and politics. Newman, on the other hand, regarded liberalism as the most dangerous of compromises, and set himself the task of holding back "the tide of social dissolution" in intellectual and social life.

In his *Apologia Pro Vita Sua*, Newman provides a revealing commentary on the subsequent struggle, and shows clearly how the Oxford Movement (Tractarians) developed as a defensive reaction to the growth of liberal sentiments within the university. So far as university education was concerned, those who stood for the primacy of reason, of the intellect—for freedom of speculation—inevitably also stood for changes in the methods and content of education. As Newman saw it, the reformers (justifiably enough) began to look upon themselves as an *élite*. They began to stress the teaching function of the university, to feel "they had a career before them, as soon as their pupils, whom they were forming, came into public life"; so they became "exposed to the temptation of ambitious views, and to the spiritual evils signified in what is called the 'pride of reason'." In these men, Newman writes, "the direct instruments and the choice fruits of real university reform, we see the rudiments of the liberal party".[1]

These were the men first responsible for internal reform at Oxford —so far as they were able. Newman found this group in being when he was made a fellow; they were "much thrown together", "banded for mutual support"—these men were the "first instruments of change." But Newman did not share their liberalism, and political events rapidly crystallised his attitude. In 1829 he is to be found throwing all his weight behind the struggle to get the high Tory Sir Robert Inglis elected to Parliament for Oxford University. In France, the Bourbons were overthrown: "I held it was unchristian for nations to cast off their governors and, much more, sovereigns who had the divine right of inheritance";[2] at home the Reform agitation (as he put it) was threatening the liberalisation of the Church. Newman's strongest objection was to the sin of spiritual pride, the elevation of the "pride of reason" as the ultimate good: "liberalism", he wrote, "is the mistake of subjecting to human judgment those revealed doctrines which are in their nature beyond and independent of it, and of claiming to determine on

---

[1] Newman, *op. cit.*, 316-18.   [2] *Ibid.*, 34.

intrinsic grounds the truth and value of propositions which rest for their reception simply on the external authority of the Divine Word".[1]

There was no one to oppose this dangerous doctrine of a party which, with its intellectual distinction, engrossed the mental energy of the university, except "the thoroughgoing Toryism and traditionary Church of Englandism of the great body of the Colleges and Convocation". For the most part easy-living, port-drinking, philistine, such present and past members of the university presented no effective intellectual opposition. Following in the steps of Keble, who was the first to "turn the tide", and bring "the talent of the University round to the side of the old theology", Newman undertook the task of providing an effective challenge. The instrument was the Oxford Movement, which stood for faith before reason, authority as against democracy; which was, as Newman summarised Keble's standpoint, united in hatred of "heresy, insubordination, resistance to things established, claims of independence, disloyalty, innovation, a critical censorious spirit".[2]

In furthering the Oxford Movement, Newman brought his intellectual powers to bear to such effect that "the mental activity of Oxford" began to flow in the opposite direction, that of "tractarianism." Not only was the climate of university life fundamentally affected, but also the Church of England was, for a time, shaken to its foundations.

This is not the place to trace the history of the Oxford Movement, that tortuous and tortured attempt to spiritualise what was seen as a predominantly materialist and opportunist church and so to reinstate its authority in intellectual, social and public life. But it must be recorded that, for a time, this appeal was almost irresistible in a university which had, since its inception, been identified with ecclesiastical doctrines and politics. For twelve to fifteen years the Oxford Movement—above all Newman in his tracts, books, sermons at St. Mary's Church—dominated the thought and activity of Oxford intellectuals. Many of the most brilliant were closely involved; few were free from its challenge.

Yet, for all its appeal and influence, this movement failed to stem the tide of liberalism. "The party grew, all the time I was at Oxford," wrote Newman later, "even in numbers, certainly in breadth and definiteness of doctrine, and in power. And what was a far higher consideration, by the accession of Dr. Arnold's pupils, it was invested

---

[1] Newman, *op. cit.*, 318.   [2] *Ibid.*, 319-21.

with an elevation of character which claimed the respect even of its opponents."[1] In fact, while Newman was attempting to dam the tide, his contemporary Thomas Arnold was swelling the flood with new recruits from Rugby.

Appointed headmaster of Rugby in 1828, Arnold had at once begun to build up, within the public school system, a new pattern and ethos; and had done so with a success which greatly added to his reputation and extended his influence to wider fields. His activities were inspired by a design opposite to that of Newman. While the latter stressed the need to build up the church's authority and clarify its doctrine, drawing a sharp distinction between established church and dissent, Arnold worked for the inclusion of both within a broad, national church. While Newman held that revealed doctrine was beyond human judgment and based the church's claims to authority on this ground, Arnold accepted the validity of historical criticism of the Bible and of the scientific approach to knowledge, believing that if Christianity was to survive in the modern world, it must come to terms with science and take account of social change.

The same approach characterised the reorientation of Rugby School. No less aware of the danger of social revolution than Newman himself, Arnold directed his efforts to preventing the division of society into two fundamentally hostile classes, as described by Disraeli. As he saw it, boys attending public schools—now drawn not only from among the sons of the aristocracy, gentry and parsons but also, increasingly, those of the new industrialists—must learn that they had responsibilities to "the people"; this alone could ensure social harmony in the new conditions of a deeply class-divided society. In short, realising that no ruling class could now maintain its supremacy unless it recognised its "obligations", Arnold set out to modify overbearing upper-class attitudes and the impulse to raw exploitation among industrialists by inculcating in both the ideal of the "Christian gentleman". In so doing he provided a form of education designed to fuse aristocracy and bourgeoisie, to make the aristocracy more useful and the bourgeoisie more polished—one which corresponded exactly with, and in turn helped to form, the outlook and aspirations of the Victorian upper-middle class.

When appointed Professor of Modern History at Oxford in 1841, Arnold drew large audiences to his lectures which brought "a new breath of vigour and enthusiasm into an atmosphere heavy with the

[1] Newman, op. cit., 322.

dust of theological disputes".[1] In the intervening years much dust had indeed been raised, not only on theological questions but also on matters with a crucial bearing on the character of the University. In 1834-5, liberals and Tractarians had clashed over the proposal to abolish religious tests for entrants to the university, when the liberals had been defeated in Convocation by a majority of eight to one. Later, high feelings had been aroused when the Whig government forced through the appointment of the liberal churchman R. D. Hampden as Regius Professor of Divinity in the teeth of violent opposition from Newman and his supporters.[2]

These campaigns, which aroused much heat and fury at the time, were skirmishes in the long ideological battle which reached a culmination in 1840 with the issue of the famous Tract 90 with its strong overtones of Roman Catholicism. By now Newman had reached a point when he was beginning to see the Roman Catholic Church as the only body strong enough to withstand the leagues of evil; these he defined as the socialists, Thomas Carlyle, Thomas Arnold and his followers, the political economists, and the misery of the world—which he seemed to face alone, armed only with distrust of his age and of himself. In 1841 Newman was, in his own words, driven from Oxford by the liberals, who had opened the attack on Tract 90. "I found no fault with the liberals," he wrote later, "they had beaten me in a fair field."[3] In 1845 he joined the Roman Catholic Church.

Others had already taken this step, more were to follow. In essence, this was a confession of defeat, a renunciation of all influence over both Oxford and the Church of England. Though Keble and Pusey held to the Church of their fathers, with Newman's departure the tide of liberalism could no longer be stemmed and with it there arose new, and more clearly formulated, demands for educational reform.

Mark Pattison, fellow of Lincoln College and himself at one time deeply affected by Newman's teaching, recalling this period in later life, described the departure of the Tractarians as "deliverance from the nightmare which had oppressed Oxford for fifteen years". During all this time attention had been focused on unprofitable discussions which "had entirely diverted our thoughts from the true business of the place" and reduced scholarship to a low level. "By the secessions of 1845 this was extinguished in a moment, and from that moment dates the regeneration of the university."

[1] C. E. Mallet, *A History of the University of Oxford* (1927), Vol. III, 270.
[2] *Ibid.*, Vol. III, 257ff.   [3] Newman, *op. cit.*, 237.

Setting about their proper work, members of the university became acutely aware "how incompetent we were for it, and how narrow and inadequate was the character of the instruction with which we had hitherto been satisfied".

> "We were startled when we came to reflect that the vast domain of physical science had been hitherto wholly excluded from our programme. The great discoveries of the last half century in chemistry, physiology, etc., were not even known by report to any of us. Science was placed under a ban by the theologians, who instinctively felt that it was fatal to their speculations."

This, Pattison ascribed in great part to Newman who claimed revealed truth to be absolute, all other truth relative—"a proposition that will not stand analysis, but which sufficiently conveys the feelings of the theologians towards science". This outlook also found expression in abject deference to authority "whether of the Fathers, of the Church, or the Primitive Ages", a standpoint "incompatible with the free play of intellect which enlarges knowledge, creates science, and makes progress possible". Deliverance from Tractarianism, therefore, was deliverance from obscurantism "which had cut us off from the general movement". As a result there was a "flood of reform . . . which did not spend itself till it had produced two Government commissions, until we had ourselves enlarged and remodelled all our institutions".[1]

In fact, after 1845, the reform party at the universities increasingly added its voice to those outside who were pressing for government interference. This pressure had been exercised for a decade or more—since the appearance of Hamilton's violent attacks in the *Edinburgh Review*—and was directed particularly to securing abolition of subscription to the Thirty-nine Articles as a condition for entry. Recently, members of the universities had taken the first steps and found support in the Commons, only to be met with solid resistance from the Tory clergy among the teaching body and in Convocation, and in Parliament. In 1834, after a petition against subscription signed by sixty-three members of the Cambridge Senate had been rejected, a debate on the subject took place in the Commons. This brought an immediate reaction from the Church and Tory party in the universities. A manifesto circulated at Oxford attracted many signatures in support of the view that in those who have a "solemn duty to provide for a Christian education . . . uniformity of faith upon essential points is absolutely

[1] Mark Pattison, *Memoirs* (1885), 236-8.

necessary". The temper of this opposition is revealed in the famous statement by William Sewell, fellow and tutor of Queen's College, Oxford:

"I deny the right of liberty of conscience wholly and utterly. I deny the right of a child to poison itself; the right of a man to ruin himself; the right of a nation to indulge itself in any caprice or madness. . . . I deny the right of any sect to depart one atom from the standard which I hold to be the truth of Christianity. And I deny the right of any legislative power, of any Minister of God, of any individual on earth, to sanction or permit it, without using every means in my power to control and bring them back from their errors."[1]

In spite of this opposition, the question was raised again in 1835 when Lord Radnor, an advanced liberal, brought in a bill to abolish subscription for entrants to the Universities—a step recommended by the Heads of Oxford Colleges but rejected by Convocation; the House of Lords similarly rejected it by 163 votes to 57. Two years later, Radnor moved for a Select Committee to enquire into the statutes of colleges and halls, and determine whether any legislative action was necessary; but withdrew the motion on an assurance from the Chancellors of both Universities (the Duke of Wellington and Marquis Camden) that most of the Colleges were willing to revise their statutes themselves. In the same month George Pryme, Professor of Political Economy at Cambridge University and Member of Parliament for the borough since 1832, moved in the Commons for a commission to enquire into the state of the Universities; a motion also withdrawn on the assurance of Goulbourn, member for Cambridge University, that the university would make such changes as were necessary.[2]

With the fall of the Whigs and the return of the Tories under Sir Robert Peel in 1841, the prospects of Parliamentary action declined. When, in 1844, W. D. Christie, member for Weymouth, again moved for a commission of enquiry, the House was counted out; renewal of the attempt in April 1845, with the support of Thomas Wyse and Joseph Hume, brought the rejection of the motion by 143 votes to 82.[3]

Christie's attempts to raise the question in the House of Commons had had the support of Benjamin Jowett, fellow of Balliol and one of

---

[1] Quoted by J. W. Adamson, *English Education, 1789-1902* (1930), 71-2.
[2] A. I. Tillyard, *A History of University Reform* (1913), 60-1.   [3] *Ibid.*, 102-3.

the leaders of the liberals in Oxford, who was closely concerned with university teaching and curricula. By this time Jowett, and those who thought like him, were firmly convinced that only a sharp jolt from outside could lay the basis for the changes they considered essential. In 1848, writing to another Member of Parliament (Roundell Palmer), Jowett made it clear that internal efforts were not enough—"It is nobody's fault—we cannot reform ourselves,"—and described Oxford University as "the one solitary, exclusive, unnational Corporation" whose enormous wealth had no manifest useful purpose.[1]

The distinguished geologist Sir Charles Lyell, in common with many other professors at both Universities (especially those teaching science), had also given up all hope of internal reform and was appealing to external authority to assist in the development of the university by removing the dead hand of the colleges. These, already responsible for most of the teaching of students (as opposed to the university professors) had actually extended their control in the 1820s, with the result that Lyell's crowded audiences of the mid-1820s had been reduced to ten or a dozen.[2] An attempt by the Oxford Hebdomadal Board to create new Professorships and require students to attend their lectures—"a last and most vigorous attempt" as Lyell described it, "to restore the functions of the professorial body"—had been thrown out by Convocation in 1839; similar attempts at Cambridge in 1843 also failed.[3]

Since science was not included in the degree courses, nor therefore taught by the colleges but only by university professors, this meant that by 1845 it was "virtually exiled from the university". "Appeal under such circumstances must therefore be made to an external authority. A Royal Commission like those which have more than once visited of late years the Universities of Scotland, might prove a sufficient counterpoise to the power and *vis inertiae* of forty learned corporations."[4]

It was, in fact, only in 1849 that optional schools in natural science, law and modern history were initiated at Oxford. Even then, every candidate for a degree must first have passed an examination in classics and must continue to study classics together with one of the new subjects for his finals.[5] This was no more than a belated and inadequate

---

[1] Geoffrey Faber, *Jowett* (1957), 195-7.   [2] Tillyard, *op. cit.*, 74.

[3] *Ibid.*, 72; Baden Powell, Savilian Professor of Geometry, who lectured on mathematics, never had more than seven students at his lectures between 1830 and 1849. In several years he had none at all. *Report of Oxford University Commission* (1852), Evidence, 258.

[4] *Ibid.*, 75.   [5] Mallet, *op. cit.*, Vol. III, 297.

gesture to appease public opinion in an attempt to stave off more fundamental reforms, and it was not to be successful. In 1846 the Whigs had returned to power, and there were signs that the universities' desire to reform themselves would no longer be accepted as an argument against a thorough enquiry and intervention from outside.

The need for external action was also accepted by many of the most outstanding younger fellows of colleges and professors at both Oxford and Cambridge; not only by Pattison, Lyell, Jowett, Stanley—then at the height of his fame as author of the *Life of Thomas Arnold*—but also such men as Tait, earlier a fellow of Balliol, who followed Arnold at Rugby and became Archbishop of Canterbury, Adam Sedgwick, the respected Professor of Geology at Cambridge, Goldwyn Smith, fellow of University College, Oxford, who was to act as assistant secretary to the Oxford Commission, Bonamy Price, later to become Professor of Political Economy at Oxford, and many others. For years these men had worked for reforms, to no real purpose. In spite of the "interminable discussion, . . . ceaseless output of articles and pamphlets, (and) abortive attempts in both Houses of Parliament", writes the historian of Cambridge reform, there had been "exceedingly little practical action".[1] All progressive proposals had been blocked, in the last resort by the country clergy who voted *en masse* in Convocation and Senate against any material change.

In such a situation, even though the protagonists of reform were themselves in orders, the struggle to introduce changes necessarily took on an anti-clerical character; and this was enhanced by the fact that the changes desired could only be brought about by breaking down the semi-ecclesiastical character of the colleges and the hold of the Church hierarchy over the university. It was, above all, to this that younger members of the reform party attributed the decay of learning, the failure to move with the times. It was not primarily the power of the colleges over the university that prevented change, wrote Mark Pattison later, but another reason altogether—"The grasp of ecclesiastical tyranny was on its throat" and, with this, Tory influence which left it "without independence, without the dignity of knowledge, without intellectual ambition, the mere tool of a political party". So also Goldwyn Smith ascribed the decline of learning to "the exclusively clerical character of the University that shut the door against science" and brought its teaching into disrepute:

"The conjoint operation of celibacy, clericism and sinecurism

[1] Tillyard, *op. cit.*, 100.

reduced the educational staff of the colleges . . . to a few clergymen waiting in colleges for college livings, and filling up the interval by a perfunctory discharge of the duties for which they received tutor's fees."[1]

The foremost need, if there was to be a fundamental change in the organisation and teaching of the universities, was that ecclesiastical control over their organisation and curriculum should be broken; that they should no longer be confined to those who subscribed to the doctrines of the Church of England and regarded as training centres for the clergy, but should be opened up as national institutions of higher education. This could only be achieved through the direct intervention of the state.

(ii) *Parliamentary Action*

In April 1850, a decisive motion, proclaiming the necessity for a reform of the ancient universities, was introduced in the House of Commons. Significantly, this step was taken by James Heywood, M.P. for North Lancashire, a Unitarian who, although he had studied at Cambridge, had been unable to take his degree because of the religious test. The motion was sufficiently comprehensive, and comprised in particular the demand for a Royal Commission to enquire into the Universities of Oxford, Cambridge and Dublin "with a view to assist in the adaptation of those important institutions to the requirements of modern times". This outright approach drew the strongest opposition from William Gladstone, at that time still a Tory and member for Oxford University, who "rose in his place and denounced the proposed commission as probably against the law, and certainly odious in the eye of the constitution".[2] The debate was adjourned, but not before the Prime Minister, Lord John Russell, had "startled the House of Commons, and delighted the liberals" by announcing the government's decision to set up a commission of enquiry "to receive evidence voluntarily given". The longstanding demand of the Radicals had at last been met.

With this definite step a new stage in the struggle began; the old order was at last on the defensive against the combined forces of liberals within and government without. Initially the university authorities still clung to their former arguments. Both universities officially objected to the proposed commissions on the familiar grounds that

[1] Quoted by Tillyard, *op. cit.*, 62-3.
[2] John Morley, *Life of Gladstone* (1903), Vol. I, 497.

they were quite capable of reforming themselves, indeed were doing so quite adequately. Time was needed, said a Cambridge remonstrance, to assess the effect of improvements recently made. Any attempt at interference with the colleges by an "extraneous power" would be "altogether destructive of their just and ancient corporate rights."[1] At Oxford, the Hebdomadal Board proclaimed entire satisfaction with the continuous improvement in studies, adding that a Royal Commission could only obstruct this natural progress of academic reform, based on the "recent" reorganisation of the university by Archbishop Laud:

> "Two centuries ago—in 1636—the University revised the whole body of its statutes, and the academic system of study was admirably arranged at a time when not only the nature and faculties of the human mind were exactly what they are still, and must of course remain, but the principles also of sound and enlarged intellectual culture were far from imperfectly understood."[2]

This was not an argument calculated to appease those who felt that the university was out of touch with modern thought, and the government was now determined on action. An amendment opposing the appointment of Commissioners was debated in the House of Commons in July, Gladstone once more in strong support, but although this debate was adjourned by a narrow majority (160 to 138) the Royal Commission was issued in August.

An assurance had been given by the Prime Minister that those appointed to the commissions would be very carefully chosen as men not only well qualified, but also inspiring confidence and respect. Yet when the seven Oxford Commissioners in particular were announced the names aroused the strongest opposition. All were Oxford men; but all without exception were "notoriously liberal in politics".[3] Among them were Tait and Baden Powell, both known as strong reformers (the latter a Professor whose criticisms had met with the full approval of *The Quarterly Journal of Education*[4]), while Thomas Arnold's chief disciple, Arthur Stanley, was appointed to the key job of Secretary to the Commission. The Cambridge Commission of five included two scientists—Sir John Herschell and Professor Adam Sedgwick. The universities prepared to make a last ditch stand.

The first action of both Commissions was to write to the chancellors,

[1] Tillyard, *op. cit.*, 105-6.
[2] *Report of the Oxford University Commission*, (1852), Appendix A, 4.
[3] Mallet, *op. cit.*, Vol. III, 299.   [4] See p. 92.

vice-chancellors, professors, proctors and other public officers of the universities, and also to the visitors and heads of colleges and halls, enclosing a copy of the commission and requesting co-operation and information. At once the strength of the resistance became apparent. From Cambridge the vice-chancellor replied that the commission was unconstitutional "and of a kind that was never issued except in the worst times"; it was therefore his "public duty to decline answering any of the questions" sent him.[1] From the Oxford vice-chancellor came only the curtest of acknowledgements, followed by silence.

Five months later the Chairman of the Oxford Commission, Dr. Hinds, Bishop of Norwich, again wrote to the vice-chancellor requesting "the favour of an early reply". This came in the form of a challenge to the legality of the commission, buttressed by a statement from "the most eminent counsel of the day", which commenced:

> "We are of opinion that the Commission is not constitutional, or legal, or such as the University or its members are bound to obey; and that the Commission cannot be supported by any authority of the Crown, either as Visitor, or under any prerogative or other right."[2]

In fact the university had determined on petitioning the Queen in Council, praying that the Commission "may be recalled and cancelled". This move was not unexpected and matters took their course. The Law Officers of the Crown submitted a contrary opinion that the Commission was "not in any respect illegal or unconstitutional."[3] Convocation, by 249 votes to 105, reiterated that it was not only illegal but "improvidently issued" and likely "to impede the course of improvement, and to destroy that confidence and stability which are essential for the well-being of an University". The Privy Council responded, in July 1851, with an order in council which concluded that "it would not be advisable for Your Majesty to comply with the prayer of the said petition".[4]

The direct appeal against the legality of the commission had failed, but the universities could continue to offer passive resistance. The Bishop of Bath and Wells and the Earl of Pembroke, both visitors of Oxford Colleges, and the Dean of Christ Church among Heads of Houses, failed even to acknowledge communications from the commissions.[5] The Bishop of Exeter likewise refused all co-operation,

[1] *Report of Cambridge University Commission* (1852), Correspondence, 2.
[2] *Report of Oxford University Commission*, Appendix B, 21, 25.
[3] *Ibid.*, Appendix B, 32.   [4] *Ibid.*, Appendix B, 35.   [5] *Ibid.*, Appendix B, 8-9.

expressing his deep concern and astonishment at the use of "the name of our present Gracious Sovereign" to authorise an inquisition which no precedent could justify and which had "absolutely no parallel since the fatal attempt of King James II to subject (the colleges) to his unhallowed control".[1]

The colleges themselves for the most part took the same stand. Basing their refusal to give evidence on their secret oaths, many made only a simple acknowledgement of the letters sent out, and took no further action. In Oxford, only seven of the nineteen colleges were prepared officially to co-operate. "From the majority of the Colleges, as Societies, we have received no assistance", wrote the Oxford Commissioners, while the governing body of the university also withheld information. As a result, the Oxford Commission was able to gain "little authentic information" as to the finances of colleges or university.[2]

A few university professors at Oxford also expressed the strongest objections to the enquiries addressed to them. The Margaret Professor of Divinity protested that the appointment of a commission was "an unconstitutional stretch of prerogative, fraught with immediate evil, and still more dangerous as a precedent". To the Professor of Poetry it represented a "revolution", a "dangerous principle and ill-omened precedent . . . a despotic stretch of antiquated prerogative", a remark which did not prevent him from appealing to and upholding still more ancient rights: "the rights of property, the independent action of the Universities within their immemorial educational province, and the distinctive religious and Church character which has from the earliest times consecrated and moulded, happily for the nation, our academic studies, must be held inviolate". Never was interference "more ungracious, impolitic or self-destructive".[3]

But, such exceptions apart, both commissions obtained full co-operation from the university professors who, as a group, had long been in favour of reform but powerless to bring it about. So also, younger members of the university grasped the opportunity to give evidence. Thus Mark Pattison appealed to the Commissioners: "We, in Oxford, are weary of scheming, suggesting and pamphleteering. Give us leave to be doing something."[4] If University College refused all co-operation, A. P. Stanley, secretary of the commission, could fill the gap; in the same way, Benjamin Jowett provided information

[1] Report of Oxford University Commission, Appendix B, 7.   [2] Report, 1.
[3] Ibid., Appendix B, 13-14.   [4] Ibid., Evidence, Part I, 44.

which was refused by Balliol as a society. In the outcome, a considerable body of information and comment was accumulated and published as part of the reports in 1852.

Of the two reports, that on Oxford was the more outstpoken, uncompromisingly exposing abuses and advancing radical proposals for reform. From the outset it established the point that the universities were national institutions requiring reform, that the colleges were "wholly unable" to take the necessary steps, that the government of the university was in the hands of "a narrow oligarchy" and that Parliament had every right to intervene.

It went on to outline deficiencies in corporate life and discipline. The number of students was small because the education offered was irrelevant. Students who did attend did so, for the most part, because they wished to enter the Church for which a degree was a vocational necessity, regardless of the quality of the teaching. Since there was little encouragement to work students tended to be idle and college life was apt to degenerate into lounging and indolence, gambling and vice: "the three great temptations of the place", the report quoted from Mark Pattison's evidence, were "fornication, wine and . . . betting". Outmoded distinctions of rank were retained, while insistence on subscription to the Thirty-nine Articles led to "sophistry in the interpretation of solemn obligations".

In their criticism of the curriculum, the commissioners were no less direct. They found that the stimulus of examinations had had a good effect on those working for honours, but for the majority of students reading for an ordinary degree "the minimum of knowledge acquired is so scanty as to leave all but the dullest and most ignorant unoccupied for the greater part of their academical course"; moreover since examinations had been established, attendance at professorial lectures covering a wider range of subjects had almost entirely ceased. Any kind of preparation for professional life was "completely neglected"; there were "no efficient means" of training whatsoever, even for the clergy, while "Oxford had altogether ceased to be a School of Medicine" and legal studies were at a very low ebb. Of the compulsory subjects, some were futile. Oxford logic, for instance, "has scarcely emerged from the obsolete philosophy of the Mediaeval Schools, and has served rather to promote than destroy the dominion of spurious science"; yet until very recently students, by mastering "a miserable pittance of logic", could abjure all mathematics.

The Commissioners declared roundly that the whole system of

collegiate instruction was ineffective. Further, in a masterly and un-compromising survey, they showed that, in almost every respect except where the personal interest of the fellows was concerned, the colleges paid no attention whatsoever to their statutes. This was perhaps the unkindest cut of all, since the colleges based their refusal to co-operate with the commission on respect for statutes. They were, therefore, open to the charge that this refusal was simply another example of irresponsibility.

It would be tedious to detail all the Commissioners' strictures and recommendations. It is enough to note that their criticisms, though phrased in statesmanlike language, were fully as outspoken as anything that had appeared in the *Quarterly Journal of Education* or the *Westminster Review*.[1] The recommendations sought to open the way to changes in government, teaching and recruitment of students. They proposed broadening the base of university government, particularly by the inclusion of the professoriat, and a strengthening of the university *vis-à-vis* the colleges, notably by building up a core of *university* teachers. They advocated a transformation of the content of education to allow for a certain degree of specialisation, including mathematics and science, stress being laid on the need for better facilities for teaching these subjects. Finally, they recommended abolition of special privi-leges open to "founders' kin" and the breaking of local restrictions on scholarships and fellowships, in favour of open competition. Certain measures were also suggested to cheapen university education in the interests of the less wealthy middle-class student.

In the meantime, Lord John Russell's government had fallen; "but things had gone too far for their successors to burke what had been done" and the Tories, under Lord Derby, invited the universities to examine the recommendations. In December 1852, the Whigs returned in Aberdeen's coalition government with Gladstone now Chancellor of the Exchequer. Convinced that reform was now inescapable, Gladstone "submitted to it in order to avert a greater evil", telling his Oxford constituents that if the Bill he drafted were thrown out, "no other half so favourable would ever again be brought in". In none of the enterprises of his life, writes his biographer, was Gladstone more

---

[1] An interesting sidelight on this is given in Stanley's remark to Jowett: "When you consider the den of lions through which the raw material had to be dragged, much will be excused. In fact the great work was to finish it at all. There is a harsh, unfriendly tone about the whole which ought, under better circumstances, to have been avoided, but which may, perhaps, have the advantage of propitiating the radicals." (R. E. Prothero. *Life of Stanley* (1893), Vol. I, 432; quoted in Morley, *op. cit.*, Vol. I, 499.)

industrious and energetic.[1] In March 1854, the Oxford University Bill was laid before Parliament, and, after a somewhat stormy passage, eventually passed through both Houses of Parliament and received the Royal Assent in August. The Cambridge Bill, which had a much easier passage, followed in 1856.

It was Gladstone's view that to legislate in the spirit of the Commissioners would be "madness". The procedure utilised, originally suggested by the Cambridge Commission, was the appointment of Executive Commissioners with statutory powers. These were able to insist on the production of documents and accounts, and, unless the universities and colleges satisfactorily recast their own statutes by a given date, were empowered to frame them themselves. Further, although this had not been proposed either by the Commissions or the government, the House of Commons (much to Gladstone's distaste) had insisted on the abolition of tests for matriculation and the Bachelor's degree (and, in the case of Cambridge, for the Master's degree). Thereby one of the key demands of the nonconformist middle class, actively advocated for almost a century, was at least partially won. Yet while a nonconformist could now gain a degree at Oxford and Cambridge, "he remained entirely shut out from all participation in the government of the University".[2] It was not until 1871 that the abolition of further tests made it possible for all teachers, whatever their beliefs, to sit on the governing bodies of the universities.[3]

The measures enforced by the Executive Commissioners, closely following the Royal Commissions, laid the basis for a transformation of the universities. Government was rendered more democratic; the way was cleared for the development of science and modern studies and the professorial system was reorganised and strengthened. College statutes were recast and "vested interests, obsolete regulations, encumbering restraints, were swept aside".[4]

Without exaggerating the speed of change—which is not the important aspect—it may be said that the Royal Commissions inaugurated, in both universities, "a quiet revolution". The 1850s, according to Mark Pattison, saw "more improvement in the temper and the teaching of Oxford" than the three centuries which went before.[5] A later Cambridge observer remarked that "the work of the Royal

---

[1] Morley, op. cit., 499-504.   [2] Tillyard, op. cit., 151.

[3] Even then, as A. V. Dicey pointed out in an analysis of the long struggle to abolish tests, the Church of England still occupied "a position of pre-eminence and predominance"; Law & Public Opinion in England (2nd edn 1914), 348.

[4] Mallet, op. cit., Vol. III, 327.   [5] Ibid., 330.

Commission appointed in 1850 bore fruit some years later in the shape of a new and surprising increase in the number of students, and in the altered conditions of academic life and study which were brought to pass. . . . There can be little doubt but that the commission was the direct cause of the extraordinary rise in numbers which followed."[1]

In sum, the university Acts, by removing the stranglehold of ecclesiastical control and the deadweight of clerical place-seekers, gave the universities scope for development as educational institutions; and there were many men at both Oxford and Cambridge ready to take advantage of new opportunities, to prosecute changes which would help the universities—like Rugby school—to serve the needs of the new upper middle class. In the outcome, though improvements were also made in university teaching, the colleges were preserved and turned to the end of providing a sound training in manners and morals as well as in classics and mathematics. Tutors such as Jowett at Oxford and, later, Oscar Browning at Cambridge—prototypes of a new race of university teachers—consciously set themselves the task of forming the character and intellect of the "enlightened rulers" as Arnold had done before them; of making the colleges centres for the formation of a gentlemanly ruling class. At Balliol, Jowett took care to know his students intimately and brought the aristocracy and middle class together in tutorials and vacation reading parties; his biographer cites as typical a party of four, consisting of an athlete, two elder sons of peers "and a clever hard-working Scot, educated in Glasgow".[2] A list of his pupils yields "a catalogue of names; many of them once famous, some famous still (embracing) statesmen, proconsuls, politicians, judges, lawyers, civil servants, clerics, scholars, historians, philosophers, landowners, farmers, poets". Meanwhile Oscar Browning drew into his discussion club at Cambridge such diverse elements as the aristocratic Alfred Lyttleton and the eldest son of the Radical Birmingham industrialist, Joseph Chamberlain; a young man who was later to make his name as a cultured conservative politician, conversant with and acceptable to both the social and the business world.[3]

So far as developments in the curriculum were concerned, both universities, but more particularly Cambridge, began to develop the sciences and even technology; they also evolved new Arts courses—Ancient Greats (classics) at Oxford and history at Cambridge—which

[1] Tillyard, op. cit., 156.   [2] Faber, op. cit., 165, 328-9.
[3] Oscar Browning, *Memories of Sixty Years* (1910), 235ff. The reference is, of course, to Austen, not Neville Chamberlain. The latter had a very different education in preparation for business, not for Parliament.

had as their overt aim that exclusive education for an élite of statesmen which Gladstone had seen as the supreme function of the universities.[1] Such an education could produce qualities of a kind necessary at this stage to the ruling class, and was well calculated to civilise recruits from the industrialists' camp. Significantly it had been Arthur Clough, one of Arnold's most distinguished Rugby pupils, who, in his evidence before the Oxford Commission, had recalled his headmaster's success, and urged that "more and more young men, sons of the more affluent parents, destined for business", should be "brought under the influences of the ancient national education". The Commission had echoed the sentiment: "It is certainly desirable that the manufacturing and mercantile, which has arisen by the side of the landed aristocracy, and which is exercising a great influence on the public counsels, should seek to have its sons brought up where so many eminent statesmen of past and present times have been trained; and that the Universities should not cease to send forth a succession of persons qualified to serve God in the State as well as in the Church."[2]

There can be no doubt that the appointment of the University Commissions marked the end of an epoch, and opened a decisive period of change in English education. In tackling first the centre of clerical power and control of education, the government opened the way for the transformation of the educational system as a whole. Whatever the limitations of the reforms achieved after 1854, from this time the universities increasingly reflected a cautious middle-class rationalism, and began to turn their attention from the narrow concerns of prelates and clerics to the great world outside—the world of diplomacy and politics and, though to a lesser extent, of commerce and Empire. In so doing they attracted more students, particularly from the rapidly developing proprietary boarding schools such as Cheltenham, Haileybury, Malvern, and Rossall, whose pupils were now brought together at Oxford and Cambridge with the products of the older "public" schools.

Nevertheless this very reorganisation made the universities more exclusive in terms of class than they had ever been. From 1854 to 1904 was the most difficult time for the poor scholar to make his way to Oxford and Cambridge.[3] In fact, in opening up the universities in ways conducive to attracting the middle class, the Executive Commissioners

[1] Thus J. R. Seeley founded the Historical Tripos "with that particular view". *Ibid.*, 234.
[2] *Report of Oxford University Commission*, 19; see also Evidence, Part I, 212.
[3] A. Mansbridge, *The Older Universities in England* (1923), 108-9.

effectively closed them to the poor. The colleges founded at both universities from the fourteenth to the sixteenth century were intended to provide places for the scholar unable to pay for his own board and tuition; after the Reformation there had been an influx of sons of the nobility and gentry but subsequently additional scholarships and exhibitions for the poor student had been established, particularly in the seventeenth century, often attached to local grammar schools. Many of these reserved places were now swept away; only where vested interests were powerful, as in the case of Winchester and Eton, were they maintained. The poverty clauses governing the award of scholarships and exhibitions were abolished, as well as those confined to particular districts and families. Instead, awards were thrown open to competition on the basis of "merit"—a step which naturally favoured the wealthier schools and pupils.[1] This was done on grounds of efficiency, and certainly with some justification.

But whatever their intentions as regards easing the way for the more indigenous middle-class student, the idea that a working-class child should get to Oxford or Cambridge never crossed the minds of those introducing reforms. Their avowed concern was to sweep away clerical privileges and restrictions and to create truly national universities. But the objective result of their efforts was the erection of new and impassable class barriers which prevented the entry of the poor scholar. So far as the working class were concerned, for one exclusive monopoly was substituted another, even harder to break. In *Jude the Obscure*, Thomas Hardy imaginatively interpreted the significance of this final exclusion.

2. REFORM OF THE PUBLIC SCHOOLS

Seven years after the passing of the Oxford University Act the Clarendon Commission began its enquiry into the nine "great" or "public" schools. In the interim not only had the universities become more efficient but reform of the civil service, including the introduction of a system of competitive entry, had mitigated the nepotism and patronage of the past; certain changes had also been introduced in the qualifications required for the army and the practice of medicine and

[1] An investigation of a sample of Cambridge students shows that the proportion coming from grammar schools fell from 16 per cent. in the period 1752-99 to 7 per cent. in the period 1850-99. Of the remaining 93 per cent in the latter period, 82 per cent. came from public schools, 11 per cent. from private schools. Hester Jenkins and D. Caradog Jones, "Social Class of Cambridge Alumni", *British Journal of Sociology*, Vol. I, No. 2, June 1950.

law. Against this background the shortcomings of schools which had made little or no attempt to adapt themselves to the times, whose curriculum remained centred on the classics and whose administration was sometimes riddled with abuses, stood out all too clearly.

The schools picked for investigation had one thing in common—all had at one time or another achieved a reputation for educating the sons of the aristocracy and gentry; in this sense, they had come to be regarded as "national" institutions. Otherwise they differed considerably. Winchester and Eton, apart from their link with colleges at Oxford and Cambridge, were part of semi-ecclesiastical collegiate foundations which had escaped dissolution at the Reformation. As such, they were open to much the same kind of criticism as the colleges at the universities. At Winchester, for instance, the warden and fellows exploited the revenues for personal gain, leaving the headmaster starved of funds for the school. Not only were boys badly fed and looked after but, with only two masters in charge of the teaching of 200 pupils, none but those with a desire to learn was likely to be educated:

> "The curriculum was almost exclusively classical. It was bound to be as long as there was no money available to pay specialists in other subjects; nor indeed were the specialists then available. From about 1820 it was possible to learn French as an 'extra' out of school hours, and Mathematics from the writing master, a despised functionary whose main duty was to clean the slates and mend the pens. There was, of course, no Science. All this rested upon the belief, typical of an aristocratic age, that in the Classics were to be found, perfectly expressed, all the principles and mental discipline required to train the statesman, the divine and the gentleman; for travel on the continent, for coping with 'those damned dots' or for the solution of practical problems, the courier, the clerk or the plumber would always be available."[1]

Education at Eton was no better, but as the recognised centre of upper-class education and training ground of statesmen—the school of Robert Walpole, William Pitt and Charles James Fox, of the Duke of Wellington, of Canning, Melbourne, Derby and William Gladstone—its appeal survived all educational deficiencies. In the 1860s it had 850 pupils.

These two schools, founded in the fourteenth and fifteenth centuries, had always been referred to as "great" schools. But after the

[1] J. D'E. Firth, *Winchester College* (1949), 107.

Reformation, when the sons of the gentry invaded the grammar schools, Westminster (1560) had come to the forefront; while two London schools administered by City companies—St. Paul's and Merchant Taylors'—also drew pupils from far afield and gained a national reputation. Another foundation in the city of London was Charterhouse (1619), established as a refuge for old men with a school attached and governed by an illustrious body which included the Queen, the Archbishop of Canterbury and sundry earls and dukes.

But by the 1860s, though Eton retained its numbers, Winchester was hardly prosperous and Westminster and Charterhouse were declining disastrously; at Westminster, for instance, there had been a drop from 300 in 1825 to 120, at Charterhouse from 480 to 140. The city company schools, meanwhile, still provided a free, or very cheap education for the numbers prescribed at their foundation. But at St. Paul's 153 boys were all taught in one room and the chief textbooks for classics were those suggested by the founder in 1512; Merchant Taylors' School also provided for only 250 boys as laid down in 1560. At both these schools, the nomination of pupils was in the hands of members of the companies, but, with the depopulation of the city as a residential area, they now provided mainly for the professional middle class, who were only too glad to make use of these facilities. Thus, of the boys at St. Paul's, 100 were sons of members of the learned professions, 50 of the London clergy, with a handful of sons of tradesmen.[1]

The remaining three schools were outside London. Shrewsbury 1552), though it had originated as a borough school, had early become a centre for the education of the nobility and gentry of the west country.[2] After eclipse in the eighteenth century, it had once more achieved a reputation under the headmastership of Samuel Butler (1798-1836), but by the 1860s had little over 100 boarders out of a total of 140 pupils. On the other hand, Harrow, founded by a sixteenth-century yeoman for inhabitants of the parish, had already in the late eighteenth century become virtually an upper-class boarding school; by contrast with the Church and Tory flavour of Eton, this was the favoured school of the Whig aristocracy and gentry, and numbered

[1] M. F. J. McDonnell, *The History of St. Paul's School* (1909), 406.

[2] Ordinances drawn up by the bailiffs of the town in the sixteenth century lay down the following entrance fees: a lord's son 10s., a knight's son 6s. 8d., a gentleman's heir 3s. 4d., gentlemens' sons 2s. 6d., anyone below this degree 2s., inhabitants of Shropshire 1s., burgesses' sons 4d., sons of other inhabitants of the borough 8d. Howard Staunton, *The Great Schools of England* (1865), 420.

nearly 500 in the 1860s. Finally, there was Rugby, rehabilitated by Dr. Arnold (1828-42) and still basking in the aura of his reputation even though it may not have lived up to his ideals in all respects. Here was a prototype of the kind of school desired by the Victorian upper-middle class.

But, if Rugby provided a model for reform, it was not the only challenge to the old order. There were also the proprietary boarding schools which had sprung up since the 1840s; though these were, in many respects, organised on the "public" school model, they were run on business-like lines and provided a relatively efficient education in preparation for professional, even business, careers. Middle-class parents had been seeking a useful education in growing numbers since the beginning of the century. Now the introduction of competitive entry to the civil service and reform of the army placed a new premium on reasonable educational standards. It was for this reason that, while Westminster, Shrewsbury, Charterhouse, emptied, Cheltenham (1841), Marlborough (1843) ,Rossall (1844), Wellington (1853) were full to bursting; preparing pupils for Sandhurst, Woolwich, the civil service, colonial administration, business, as well as for the church.

In addition, certain day schools had grown in numbers and developed in efficiency, following in the steps of the City of London School, founded in 1836 under the direct influence of Brougham and his circle.[1] Moreover, London University had now for three decades or more provided a new focus for higher education, a new goal for which schools could work, though its development had not been without setbacks. As the Clarendon Commission was to find, its matriculation requirements for all faculties including Arts were altogether broader and of a higher standard than those of Oxford and Cambridge, covering not only mathematics but also a reasonable knowledge of mechanics and of physics and chemistry.[2]

In 1863, the modern ("military and civil") side at Cheltenham catered for 276 boys, almost half the school—the curriculum covering mathematics, science and modern languages with only a little Latin and no Greek.[3] Wellington, partly under the influence of the Prussian *Realschulen* and with entry to Sandhurst and Woolwich in view, organised varied modern courses around a common core of Latin, divinity and modern languages. At Rossall, in addition to the

[1] A. E. Douglas Smith, *City of London School* (1937), 65-9.
[2] *Report of the Public School Commission* (1864), Vol. II, 48-9; Vol. IV, 363-4.
[3] *Ibid.*, Vol. II, 546-50.

classical side, the school provided five classes with different aims in view: military, naval, civil service, civil engineering and mercantile.[1] As the headmaster of Marlborough put it, such schools could ensure "a definite and successful preparation for a large and increasing number of openings in life . . . secured at much smaller outlay than at a private tutor's, and with all the advantages of public school life".[2]

In short, a new system of schools was developing which bid fair to oust the lesser ancient foundations whose teaching still revolved around the classics; while it also provided for the middle class a far sounder education than that to which aristocrats had access at such schools as Eton and Harrow. If the aristocracy was to maintain its position of superiority in the modern world—and the "respectable" middle class had no desire to do away with it[3]—then it must, at all costs, be decently educated. In the light of this consideration, the task was to modernise and improve the "great" schools, while at the same time bringing the lesser public schools up to a standard which met the needs of the middle class, who wished their sons to have a reasonably useful education. Thereby Eton and the rest could once more take their place at the head of a system of upper-class schools.

This task was not so extensive, nor so delicate, as that of reforming the universities; no head-on challenge to the Church was involved, while the schools were not banded together as the colleges had been. Moreover, the university commissions had broken the ice of non-intervention and illustrated that reform need not undermine all privilege; that, on the contrary, it was necessary to retain it. This time, therefore, when radical criticism of the public schools became outspoken, supporters for a new enquiry by Royal Commission were to be found even in the Tory camp.

The new campaign of criticism opened in 1860 with an attack on Eton, launched specifically from a middle-class standpoint and exposing its educational inefficiency and financial corruption. In 1861, an important article in the *Edinburgh Review* was demanding a Royal Commission with a view to establishing new governing bodies for the public schools: when Sidney Smith had criticised these in 1810,

---

[1] Staunton, *op. cit.*, 494-5.   [2] *Report of the Public School Commission*, Vol. II, 512.

[3] "The aristocratical element has immense force in England. The English aristocracy is the only aristocracy in Europe which is still powerful, and even the progress of democracy adds seemingly to its strength. The aspiration of the English aristocracy is to be, not the best educated, but for practical purposes the most cultivated . . . it exists that it may be the national ornament and bulwark; it exists that it may crown that social hierarchy which should symbolise the hierarchy of nature." This, the outlook of a contemporary writer on education, was a not uncommon view. (Staunton, *op. cit.*, xx.)

the author remarked, they were at least the best schools there were—
now "we are very much inclined to suspect that they are nearly the
worst".[1] Equally sharp criticism came from the *Westminster Review*,
still, as before, voicing the views of the Radical middle class.

But when the commission was eventually appointed, in 1861, its
chairman was the Earl of Clarendon, who believed that the public
schools needed reform because their inefficiency placed the "upper
classes in a state of inferiority to the middle and lower";[2] while among
its members were the Tory Sir Stafford Northcote, Halford Vaughan
(a relative of Charles Vaughan, the reforming Headmaster of Harrow
and, between 1848 and 1858, Professor of Modern History at Oxford),
and others who ardently desired the maintenance and rehabilitation,
rather than any radical reorientation of the public schools. With the
exception of Clarendon and one other, all were themselves products of
the schools they were to investigate.

This did not prevent the headmasters of the leading schools, Good-
ford of Eton, Moberley of Winchester, Scott of Westminster—who
had at first stoutly resisted the appointment of any commission—
from denying before it that anything needed putting right. As E. C.
Mack, the historian of the public schools of this period, writes: "They
filled the public prints with passionate denials of the need for a Parliamentary investigation. When, despite their efforts, the commission
was appointed, they continued before that august body their frantic
defence of their institutions", maintaining a "blanket refusal to admit
evils and a complacent assertion that the public schools did all that
was expected of them by their critics".[3]

But in spite of this attitude on the part of the heads, or perhaps
partly because of it, the Commissioners conducted an extraordinarily
thorough, even microscopic examination of the position in each of
the schools. The detailed enquiries and often sharp cross-examinations
of the witnesses serve to make their approach to the problem before
them absolutely clear. Mack sees them as thorough-going political
reformers "anxious to preserve the public schools by bringing them
up to date"; as providing "a concensus of upper-class opinion, a compromise between the educational ideas dominant among the mid-
Victorian middle class and the aristocracy".[4]

The nature of this opinion is perhaps best expressed, in a letter to

---

[1] *Edinburgh Review*, Vol. CXIII, No. 230, April 1861, 368; quoted by Edward C. Mack,
The Public Schools and British Opinion since 1860 (1941), 27.

[2] Quoted by Mack, *op. cit.*, 27.   [3] *Ibid.*, 19-20.   [4] *Ibid.*, 29-30.

the Commissioners, from Gladstone, son of a Liverpool merchant, but also an old Etonian and shortly to become leader of the Liberal Party. Describing the public schools as "public property", he urged them to set aside private interest for the public good, fearlessly to "lay open the whole case, and set out the full extent of what is to be desired by way of remedy".[1] But, in Gladstone's view, as in that of many others, the public good demanded not only business efficiency in organisation and modernisation of studies, but also the maintenance of aristocratic exclusiveness—of a form of education which was markedly different from that available to other classes. It was to this end that, in the same letter, he strongly advocated retention of the classics as "the paramount matter of education" for "that small proportion of the youth of any country who are to become in the fullest sense educated men". This was a view with which the Commission was to find itself in full agreement.

The passages relating to changes in the curriculum are full of interest; illustrating clearly that the main preoccupation of the Commission, and many of its witnesses, was not so much with educational considerations as with the class issues underlying educational reform. A substantial extract will serve to convey the sense of many passages; it concerns the evidence of Sir Charles Lyell, the geologist, who was arguing in favour of increased teaching of science, and is here being questioned by the commissioner, Halford Vaughan.

Question 77: (Mr. Vaughan): Have you any means of knowing whether in the middle classes there is a greater knowledge on the (scientific) subjects at present than in the upper classes?—It is a very remarkable fact that if a scientific book is published it depends more for its sale on the middle classes of the manufacturing districts than on the rich country gentlemen and clergy of the agricultural parts of the country, and, therefore, if there is a distress like the present in Lancashire, the publisher would say "Do not bring out your book now".

Question 78: In a political point of view, is not that not only an unhealthy but also a dangerous state of things in some respects, that the material world should be very much better known by the middle classes of society than by the upper classes?—Certainly, and I think it is particularly so in reference to the teaching in this country

[1] *Report of the Public School Commission*, Vol. II, 42.

by the clergy, and a vast proportion of the university men are going in to the Church. In order to bring their knowledge more into unison with that of the artisans, it is particularly desirable that a certain portion of science should be taught. Medical men would of course be required to know some science, natural history, comparative anatomy, or something equivalent, but they would say it is not necessary for the clergy. I think it is particularly desirable that the clergy should have some initiation into these things.

Question 79: Does not the absence of knowledge in these branches of learning tend to disturb the relation which the social position of the two would in itself rather tend to produce, and the respect of the middle classes for the upper classes?—Yes, I think it must, but I do not feel very strongly on that question because the aristocracy of this country, in spite of the system of education being somewhat narrow, get their education in other ways, and, therefore, they are greatly respected; but I think the clergy would be particularly benefited by any change you could make by introducing these things into public schools. I feel that there is a dangerous want of sympathy at present between the better informed working class of the manufacturing districts and the clergy.

Question 80: I do not by any means ask whether they do not generally on many accounts meet with respect, but whether the absence of that knowledge on the part of the upper classes which the middle classes appreciate and possess does not tend to diminish the respect so far?—Certainly, so far.

Question 81: And whether it does not also tend to put a certain amount of power into the hands of the middle classes, which the upper classes have not?—Yes, I think so.

Question 82: (Sir Stafford Northcote): But if the upper classes, in acquiring a greater amount of this knowledge of the physical world were to lose any of their literary and intellectual superiority, might they not thereby endanger their pre-eminence as much in the one way as they would gain in the other?[1]

The upper classes must vie with the middle classes on their ground, but they must also retain a special ground of their own if their

[1] *Report of the Public School Commission*, Vol. IV, 374.

pre-eminence was not to be endangered. This attitude, expressed here by a Tory representative on the commission, had been reinforced by Gladstone's instructions; by his rejection of "the low utilitarian argument for giving what is termed a practical direction to education" and his strong rebuttal of the inference that science and modern subjects were on a parallel with divinity and the classics—when they were, at most, "ancillary" to this traditionally basic core which also lay at the heart of all national institutions. The same attitude permeates other commissioners' questions and is reflected in the eventual finding that the classics must remain the principal study of public schools, that classical literature, which "has had a powerful effect in moulding and animating the statesmanship and political life of England", should continue to fulfil this role.

It was in this prevailing atmosphere that the scientists were forced to frame their arguments, for all the leading scientists of the day— Hooker, Owen, Airy, Lyell, Faraday, among others—were called to give evidence. They advanced two main lines of argument in favour of teaching science; first, that science was an effective means of "training the mind", and second, that the ruling class must know something of science in order to preserve its position. Thus, according to Hooker, the teaching of science was the best way of training the mind, study of the classics the worst,[1] while Sir John Herschel pleaded for science not on "mere utilitarian considerations" but as an aid to acquiring habits of "concentrated thought", to the "contemplation of abstract truth".[2]

Others deplored the lack of scientific knowledge among the middle and upper classes on the same grounds as Vaughan. One reason why Oxford had "gone to the labour and great expense of increasing its means of scientific study", said Acland, Professor of Medicine, "is found in a sense entertained there of the importance to the clergy and upper classes of England generally of more extended knowledge, in order to retain their proper relations to the lower and middle classes who have this knowledge".[3]

Both these lines of argument could be described as opportunist; in any case they played into the hands of the classicists. Hooker might claim that science was a better training of the mind than classics, but other scientists did not agree with him or at least did not say so. This left the way open for arguing that the classics did the job better and

[1] *Report of the Public School Commission*, Vol. IV, 382ff.   [2] *Ibid.*, Vol. II, 47.
[3] *Ibid.*, Vol. IV, 410.

must, therefore, be retained on these grounds, with science as a "respectable" adjunct, fulfilling the same function at a lower level. The second approach also led inescapably at that time to the continued supremacy of the classics. If a knowledge of science was only needed to prevent the upper classes from appearing too ignorant, then a modicum would suffice while retaining the classical "mystery" as the main mark of social superiority.

Among the scientists only Faraday (who had come up the hard way) tore through these arguments and passionately put the case for science as the central core of education in its own right. Asked whether science "trained the mind" he launched a frontal attack on this whole approach to education, exposed this theory for the nonsense it has since been shown to be, and asked:

"Who are the men whose powers are really developed? Who are they who have made the electric telegraph, the steam engine, and the railroad? Are they the men who have been taught Latin and Greek? Were the Stephensons such? These men had that knowledge which habitually has been neglected and pushed down below. It has only been those who having had a special inclination for this kind of knowledge have forced themselves out of that ignorance by an education and into a life of their own."[1]

As for those with a classical education, they had no compunction in arguing with him about matters on which, though they claimed to have knowledge, they were utterly ignorant; but they were even "ignorant of their ignorance at the end of all that education". Rebutting the proposition that the classic with a "well-trained mind" can easily master science, Faraday asserted that the truth was the very contrary—in fact, they acquired a strong prejudice against science which reinforced and perpetuated ignorance. Was there enough material to make a whole-time course out of science? "Our life, our time, our faculties wear out," he replied, "men have worn out, but the matter of *this* education, with all its developments and all its rewards, is ever there, growing into the future."

After the freshness of Faraday's approach, concerned as he was predominantly with educational considerations, it comes as no surprise to learn that he was unaware that the commission's enquiry was restricted to upper and middle-class education—"I expected you were taking *all* classes", he said.[2]

The commissioners were not impressed by such arguments. What

[1] *Report of the Public School Commission*, Vol. IV, 377.   [2] *Ibid.*, Vol. IV, 374ff.

did impress them, and very unfavourably, was the prevailing low level of classical studies as elicited by their searching enquiries. Convinced that the classical curriculum must, at all costs, be renovated and retained—that the upper class must be provided with an education suitable to its station in life—they had no hesitation in exposing and commenting on the outstanding weaknesses before outlining the steps that should be taken to raise standards.

The sections of the evidence dealing with Eton and Winchester run to almost half a million words, and include some strong criticism by university tutors who had to cope with the products of the schools and could compare them with those of newer foundations. Thus Charles Neate, fellow of an Oxford college, claimed that not only were the majority of public school boys "almost incredibly ignorant" of English, modern languages, mathematics, natural history and modern history, but also, after up to twelve years spent in exclusive study of Latin and Greek, were "unable to construe off-hand the easiest passages"; while "their Latin writing is almost invariably such as would under the old school system have subjected them to a flogging as boys of 12 years old".[1]

"Very few . . . can construe with accuracy a piece from an author whom they profess to have read", wrote the Senior Censor of Christ Church. "We never try them in an unseen passage. It would be useless to do so."[2] The Professor of Natural Philosophy at Cambridge, Bartholomew Price, F.R.S., found "a very marked difference" between the public school products and those from other schools and private tutors. "Seldom do I meet with young men from the public schools who know more than the bare elements of mathematics." The standard of boys from "middle-class schools" was "far superior" to that of public schoolboys; "these latter can in many cases scarcely apply the *rules* of arithmetic, and generally egregiously fail in questions which require a little independent thought and common sense".[3]

The Commissioners' summary of this and other evidence was damning. Average attainment in classical scholarship was, they concluded, low, while "in arithmetic and mathematics, in general information, and in English, the average is lower still, but is improving". However, "in arithmetic and mathematics the public schools are especially defective" by comparison with others; and "of the time spent at school by the generality of boys, much is absolutely thrown

[1] *Report of the Public School Commission*, Vol. II, 49.
[2] *Ibid.*, Vol. II, ii.　　　[3] *Ibid.*, Vol. II, 24.

away as regards intellectual progress, either from ineffective teaching, from the continued teaching of subjects in which they cannot advance, or from idleness, or from a combination of these causes".[1] "If a youth," they add, "after four or five years spent at school, quits it at nineteen, unable to construe an easy bit of Latin or Greek without the help of a dictionary or to write Latin grammatically, almost ignorant of geography and of the history of his own country, unacquainted with any modern language but his own, and hardly competent to write English correctly, to do a simple sum, or stumble through an easy proposition of Euclid, a total stranger to the laws which govern the physical world and to its structure, with an eye and hand unpractised in drawing and without knowing a note of music, with an uncultivated mind and no taste for reading and observation, his intellectual education must certainly be accounted a failure, though there may be no fault to be found with his principles, character or manners." This last was a concession to the last ditch argument that, whatever their other failings, the public schools did, at least, "train character". But the Commissioners were not disposed to let this pass as a cover for a large measure of inefficiency in teaching. If, they conclude, their summary does not represent the ordinary product of public school education, "we must say that it is a type much more common than it ought to be".[2]

So far as school organisation and government were concerned the Commissioners did not hesitate to uncover abuses—particularly at Winchester and Eton. Here action had been forecast by the university commissions and the Clarendon Commission followed this up by recommending "a ruthless and complete transformation of governing bodies" so that these should be composed of "trustees without pecuniary interest";[3] proposing, in effect, that the grasping fellows of the original foundations, who performed no useful function, should be replaced by governing bodies of "men conversant with the requirements of public and professional life and acquainted with the general progress of science and literature".[4] Such men would be capable of

[1] *Report of the Public School Commission*, Vol. I, 26.
[2] *Ibid.*, Vol. I, 31.   [3] Mack, *op. cit.*, 31.
[4] *Report of the Public School Commission*, Vol. I, 6. In the event, the old collegiate body at Eton was swept away in 1872 and the original statutes were repealed. The new governing body was to consist of up to eleven members, of whom five were to be nominated respectively by the universities of Oxford and Cambridge, the Royal Society, the Lord Chief Justice and the masters. H. G. Maxwell Lyte, *Eton College* (1877), 479. A similar change was effected at Rugby W. H. D. Rouse, *History of Rugby School* (1898), 301-2), and elsewhere.

deciding on new studies to be introduced and the suppression of old.

But in this last matter the report gave guidance at some length. Though the classics must be retained as the central core of education, more attention should be paid to the content of the works studied, less to grammar and philology. In addition, courses must be "extended" by the introduction of the elements of science and modern languages; "class teaching for an hour or two in the week, properly seconded, will be found to produce substantial fruits". Some attempt must also be made "to meet the case of that large class of boys, who are destined not for the universities, but for early professional life", in this case, while rejecting the idea of a "modern" side parallel to the classical side, the commissioners argue that in what are "essentially classical schools" some deviations from the course should be allowed in certain cases. Even this suggestion is hedged around with various qualifications. But, in general, the Commissioners supported the introduction of modern studies, proposing the inclusion not only of mathematics and a foreign language but also of music, drawing, history geography, English composition and spelling and natural science— at that time taught only at Rugby. All these should go to make up a regular course of study, in which classics (with classical history and divinity) should be allotted just over half the total time, science no more than one-eighth.

As for teaching method and school organisation, the Commissioners were certainly shocked by what they found, and openly said so. "We have been unable to resist the conclusion that these schools, in very different degrees, are too indulgent to idleness, or struggle ineffectually with it, and that they consequently send out a large proportion of men of idle habits and empty and uncultivated minds."[1] Once more proposals are framed to increase the efficiency of the schools; proposals concerning promotion of pupils, prizes, the need for daily marking of work done, periodic examinations, entrance examinations, superannuation schemes—these have quite a Benthamite ring. Otherwise, however, the Commissioners favoured prevailing methods of public school discipline, approving fagging (with qualifications) and the prefect system which has borne "excellent fruits and done most valuable service to education". They also held that the tone of moral and religious education had improved considerably in the last thirty years, a tribute to Arnold's influence. Finally, forgetful of earlier strictures and imbued rather with a sense of what was needed, the

[1] *Report of the Public School Commission*, Vol. I, 55.

report concludes with what is nothing less than a paean in praise of
the public schools, "the chief nurseries of our statesmen", where "men
of all the various classes that make up English society, destined for
every profession and career, have been brought up on a footing of
social equality". "It is not easy", the Commissioners conclude, "to
estimate the degree in which the English people are indebted to these
schools for the qualities on which they pique themselves most—for
their capacity to govern others and control themselves, their aptitude
for combining freedom with order, their public spirit, their vigour
and manliness of character, their strong but not slavish respect for
public opinion, their love of healthy sports and exercise." All this
could be summed up in one phrase: the public schools "have had
perhaps the largest share in moulding the character of an English
gentleman".[1]

One other set of recommendations remains to be examined, which
shows, more clearly than the rest, the Commission's overriding concern to establish an exclusive upper-class system of education; one
which could stretch to include the sons of wealthy industrialists and
professional men, but which must at all costs be kept free from the
encroachments of tradesmen and the lower orders beneath. This was
the authority given to ignore founders' provisions relating to "poor
scholars" or "free" pupils from the localities, in favour of streamlining
the schools as boarding establishments with high fees.

All the schools which were part of a large composite foundation
had a certain number of places "on the foundation", intended to provide a free board and education for poor and deserving scholars;
Winchester and Eton had 70, Westminster 40, Charterhouse 44. But
the statutes allowed also for additional boarders and day boys, paying
fees for board and tuition, and it was envisaged that the former would
be drawn from the nobility and gentry. At the other end of the scale,
what were originally small local grammar schools—such as Rugby
and Harrow—had been founded to provide a free education for the
children of inhabitants of the parishes concerned; though there was
sometimes a proviso that the master might take a few additional
pupils from outside, boarding them if he chose in his own house,
and might in these cases charge fees.

Whenever a school became sought after, the number of fee-paying
pupils usually grew to exceed those on the foundation. Further, places
on the foundation of collegiate schools—which were disposed of

[1] *Report of the Public School Commission*, Vol. I, 56.

under the guidance of governing bodies or by individual governors —were usually awarded by patronage or nepotism without any regard to the poverty or worth of the pupil, while various fees and perquisites were gradually required of foundationers. These were longstanding abuses of original statutes and intentions which had persisted through the centuries. Likewise, if a local grammar school was well situated, an energetic master might achieve a personal reputation and build up a considerable boarding establishment; the master's own "private" school in contrast to the free pupils from the locality. Sometimes, as at Harrow, a tuition system—where the real business of the school went on—was developed in the Head's school from which the foundationers were excluded. The determined refusal to depart from a strictly classical education (as has been noted earlier) also had the effect of excluding the local tradesmen, farmers and artisans. If, in addition, the endowment greatly increased in value, as, for instance, in the case of Rugby where the land lay in the city of London, all the conditions existed for the alienation of the school from the locality, its transformation from a simple local school into something approximating to the style of a Winchester or an Eton.

But the presence of local boys lowered the social tone of a school aspiring to attract the upper classes, and so militated against the development of a "national" public school. Hence the tendency, during the nineteenth century, to demand fees from local children. While the term "free" education was a loose one, sometimes covering payment of varying sums for entrance and extras, the extortion of substantial annual fees, a step which excluded most local children, was certainly not normally in accord with the founders' intent.

It is characteristic that Arnold's first step, on his appointment to Rugby, was to double the fees for "free" scholars, putting them at twelve guineas.[1] At Harrow, compulsory private tuition and extras amounted in 1862 to 17 guineas. Added to this, the masters and boys of schools which were now setting out to educate Christian gentlemen spared no efforts to put "outsiders" where they belonged—outside. Anthony Trollope describes in his autobiography the tribulations, great and small, which made the life of a genuinely poor foundationer at Harrow intolerable.[2]

Local residents at Harrow, Rugby and elsewhere had protested strongly at these developments in the early nineteenth century. Thus in

[1] Rouse, op. cit., 235.
[2] Anthony Trollope, An Autobiography (1946 edn), 23-4, 29-31, 33-4.

a case brought before the Roll's Court in 1810, local residents claimed "that the children of Harrow parish cannot be sent safely or properly to the school, on account of the number of foreigners who are chiefly the sons of the nobility and gentry of the kingdom, and who constantly scoff at and ill-treat the other boys". They further complained that local children, if sent to the school, "are apt to imbibe the extravagant and expensive ideas, as well as the pernicious habits, of the young men of fortune admitted to the school". Such protests had been quashed by legal decisions. These established the right of the governors to make large scale provision from the endowment in favour of the wealthy scholars.[1] This, of course was the main point at issue, and these legal decisions cleared the way for a further advance.

Taken all together, these tactics were extremely effective. The headmaster of Harrow was able to assure the Commission that "in no instance is any son of a Harrow tradesman now a member of the great school".[2] This final transformation had been effected with great skill against strong opposition from local townsmen, determined to maintain their privileges. Vaughan, headmaster from 1844 to 1859, by a series of petty restrictions, tried to make it impossible for local boys to attend unless they lived adjacent to the school itself. He did this by issuing edicts that no boys could ride to school, and insisting on school call-overs three times a day, one immediately after the midday meal (which day-boys took at home). In an attempt to divert the anger of the inhabitants he started, in 1853, an "English Form" where, at £5 a year, local boys could learn elementary Latin grammar, English, history, geography and mathematics. This is described as "housed in a humble tenement, limited in numbers owing to inadequate funds, and generally worked at a disadvantage".[3] Among the rules of the school one stated bluntly: "The boys will regard themselves as entirely separate in all respects from those of the Public School: they will on no account mix themselves with the games, and etc., of the Public School", a rule, Vaughan announced, made entirely for the benefit of the new form "to secure them from any interference or annoyance from the Public School".[4] In his evidence before the Commission, Butler, then head, announced that he was

[1] For a report of the judgment on the Harrow case (1810) see N. Carlisle, *Endowed Grammar Schools* (1818) Vol. II, 138ff, and *Quarterly Journal of Education*, Vol. IX, No. 17, January 1835, 80-1; the Harrow judgment was based on an earlier judgment in the case of Rugby.

[2] *Report of the Public School Commission*, Vol. IV, 159.

[3] E. Graham, *The Harrow Life of Henry Montagu Butler* (1920), 197.   [4] *Ibid.*, 197.

quite satisfied with the education of the twenty-two boys in the English form; questioned, he said that the schoolroom "is a humble room". "Is it a decent place?" "It is a very common room—I do not know how to describe it more accurately."[1]

The extent to which, by 1860, the headmasters of prosperous schools had built up a body of fee-paying pupils, and the position at other schools, is shown in the following table compiled by the commission:[2]

Nos. of pupils in 1862	Foundationers	Non-Foundationers	Total
Eton	70	770	840
Harrow	32	449	481
Rugby	61	402	463
Winchester	70	146	216
Shrewsbury	26	114	140
Westminster	40	96	136
Charterhouse	44	92	136

It was also made clear to the commissioners that foundation scholars paid various fees and extras amounting to up to £20 and that, in admitting them, little or no regard was paid to the poverty qualification. The situation was summed up by the commission as follows. At Westminster the poverty qualification was considered obsolete; at Winchester, financial means were only taken into account "other things being equal"; at Eton, parental circumstances were not investigated. Only at Charterhouse were the sons of "really poor" people usually selected but these were also "persons exceedingly well-connected".

This time the commissioners evinced no shocked surprise; on the contrary they found that various circumstances had tended, and would continue "to render the qualification of indigence practically inoperative," adding "we do not think it necessary to recommend any changes in this respect".[3] In fact, they were to lend a helping hand by recommending the sweeping away of all such obsolete requirements and the opening up of the schools to competitive examination. This step had already been taken at Eton and Winchester in the 1850s, at the instigation of the university Commissions which dealt with these schools as adjuncts of Kings and New College respectively. Now it was recommended for all.

[1] Report of the Public School Commission, Vol. IV, 160. [2] Staunton, op. cit., 19.
[3] Report of the Public School Commission, Vol. I, 10.

"Short of destroying entirely the upper-class character of the schools, which, of course, they had no intention of doing," writes Mack, the commissioners felt that

"the best way to cut the Gordian knot was to abolish entirely the traditional rights of the poor. They did this by recommending that entrance to the foundations of all schools be made a matter of competitive examination, a solution both entirely in accordance with the laisser faire business ideals of the Victorian upper classes and singularly effective for securing its end, since a good deal of expensive preparation was necessary to pass public school entrance examinations."

To the protests of local residents which had continued to smoulder and to break out now and again into impassioned denunciations of the alienation of endowments, the commissioners were necessarily deaf; they were "determined to wipe out class differences in the schools, and, like all ruling classes, they intended to do so by destroying the privileges of all but their own class".[1]

In fact, the commission did not stoop to call representatives of local interests as witnesses. Instead, it carefully worked out stages whereby local privileges could be altogether abolished; thus, it proposed that such foundationers at Rugby be reduced to twenty-five by 1873 and eliminated altogether by 1883. Nevertheless, the final solution needed some diplomacy. At Harrow, Montagu Butler called together the parishioners and "acknowledging with sympathy the justice of their grievance . . . reminded them that the Founder's estate was still devoted to giving a free education, though now to boys of a higher class". To make the position doubly sure, while at the same time reducing cause for complaint, he transformed the "English" form into "The Lower School of John Lyon" which maintained some links with the original endowment while finalising the exclusion of the tradesman's son from "the great school". In 1876, in his concern for the advancement of the poor, Butler offered two scholarships from the new elementary Board schools to the "Lower School"—so inserting a rung at the bottom of the scholastic ladder "as a *solatium* to any outstanding grievance felt by the poorest class of inhabitants by their exclusion from a share in the bounty of John Lyon".[2]

Elsewhere, a similar solution was found. Rugby still has its Sheriff's grammar school (also named after a founder who had originally established his school for the inhabitants of Rugby and Brownsover); at Oundle, Laxton's school recalls the worthy London grocer who

---

[1] Mack, *op. cit.*, 32-3. [2] Graham, *op. cit.*, 201, 211.

wished to benefit the poor of his native parish. So consciences were salved, while rigid class divisions were safely ensured. The reform of governing bodies aided this development by excluding local men in favour of men of the world who knew what they had to do. So the upper-middle class divested itself of all likelihood of social contamination while the public schools, originally intended for all classes above that of the Elizabethan pauper, became the monopoly of one.

The Clarendon Commission submitted its recommendations in 1864; as in the case of the university commissions, its powers ended here. There followed four years of controversy, when various attempts to introduce legislation failed. Finally, in 1868, the Public Schools Bill was introduced to give effect to the commission's recommendations. Inevitably, it met with attack from the right, from all those who thought interference dangerous and unnecessary, and also from the Radicals who, with reason, regarded it as "one of the most delusive and reactionary measures ever put before the country".[1] Nevertheless, it became law, ensuring, once more, the appointment of an executive commission with powers to transform governing bodies and to draw up new statutes.

Meanwhile, in response to the pressure of public opinion and the suggestions of the commissioners, the schools themselves had been taking action. Indeed, the ideas advanced by the commission in the sixties began to find expression as early as 1862, reform "developed considerable momentum in the last years of the decade, and was virtually completed by the early seventies . . . the public schools . . . put their house in order with almost unparalleled speed".[2]

So far as studies were concerned, it was the old house that was reordered; the classics remained the staple of the structure and science was only an annexe. But discipline and organisation now tended to approximate more to the Arnold pattern and the public schools became respectable—the nucleus of what was to grow into an organised educational system which could confer particular privileges in a new way. The cult of athleticism, the first signs of which are discernible in the '50s, grew apace. The morality now prevailing was less narrowly religious (though Church of England doctrines were still actively propagated) and more concerned with loyalty and *esprit de corps*— "Fear God, Honour the King" was Montagu Butler's text[3]—with the unspoken addition that the lower classes were also to be feared and wooed. Indeed, Arnold's conception of obligation to the poor was to

[1] Quoted by Mack, *op. cit.*, 49.   [2] *Ibid.*, 91.   [3] *Ibid.*, 99.

find a new direction with the foundation of public school missions in the poorer parts of London; so Butler started the Harrow mission in 1882

> "to give the upper classes a chance to exercise their obligations by teaching the lower classes the moral virtues; (while) the lower classes were given the privilege of getting to know their betters and to love them for their condescension."[1]

So schools which had in the past bred statesmen and Churchmen for the tasks of government were successfully adapted to train a new kind of ruling class. In the coming years, not only were they to prosper but also more aspiring grammar schools were to become minor "public" schools and the upstart proprietary schools were to be drawn in to swell the galaxy. Indeed, it was these last—truly middle-class foundations—which perhaps best gave expression to the public school ethos in the golden age of the system, from 1880 up to the first world war; Cheltenham, whose prospectus proclaimed it to be a "training place beyond compare for the defenders of Empire", the Haileybury and Marlborough beloved by Kipling for providing "chaps who went out to Boerland and Zululand and India and Burma and Cyprus and Hong Kong" and "lived and died as gentlemen and officers", the Clifton of Newbolt, who wrote with such deep emotion of the cricket field and the thin red line.

All in all, by insisting on the preservation of the classics as the main core of teaching, and by ensuring the final separation of the public schools from those for other classes, the Clarendon Commission created an efficient and entirely segregated system of education for the governing class—one that had no parallel in any other country. The Commissioners had done what was required of them, and had done it well.

3. ADAPTATION OF THE GRAMMAR SCHOOLS

In the same year that the Clarendon Commission reported its findings, a new Commission was appointed to examine the state of education for "those large classes of English society which are comprised between the humblest and the very highest", and to recommend "practicable and expedient" reforms.[2] This time the target was the bulk of the old endowed schools.

[1] Mack, *op. cit.*, 100.
[2] The Schools Inquiry Commission, known, after the Chairman, as the Taunton Commission.

The profound dissatisfaction of the industrial and commercial class with the state of the grammar schools, their frequent attempts to transform them during the first decades of the century, have already been described. These had led, in 1840, to the passing of Eardley Wilmot's Grammar School Act, which, by legalising new schemes for the introduction of modern subjects, allowed for the modification of the purely classical curriculum in individual schools. But, since the Act laid down that such steps could only be taken on the death of the master, it did not affect the majority of the schools. No overall reform was, therefore, possible.[1]

Many schools, therefore, still remained peacefully in their former state of stagnation. They were no longer to do so. A ruling class which had achieved repeal of the statutes of Eton and Oxford colleges, and laid down in detail the lines for their future organisation and development, was unlikely to deal gently with much lesser institutions. In fact, the Taunton Commission was the most determined and unceremonious of all the educational enquiries; it included, together with such men as Northcote and Lyttleton who had served on the Clarendon Commission, the liberal leader W. E. Forster and the Radical nonconformist Edward Baines, directly representing the industrial middle class.

This Commission conducted what was certainly the most far-reaching educational enquiry ever to have been undertaken. With the exception of the nine public schools already dealt with, and, at the other end of the scale, the attenuated system of elementary schools for the working class, it covered all the schools in the country. The bulk of the necessary work was done by twelve assistant commissioners, whose task it was to make a detailed investigation of school provision in every area. They personally examined nearly 800 endowed schools, making outspoken criticisms and assessments of each, coupled with what were often radical proposals for reform of the school and use of the endowment. Private and proprietary schools were also visited, so that middle-class schooling was considered as a whole. Among the assistant commissioners were such men as James Bryce and T. H. Green, later to become famous in other fields. Their reports, the evidence and the findings of the Commission were published in full in twenty large

---

[1] As was pointed out by Patrick Cumin, Secretary to the Committee in Council, in his evidence to the Newcastle Commission. He notes that Eldon's judgment in the case of the Leeds Grammar School was "curiously strengthened and confirmed "by the 1840 Act (*Report of the Commissioners appointed to inquire into the State of Popular Education in England*, (1861), Vol. IV, 294). Robert Lowe also stressed the need to amend this Act, regarding it as "a cumbrous piece of machinery . . . clogged with provisoes and provisions" (*Ibid.*, Vol. IV, 629).

volumes, ten of which are devoted entirely to reports on individual grammar schools. These provide the most complete sociological information pertaining to education ever assembled in this country.

The main justification for state intervention in the affairs of all endowed educational institutions was the argument that these endowments were made in the interests of the nation as a whole, rather than in those of particular groupings. The Taunton commission emphasised this interpretation. "The whole country", it insisted, "has an interest in these endowments, and has a right to know how the property is used, and whether the results produced are commensurate with the means. If the endowed schools are not doing good, they must do harm, by standing in the way of better institutions. The public has a right to see that they are doing good, and not harm." The state of affairs they were to disclose, on behalf of the public, they found to be "discreditable and injurious to the country itself".[1]

There is no need to go once more into the defects of the endowed schools. The Commission described their work as "very unsatisfactory", the whole system—or lack of system—as "chaotic".[2] These failings were due to "untrained teachers, and bad methods of teaching, uninspected work by workmen without adequate motive, unrevised or ill-revised statutes, and the complete absence of all organisation of schools in relation to one another".[3] The assistant commissioners dramatically describe the decay of the whole system. The Lancashire towns, wrote Bryce, are not the most beautiful in England; but in spite of the general air of ugliness, "the public buildings are seldom mean, even the mills and warehouses, as well as the private houses of the richer people are spacious, solid, and comfortable. Only one class of buildings remains uniformly mean, confined, unsuited to their purpose, and these buildings are the grammar schools".[4] Of some sixty or seventy, only two were satisfactory.

In contrast, the Commission found that "the educational character of the proprietary schools stands very high".[5] Developed some thirty or forty years earlier, when the traditional methods of instruction "were undergoing a severe and almost revolutionary criticism", these schools had helped to solve several educational problems. Their history "is in a great degree the history of recent struggles for the improvement of secondary schools", and although not always successful commercially, they have "very largely succeeded" educationally,

[1] *Report of Schools Inquiry Commission*, Vol. I, 619, 661.   [2] *Ibid.*, Vol. I, 112.
[3] *Ibid.*, Vol. I, 139.   [4] *Ibid.*, Vol. IX, 490-1.   [5] *Ibid.*, Vol. I, 310-22.

"the reforms which they were intended to introduce have in a great degree become recognised as in the main right".[1] Private schools were also a living proof that the middle class had lost confidence in the grammar schools. These were still very numerous—Bryce comments on their "prodigious number" and "extreme diversity", "in the out-skirts of Manchester and Liverpool they lie very thick". But, though some which catered for the professional and upper-middle class were very good, most were unspeakably bad; in fact, the majority were "mainly or wholly commercial" and exhibited all the worst vices of the small school system. Not only was the education meagre, but the rooms were poor, the air "of course, unsupportably fetid".[2]

This was but one example of an increasing class stratification of schools, which corresponded to changes in the social structure during the nineteenth century. Bryce noted that Manchester had been trans-formed during the past thirty years from a factory centre into the metropolis of a vast manufacturing district. Whereas in the 1830s two classes, operatives and mill-owners (who had themselves risen from the ranks) faced each other, by the '60s, there had grown up "a large and tolerably well-defined class of wealthy merchants, com-mission agents, cotton spinners, and calico printers"; below them was a class of warehousemen, clerks, etc., earning salaries of £60 to £500, to which must be added a growing number of professional men and shopkeepers.[3]

Where did these various classes and groupings look for the educa-tion of their families? Taking Manchester and Merseyside, Bryce found that the richest, perhaps some 500 or so, sent their children away to be educated in public and other boarding schools. In Liverpool, those who remained of this class went to the two proprietary schools—Liverpool College and the Royal Institution—while the private schools were filled "by a somewhat poorer class". In Manchester "professional people prefer the grammar school, and the richer mercantile men the private schools, several of which are worthy of their confidence. In the manu-facturing towns the grammar school is usually the more genteel place of education, and the private schools are filled by the children of the

---

[1] Though the Commission also noted that under prevailing influences, some such schools were departing from their original educational principles; thus, quoting Bryce on the Liverpool Institute schools, "Someone in Liverpool remarked to me, 'The Institute was meant to be a place of modern education, and it now teaches classics to the whole of its upper school; its discipline was to be maintained without corporal punishment, and the cane is now in regular use; it was to be purely secular, and its late and present head-masters are clergymen of the Church of England'." (op. cit., Vol. I, 314).

[2] Ibid., Vol. IX, 534-6, 546.   [3] Ibid., Vol. IX, 712.

smaller tradespeople and clerks, with perhaps a few of the best paid artisans."[1] The private schools he classified in two groups: a select group of "respectable" schools (there were only three or four such schools in Lancashire with more than 100 pupils) and a general group of mainly or wholly commercial schools which were, in general, very poor. As for the working class, their children went to the local elementary schools, that is, the National and British schools, which were also patronised by the tail of the lower-middle class, lesser shopkeepers, warehousemen and clerks.[2]

The final Report underlines the extent to which sharp class distinctions had penetrated the private and proprietary schools themselves. Classifying the latter in three classes, corresponding to occupational groupings, it remarks that such schools set up strong "distinctions of social rank", often specifically excluding those not socially acceptable. The three schools composing Liverpool College "correspond, as a matter of fact, to three divisions of society, and the scholars are kept quite apart from one another, except at the daily prayers at opening the school".[3] (Bryce found only one good private school in a new manufacturing town which took in all classes; such a school, he comments, "is only to be found in an unformed society before the distinction of ranks has begun to grow sharp."[4])

It is against this background that the Commission's proposals must be assessed. Its aim was to secure an efficient education for the "middle classes" as a whole, one which made due provision for class distinctions while at the same time allowing for a strictly controlled degree of upward mobility. Such a development required that schools be integrated into a cohesive system, and, above all, operated efficiently and according to plan. In some places the country was thickly dotted with grammar schools which had fallen into decay because they taught what no parents near them wished their children to learn. Such aimlessness must be put an end to once and for all. The schools "need to have their work defined and then to be kept to that work . . . each kind of school should have its own proper aim set before it, and should be put under such

[1] *Report of the Schools Inquiry Commission*, Vol. IX, 536.

[2] *Ibid.*, Vol. IX, 543, 546, 713.

[3] *Ibid.*, Vol. I, 317. The same class differences were provided for in the boarding schools. Thus Nathaniel Woodard founded several Church of England boarding schools after 1850 specifically for different levels of the middle class, with fees graded accordingly. Among these, Lancing was founded for the gentry, Hurstpierpoint for the upper-middle class, and Ardingley for the lower-middle class. (K. E. Kirk, *The Story of the Woodard Schools* (1937), *passim.*)

[4] *Ibid.*, Vol IX, 561-2.

rules as will compel it to keep to that aim."[1] These words indicated a certain determination.

What different schools should there be and how should they be differentiated? Here the Taunton Commission followed the Clarendon Commission's lead—the question must be decided in terms of class and the relations between classes. Lord Harrowby, they reported, precisely defined the line of advance in his evidence when he said: "I should like to club the grammar schools with some relation to locality, and I should like to say, you shall be a good lower middle-class school; you shall be a middle middle-class school; and you shall be a higher middle-class school, that which is now called a grammar school".[2] Such, accordingly, was the solution recommended by the Commission which the Endowed School Commissioners later attempted to put into effect.

Briefly, three grades of school were advocated, each charging a defined fee, each having a specific purpose, and, most important, each having a definite leaving age which should be strictly enforced, since "the fixing of the age would be the most certain means of defining the work which the school had to do, and keeping it to that work".[3]

Schools of the first grade would aim at the university. The proprietary boarding schools, like Haileybury, Malvern and Clifton, and certain grammar schools aspiring to public school status, such as Repton and Oundle, came in this category. These would serve the upper-middle and professional classes; first, those with large unearned incomes, successful professional men, and business men "whose profits put them on the same level", second, the clergy, doctors, lawyers, and the poorer gentry, who "have nothing to look to but education to keep their sons on a high social level", and who needed a relatively cheap form of education which was also socially acceptable.[4] The Commissioners noted that the latter proviso was often associated with a classical education, but that there was an increasing demand for modern studies; it also stressed the desire for boarding schools. In fact, such schools as Marlborough—with reduced terms for clergymen's sons, accommodation in hostels instead of in masters' houses and a huge hall to accommodate younger boys during the greater part of the school day in place of individual studies—met the need defined by the Commissioners' suggestions for boarding schools offering a respectable, but at the same time not too expensive, education.

---

[1] *Report of the Schools Inquiry Commission*, Vol. I, 576-8.   [2] *Ibid.*, Vol. I, 579.
[3] *Ibid.*, Vol. I, 583.   [4] *Ibid.*, Vol. I, 16, 18.

Second grade schools were for those leaving at sixteen. These should be day schools, to be established in every town with a population of over 5,000. They would prepare for the army, the medical and legal professions, the civil service, civil engineering, business and commercial life; and, it was envisaged, would be patronised largely by the mercantile and trading classes—larger shopkeepers, rising men of business, substantial tenant farmers. Since, the Commissioners felt, some of these "are not insensible to the value of culture in itself, nor to the advantage of sharing the education of the cultivated classes",[1] Latin might be included in the curriculum, though not Greek. Otherwise, English literature, political economy, mathematics and science (with a practical slant) should be the staple of studies.

The third grade of education "which stops at about fourteen, belongs to a class distinctly lower in the scale"—smaller tenant farmers, small tradesmen and superior artisans.[2] The establishment of good schools of this grade was, the Commission stressed, of the first importance. Their curriculum should include the elements of Latin or a modern language, English, history, elementary mathematics, geography and science. But education for boys of this class was to be strictly limited; none must be permitted to stay beyond the age of fourteen, or the school would tend to encroach on the work of schools of the grade above.

In this respect, a key point was the charging of suitable fees for each grade of school. Thus the third grade school should charge no less than two guineas, but no more than four as this "would put it out of reach of the class for which it was intended";[3] the first grade boarding school fees should vary between £60 and £120 per annum. This regulation of fees, leaving age, and curriculum, was consciously designed to delimit the class attending the school, and ensure that it kept to its intended grade. Nothing could be worse, from the Commission's point of view, than a school which gave a free education to children from a particular area. It was this that prevented many grammar schools from maintaining their status and providing a high grade of education. Even a few working-class boys "seem to form an obstacle to the schools becoming attractive to others".[4] In such schools, said the Commissioners, class divisions inevitably arose. What better way of ensuring the abolition of such divisions than by the removal of working-class children? To this end it must be argued that endowments originally given to ensure a free education for local

[1] *Report of the Schools Inquiry Commission*, Vol. I, 20.   [2] *Ibid.*, Vol. I, 20.
[3] *Ibid.*, Vol. I, 583.   [4] *Ibid.*, Vol. I, 152

children should be turned to providing efficient schools for the middle class. As the Commissioners put it: "If a school is to be a high grammar school the requisite funds must be procured, and it is most unwise to squander the endowment on the indiscriminate admission of those who do not require such an education and cannot profit by it".[1]

The Taunton Commission, therefore, faced the same problem as the Clarendon Commission, only in a heightened form; it had not only to abolish local privilege, but also other forms of free education laid down in the statutes of the endowed schools (for instance, some schools were free to all comers, or to all without distinction up to a certain number).

On this point the Commission had determined views. "Indiscriminate gratuitous instruction" (the Commission's euphemism for a free education) was a waste of endowments, "as invariably mischievous as indiscriminate almsgiving", and should be abolished. Typical of free schools was "slovenly management, irregular attendance, scholars unfit for instruction, and contempt from the parents". So low was the character of these schools that even "the humbler class" was deprived of any real benefit.[2] In particular, restriction of the foundation (i.e. the facilities for a free education) to one locality was highly undesirable—the wider the area on which a school drew, the more competitive would be the entry, and the more efficient the school. "We are decidedly of the opinion", conclude the Commissioners, "that even in the interests of the poor themselves, and still more in the interests of education generally, no such (local) restriction should be maintained." Instead of a free education for all, fees should be charged, and exhibitions provided open to competition. This change would greatly benefit the poor: a boy who comes in through open competition compels respect, "the close foundation too often inflicts a kind of stigma. And these class distinctions within any school are exceedingly mischievous both to those whom they raise and to those whom they lower".[3]

The Commissioners may sincerely have felt that by excluding the poor from their historic rights, and so from the grammar schools, they were abolishing class distinctions and doing the working class a service; as we shall see later, however, this was not the view of their victims. The Commission was concerned specifically with middle-class education; the endowed schools, they claimed, should undoubtedly be

<hr/>

[1] *Report of the Schools Inquiry Commission*, Vol. I, 154.
[2] *Ibid.*, Vol. I, 593-4.   [3] *Ibid.*, Vol. I, 596.

middle-class schools, their job was to get the endowments back for this class, which needed them. The poor, whose education was provided by the National and British schools, normally paid for their education—usually anything from a penny to threepence or fourpence a week. Why, then, should the poor get a free education in what should be middle-class schools?

In any case, it was in the interests of the poor to abolish free education and to open entry to a general competition, since only the sweeping away of mediaeval forms of privilege could ensure the free and beneficent working of the laws of competition, whereby the worthiest invariably came to the top. The poor were not, of course, to be altogether excluded from higher grades of school; they had but to prove their worth to secure a more extended education and so to step into another class. But to do this they must compete with members of the class to which they aspired. Since the object of such competition "is to select those who are to make education a means of rising, the best test of all is that the competitors should be pitted against other boys of the very class into which they are to make their way. A boy who has only beaten other boys of the same class does not prove thereby that he is fit to receive the education of another class. But if all classes have entered into the competition the selection is sure to be right. If the son of a labourer can beat the sons of gentlemen that goes a long way to prove that he is capable of using to advantage the education usually given to gentlemen."[1]

There followed proposals for an elaborate scheme of scholarships (exhibitions) to be financed out of the endowments previously used to provide a free education, or from endowments originally intended (according to the Commission) for advanced education which had "sunk to the purposes of elementary education". (The latter, they claim, "as long as they are devoted to elementary education, . . . are practically diverted from the poor altogether"[2] a somewhat tortuous argument). Scholarships should aid passage from the local elementary schools to a third grade school, from a third grade school to a second, and so on; while some should be awarded for various forms of higher education. If, for every forty paying scholars in a first grade school, there were three exhibitions—one ensuring a free education and two a reduction of fees by a half—this would "enable poor boys to rise", and so adequately protect the rights of the poor in general.

But middle-class education required subsidy. Indeed, the higher the

---

[1] *Report of the Schools Inquiry Commission*, Vol. I, 596.   [2] *Ibid.*, Vol. I, 624.

class for whom education was provided, the more the expenditure required and the greater the subsidy necessary. So, at least, the Commission argued: "an application of endowments becomes increasingly needful as the education becomes higher". A third-grade school would need little help from an endowment—parents could cover most of the cost; a second-grade school would require more help, a first-grade school "requires more still". This, as the Commission points out— true to form—is in the interests of the lower classes who might conceivably rise to these heights.[1]

What happened when these precepts were applied to particular cases can be seen in the case of two educational endowments at Tonbridge and Bedford. Tonbridge school had been founded by a London skinner in the sixteenth century, and was required to give a free education to children living within ten miles of Tonbridge church. The Commissioners, proposing the abolition of this privilege, "venture to recommend" that places on the foundation be awarded on a competitive examination open to all England as in the case of Eton and Winchester;[2] a finding which well suited a school treading in the footsteps of Harrow and Rugby. At Bedford, what had become a very large endowment was maintaining seven schools, of which one was a grammar school. Here the Commissioners, again following the lead of the Clarendon Commission in the case of Harrow, Rugby, and Shrewsbury, "advise that, after the lapse of a certain number of years, the exclusive privilege of the town of Bedford should cease". We should then, they continue triumphantly, "have an educational endowment of £10,000 a year to be made the most of, freed from local restrictions as to those who are to benefit from it". Learning that "gentlemen of the neighbourhood" had begun to establish a school "to be founded out of their own resources", they ask them to pause, to "amalgamate" with this freed endowment, and to set up their school in this way. So a new school "for the extension of middle-class education" could be largely financed from an endowment intended to provide a free education for the people of Bedford.[3]

If this transfer of endowments was the key question, other proposals were in line with the Commissioners' determination to promote efficiency and co-ordination on a national scale. Briefly, these covered the setting up of effective governing bodies (involving the diminution of clerical control), the ending of the master's freehold, the

[1] *Report of the Schools Inquiry Commission*, Vol. I, 167.
[2] *Ibid.*, Vol. I, 528.   [3] *Ibid.*, Vol. I, 534-5.

establishment of examinations, inspection of all endowed schools, and the formation of effective regional and national authorities to exercise control over the whole system.

This challenging report was published in 1868; a year later the Endowed Schools Act became law. Though this did not attempt a complete reorganisation under direct state control, as some would have liked, it provided for the appointment of three Endowed Schools Commissioners with very wide powers indeed, and with instructions (under the Act) to work according to the recommendations of the Taunton Commission. One of these was Lord Lyttleton himself, who had sat on both the Clarendon and the Taunton Commissions, and who therefore took a leading part in the working out of the Commission's recommendations in practice. The Commissioners, with the aid of seven assistants specifically appointed for the tasks ahead, got to work immediately. Within four years they published 317 schemes for particular schools, ninety-seven of which had been before Parliament, and were formulating many more. By this time they had aroused considerable resentment, in particular because the re-modelling of governing bodies had touched the interests of both the Church and dissenting groups. Both sides accused the Commissioners of showing "preference", and protests reached a volume sufficient to bring about the appointment in 1873 of a Select Committee to examine the workings of the Endowed Schools Act.

The Committee found that much good work had been done, but admonished the Commissioners for being too outspoken and over-zealous in other cases.[1] In 1874, on the accession of a Tory government headed by Disraeli, an Amending Act transferred the functions of the Endowed Schools Commissioners to the Charity Commission;[2] so, in effect, securing the dismissal of Lyttleton and Roby, two of the paid Commissioners. Such, however, was the opposition to the actions of the Charity Commissioners that another Select Committee was

---

[1] "The published opinions of some of the Commissioners on the subject of endowments have caused alarm, and have, in some cases, seriously impeded the harmonious action which might otherwise have been secured between them and the Governing Bodies of the Charities with which they have had to deal. Their own experience, as they state, in attempting to work the Act, has convinced them that the country was hardly prepared for its reception; and it is to be regretted that some of the changes proposed by them, especially in the cases of certain good schools, should have been such as to hinder the hearty co-operation of those who had heretofore worked to render them efficient. It must, however, be acknowledged much sound and good work had been done. Many schools which had fallen into decay have already received new life, and become valuable and prosperous institutions." *Report of Select Committee on Endowed Schools Act (1869) (1873)*, iii.

[2] Set up as a result of the Charitable Trusts Act of 1853.

appointed in 1886, and re-appointed in 1887. What, then, had been going on?

This fresh outcry was due primarily to the ruthless action of the Charity Commissioners, who, travelling the country, were evolving new schemes for the administration of endowments. These involved the transfer of these endowments from elementary to higher education, so ending all forms of "indiscriminate gratuitous instruction".[1] In more and more places, the implications of the Endowed Schools Act were being forcibly brought home to the local population. As a result, working-class and other organisations were registering strong protests. To appreciate the full implications of this Act, it is necessary to look ahead to the '80s and consider some of these protests and their cause.

The Endowed Schools Commissioners had been empowered to carry out "the main design of the founders" of schools "by putting a liberal education within the reach of all classes". In effect this meant, of course, abolishing free places and imposing fees. Many schools, founded in the sixteenth or seventeenth century, were giving a free education—sometimes elementary—to children living in the area defined by the founder; and in some cases had been doing so for centuries. In such cases, the Commissioners made a scheme substituting for free places a limited number of exhibitions to be awarded on merit. These were of the kind advocated by the Taunton Commission: either to provide a place at the local school (if it was continued)— in which case they were worth about £2, or an exhibition of about £25 to aid transfer from an elementary school to a higher grade school; both these sums had to be paid out of the school's resources, which included the original endowment. Such schemes, according to the Commissioners, achieved the aim of the Act; free education was abolished, but a "liberal" education *was* put within the reach of all through the larger exhibitions available to higher grade schools, while the rights of the poor were specifically met by the lesser exhibitions at the elementary level.

Matters did not appear in the same light to those whose children had been attending free schools but who must now pay fees. The Select Committee of 1887 examined some typical examples, in particular the cases of Scarning in Norfolk, Kendal and Sutton Coldfield. At Scarning there was organised local opposition to a scheme which abolished the free elementary education enjoyed by the people for

[1] See *Report of Select Committee on Endowed Schools Act (1869), (1887)*, iii.

a very long period. William Taylor, a working man who described himself as "a platelayer on the railway; foreman on the line; what is commonly called a ganger", told the Committee what had taken place.[1] As soon as the scheme became known a protest meeting against the charging of fees was called at which he had taken the chair. Asked whether there was any difference of opinion at the meeting he replied: "No; all the working men, to a man, and I believe three parts, or 19 out of 20 of the farmers, strongly protested against the scheme". Their objection was "that the people of Scarning who have a right to free education are compelled to pay the school fee"; it was an objection in principle, "we consider it a great wrong".

Further, the workers protested strongly that the £2 exhibitions were awarded, not to the working class, but to a higher class: "I believe," said Taylor, "that from the time the scholarships have been awarded, the higher class have received the more part of them, I believe three-fourths of them."[2] In addition, the £25 exhibition to a higher school had never been awarded, owing to the passive resistance of the governors. Even if it had been, it would not have benefited the workers, since it was quite insufficient to cover full board and expenditure on clothing. Asked directly whether this scholarship would be of any use to the agricultural labourers of Scarning, Taylor replied: "Not to one, without any exception".

Following the protest meeting the workers, evidently with outside support, had taken further action. On receipt of a circular from the governors saying that no child would be admitted without a school fee, "we sent our children, and three men were sent to accompany the children and conduct them to school. We spoke to the schoolmaster, asking him to admit them free, as on other occasions. The schoolmaster would not take the trouble to listen to what we had got to say in reference to this". When the boys wanted to enter, he pushed them back.

Determined not to give in, the workers proceeded to open their own school in a Primitive Methodist Chapel; this was a free school, maintained by voluntary subscriptions from all over Norfolk: "The money came in; we had enough to pay our way". On a report of the school attendance officer, proceedings were taken against thirty-seven parents for not sending their children to school. This step was

---

[1] *Report of Select Committee on Endowed Schools Act (1869)* (1887), 18-30.

[2] In fact the schoolmaster's sons had got seven exhibitions; of thirty-five awarded, twenty-one had gone to non-labourers, fourteen to labourers. Of the latter fourteen, five went to one family only.

apparently unsuccessful.[1] But finally the parents had been forced to give in and pay fees at the local school. That they still held that a great injustice had been done was made apparent to the Committee. A memorial was presented, signed, in one day, by a large number of inhabitants: "We, the undersigned ratepayers of Scarning, feeling that we have been greatly wronged, have protested, and still do protest, against the unjust scheme of the Charity Commissioners, which has robbed us of a free school".[2] The essence of the objection to all such schemes was summed up in a question put by Jesse Collings, who had presented the memorial:

> "Can we want any more evidence of the fact that the poorer classes of Scarning have, if the scheme is carried out, had their educational advantages on the one hand, and their money payment on the other hand taken away from them for the benefit of the children of the better class people?"[3]

Jesse Collings, Radical, ex-Lord Mayor of Birmingham, and outspoken opponent of the alienation of the rights of the poor by the Charity Commissioners, brought several other cases to the notice of the Committee.[4] The scheme at Lewisham, which the Commissioners cited as a model showing their capacity for harmonious negotiations, had profoundly affected the rights of the poor. It had been carried out, as was the general rule, without any reference to the poorer classes whatsoever: "they are not consulted, or represented, or their case put in any way . . . the rights of the poor are dealt with in any fashion without their consent and it may be without their knowledge".[5]

At Sutton Coldfield, where there were considerable endowments designed for the poor and where elementary education had been free until the Commissioners' scheme was introduced, £15,000 had been appropriated to build a grammar school—"a high school for well-to-do children"—while it was proposed to appropriate a further £17,000 to build and endow a high school for girls. Here also an agitation was going on. A deputation of working men as well as the Corporation as a whole "strongly pressed the desirability of having no fees in the elementary schools".[6] Petitions had been organised, and

---

[1] *Report of Select Committee on Endowed Schools Act (1869)* (1887), 5.

[2] *Ibid.*, 55.   [3] *Ibid.*, 12.

[4] Collings had been Secretary of the National Education League, set up by the Birmingham Radicals in 1869 to achieve a national system of free unsectarian education; in this capacity he worked closely with Joseph Chamberlain (see Ch. 7, pp. 363-4).

[5] *Ibid.*, 44.   [6] *Ibid.*, 110.

protests made by the people against their deprivation of the endowments administered by the Corporation, against charging fees in the elementary schools, "and altogether complaining that the rights of the poor were dealt with in such a manner".

At Kendal, where endowments which had provided a free education in a Bluecoat school were to be utilised, among other things, to develop boarding facilities for the well-to-do in the local grammar school,[1] strong local opposition had persisted for years. Collings reported: "The poorer classes themselves (when I say the poorer classes I mean the labouring class and the working class as well) agitated very strongly against the scheme. There were several town meetings held against the scheme, and resolutions passed against it, which were forwarded to the Charity Commissioners". A unanimous resolution had, in fact, been passed at a public meeting, under the presidency of the Mayor, as soon as the scheme was formulated in 1881. "A petition was sent up signed by 6,000 men and women from Kendal against the scheme", and further protest meetings were held in succeeding years—all to little avail, as the resolution passed at a public meeting in 1883 makes clear:

"That this meeting views with alarm that, notwithstanding the protests of the inhabitants of Kendal by petition and in public meeting assembled, the Charity Commissioners persist in their scheme which appropriates the funds of the Bluecoat School for purposes other than the education of the poor, and contrary to the will of the founder. That the town council be asked to withhold its approval to any scheme which so flagrantly interferes with the rights of the poor, and requests that they will take steps which will secure to the poor of Kendal all the benefits intended by Thomas Sandes, the donor."[2]

The town council, added Collings, had adopted this policy. The agitation continued. A public meeting in 1884, reflecting, according to Jesse Collings, the "very great feeling on the subject", heard a report from a committee appointed to secure modifications in the scheme. The report concluded: "The interference by the Commissioners, here and in many other places, has aroused the people to action in defence of their rights, which can be maintained by united

[1] The Bluecoat School, which educated seventy-five to eighty poor children, had an endowment worth £518 per annum—the whole of which was to be appropriated for the grammar school. *Report of Select Committee on Endowed Schools Act (1869)* (1887), 50.
[2] *Ibid.*, 47-8.

action by using every constitutional means, which in the end cannot fail to receive justice".[1] This hope was not to be realised.

Under examination, the Commissioners responsible did not seek to deny the charges. Indeed, they were extraordinarily frank. First, they pointed out that both the Taunton Commission and the earlier Newcastle Commission were opposed to free education. Second, they claimed that the recent Education Act of 1870 ensured that elementary schools should be provided for the poorer, or working class "at the cost of their richer neighbours"; and that, as soon as this was done, the financial benefit from an endowment "at once shifts to the classes which are bound to provide the elementary education", that is, "to the classes who are not commonly called poor".[2] Finally, the original founders of these schools had not specified that a particular class should benefit from the endowment, so that it would ill become the Commissioners "to proceed gratuitously to narrow it to any single class", while it was disputable that the word "free" meant free from payment. Here the Commissioners claimed (with Kennedy, head of Shrewsbury) that a free school meant one "free from interference".[3]

Leaving aside the fact that the Commissioners were, in effect, confining grammar schools to one class—the middle class—the most important of these arguments was the second. It was left to Jesse Collings to point out that "the poorer classes and the working classes are large payers of rates"; as large payers "in the aggregate . . . as any other class, or larger in some parts". The argument that "because the elementary schools are supported out of the rates, therefore the better-to-do classes have a sort of right to monopolise" endowments thereby fell to the ground.[4]

The Commissioners, naturally reluctant to admit the real implications of their work, constantly fell back on the exhibitions which provided a ladder enabling the poor to rise, so guaranteeing their rights. Yet the Select Committee found that of 2,989 exhibitions awarded at schools of higher grades in 1882, less then half (only 1,145) were held by children from elementary schools—and then there was no indication as to whether these were working-class children.[5] Challenged by Jesse Collings, D. C. Richmond, the Secretary

---

[1] *Report of Select Committee on Endowed Schools Act* (1869) (1887), 48.   [2] *Ibid.*, 25.

[3] In answer to this A. F. Leach, though himself a Charity Commissioner, affirmed that "a free school meant undoubtedly a school in which, because of the endowment, all, or some of the scholars, the poor or the inhabitants of the place, or a certain number, were freed from fees for teaching". *English Schools at the Reformation* (1896), 114.

[4] *Ibid.*, 81.   [5] *Ibid.*, v-vi.

of the Commission, claimed that it was only just that endowments, which had gone solely to the poor, should be made more widely available; but then denied any knowledge that these endowments had provided a free education for large numbers:

8068 (Jesse Collings): It is not now a question of what is just. I only want to ask your opinion whether, rightly or wrongly, the class that I speak of have enjoyed for this very long time, for generations, and sometimes for hundreds of years, these privileges which are now taken from them?—I am afraid I cannot accept the question in that way, "which are now taken from them".

8069 Then shall I put it more in the concrete. Have not the people of Birmingham enjoyed free education for 300 years, until the Scheme of the Charity Commissioners was made?—Very likely, as far as I know.

8070 And by the Scheme of the Charity Commissioners they no longer enjoy free education?—No; they have fees.

The fees imposed on the grammar school at Birmingham, according to Collings, an ex-governor of the school, "have done us no good whatever". Further, "to put a fee on for education where one has not existed before will, when anybody writes about it 300 years hence, be quoted as a mark of the barbarism of our day".[1]

Though the Select Committee finally reported that the Charity Commissioners had faithfully carried out the requirements of the Endowed Schools Act (which were themselves "sound and just"), the effect of their work was to cut away the traditional rights of the poor and other local inhabitants, and to separate the working class from any organic connection with higher education in grammar or public schools. By taking over and rationalising all available endowments, the Commissioners endeavoured to construct an effective system of middle-class education, adapted to particular sections of this class on the pattern which had already been developed in the network of private and proprietary schools. From 1869 until the close of the century the Commissioners tirelessly travelled the country, holding meetings, negotiating with local interests, formulating schemes and seeing they were put into effect. Every school history gives the details of these visitations; governing bodies were reorganised, local privileges and free education abolished and fees imposed or regularised, competitive

[1] *Report of Select Committee on Endowed Schools Act (1869)* (1887), 80.

entrance and exhibitions established, the master's freehold abolished and new conditions of appointment substituted, the curriculum modernised, and entirely new schools set up from available "wasted" endowments.

The Commissioners were, indeed, excellent servants of the state. As a result of their labours, some grammar schools now began to provide a more effective, and often a cheaper education than the private schools. Others, such as Repton, were enabled to climb beyond all reach of the poorer classes into the ranks of the "public" schools.[1] As a result, by the 1890s, the middle classes enjoyed a subsidised system of secondary education.

Moreover, the principle of the educational "ladder" had been established—as one which covered lower grade schools while carefully excluding the public schools. This narrow ladder was all that was left of foundations, which for the most part were designed to finance a common local school for all who could attend, not excluding the "poor and indigent", and sometimes specifically intended for the poorest. Meanwhile the secondary school system had been remodelled to underline and reinforce class distinctions. In particular, the vast majority of working-class children were consciously debarred from receiving an education above their station. The handful who might in future succeed in making their way upwards would inevitably do so—and this was the intention—at the cost of alienation from their own class and local community.

These final examples extend beyond the period with which this chapter has been primarily concerned. But they serve to underline the significance and direction of the reforms undertaken. The Universities Acts of 1854 and 1856, the Public Schools Act of 1868, the Endowed Schools Act of 1869 and the subsequent activities of the Endowed Schools Commissioners—all these operated to establish a firmly based, and, by comparison with the past, a rationally organised system of secondary and higher education; one primarily designed for the benefit of the Victorian upper-middle class but which ensured the preservation of aristocratic privileges and pretensions while also opening new opportunities to professional men and the more prosperous tradesmen.

This system was established at the expense of the working class, who were edged out of grammar schools where a free education had hitherto been available—whatever may have been its quality—and left only elementary schools provided and administered by voluntary bodies

[1] A. Macdonald, *A Short History of Repton* (1929), 191-4.

or small private schools of little value; schools which now contrasted not only with a flourishing system of boarding schools, but also with the rising standards of some of the reorganised and newly established grammar schools. The very success of the far-reaching organisation of secondary education, therefore, served to throw into ever sharper relief the educational deprivation of the majority.

CHAPTER VII

THE STATE AND EDUCATION (II), ELEMENTARY SCHOOLING FOR THE WORKING CLASS

OF the Royal Commissions appointed during the years after 1850, only one, set up to consider elementary instruction, found no cause for any fundamental change in the existing system of voluntary schools. Yet, less than a decade after the commission reported, the most extensive Education Act of all was to be passed, marking a decisive intervention by the state to ensure universal education for the working class. In order to examine this course of events we must first turn back to consider the demands that were being advanced in this field in the 1850s and the response of the Newcastle Commission. It will then be necessary to outline the progress of that political movement of the 1860s which marked a rapprochement between the organised working-class movement and the Radical middle class and culminated in the winning of the Reform Act of 1867. Closely associated with the demand for the vote was the demand for a national system of schools which was subsequently taken up by the National Education League in 1869. Other influences were also at work which throw further light on the nature of the Education Act of 1870, the crown of the programme of educational legislation initiated in mid-century.

1. THE POSITION IN THE 1850s

(i) *The Voluntary System*

There were, as we have seen earlier, conflicting attitudes on the question of education for the working class. Elementary schools, provided by religious bodies and maintained by voluntary subscriptions and school fees, were, if they qualified, directly subsidised by Parliament (through the Committee of Council). The Tory tendency was to uphold the interests of the Church of England which controlled the majority of these schools, and to oppose government intervention in education beyond the handing out of money to such schools. This attitude had been castigated by Kay-Shuttleworth, in a semi-official document published in 1839, which represented sufficiently clearly the outlook of such Whig ministers as Lord John Russell.

"We confess that we cannot contemplate with unconcern the vast physical force which is now moved by men so ignorant and so unprincipled as the Chartist leaders; and without expecting such internal convulsions as may deserve the name of *civil war*, we think it highly probable that persons and property will, in certain parts of the country, be so exposed to violence as materially to affect the prosperity of our manufactures and commerce . . . and to diminish the stability of our political and social institutions. . . . It is astonishing to us that the party calling themselves Conservative should not lead the van in promoting the diffusion of that knowledge among the working classes which tends beyond anything else to promote the security of property and the maintenance of public order. . . . If they (the working classes) are to have knowledge, surely it is the part of a wise and virtuous government to do all in its power to secure them useful knowledge and to guard them against pernicious opinions."[1]

Kay-Shuttleworth himself had, of course, long been a leading exponent of the view that working-class conditions, including education, must be improved as a means of averting social revolution; and to this view he still held after the immediate menace of Chartism had receded. Convinced that all education for the workers must "be hallowed by the influence of religion", he was yet fully aware—as secretary of the Committee of Council which administered the meagre Treasury grant to the voluntary schools—that these barely conducted their religious teaching effectively while they often taught little else. Moreover, they were far too few, and subscriptions showed signs of falling off. He saw state intervention as the necessary means of providing an adequate education.

But it was not only Anglicans and Tories who opposed this; many nonconformists and Liberals reacted equally strongly. Since Anglican schools were far more numerous than those supported by any other denomination, Free Churchmen feared that, if the state took over the voluntary schools, Anglican doctrines would predominate in any national system of education which resulted. Some nonconformist bodies even refused to share in the Treasury grant on the principle that no state interference of any kind could be accepted. Though by this time a number of religious, or semi-religious, bodies claimed a

---

[1] J. Kay-Shuttleworth, "Recent Measures for the Promotion of Education in England", *Four Periods of Public Education* (1862), 231-2. Dr. J. Phillips Kay had become an assistant Poor Law Commissioner in 1835. In 1839 he was appointed Secretary to the Committee of the Privy Council on Education, a post he held for 10 years. In 1842 he married a wealthy heiress, and assumed her name.

share in this grant, the Congregational Board of Education and the Voluntary School Association still stood aside.

A more fundamental reason for the failure to move towards a national system of elementary schools underlay the conflicts between contending denominations and their exploitation by political parties. If the middle class were determined to carve out a place for their own children in the established schools of the country, and used their new influence to this end, many industrialists were opposed to an extension of education which might restrict their right to employ the children of the workers as and when they required. This danger was obviously implicit in the principle of publicly administered schools which might also enforce compulsory attendance. This view was to find full expression in the report of the Newcastle Commission.

Meanwhile the battle was fought out mainly on the plane of religion and denominational politics, both in Parliament and outside. That working-class children should be brought under religious influences, all parties—even the Radicals—were now agreed. Rationalism, even atheism, may have characterised the outlook of an earlier age but it was now, under the pressures of the time, being abandoned in favour of a general turn towards religion. Radicals might retain their animosity to the doctrines and policies of the Church of England and advocate a national system of education—a secular system under public control —but to many this meant primarily replacement of an inefficient voluntary system and putting an end to quarrels which brought religion itself into disrepute. Only in the working-class movement was the fully rationalist approach preserved—in terms of a demand for enlightenment in place of indoctrination.

In the House of Commons, such was the organised opposition from Anglican-Tory and Liberal-nonconformist camps, at a period of shifting allegiances, that even attempts to make minor advances failed; for instance, to initiate a college free from denominational control for the training of teachers, in an effort to improve the qualifications of the profession. While the activities of the Committee of Council were criticised by Liberals as being carried on without the assent of Parliament, any step towards extending public control over education was equally anathema. If any form of national system were introduced funds would have to be provided not only, as hitherto, by direct Treasury grant, but also from the rates; and the principle of rate aid for local schools necessarily brought in its wake the issue of control of the schools by locally elected committees of one kind or another—in short, control by laymen rather than the Churches with the attendant menace of too great a degree of popular influence.

(ii) *The Call for a National System of Education*

This, of course, was the policy advanced by the London Working Men's Association in the *Address* of 1837 and reiterated by Lovett and Collins in *Chartism*—the provision of schools financed from public funds, free from all religious teaching and administered by democratically elected local committees. The W.M.A. had attacked the "selfish desires and sectarian jealousies" which suffered "ignorance, vice and disunion to prevail" in place of pursuing the true end of education which was to bring up children "to dwell in peace and union".[1] So also, in the 1840s, Samuel Bamford, holding out the prospect of a true education for the people, wrote searingly of "the priesthood, scrambling for worldly gain, and squabbling as to which sect or party shall have most hand in moulding the brains of the rising generation".[2]

At this period the working-class demand for education had been integrally linked with the political campaign for the People's Charter or with Owenite propaganda for a socialist order. But, when the political movement declined and socialist ideas receded into the background, the programme of a national system of secular education was not lost to sight. Only when religious indoctrination of the young was excluded could education be enlightened and scientific. This view had consistently been propagated by Tom Paine, Robert Owen, Richard Carlile, the organisers of the Hampden Clubs and Union Societies— not to mention James Mill and Jeremy Bentham; all had pointed to the inculcation of religious dogma as the main cause of erroneous ideas and so of social backwardness and oppression, and had argued the case for universal secular education.

In 1847 the campaign for secular schools financed and controlled locally was taken up afresh by the Lancashire Public School Association, founded by Manchester Radicals under the leadership of Richard Cobden. Its programme held that no religious instruction whatsoever be given in such schools but that these might be closed at stated times in order that parents or religious teachers could give this instruction. This programme received considerable support from other parts of the country and in 1850 the association widened its basis, assumed the title of the National Public School Association, and launched a national

[1] William Lovett, *The Life and Struggles of William Lovett* (1876), 146.
[2] Samuel Bamford, *Passages in the Life of a Radical* (ed H. Dunckley 1893), Vol. II, 344.

campaign. Its propaganda was countered by another body, the Manchester and Salford Committee on Education, which also accepted the principle of rate aid but argued that the voluntary system and control by the religious bodies be maintained. Bills were introduced in Parliament representing these various points of view but none received adequate support. Indeed, Parliament achieved at this period the reputation of being "the great cemetery for the interment of defunct Education Bills".[1]

Cobden himself, increasingly impatient of sectarian strife, felt the "danger of alienating the great mass of the people in these manufacturing districts from every religious communion, and even estranging their minds from every principle of Christianity, if we allow this unseemly exhibition to go on—of men squabbling for their distinctive tenets of religion, and making that a bone of contention, and a means of depriving the great mass of the people of the knowledge that is necessary for them to gain their daily bread, or to preserve themselves in respectability". "The great mass of the people", he affirmed, "want education for their children; they are sick to death of these obstacles you throw in their way."[2]

The demand for a publicly provided system of secular schools was, in fact, being advanced by various working-class organisations. In 1847, the Miners Association of Great Britain and Ireland had included in a comprehensive petition to Parliament on industrial conditions a demand for education; a similar petition a decade later specified compulsory education for all children under fourteen; throughout this period the miners consistently advocated reform.[3] The programme of the Metropolitan Trades Delegates, issued in 1849, coupled with demands for nationalisation of the land and manhood suffrage a call for a national system of secular education. Those who were endeavouring to maintain forms of Chartist organisation, such as Ernest Jones, and Julian Harney who launched the "National Charter and Social Reform Union" late in 1850, included educational reform as an integral part of their programmes.[4] Universal education was one of the points in William Newton's address when he stood as the first independent

[1] Quoted by F. Smith, *The Life of Sir James Kay-Shuttleworth* (1923), 257.

[2] John Bright and Thorold Rogers (ed), *Speeches by Richard Cobden M.P.* (1878), 596, 608.

[3] R. Page Arnot, *A History of Scottish Miners* (1955), 35; see also *Trade Societies and Strikes*, a Report of the Committee on Trade Societies appointed by the National Association for the Promotion of Social Science (1860), 41-2.

[4] F. E. Gillespie, *Labor and Politics in England, 1850-1867* (1927), 38-9, 72.

Labour candidate against both political parties in 1852 and won extensive support.[1]

Newton was one of the founders of the Amalgamated Society of Engineers, established in 1850, the first of the great new combined unions which brought together scattered craft societies and which were henceforth to be the main focus of working-class activity. Writing in his journal, *The Englishman*, he expressed the workers' indignation at the diversion of endowments from free schools to provide education for the upper class—a protest which was henceforth to be a permanent feature of working-class educational propaganda. "It is well known", he writes, "that such schools as Eton, Rugby, and Harrow are exclusively kept for the education of the aristocracy. In these and other ways a million of money is annually perverted from its proper use—the education of the poor." While "the 'well-to-do' classes of society" monopolised the benefits of endowments, "the miserably supported" schools are "those where the children of the labourer are not educated but confined during certain hours of the day to keep them out of mischief". He advocated (as William Thompson and Henry Brougham had done earlier) that these endowments be taken over to provide schools for the people.[2]

"We will not speak of the endowed schools", ran a *Declaration of Views and Principles* issued by the Working Men's Association for Promoting National Secular Education in the early 1850s, "we have neither the interest nor the art necessary to penetrate the strong barriers by which greedy selfishness had hedged them in for its own purposes." This remarkable document, signed by over 400 London workers at a time when the university commissions were bringing to light the evils of clerical control at Oxford and Cambridge, categorically rejects the various "charity" schools provided for the workers as "objectionable on account of their sectarian character". For years religious interests have fought for control over the education of the people, but "none of them have ever dreamed of ascertaining our opinions, or consulting our wishes, as to what should be done with our children". The working class have their own views; they want schools to educate the child in truth, to unite humanity instead of dividing people from each other—in short, "a good system of secular education".

The evils of religious indoctrination are once more exposed. "We cannot consent that our children should be apportioned among the

[1] James B. Jefferys, *The Story of the Engineers* (1945), 47.
[2] *The Englishman*, No. 10, March 11th, 1854.

religious sects, that their plastic minds and nascent judgments should be subjected to an external pressure which would give them a permanent bias towards peculiar notions"; working-class children "have been treated like raw material, which each sect claims the right to work up after its own design". What is required is a system which provides a sound secular education for all children as a right. "We do not appeal to public compassion and benevolence for the education of our children; we stand upon the higher ground of justice, and demand it as a debt due to us from the nation."

Yet again there is thrown back, in this context, the well-worn argument that the workers are ignorant and so have no right to a voice in affairs, to the vote. Why are they ignorant? Because "the present arrangements of society prevent the working man from obtaining education for himself and deprive him of the means of educating his children". He would gladly devote money to his children's schooling but low wages and high taxation mean that money "is wrested from us, and added to the public revenue" while, as for the children, "we are compelled, by physical necessity, to put them to labour at the earliest possible moment, in order that by earning some trifle they may eke out our wretched means of keeping bodies and souls together". In the midst of England's "unparalleled wealth, luxury and power", those in authority have defrauded the labourers and reduced them to an animal existence. It is, then, the government's responsibility to set a tax on the property of the country to raise the funds for a national system of secular education for the people.[1]

William Newton likewise stresses that religious interference has prevented educational advance and kept the people "in that state of ignorance which is made the ground of their exclusion from political power", and characterises the voluntary system of schools as "one of the greatest shams of the age".

> "In the first place it teaches the people to rely for one of their greatest necessities upon the charitable support of those in better circumstances than themselves, and to accept as a boon that which belongs to them as a right; and secondly, it gives to those who subscribe the full power of dictating the nature of the education the people shall receive."

No doubt this is the chief argument for the voluntary system, "that it gives to bigoted but wealthy people the privilege of confining the

[1] *Declaration of Views and Principles, passim.* This pamphlet is undated; there is a copy in the University of London Library bound with other pamphlets of the early 1850s.

system of education to one of an illiberal and intolerant nature". There could be no more dangerous thing.[1]

At this same period the Owenite and Chartist agitations of the 1840s were giving place to the great secularist movement led at first by Holyoake. When, in 1853, a national organisation was established, branches sprang up in all the larger industrial towns, in some taking over Owenite Halls of Science, elsewhere establishing new centres, many of which still exist. "Secularism was embraced by thousands and tens of thousands of the working classes", wrote a contemporary historian; it was immediately successful because "great masses of the working classes, especially in the large manufacturing towns, were already lost to Christianity" and looking for an alternative.[2]

Holyoake, and after 1860 Bradlaugh, attracted huge audiences to their lectures and especially to debates with Anglican and other ministers of religion in meetings which sometimes lasted several evenings. What made this development the more menacing, from the point of view of the authorities in both church and state, was that secularism derived its main support from the more privileged section of the workers. "In very large proportion, probably the majority of the operative classes in towns are total unbelievers," declared W. R. Greg, an eminent Liberal writer, "and these are not the reckless and disreputable, but on the contrary, consist of the best of the skilled workmen." Scepticism among the working class "is for the most part absolute atheism, and is complicated by a marked feeling of antagonism towards teachers of religion, a kind of resentment growing out of the conviction that they have been systematically deluded by those who ought to have enlightened them".[3]

Warnings had already been sounded on this subject, and not only by such men as Cobden. In September 1851, *Robert Owen's Journal* (successor to the *New Moral World*) called attention to a "remarkable" leading article in *The Times*; remarkable because it gave expression, in an unexpected quarter, to the Owenite idea that man's character and thoughts are determined by his circumstances. It is noteworthy also as a comment on the prevailing situation.

The education of the people, the writer begins by noting, has been constantly discussed for many years but the power of the state has been paralysed because education is a subject of "bitter dispute and fierce

[1] *The Englishman*, No. 2, January 4th, 1854; No. 10, March 11th, 1854.
[2] Quoted by Joseph McCabe, *Life and Letters of George Jacob Holyoake* (1908), Vol. I, 210, from W. N. Molesworth's *History of England 1830-1874*, Vol. II.
[3] Quoted by S. Maccoby, *English Radicalism 1853-1886* (1938), 133.

animosity"; Church and dissent have either regarded all proposals as "plans for the maintenance of some exclusive ecclesiastical domination", or as a "wicked device . . . for the utter destruction of all religious belief among the people generally". Meanwhile the character and conduct of the people are constantly being formed under the influence of their surroundings; "while we are disputing which ought to be considered the most beneficial system (of education), we leave the great mass of the people to be influenced and formed by the very worst possible teachers".

Certain teachers, indeed, could be called "instructors . . . for evil". The Chartist movement might no longer be the dangerous presage of civil strife denounced by Kay-Shuttleworth in 1839, but in 1850 Harney's *Red Republican* had printed in full "The Communist Manifesto" supporting "every revolutionary movement against the existing social and political order of things" and calling on working men of all countries to unite; the National Reform League led by Ernest Jones and Bronterre O'Brien was campaigning for the nationalisation of the land, atheism was being actively propagated. With such evidence before him the writer concludes that "in the very heart of this apparently well ordered community" enough evil teaching is actively going on "to startle, if not to alarm, the most firm minded".

"Systems the most destructive of the peace, the happiness, and the virtue of society, are boldly, perseveringly, and without let or hindrance, openly taught and recommended to the acceptance of the people with great zeal, if not with great ability. Cheap publications containing the wildest and most anarchical doctrines are scattered broadcast over the land, in which religion and morality are perverted and scoffed at, and every rule of conduct which experience has sanctioned, and on which the very existence of society depends, openly assailed, while in their place are sought to be established doctrines as outrageous as the maddest ravings of furious insanity— as wicked as the most devilish spirit could possibly have devised."

The middle classes "who pass their lives in the steady and unrepining duties of life" may find it hard to believe in such atrocities. Unfortunately they know little of the working class: "only now and then, when some startling fact is brought before us, do we entertain even the suspicion that there is a society close to our own . . . of which we are as completely ignorant as if it dwelt in another land and spoke a different language; with which we never conversed; which, in fact, we never saw". Only in one way could this great danger, "this great

evil . . . be counteracted". The religious sects must bury their differences. "Let a prudent spirit of conciliation enable the wise and the good
to offer to the people a beneficial education in place of this abominable
teaching."[1]

(iii) *The Newcastle Commission*

This was only to echo what the more far-sighted ministers of governments and their officials had been saying for a decade or more. In the
meantime some minor advances had been made in the Committee of
Council's work. Kay-Shuttleworth had ceased to be secretary but,
before he retired in 1849, its yearly grant had reached £125,000, a
considerable increase on the original £20,000 if still altogether
inadequate. There had also been some attempt to introduce minimum
standards which schools must reach before they qualified for grant.
In 1853 a more general attack on the problem was made when Lord
John Russell introduced an Education Bill proposing, among measures
to improve technical and scientific education prompted by the Great
Exhibition of 1851, that boroughs with a population of 5,000 and over
be empowered to levy an education rate. Nothing came of the latter
proposal but a Science and Art Department was set up which was
later merged with the Committee of Council to form a new Education
Department; this for the first time was controlled by a member of the
government sitting in the House of Commons. Grants were now made
to additional schools and by 1858 the Treasury was disbursing over
£663,000 for education.

In 1855 yet another Education Bill was brought in by Sir John
Pakington, a Tory who had once acted as Secretary for War. He
argued that "by the voluntary principle alone we cannot educate the
people of this country as they ought to be educated; you can no more
do it than you can carry on a great war or defray all the annual expenses
of Government by a voluntary contribution instead of taxation".[2]
The comparison was apt if only because the Crimean War was at its
height, but the Bill, granting permissive powers to borough councils
to provide schools, came to nothing. Pakington's next attempt met
with more success, a resolution in the Commons in February 1858, for
the appointment of a commission of enquiry into elementary education.
A few days later the Palmerston ministry had fallen to be replaced by a

---

[1] *Robert Owen's Journal*, Vol. II, No. 47, September 20th, 1851, 166-8, quoting from
The Times, September 2nd, 1851.

[2] Quoted by Adamson, *op. cit.*, 152.

shortlived Derby ministry. It was, therefore, under Tory auspices that, in June, a Commission was issued to "enquire into the present State of Popular Education in England, and to consider and report what Measures, if any, are required for the Extension of sound and cheap elementary instruction to all classes of the People".

This Commission, under the chairmanship of the fifth Duke of Newcastle, one of the largest landowners in the country, enquired into the state of the schools for the next three years, during which other action was suspended. When it reported it was to a new ministry in which Gladstone, as Chancellor of the Exchequer, was committed to a policy of retrenchment; expenditure on the armed forces now stood at some £24 millions, that on education was approaching £1 million—it was agreed on all sides that economies must be made.

When the Treasury grant to schools increased more than fourfold between 1851 and 1858 voices had been raised to protest that these funds were being squandered on paying unqualified teachers to give education of doubtful value. The report of the Newcastle Commission threw light on what, in fact, was taking place. First, it estimated that 860,000 children attended private schools, which received no state aid, the majority of which were bad. Some 1,675,000 were educated in schools run by religious societies or other non-profit making bodies, but of the 24,500 schools concerned more than two-thirds received no support whatsoever from public funds; most of these were in poor areas and rural parishes and of too low a standard to qualify for grant. Of the remaining voluntary schools which did receive grant, over 80 per cent were maintained by the Church of England. But children's attendance was very sporadic and only 20 per cent stayed in school after the age of eleven; the average school life was "about four years".

The Commission, however, on the basis of some very doubtful statistics, found that there was no cause for concern about the state of education as compared with other countries; enough school places appeared to be provided under the voluntary system. On the other hand, school life was too short and the commissioners commented critically on the fact that teachers concentrated chiefly on the 20 per cent of children who remained after the age of eleven. They rejected, however, any suggestion that attendance be made compulsory or extend beyond this age, quoting with approval the outlook on the education of the working-class child expressed by James Fraser (an assistant commissioner and future Bishop of Manchester)—"We must make up our minds to see the last of him, as far as the day school is concerned, at 10 or 11."[1] Any deficiency there might be could be remedied in evening school, after work.

"The peremptory demands of the labour market", the Commission's own report remarked, required the employment of children at this age; and "if the wages of the child's labour are necessary, either to keep the parents from the poor rates, or to relieve the pressure of severe and bitter poverty, it is far better that it should go to work at the earliest age at which it can bear the physical exertion than that it should remain at school."[2] When their attention was drawn to a desire for compulsory education expressed by the miners of Durham and Bristol, the Commissioners could only feel that this would entail "much difficulty and danger", and would give a great "shock to our educational and social system"; it would, of course, have imposed on the government the task of providing sufficient schools; enforcing attendance and maintaining children whose parents could not afford fees. But if the peremptory demands of the labour market, and the pressures of dire poverty, had their respect, the Commissioners wanted nothing to do with any other form of compulsion; in their view, attendance at school could be improved equally well through the "moral pressure" of "right-minded employers, landowners, clergymen, and other persons of local influence".[3]

In the final outcome, the Commission came down on the side of those who had advocated the levying of a county rate for education while leaving the voluntary system in being in so far as control by religious bodies was concerned; the latter being considered essential as the only method "to secure the religious character of popular education". Besides this, the Commission expressed concern that the majority of children who left school before 11 and never reached the first (or top) class should be better instructed. To this end they proposed that grants should only be given to schools if the level of attendance was satisfactory and if, on examination, each child showed adequate proficiency in reading, writing and arithmetic. Since they regarded it as mainly the teachers' fault that younger children had less attention (disregarding the fact that it was only with the smaller numbers in the top class that education worth the name could begin) they proposed making teachers' salaries partly dependent on the children's results.

---

[1] *Report of the Commissioners appointed to inquire into the State of Popular Education in England* (1861), Vol. I, 243.

[2] *Ibid.*, Vol. I, 188.   [3] *Ibid.*, Vol. I, 200-1.

Here was a recommendation which held out the promise of satisfying the critics and relieving the Exchequer. The proposal to levy a county rate was shelved, but in July 1861, Robert Lowe, who was now in charge of the Education Department, announced a scheme, which was to become known as "payment by results". Not only were grants in respect of the majority to be meted out on the basis of individual examination of children by inspectors, but also those previously payable in respect of older children were abolished and those to training colleges for teachers (which were said to be engaged on too advanced work) reduced. "I cannot promise the House", said Lowe, "that this system will be an economical one, and I cannot promise that it will be an efficient one, but I can promise that it shall be one or the other. If it is not cheap, it shall be efficient; if it is not efficient it shall be cheap." "I have the greatest hopes," he added, "of the improved prospects of education, if this principle is sanctioned."[1]

Sound and cheap elementary instruction had been the aim set before the Newcastle Commission. The system of payment by results, one of its few positive proposals and the only one to be adopted and incorporated in a Revised Code (1863), admirably served the latter end. In 1861 the Treasury grant had topped £800,000, but four years later Mr. Gladstone was only called upon to disburse some £600,000 towards the education of the workers' children. Moreover, a mechanical system of rote teaching confined mainly to the three Rs had been fastened on the schools. So ended the Newcastle Commission, the only Royal Commission of this period which had no outcome in legislation, and introduced no fundamental reform.

Thus, at a time when steps were being taken to transform and extend the whole system of secondary schools and the universities for the benefit of the middle and upper classes, the schools for the working class were if anything more severely circumscribed than before—and the voluntary system was left in being. Despite such warnings as those voiced by *The Times* and Cobden, and the opposition of Kay-Shuttleworth who correctly foretold what "payment by results" would mean, complacency was not shaken. Over ten years had passed now since 1848; despite the conflicts taking place over wages and hours in certain industries, in general the working class no longer appeared as a potentially revolutionary force. It had not been proved that English education lagged behind that of other countries, and meanwhile industry was prospering and profits rising. Where, then,

[1] Quoted by Adamson, *op. cit.*, 230.

was the need to give the workers any more education than that to which they already had access? Why, the *Edinburgh Review* commented in 1861, they got "a much better education" for 2*d.* a week in the voluntary school than many other schools offered for two shillings.[1]

Only nine years later this complacency had been rudely shaken; so much so that a comprehensive Education Bill requiring the levying of a local rate and local control of schools was accepted on all sides as a political necessity and rapidly passed into law. To review the factors which so materially changed the situation we may first turn to the political scene and then consider the renewed campaign for a national system of education in the late 1860s.

2. POLITICAL REFORM AND ITS EDUCATIONAL AFTERMATH

(i) *The Struggle for Reform*

The Reform Act of 1832 had been strictly limited in itself, but in the subsequent decades there had been shifts of population which made the distribution of seats a complete anomaly; Cornwall, for instance, boasted as many M.Ps. as Middlesex and the London boroughs north of the Thames. In general, of five million adult men, less than a million—only one in six—had the vote. If, then, the working class was almost completely excluded from the franchise, the capitalist class of growing industrial towns also had a strong grievance; while their own voice in affairs was stifled, the strength of the country vote ensured the continued influence of the traditional governing class, the Whig aristocracy. This was the background of the renewed agitation for Parliamentary reform after 1857, a year when checks to trade brought trade union action on the industrial front and a new revolt against the inefficiencies of aristocratic government from the Radicals.

During the previous five years the unions had consolidated their position and won improved conditions. Now they brought their new strength to bear in action which culminated in the great builders' strike and lockout of 1858-60. As a result of this movement, which was predominantly directed to winning the nine-hour day, a second great amalgamated union was established on the same model as that of the Engineers—the Amalgamated Society of Carpenters and Joiners, of which Robert Applegarth became secretary. Now, too, the London Trades Council, which was to play an important part in working-class politics during the next decade, came into being; acting as an

[1] Adamson, *op. cit.*, 225.

unofficial co-ordinating body of union activities, it brought together what has been dubbed the Junta—the group of influential secretaries of the Engineers, Carpenters, Ironfounders, Bricklayers and Shoe-makers unions—and other leading officials.

The leaders of the new unions of skilled workers were determined to secure for the workers a "fair share" of the fruits of industry and were prepared if necessary to use the strike as a weapon—in fact, some of the strikes of this period were very bitter and prolonged. But in general they held that workers and employers must work together to develop production and trade in the face of competition from other nations; that co-operation between masters and men, rather than in-dependent working-class action, was the best means to prosperity and the securing of a just society. If, however, disputes were to be settled by arbitration and conciliation it was necessary to win for the unions a secure legal position and definite bargaining rights. In prac-tice, therefore, union leaders sought to build up the strength of their organisations, accumulate funds and use these resources both to appease rank and file members and to meet the employers. In effect this amounted to action to secure freedom of organisation and, were there any threat to this, the unions could be counted upon to move into action in the political field. Closely allied with this question, of course, was that of the right to the franchise.

With the strengthening of unionism on craft lines went also a new development in co-operation with the foundation of retail societies; by 1863, 450 or more stores had been founded on the pattern of that established by the Rochdale Pioneers. At the same time Friendly Societies began to prosper among the better paid workers and to attract their energies, some reaching a membership of 200,000. Ab-sorbed in the conduct of these various organisations in different fields, the working-class movement in fact paid little attention to the ques-tion of the franchise before 1859; though this was a period when the Lancashire cotton manufacturer, John Bright, was conducting an intensive campaign for a redistribution of seats and extension of the right to vote in industrial towns, specifically in the interests of the capitalist class.

It was now accepted on all sides in Parliament that reform of some kind was inescapable, but the provisions of a Whig Bill introduced in 1854, and a Tory Bill in 1858, had caused divisions which brought down the respective ministries, and it was without much conviction that the Palmerston administration introduced yet another measure providing for partial reform in 1860. This time, however, the working-class movement began to make itself felt. In the previous two years great industrial struggles had been fought and now, after holding out for eighteen months, the building workers were finally forcing the employers to withdraw. In this new atmosphere of militancy the old Chartist call for manhood suffrage rose again, and there were mass meetings in support of a full extension of the franchise. This was enough to convince all parties in the Commons that, whatever the anomalies, this was not the moment for any measure which would increase the working-class vote. The Reform Bill was this time withdrawn; in an atmosphere of "intense and newly augmented dread of conferring political power upon the working classes", the "overwhelming majority of the House of Commons, by tacit consent, set themselves to hold the line for as long a period as they might be able".[1]

This was not to be for long. In the House of Commons Bright alone had protested against the betrayal, but behind him were ranked forces which could not be withstood. In 1857 he had left his Lancashire constituency on the invitation of Birmingham Radicals and had been returned unopposed as member for Birmingham. From now on this city, the centre of small-scale industry and engineering, took over from Manchester as the seat of Radical activity. Here the division between capitalist and worker was not so acute as in the Lancashire cotton areas, and there was a foretaste of the alliance which was to bring victory in 1867. It was henceforth from Birmingham that Bright conducted his campaign for household suffrage, with the aim of strengthening urban as against rural representation and winning for the industrial middle class the dominant voice in the House of Commons.

From 1860 the working class also increasingly pressed the claim for the vote, but their aim was full manhood suffrage. If on the industrial front there might be renewed struggle with the employers, on this issue of the extension of the franchise interests coincided. In 1862 Applegarth and his colleagues established the "Manhood Suffrage and Vote by Ballot Association" to win trade union members to the fight; its address claimed that "all the evils under which we suffer have a common origin, namely, an excess of political power in the hands of those holding a higher social position".[2]

Meanwhile events abroad sharpened attitudes and broadened the outlook of the working class. The widespread support for the North

---

[1] Gillespie, *op. cit.*, 188-9.   [2] *Ibid.*, 212.

in the American Civil War, despite the sufferings of the Lancashire cotton operatives, the upholding of the Polish fight for independence in 1863, the mass popular enthusiasm aroused for Garibaldi on his visit to London in the following year—these culminated in the founding, in September 1864, of the International Working Men's Association (or the First International), with which Karl Marx was closely associated. To the new organisation, leading trade unionists—including Applegarth and Odger, secretary of the London Trades Council—gave their adherence; if they did not support its full programme they were thereby brought into contact with a growing movement in other countries and so more fully into the struggle for political democracy at home.

It was members of the International who played a leading part in the formation of the National Reform League in 1865 with a platform of manhood suffrage—the workers' counterpart to Bright's National Reform Union. In the collaboration of these two bodies in the closing stages of the battle for reform was epitomised the *rapprochement* of the organised working class seeking the right to vote and the Radical manufacturers and industrialists seeking access to power.

The death of Palmerston in 1865 removed one of the chief Parliamentary obstacles to the enactment of reform and, with mass working-class pressure growing in the country, the new Russell ministry brought in yet another Reform Bill. Once more, however, Tories and right-wing Whigs combined to bring about the fall of the administration—Robert Lowe, architect of the Revised Code for elementary schools, being one of the most unyielding opponents of any measure which would extend the vote to the workers.

Now indignation in the country reached new heights; the Reform League launched a massive campaign among the workers and within a year had 107 branches in London and 337 in the provinces.[1] It was at this point that the full weight of the organised trade union movement was brought to bear. Indeed, in 1867, two events "brought to a focus all the energies of organised labour, both industrial and political". First, in an attempt to curb the growing power of the unions, the Derby administration set up a commission to investigate their organisation; secondly, a judicial decision demonstrated that the unions had no legal status and could claim no protection for their funds.[2] This new offensive ensured that the strength of the unions was brought, at a critical moment, into the mass agitation for political reform; it was sufficient to turn the scale and ensure success.

[1] Gillespie, *op. cit.*, 279-80.   [2] *Ibid.* ,232.

After the defeat of the Bill of 1866 the Reform League had called out the workers and a rally of 200,000 had stormed Hyde Park, the gates of which had been closed against them. Now there were vast mass meetings in Birmingham, Manchester, Leeds, while Glasgow saw "the greatest political demonstration that had ever been held in Scotland" with 30,000 men from the workshops, mines and foundries marching in a procession five miles long through the city streets.[1] As alarm within Parliament increased correspondingly, Disraeli's Tory ministry—which had come to power on the defeat of a reform bill—was forced to introduce one of its own.

On the day its terms were to be announced thousands of London trade unionists staged a march from Trafalgar Square to Islington. The terms were, in fact, originally less favourable than those of the earlier Whig measure but concession after concession had to be made until the Act of 1867 ended in providing a form of household suffrage; it enfranchised the lower middle class and the better off workers, while also redistributing seats in favour of the towns, adding, in all, close on a million voters to the lists.

If the gains were still limited they yet ensured that working-class voters were in the majority in the towns; while the possibility loomed of a further extension of the franchise which would give the workers the opportunity of gaining full control of Parliament. It was also clear that it was the pressure of the organised working-class movement that had turned the scale and enforced this concession. The implications were generally recognised. A new phase of British politics had opened, one in which the question of educating the lower classes assumed a fresh and urgent importance.

(ii) Education as a Political Necessity

One of the first to react was Robert Lowe, who had been largely responsible for the defeat of his own party's Reform Bill in 1866. Deprecating the "intense tendency" of the English working class "to associate and organise themselves" he had argued that organisations now used for strikes would certainly also be used for political ends. "Once give the men votes, and the machinery is ready to launch those votes in one compact mass upon the institutions and property of this country."[2]

[1] Gillespie, op. cit., 272-3.
[2] A. Patchett Martin, *Life and Letters of the Right Honourable Robert Lowe Viscount Sherbrooke* (1893), Vol. II, 262.

This view was not shared by other sections of Liberal opinion. Such men as Bright himself, Edward Baines, A. J. Mundella, W. E. Forster, John Stuart Mill, believed that once the workers were brought within the framework of the constitution the more moderate elements would prevail and the way be clear for developing co-operative relations between capitalist and worker. Mill, at this time M.P. for Westminster, reiterated an argument earlier used by his father. Experience showed that working men usually voted for great employers of labour; if they had the chance of returning 200 members to the House "there would not be fifty of that number who would represent the distinctive feelings and opinions of working men, or would be, in any class sense, 'their representatives'".[1]

To this Lowe rejoined that, as a majority, the working class would have the power of "becoming masters of the situation", a power of which they would not long remain ignorant. Nothing could be worse than, by extending the franchise, "to subvert the existing order of things, and to transfer power from the hands of property and intelligence, and so to place it in the hands of men whose whole life is necessarily occupied in the daily struggle for existence". A conspiracy of the "unfit" would swamp and obliterate not only property but intelligence, culture, toleration, patriotism.[2]

Faced with the reality of 1867, however, Lowe was himself to apply the teaching of Bentham and James Mill—education is the essential concomitant of the suffrage—and to advance this view with equal force. "I believe", he said, "it will be absolutely necessary to compel our future masters to learn their letters."[3] Forthwith, in a series of speeches and pamphlets, he launched an educational campaign.

Education, Lowe affirmed, is divided into two distinct branches—"the education of the poor or primary education, and the education of the middle or upper classes". Both need reform. As for the former, he is categoric that the voluntary system has become out of date. "The voice potential in the government" has been placed in the hands of the working class; the provision of compulsory education is therefore "a question of self-preservation . . . a question of existence, even of the existence of our Constitution." The state must, if necessary, compel the foundation of schools, levying a compulsory rate for their maintenance; schools once established, compulsory attendance must be enforced. Anyone who obstructs such necessary measures will, warns

[1] Martin, *op. cit.*, Vol. II, 281.   [2] *Ibid.*, Vol. II, 281-2, 263-4, 261.
[3] *Ibid.*, Vol. II, 323.

Lowe, bear the heaviest responsibility "that mortal man can possibly lie under".[1]

A radical reform of upper-class education is urged on the same grounds. If the lower classes must now be educated "to qualify them for the power that has passed . . . into their hands", then the higher classes must be educated differently because power has passed out of their hands—in short, they must preserve their position by "superior education and superior cultivation". Above all, this education must be up to date so that they "know the things the working men know, only know them infinitely better in their principles and in their details"; thereby they can "assert their superiority" over the workers, a superiority ensured by "greater intelligence and leisure", and so "conquer back by means of a wider and more enlightened cultivation some of the influence which they have lost by political change".[2]

Lowe is quite clear that political reasons must dictate educational change, and equally clear about the political end educational reform is to serve. If the lower classes must now be educated to discharge their new duties, they must also "be educated that they may appreciate and defer to a higher cultivation when they meet it; and the higher classes ought to be educated in a very different manner, in order that they may exhibit to the lower classes that higher education to which, if it were shown to them, they would bow down and defer".[3]

His past dealings with education, his position as Chancellor of the Exchequer in the Gladstone administration formed in December 1868 —which had, incidentally, been brought into office on the crest of a substantial Liberal majority returned under the newly enlarged franchise—ensured that Lowe was influential in the events leading to the passage of the 1870 Act.

Kay-Shuttleworth also once more entered the field. He had been a strong opponent of Lowe's Revised Code, which necessarily reduced elementary education to the three Rs, for he held to James Mill's view that the overriding need was to enlighten the workers as to their "true" interests, while also laying his hopes on the efficacy of religious teaching. In a sustained onslaught on the Code in 1868, prompted by the passing of the Reform Act, he develops these points at length. A purely mechanical education, he argues, will do nothing to open the minds of the workers to the economic theories and religious principles they need to imbibe. The recent trade union commission indicates "the anti-social doctrines held by leaders of trades unions as to the relations of

[1] R. Lowe, *Primary and Classical Education* (1867), I, 8-10.   [2] *Ibid.*, 31-2.   [3] *Ibid.*, 32.

capital and labour. . . . Parliament is again warned how much the law needs the support of sound economic opinions and higher moral principles among certain classes of workmen, and how influential a general system of public education might be in rearing a loyal, intelligent, and Christian population".[1]

Kay-Shuttleworth is hopeful that, by contrast with the 1840s, when there was no sign that public opinion had been roused to the importance of educating "the manual labour class", there is now "a more general sense of the political necessity that Parliament should make adequate provision for the education of the people".[2] This hope rested in part on the change of front of that section of the dissenting interest which had formerly rigidly opposed state intervention. In fact the influential Free Church leader, Edward Baines, was now affirming the conviction of the middle and upper classes that education of the workers "now introduced in such numbers to political privileges and to great influence in the choice of law makers is a matter of pressing necessity for the safety of the Empire".[3]

Kay-Shuttleworth had no compunction about playing on the fears of the propertied. Only "by experience and education", he had argued earlier, "can the workmen be induced to leave undisturbed the control of commercial enterprises in the hands of the capitalists".[4] On the other hand, should the working class legislate in their own interest, "our entire system of industry and commerce would undergo a revolution, and with it every institution of property"; if the manual labour class "usurped such a predominance as to give it the practical control of the House of Commons", the resultant evils would "assume the monstrous proportions of a destructive revolution".[5] The workers must, then, be educated to vote for their betters. Finally, he made the telling point that the working class were themselves demanding education and, now enfranchised, would inevitably attain it. This, then, was the moment to ensure, before it was too late, that education was provided in "the form most consistent with the traditions and permanent interests of the country".[6]

[1] J. Kay-Shuttleworth, "Memorandum chiefly on the Influence of the 'Revised Code' on Popular Education, written in 1868", *Thoughts and Suggestions on Certain Social Problems* (1873), 194.

[2] *Ibid.*, 260.

[3] Quoted by S. E. Maltby, *Manchester and the Movement for National Elementary Education*, (1918), 102.

[4] "Address on the Correlation of Moral and Physical Forces", *Social Problems*, 328.

[5] "The Political Aspect of the Progress of the Working Class", *Ibid.*, 51.

[6] "Memorandum on the Revised Code", *Ibid.*, 275-6.

Others, who had also strongly opposed Lowe's attitude to the franchise, took a similar view; for instance, the Christian Socialists who had conducted educational activities among the working class for some twenty years—activities which were, in effect, an up-to-date version of those once undertaken by the Society for the Diffusion of Useful Knowledge under Brougham's direction. Learning from the earlier failure of the Mechanics' Institutes, the leaders of this movement endeavoured to avoid any tinge of patronage, to create the impression of meeting the workers as equals and respecting them as individuals. The London Working Men's College, founded in the early 1850s, was based on the idea that no education could be good for the workers "which did not recognise them as English citizens, and did not aim directly at the object of qualifying them to perform their duties as citizens". These views were set out by Frederick Denison Maurice on the eve of the Reform Act in his book *Representation and Education of The People*. Through an education which covered science, politics and religion, Maurice held, workmen could learn to think of the vote as carrying obligations rather than as a means of wresting privileges from others; the aim was, in fact, to awaken the sense that the vote was a trust.[1]

Five years before the Reform Act the Working Men's Club and Institute Movement had been founded with similar aims; its leading spirit was a Unitarian minister, Henry Solly, and with the aid of donations from the aristocracy and gentry it established 116 clubs within three years. Here education was given "as by a friend", in "an easy, pleasant, perhaps conversational way".[2] The movement's journal, *The Working Man*, was also dedicated to elevating the workers and advocating co-operation with the employers. In these circles, too, there was strong advocacy of universal elementary education to extend such influences.

A change was also taking place among industrialists who had earlier presented a solid front of opposition to factory legislation which incorporated education clauses, and continued this opposition in the face of any proposals to introduce universal education. In fact, in certain industries and in particular in the larger factories now using improved sources of power and more complex machines, the employment of little children was no longer indispensable, no longer profitable; indeed, in the better organised industries children even of ten or

[1] F. D. Maurice, *Representation and Education of the People* (1866), vii-ix.

[2] B. T. Hall, *Our Fifty Years: The Story of the Working Men's Club and Institute Union* (1912), 27; Henry Solly, *These Eighty Years* (1893), Vol. II, 250.

twelve could now be more trouble than they were worth. This argument was clearly stated by the Manchester Education Aid Society in 1866.

"The first need of society is order. If order is to be produced in men and women, what kind of preparation for it is that which leaves the children as wild as young ostriches in the desert? When for the first ten or twelve years of life there has been no discipline either in life or body—when cleanliness has been unknown—when no law of God or man has been considered sacred, and no power recognised but direct physical force—is it to be expected that they will quietly and industriously settle down in mills, workshops, warehouses or at any trade in the orderly routine of any family, to work continuously by day, morning and evening, from Monday till Saturday? The expectation is absurd. Continuous labour and sober thought are alike impossible to them."[1]

It was on this foundation that a demand now came from industrial Lancashire for a public system of elementary education. For continuous work, from morning to night from Monday to Saturday, the best preparation was schools which would discipline the wild "young ostriches", make them co-operative and accustom them to sober thought.

Meanwhile other employers looked to a strong educational measure as a step towards curbing the trade unions. Thus Edward Potter, M.P. for Carlisle, saw compulsory education as one branch of a two-pronged attack on the trade union movement. Many trade unionists, he declared in 1869, "are uneducated men. The government must therefore not only legislate next year for trade unions; they must bring in a strong educational measure; for it is only by a very strong compulsory education bill—I do not care how strong—that we can hope to make much impression on trade unions".[2]

The complacency about the state of English education as compared with that in continental countries, expressed by the Newcastle Commission, had also been dispelled. The Paris Exhibition of 1867 revealed a high level of industrial technique in other countries, particularly Germany, and it had been made clear that this rested not only on a high standard of technical education but also on universal elementary schooling. The same point had been borne in directly on employers,

[1] Quoted by Maltby, op. cit., 97-8.
[2] Quoted by W. H. G. Armytage, A. J. Mundella, 1825-1897 (1951), 72.

notably in the engineering industry, that to make use of new techniques workers must have a minimum level of education. Mundella argued that even mill hands in the textile industry could with advantage have an elementary education so that a pool was provided from which to select the higher grades of workers, foremen and managers; a point of view seconded by employers in the chemical and metal industries. In mining increased mechanisation prompted the same opinions; not only was elementary education desirable for all, to provide an efficient labour force, but also it was the necessary foundation for the scientific studies which higher grades must now undergo.[1]

So it was that, when W. E. Forster carried out an enquiry among Chambers of Commerce in 1867-8, wide agreement emerged on the need for more elementary schools.[2] Kay-Shuttleworth summed up the position when he welcomed the new demand for "a superior elementary education" from leading manufacturers, who were now convinced of its necessity if they were to continue "successful competition with foreign rivals".[3] Meanwhile, as he had also noted with apprehension, the working class had educational demands of their own.

(iii) *The National Education League and the 1870 Act*

Trade union leaders also regarded education and trade unionism as allied questions. But contrary to colourful denunciations of Union spokesmen, the Junta and their allies were far from preaching defiance; rather they stressed the importance of education in furthering mutual understanding between classes. "Opposition of masters and men does not arise from a desire of either to oppress each other, but rather from ignorance", wrote Applegarth in the journal of his union, adding "I look to education to teach all parties better." Education was, therefore, "inseparable from trade unions" whose task it also was to further class collaboration. A typical trade union leader of this age, Applegarth summarised his industrial and social aims as follows in the year of the second Reform Act:

> "Let us, then, unite with dignified firmness and rest not till our Unions have that protection to which they are entitled, and I trust that, with such protection and a few more years' experience, we shall have established a new era in the history of labour, have gained

---

[1] J. A. Purton, "The Influence of Industry and Commerce on the Development of Educational Facilities in England and Wales" (unpublished M.Sc. Thesis, London University 1958), 135-8.

[2] *Ibid*, 140-4.   [3] J. Kay-Shuttleworth, *Social Problems*, 267.

the full confidence of our employers, adopted arbitration as the first resort in our differences, and freed our Unions from the expense and anxiety of strikes as far as it is possible to do so, and we might then—'material' as we are—turn our attention to the establishment of a system that would embrace education for the young, employment for our surplus labour, the erection of meeting houses apart from public houses, as well as homes for our aged members."[1]

In fact, the unions were almost immediately to take steps to promote the education of the young, and in the heat of a sharp political struggle for a far-reaching Education Act. In this, various trade union leaders played an important part; indeed, one of them, George Howell, later affirmed that it was the labour leaders who, carrying on the tradition of the Chartists and voicing the aspirations of the masses, supplied "the fervour of the movement" which others led.[2]

When, in 1868, the A.S.C. and J. initiated classes in technical instruction, Applegarth acclaimed this as the first example in the industrial history of the country of a trade union planning education for its members, adding the hope that it will "do something towards securing what the working class have so long desired, namely a national, compulsory and unsectarian system of education".[3] At every meeting of workers he had addressed during the previous twelve years, he said in 1869, he had tested the men in regard to education and never found an exception to his own opinion—that this was what was wanted.[4] In that same year the union's annual report noted "most hearty support" for the movement for national education—"in fact, the working classes generally have taken the question into their own hands, and, to all appearances, will not let the matter rest till compulsory, unsectarian, and free education be the law of the land".[5]

Perhaps the longest record in this field is that of the miners who, through their unions, had been calling for education for many years. Before the employers began to canvass the importance of elementary and technical education, the workers were urging that "ignorant miners are found to be reckless and dangerous miners" and that children should not be given responsible duties unless they had attended school.[6] In the spring of 1860 a Bill had been introduced in Parliament

---

[1] A. W. Humphrey, *Robert Applegarth; Trade Unionist, Educationist, Reformer* (1914), 29-30.

[2] G. Howell, *Labour Legislation, Labour Movement, Labour Leaders* (1902), 473.

[3] Humphrey, *op. cit.*, 195.   [4] *Ibid.*, 211.

[5] *10th Annual Report of the A.S.C. and J. (December 1868 to December 1869)*, 10.

[6] *Trade Societies and Strikes* (1860), 309.

covering conditions in the mines which included an educational clause; "no less than twenty-five petitions were presented in support, signed by over 300,000 colliers". It was this education clause in particular that was opposed in counter-petitions by the colliery owners.[1]

Alexander Macdonald, first president of the National Union of Miners in 1863, had long been the moving spirit in the miners' demand for national education. Himself sent to work at the age of eight, he had later studied on his own to gain entry to Glasgow University in 1846 and supported himself there from his savings and by working in the mines in the summer.[2] Here was one of the "uneducated" trade union leaders: Cremer, Broadhurst, Thomas Burt were others who overcame all obstacles to educate themselves.

It was in 1856 that, already known throughout Scotland as a miner's leader, Macdonald crossed the border to advocate, in his own words, "a better Mines Act, true weighing, the education of the young, the restriction of the age to 12 years, the reduction of working hours to eight in every 24".[3] But there is already clear evidence of the miners' desire for education for their children in the famous report of 1842 on Children's Employment in the Mines. The Newcastle Commission received like evidence, including a direct demand for compulsory education. Education continued to figure in nearly every contemporary demand relating to industrial conditions. It was, therefore, no idle boast on the part of Alexander Macdonald when he declared that no other class in the community had done more than the miners towards influencing public opinion in favour of an improved system of education.[4]

The importance accorded to education by individual unions ensured that this question figured largely on the agenda of the second congress of the newly formed Trades Union Congress, held at Birmingham in August 1869. A motion introduced by W. R. Cremer, and carried unanimously, declared: "this Congress believes that nothing short of a system of national, unsectarian, and compulsory education will satisfy the requirements of the people of the United Kingdom", while the President, in his address, affirmed that educational reform was the most important immediate step.[5] This was the working-class demand which

[1] R. Page Arnot, The Miners: Years of Struggle (1953), Vol. I, 52.
[2] S. and B. Webb, History of Trade Unionism (1894), 285n. On leaving Glasgow University Macdonald acted for several years as a schoolmaster.
[3] Ibid., 286.
[4] Transactions of the National Society for the Promotion of Social Science (1865), 366-7.
[5] J. B. Jefferys, Labour's Formative Years, 1849-79 (1948), 160; W. J. Davis, The History of the British Trades Union Congress (1910), 7.

Kay-Shuttleworth found so alarming; a demand, kept alive since Chartist days and now once more brought to the fore, for an education freely available to all and free, also, from religious indoctrination which fettered the minds of the young.

Later in the same year, Radicals and dissenters launched a new campaign by founding the National Education League in the centre of political radicalism, Birmingham. One of the moving spirits was Joseph Chamberlain, a young Unitarian manufacturer, who had been educated at University College school. Like others, Chamberlain held that the provision of popular education was an insurance which property must pay in order to exist; to extend power to ignorance, by giving the franchise to uneducated workers, was to him a scandal beside which "every other social question was insignificant".[1] But he was also concerned to advance the Radical interest, to build up a mass backing which would not only make possible the defeat of Church and Tory but also gain him a position of strength within the Liberal camp.

The platform of the League was for rate-aided and non-sectarian schools, free and compulsory education; a programme which could unite both workers and the more far-sighted employers, and draw in dissenters, on the paramount issue of the day.[2] It had as its chairman George Dixon, M.P. for Birmingham and, in 1867-8, its Lord Mayor, while Chamberlain held the post of vice-chairman and his lieutenant Jesse Collings that of secretary. The inaugural meeting, held in October 1869 at Birmingham, was addressed by leading trade unionists, including Applegarth and George Howell of the Operative Builders, both of whom were elected to the executive. The Labour Representation League, founded in the same year to promote the Parliamentary candidature of working men, sent its secretary, Lloyd Jones, an old Owenite and Owen's biographer. Support was forthcoming from the London Trades Council.

So the great potential strength of the working-class movement was harnessed and Chamberlain made the most of it, referring specifically in his speech to the "delegates and representatives of the great Trades Councils throughout the kingdom" and claiming that "directly or indirectly, from 800,000 to 1,000,000 working men have, at these

---

[1] J. L. Garvin, *The Life of Joseph Chamberlain* (1932), Vol. I, 89; for Chamberlain's view of education as a "ransom" or "insurance" for the security of property, see *Ibid.*, Vol. I, 549-52.

[2] The demand for a "non-sectarian" education was a compromise. The workers stood for a "secular" education which implied no religious instruction of any kind. After the passage of the Education Act of 1870, the National Education League finally took up the latter position.

meetings in Birmingham, given their support to the platform of the League".[1] "We claim to represent the determination of the laity," he wrote in the following year, "and especially of the working class, to secure at least a good primary instruction for every child in the country."[2]

As the League developed its campaign, affiliated Working Men's Auxiliary Committees were set up, particularly in the Midlands and the North. Meetings were organised in various parts of the country at which such men as Applegarth and Howell shared the platform with Jesse Collings and other middle-class supporters. A pamphlet by Applegarth, pressing the case for compulsory education, was published in half a million copies.[3] The London Working Men's Education Committee, set up by Trade Unionists and others, played an important part in the agitation which culminated in June 1870 with a mass meeting at Exeter Hall, presided over by the celebrated preacher, C. H. Spurgeon. "This meeting", declared Cremer, of the A.S.C. and J., "records its deliberate conviction . . . that the educational wants of the country cannot be supplied except by the establishment in every parish or district of free schools, at which attendance shall be compulsory, and the teaching entirely free from anything of a sectarian character."[4]

The meeting took place when the Education Bill had already been introduced in the Commons by W. E. Forster, now in charge of the Education Department in the Gladstone administration; and this complex Bill was to become law in August 1870, after only minor modifications. What were its provisions?

The complacency of a decade earlier had been swept away. Influential opinion, on all sides, was now in favour of a system of universal, if not compulsory, education for the working class. The issue was between those who, in the National Education League, were exercising mass pressure in favour of publicly provided schools with no tinge of sectarian religious teaching; and those who, brought together in the rival National Education Union, pressed the claims of the Church schools and religion.

In the circumstances the government was able to introduce a far-reaching bill of a kind which would have been rejected out of hand in 1860; but it was one which also incorporated a basic compromise and fastened a dual system of organisation on the elementary schools.

[1] *Report of the First General Meeting of the National Education League*, 215.
[2] *The Times*, January 1st, 1870.   [3] Humphrey, *op. cit.*, 227-8.
[4] *The Beehive*, June 18th, 1870.

Church schools were left in being and the Treasury grant to them was increased; but provision was made for locally elected school boards to levy a rate for education, to build schools where these were lacking, provide teachers and, if they thought proper, enforce the attendance of children under thirteen. In these schools no "catechism or religious formulary distinctive of any particular denomination" was to be taught, and it was left to the school boards to decide whether any religious instruction was to be given at all.

The principle of rate aid had been secured, therefore, if only in a limited field in so far as Church schools continued with a special direct grant (and, indeed, increased in number). The same was true so far as securing a non-sectarian education was concerned—Church schools continued to teach particular doctrines but board school religious teaching, if introduced, must be free of all sectarian bias. A step had been taken towards the principle of compulsory education (which was soon, as board schools multiplied, to be followed by more decisive ones in 1876 and 1880); but there was to be no free education —only parents who could not afford fees were exempted from payment.

With the Education Act of 1870 reorganisation of the country's educational system was completed in the light of the new conditions following the extension of the franchise. It had not been originally envisaged that the workers' education should be so extended; least of all that control of schools be handed over to elected bodies and the teaching of religion made optional. But events had forced the pace and mass working-class pressure contributed to ensuring that at least the first foundations of a universal system were laid—that education was no longer a charity but a right.

Robert Lowe, Kay-Shuttleworth and the class for which they spoke might continue with endeavours to use elementary education as a means to stabilise class society; though from the moment that the working class as a whole had access to literacy such educational aims were no longer openly proclaimed—instead, class policies were to be disguised by educational phraseology. The nature of Radical sympathy for working-class aspirations was shown by the fact that, immediately the political battle was over, Birmingham Radicals rejected an approach by working-class candidates for an alliance and put up only their own nominees for the local school board.[1] Nor, as Frederick Engels

[1] I am indebted to Mr. A. F. Taylor for my information as to this action by the Birmingham Radicals.

was to remark, was the Church slow in seeing that parsons too found a place and influence on these boards.

But the working class had at last some opportunity of exercising control over the schooling of their children. With the first school board elections working-class candidates were in the field and a few were successful. Thomas Henry Huxley, whose scientific lectures to workers had made him a popular figure since 1855, was elected a member of the first London School Board and managed to ensure that elementary science was included in the curriculum of the capital's new board schools.[1]

The movement to secure a full education for the working-class child continued, therefore, in new forms. If the first worker members of the school boards had little impact, for lack of a clear educational policy, there was once more to be a distinctive working-class approach to education when Victorian prosperity was rudely shaken and socialist ideas reborn. Meanwhile elementary schools could grow upwards in response to a direct demand, provide a fuller education for older children and so help to stake the workers' claims—not only to elementary schooling, but also to secondary education, university places, to an equal right to education of every kind. In the 1880s a member of the London Trades Council, speaking as a "representative of the working classes", is affirming to a new Royal Commission: "We believe that the children of the poor ought to be able to rise from the elementary to the secondary schools, and on to the universities . . . all educational facilities ought to be equal and open to all classes. . . . We feel that it is necessary to have all the roads to education open, free, and unfettered to the people".[2]

In the period 1850-70 a conscious effort was made to establish a closed system of schools; so to divide and differentiate the education given to different social classes that privilege could for ever withstand the pressure of the working masses. This attempt could only meet with failure, whatever the temporary respite secured and the brakes put on educational advance. From the moment of the repeal of the Corn Laws, the capitalist class could, in fact, take no step which was not conditioned by the attitude of the working class. To win the workers' support for their own ends, and curb independent action, they must always make more concessions than they wished, in the educational no

[1] Leonard Huxley, *Life and Letters of Thomas Henry Huxley* (1900), Vol. I, 337-55.

[2] *Third Report of the Royal Commission appointed to inquire into the working of the Elementary Education Acts, England and Wales* 1887), 382-3.

less than in the political field. To counter these concessions they might try to neutralise the workers' minds through carefully planned and restricted schooling and other teaching; but this was a frail enough defence. Though some working-class leaders might accept Liberal ideas, and seek to climb into the middle class themselves, under the influence of the hard facts of life the working-class movement would always rediscover its own needs and interests and take up the struggle for its own aims.

These, in the educational field, were broadly human aims, as opposed to the narrow class approach which prompted the educational legislation of this age—and much that followed later. They are summed up in general terms in the answer given to Robert Lowe's philosophy by the first Labour M.P., Thomas Burt. "We say educate a man, not simply because he has got political power, and simply to make him a good workman; but educate him because he is a man."[1] This view, as expressed in the writings of the early socialists, was inseparably connected with the belief that, for the chance to be men, the workers must established a just social order; for only in a society where all are free and equal can education, and labour too, become, in Lovett's words, "a universal instrument for advancing the dignity of man, and for gladdening his existence".

Even when this socialist perspective was obscured, the working-class movement carried on the essential struggle to shorten the working day and improve living conditions, without which education in any real sense of the word must for ever remain out of reach. The new promise of technology and science was recognised, support given to freedom of religious or non-religious belief, the demand advanced for education not as a charity but as a fundamental human and social right. In so doing the working class carried forward the ideas of the eighteenth-century forerunners and of the "practical philosophers" of the "age of reform". By such means the way was kept open for later generations to renew the call for an enlightened education as part of the continuing struggle for socialism—for a society in which classes would be abolished and the opportunity for full human development made equally available to all.

[1] A. Watson, *A Great Labour Leader* (1908), 104.

INDEX